SPEC OPS

SPEC OPS

Case Studies in Special Operations Warfare: Theory and Practice

WILLIAM H. McRAVEN

PRESIDIO

This edition printed 1996

Copyright © 1995 by William H. McRaven

Published by Presidio Press
505 B San Marin Drive, Suite 300
Novato, CA 94945-1340

Library of Congress-in-Publication Data

McRaven, William H. (William Harry), 1955–
    Spec ops : case studies in special operations warfare theory & practice / William H. McRaven.
        p. cm.
    Originally published under title : The theory of special operations.
    Includes index.
    ISBN 0-89141-544-0 (hardcover)
    ISBN 0-89141-600-5 (paperback)
    1. Special operations (Military science), Case studies. I. McRaven, William H. (William Harry), 1955–Theory of special operations. II. Title.
U262.M37 1995
356'.16—dc20   94-46452
                                              CIP

Typography by ProImage
Printed in the United States of America

Contents

Contents

1

The Theory of Special Operations

In the realm of military literature, there is much written on the theory of war, ranging from Herman Kahn's thinking about the unthinkable on the nuclear end of the spectrum to B. H. Liddell Hart's indirect warfare on the conventional end. There are theories of war escalation and war termination, theories of revolution and counterrevolution, and theories of insurgency and counterinsurgency. There are general airpower and sea power theories, and more specific theories on strategic bombing and amphibious warfare. Nowhere, however, is there a theory of special operations.

Why is a theory of special operations important? A successful special operation defies conventional wisdom by using a small force to defeat a much larger or well-entrenched opponent. This book develops a theory of special operations that explains why this phenomenon occurs. I will show that through the use of certain principles of warfare a special operations force can reduce what Carl von Clausewitz calls the frictions of war to a manageable level. By minimizing these frictions the special operations force can achieve relative superiority over the enemy. Once relative superiority is achieved, the attacking force is no longer at a disadvantage and has the initiative to exploit the enemy's weaknesses and secure victory. Although gaining relative superiority doesn't guarantee success, it is necessary for success. If we can determine, prior to an operation, the best way to achieve relative superiority, then we can tailor special operations planning

and preparation to improve our chances of victory. This theory will
not make the reader a better diver, flyer, or jumper, but it will provide
an intellectual framework for thinking about special operations. The
relative superiority graph that will be shown later is a tool to assess
the viability of a proposed special operation.

THE SCOPE OF THIS STUDY

To develop a theory of special operations I had to first limit the
scope of the problem. This required developing the following refined definition of a special operation: "A special operation is conducted by forces specially trained, equipped, and supported for a
specific target whose destruction, elimination, or rescue (in the case
of hostages), is a political or military imperative."*

My definition is not consistent with official joint doctrine which
broadly defines special operations to include psychological operations, civil affairs, and reconnaissance. The eight combat operations
I analyzed to determine the principles of special operations and to
develop the theory are more closely aligned to what *Joint Pub 3-05*
defines as a direct-action mission.† Unlike direct-action missions,

---

*The *Doctrine for Joint Special Operations* [*Joint Pub 3-05*] defines special operations as

> operations conducted by specially organized, trained, and equipped mili-
> tary and paramilitary forces to achieve military, political, economic, or
> psychological objectives by unconventional military means in hostile,
> denied, or politically sensitive areas. These operations are conducted
> during peacetime competition, conflict, and war, independent or in co-
> ordination with operations of conventional, non special operations
> forces. Politico-military considerations frequently shape special opera-
> tions, requiring clandestine, covert, or low visibility techniques and
> oversight at the national level. Special operations differ from conven-
> tional operations in the degree of physical and political risk, opera-
> tional techniques, modes of employment, independence from friendly
> support, and dependence on detailed operational intelligence and in-
> digenous assets.[1]

†*Joint Pub 3-05* states that direct action missions are "designed to achieve
specific, well defined, and often time-sensitive results of strategic, opera-

however, the eight special operations that I analyze in this book were always of a strategic or operational nature and had the advantage of virtually unlimited resources and national-level intelligence. The refined definition also implies that special operations can be conducted by non–special operations personnel, such as those airmen who conducted James Doolittle's raid on Tokyo or the submariners involved in the raid on the German battleship *Tirpitz*. Although I believe the theory of special operations, as presented in this book, is applicable across the spectrum of special operations, as defined by *Joint Pub 3-05,* it was developed solely from the eight case studies presented in this work. All usage of the term *special operations* henceforth will adhere to this refined definition.

WHY ARE SPECIAL OPERATIONS UNIQUE?

All special operations are conducted against fortified positions, whether a particular position is a battleship surrounded by anti-torpedo nets (the British midget submarine raid on the German battleship *Tirpitz*), a mountain retreat guarded by Italian troops (Otto Skorzeny's rescue of Benito Mussolini), a prisoner of war (POW) camp (the Ranger raid on Cabanatuan and the U.S. Special Forces raid on Son Tay), or a hijacked airliner (the German antiterrorist unit [GSG-9] hostage rescue in Mogadishu). These fortified positions reflect situations involving defensive warfare on the part of the enemy.

Carl von Clausewitz, in his book *On War,* noted, "The defensive form of warfare is intrinsically stronger than the offense. [It] contributes resisting power, the ability to preserve and protect oneself. Thus, the defense generally has a negative aim, that of resisting the enemy's will . . . if we are to mount an offensive to impose our will, we must develop enough force to overcome the inherent superiority of the enemy's defense."[2] Clausewitz's theory of war states that to defeat "the stronger form of warfare" an army's best weapon is superior numbers. "In this sense superiority of numbers admittedly is

---

tional, or critical tactical significance." They involve attacks on critical targets, interdictions of lines of communication, location, capture, or recovery of personnel or materiel, or the seizure, destruction, or neutralization of critical facilities.

the most important factor in the outcome of an engagement, so long as it is great enough to counterbalance all other contributing circumstances. It thus follows that as many troops as possible should be brought into the engagement at the decisive point."[3]

No soldier would argue the benefit of superior numbers, but if they were the most important factor, how could 69 German commandos have defeated a Belgian force of 650 soldiers protected by the largest, most extensive fortress of its time, the fort at Eben Emael? How can a special operations force that has inferior numbers and the disadvantage of attacking the stronger form of warfare gain superiority over the enemy? To understand this paradox is to understand special operations.

RELATIVE SUPERIORITY

Relative superiority is a concept crucial to the theory of special operations. Simply stated, relative superiority is a condition that exists when an attacking force, generally smaller, gains a decisive advantage over a larger or well-defended enemy. The value of the concept of relative superiority lies in its ability to illustrate which positive forces influence the success of a mission and to show how the frictions of war affect the achievement of the goal. This section will define the three basic properties of relative superiority and describe how those properties are revealed in combat.

Relative superiority is achieved at the pivotal moment in an engagement. For example, in World War II, when the Germans attacked the Belgian fort at Eben Emael, they achieved a decisive advantage—relative superiority—over the enemy within five minutes of the initial engagement by using gliders and shaped charges to gain surprise and speed to subdue the enemy quickly. Although the Belgians fought for another twenty-four hours, the battle hinged on the first few moments, and the outcome of the engagement was virtually assured.

In some cases, the pivotal moment comes before actual combat. In 1943 the British modified an old destroyer, the HMS *Campbeltown,* filled it with four and a quarter tons of explosives, covered it with armor plating, sailed it across the English Channel, and rammed it into the German-held dry dock at Saint-Nazaire, France.

This action rendered the dry dock useless for the remainder of the war. Although the German defenses surrounding Saint-Nazaire were the heaviest in the Atlantic, once the HMS *Campbeltown* managed to reach the outer harbor of the port (two miles from the dry dock), the Germans could not stop her. At this point, which was prior to actual hostilities, relative superiority was achieved. The point at which relative superiority is achieved is also frequently the point of greatest risk. The closer the attacking force gets, the tougher the defenses become. However, once you overcome the last obstacle the probability of success strongly outweighs the probability of failure, and relative superiority is achieved.

Once relative superiority is achieved, it must be sustained in order to guarantee victory. In an effort to rescue the Italian dictator Benito Mussolini, SS Capt. Otto Skorzeny conducted a glider assault on an Italian stronghold on top of Gran Sasso peak in the Apennines Mountains. Within four minutes of landing, Skorzeny had stormed the hotel hideout and had Mussolini in his custody. At this point he had achieved relative superiority. However, for the mission to be successful, Skorzeny had to extract Mussolini from the mountaintop and ensure the dictator's safe return to Rome. This interim period between grabbing Mussolini and mission completion required sustaining relative superiority. This was accomplished through boldness on Skorzeny's part and by reinforcing the small commando force with conventional troops.

The ability to sustain relative superiority frequently requires the intervention of courage, intellect, boldness, and perseverance, or what Clausewitz calls the moral factors. For example, during World War II, Lt. Luigi Durand de la Penne, an Italian frogman, clandestinely entered Alexandria Harbor aboard a manned torpedo. He and his second diver overcame an antisubmarine net, depth charges, picketboats, pier security, and an antitorpedo net to reach the British battleship HMS *Valiant*. All they had to do was place explosives on the hull and the mission would have been successful. Unfortunately, as Durand de la Penne dove the manned torpedo under the HMS *Valiant,* the submersible gained ballast and sank into the mud. To make matters worse, his second diver lost consciousness and floated to the surface. Although physically exhausted from the long dive and freezing from the cold water seeping into his torn dry suit, Durand de la Penne spent the next forty minutes moving the torpedo into position under the HMS *Valiant*. Only through his tremendous perseverance and courage (two of the four moral factors) was he able to sustain relative superiority and complete the mission.

If relative superiority is lost, it is difficult to regain. After the *Campbeltown* rammed the dry dock at Saint-Nazaire, the plan called for eighty commandos aboard the ship to disembark and destroy a variety of targets around the port facility. Although the commandos achieved a distinct tactical advantage when they rammed the dry dock and surprised the Germans, German sailors and soldiers intervened and slowed the commandos' progress when they attempted to destroy the targets ashore. After thirty minutes ashore, the HMS *Campbeltown* commandos were overwhelmed by German reinforcements and lost relative superiority. The engagement lasted another two hours, but the British, because of their numerical inferiority, were never able to regain the advantage. Eventually the commandos were forced to surrender. An inherent weakness in special forces is their lack of firepower relative to a large conventional force. Consequently when they lose relative superiority, they lose the initiative, and the stronger form of warfare generally prevails.

The key to a special operations mission is to gain relative superiority early in the engagement. The longer an engagement continues, the more likely the outcome will be affected by the will of the enemy, chance, and uncertainty, the factors that comprise the frictions of war.

At the end of each case study, a graph will be used to show how and when each special operations force achieved relative superiority. This relative superiority graph illustrates how special operations forces, with their cutting-edge technology, access to national-level intelligence, high-quality training, and elite troops, are able to minimize the frictions of war and achieve relative superiority. This graph is intended to be not an analytical tool but a conceptual one to help illustrate why certain missions succeed. Additionally, the graph provides a visual demonstration of the three properties of relative superiority: the pivotal moment can be seen as a dramatic rise in the probability of mission completion; sustaining relative superiority is a gradual rise from the pivotal moment to mission completion; and a decisive drop in the probability of mission completion shows a loss of relative superiority. Figure 1-1 is a representative relative superiority graph.

The X-axis is time, the Y-axis is probability of mission completion. The intersection of the axes is the point of vulnerability (PV). The point of vulnerability is defined as the point in a mission when the attacking force reaches the enemy's first line of defenses. At this point, the frictions of war (chance, uncertainty, and the will of the enemy) begin to impinge upon the success of the engagement. This point of vulnerability is somewhat arbitrary, and the exact location can be debated. Although the so-called frictions of war can affect a mission even in the planning and preparation phases, I have elected to define the point of vulnerability as an aspect of the engagement phase.

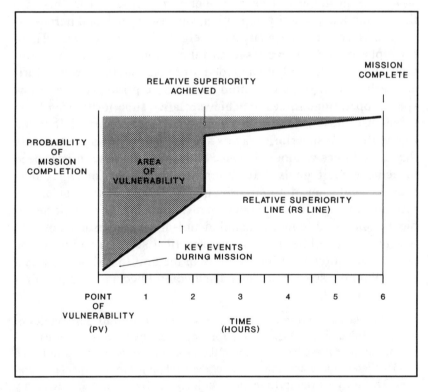

Fig. 1-1. Sample Relative Superiority Graph

The area of vulnerability (AV) is a function of mission completion over time. The longer it takes to gain relative superiority, the larger the area of vulnerability, and hence the greater the impact of the frictions of war. The graph shows that the special operations force succeeds because its inherent advantages (technology, training, intelligence, etc.) allow it to reduce the area of vulnerability, and hence the frictions of war, to a manageable level.

Although there are factors in war over which we have little control, the theory of special operations shows that there are six principles that can be controlled and that have an effect on relative superiority.

THE SIX PRINCIPLES OF SPECIAL OPERATIONS

The six principles of special operations presented in this section—simplicity, security, repetition, surprise, speed, and purpose—were derived from an analysis of eight historical cases.* These principles dominated every successful mission. If one of these principles was overlooked, disregarded, or bypassed, there was invariably a failure of some magnitude. It is these principles that allow special operations forces to achieve relative superiority. Can large forces use these principles to gain relative superiority? It is not likely. Relative superiority favors small forces. This is not to imply that large forces cannot gain some element of surprise or use speed to achieve their goals, but gaining relative superiority requires proper integration of all six principles. Because of their size, it is difficult for large forces to develop a simple plan, keep their movements concealed, conduct detailed full-dress rehearsals (down to the individual soldier's level), gain tactical surprise and speed on target, and motivate all the soldiers in the unit to a single goal. At some point the span of command and control becomes too great for

---

*Initially the cases were viewed in terms of the U.S. Army's principles of war as defined in the *Doctrine for Joint Special Operations*. After careful examination of these cases, some of the principles of war were eliminated or modified to more accurately reflect their relationship to a special operation. The army's principles include: objective, offensive, mass, economy of force, maneuver, unity of command, security, surprise, and simplicity.

a large force to effectively blend the principles of special operations. Clausewitz states the obvious when he says, "The greater the magnitude of any event, the wider the range of forces and circumstances that affect it."[4] Large forces are more susceptible to the frictions of war. The principles of special operations work because they seek to reduce warfare to its simplest level and thereby limit the negative effects of chance, uncertainty, and the enemy's will.

To achieve relative superiority, the practitioner of special operations must take account of the principles in the three phases of an operation: planning, preparation, and execution. The principles are interconnected and rely on each other for support. For example, if a plan is not simple, it will be difficult to conceal the operation's intent and even more difficult to rehearse the mission. And if the operation is difficult to conceal and rehearse, it will be nearly impossible to execute with surprise, speed, and purpose.

The Holloway Commission's *Rescue Mission Report,* which reviewed the failed attempt to rescue hostages from Tehran in 1980, shows how the principles of simplicity, security, and repetition are related. The rescue mission was aborted when, due to unforeseen circumstances, there were insufficient helicopters to continue the operation. The report noted, however, that adding additional helicopters would have increased the level of difficulty, which "would [have] result[ed] in an unnecessary increase in the OPSEC [operational security] risk."[5] The report continued, "OPSEC considerations mitigated [*sic*] against such a [full-scale] rehearsal and, while the review group recognized the inherent risk in bringing all the forces together in the western US training site, the possible security disadvantages of such a rehearsal seem to be outweighed by the advantages to be gained."[6] The correlation between simplicity, security, and repetition is clear: if a plan is complex it will require extraordinary security, and an overabundance of security hinders effective preparation.

In the preparation phase, proper security and constant repetition have a direct impact on the attacking force's ability to gain surprise and speed in the execution phase. Clausewitz in his discussion on surprise says, "Surprise will never be achieved under lax conditions [poor security] and conduct."[7] Security must remain tight in the preparation phase to prevent the enemy from gaining a disastrous advantage.

Constant repetition, as manifested in training and premission rehearsals, is the link between the principle of simplicity in the planning phase and the principles of surprise and speed in the execution phase. For example, Lt. Col. Herbert Zehnder, the pilot of the HH-3 who flew from Thailand to Son Tay, North Vietnam, had the difficult task of landing in the POW camp's small courtyard. It was considered essential to make this controlled crash in the courtyard in order to gain a few seconds of surprise. Initially, this maneuver was considered too difficult, but after hundreds of flying hours and a dozen rehearsals, the difficult landing became easier and surprise was achieved. Constant repetition made the task of landing in a confined area easier and thereby improved the opportunity for gaining surprise.

Constant, realistic rehearsals will improve the attacking force's ability to quickly execute the mission, particularly under combat conditions. John Lorimer, a crewman on the midget submarine that damaged the German battleship *Tirpitz,* said, "If you are going to do anything dangerous, the best way to accomplish it is to train, train, train, so that in the excitement of the situation you do the thing automatically."[8] Repetition, by its very nature, improves speed on target.

The last of the six principles is purpose. A sense of purpose, namely the understanding of the mission's objectives and a personal commitment to see those objectives achieved, is vital to achieving relative superiority. Although the principle of purpose is most apparent in the execution phase, all phases must focus on the purpose of the mission. Knowing the purpose of the mission will reduce the extraneous objectives, isolate the intelligence required, tailor OPSEC requirements, focus the rehearsals, and in combat ensure the efforts of the commander and the individual soldiers are centered on what is important, the mission.

All of the previous examples illustrate the relationship between the planning, preparation, and execution phases of a mission and demonstrate the synergistic nature of the six principles of special operations. The special operations model shown in figure 1-2 depicts the principles of special operations as an inverted pyramid.

The blocks within the pyramid can be constructed to reduce the frictions of war and achieve relative superiority. Although gaining relative superiority over the enemy is essential to success, it is not a guarantee. The success of the mission, like the inverted pyramid,

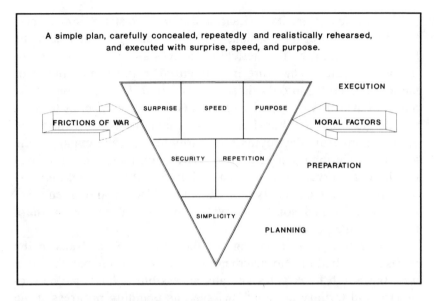

Fig. 1–2. The Special Operations Model

is precariously balanced on a slender apex. The moral factors of courage, intellect, boldness, and perseverance have to support the pyramid and prevent the frictions of war from toppling it and causing defeat. This model is a tool to help the reader analyze the historical cases and understand the relationship between the principles of special operations and relative superiority. This model also reflects the theory of special operations. It graphically represents the idea that special operations forces succeed, in spite of their numerical inferiority, when they are able to gain relative superiority through the use of a simple plan, carefully concealed, repeatedly and realistically rehearsed, and executed with surprise, speed, and purpose. Failure results when the frictions of war overcome the moral factors. Now let's examine the six principles in detail and demonstrate how they are manifested in combat.

Simplicity

Simplicity is the most crucial, and yet sometimes the most difficult, principle with which to comply. How does one make a plan simple? There are three elements of simplicity critical to success: limiting the number of objectives, good intelligence, and innovation.

The political or military situation dictates the strategic or operational objectives of the mission, but the planners generally have the latitude to determine the tactical objectives as long as the two objectives coincide. Therefore it is essential to limit the number of tactical objectives to only those that are vital. For example, at the outset of World War II, Hitler ordered German commandos to seize the Belgian fort at Eben Emael to prevent the fort's 75mm and 120mm guns from destroying the nearby bridges and engaging the advancing German panzer division. Although there were nineteen fortified artillery positions (each with two to three guns), the Germans initially attacked only nine casemates. The remaining ten casemates were aimed south and were not a threat to the northern bridges or the panzers.

Conversely, while planning for the raid on Saint-Nazaire the British identified the Normandie dry dock as the principal objective with the South Lock gates and any accessible U-boats as the secondary and tertiary targets.[9] However, as planning progressed the total number of major targets grew to eleven. By increasing the number of objectives from three to eleven, the assault force was required to add fifty more soldiers and over two hundred naval support personnel. Additionally, ten extra assault craft were added, more training was required, and the tactics had to be modified to accommodate these changes. Limiting the objectives to only what is essential focuses the training, limits the number of personnel required, reduces the time on target, and decreases the number of "moving parts."

Good intelligence is the second element needed to develop a simple plan. Good intelligence simplifies a plan by reducing the unknown factors and the number of variables that must be considered. While preparing to rescue hostages from the Entebbe Airport, Israeli intelligence personnel were able to determine the number of terrorists and Ugandan guards, their weaponry, and their general disposition. This information allowed the commander of the raid force, Brig. Gen. Dan Shomron, to reduce the size of his force to only what was necessary. This dramatically improved command and control and was essential to success. Prior to the raid on the fortress at Eben Emael, the Germans obtained engineering plans that provided a detailed description of the fort's emergency exits. This was necessary because if even a portion of the 650 Belgians inside the fort escaped, they could have overwhelmed the small German force. Armed with this knowledge, the glidermen, upon landing, quickly destroyed the emergency exits and eliminated the Belgians' capability to counterattack.

There will, however, always be gaps in the intelligence. The midget submarine crew that attacked the German battleship *Tirpitz* did not know how far the antitorpedo net extended below the water. At Son Tay, the raiders did not know exactly how many POWs there were, or how many enemy guards were inside the camp. In both cases the operators heeded the words of Clausewitz: "Many intelligence reports in war are contradictory; even more are false and most are uncertain. What one can reasonably ask of an officer is that he should possess a standard of judgement . . . He should be guided by the laws of probability."[10]

The submarine crew was prepared to cut through the net assuming that it extended to the seabed 120 feet below. Intelligence analysts studying the Son Tay camp projected the number of POWs and guards based on the number and size of the buildings. Both units built their plans around what was reasonable to expect.

The third element that contributes to simplicity is innovation. Innovation simplifies a plan by helping to avoid or eliminate obstacles that would otherwise compromise surprise and/or complicate the rapid execution of the mission. Innovation is normally manifested in new technology, but it is also the application of unconventional tactics. Fort Eben Emael was thirty miles from the German border. If surprise had been compromised, the Belgians would have had ample time to destroy the bridges crucial to the German advance. Airborne troops were unable to carry the heavy ordnance needed to destroy the casemates and parachute delivery would have produced too wide a troop dispersion. Hitler ordered Gen. Kurt Student to develop a gliderborne assault force to seize the fort. Although gliders were not a new technology, this was the first use of gliders during combat, and it surprised the Belgians long enough to allow the Germans to destroy the guns covering the bridges.

While training for the raid on the Son Tay POW camp in North Vietnam, Army Special Forces personnel had difficulty engaging targets at night. Even under the best circumstances "the accuracy of firing at night was roughly 35 percent."[11] Improving the accuracy was considered crucial to the rapid execution of the mission. Within a week of identifying the problem, Special Forces personnel found a commercially available low-light scope and accuracy rose to 95 percent.

In every case either new technology or innovative tactics were used to assist the assault element in reaching the objective and then quickly and effectively eliminating the enemy. Gliders, midget submarines, manned torpedoes, forward-looking infrared radar (FLIR)–equipped C-130Es, and modified destroyers were all new or innovative technology specially designed or configured to defeat enemy defenses and achieve surprise. Shaped charges, Bren guns, special demolitions, low-light scopes, Flash Stun grenades, and night-vision devices (NVDs) were all crucial to achieving speed on target.

Although the three elements of simplicity have their greatest impact during the execution phase, they must be identified early to help craft the plan and make it as simple as possible.

Security

The purpose of tight security is to prevent the enemy from gaining an advantage through foreknowledge of the impending attack. However, the nature of special operations is to attack a fortified position. It naturally follows that, whether in war or peace, the enemy is prepared for an attack. Therefore it is not so much the impending mission that must be concealed as the timing and, to a lesser degree, the means of insertion. For example, the students who seized the American embassy in Tehran were expecting the United States to attempt a rescue. They had covered the open area with long wooden stakes to prevent the landing of helicopter or airborne forces. The battleship *Tirpitz,* although securely nestled sixty miles up the Soroy Sound in Norway, was protected with antisubmarine nets, antitorpedo nets, and antiswimmer devices to counter any subsurface attack. The four terrorists aboard Lufthansa flight LH181 knew that both Germany and Israel had counterterrorist units capable of quickly assaulting an airliner. The terrorists were armed with automatic weapons and grenades and could easily have prevented GSG-9 from entering the Boeing 737.

In most of the historical cases the enemy personnel at the targets were adequately prepared to defend themselves against just the type of attack that occurred. Nevertheless, the assaults were mainly successful. Why? Security on the part of the attackers prevented the enemy from knowing the time, and in some cases, the method of the attack, although it did not prevent the enemy from preparing for an assault. Special operations succeed in spite of defensive preparation on the part of the enemy. Security should be as tight as possible, without unduly impeding the preparation or execution of operations. It is important in achieving relative superiority because it prevents the enemy from gaining an unexpected advantage. A prevailing reason for the success of special operations is the ability of the attacking force to know what defenses the enemy has prepared. A failed security effort could result in the enemy preparing a surprise of his own and subsequently preempting the attack or reducing the speed on target, both of which would dramatically reduce the possibility of achieving relative superiority.

Repetition
In the preparation phase, repetition, like routine, is indispensable in eliminating the barriers to success. When the air force task group involved in the Son Tay raid first attempted to fly the UH-1H in formation with the C-130, they found flying in such a tight formation so difficult that it was not within the "capability of the average Army aviator." After hundreds of hours of flying the same profile, however, "the tactics of drafting with the . . . UH-1H [were] proven and [could be] applied in future plans."[12]

General Joshua Shani, the lead C-130 pilot on the Entebbe raid, had only one opportunity to rehearse his short field landing prior to the mission, but to Shani it was not an issue. He said, "I had done hundreds of short field landings. They are part of basic training . . . it was routine."[13]

Certain combat units, such as counterterrorist teams, strategic bombers, and SEAL delivery vehicle teams, perform standard mission profiles as a matter of routine. This routine hones those tactical skills to a degree that allows quick reaction to a threat, provided that threat fits within the standard scenario for which the unit has been practicing. Most special operations, however, vary enough from the standard scenario that new equipment and tactics must be brought to bear on the problem. When this occurs it is essential to conduct at least one, and preferably two, full-dress rehearsals prior to the mission. The plan that sounded simple on paper must now be put to the test. The need for a full-dress rehearsal is borne out time and again. Invariably when a certain aspect of an operation was not rehearsed, it failed during the actual mission.

For example, the British had eighteen months to prepare for the attack on the German battleship *Tirpitz*. The mission called for the small dry submersibles, the X-craft, to be towed for eight days across the North Atlantic by conventional submarines. Towing was particularly taxing on the crews and therefore was only conducted for short durations during the rehearsals. On the actual towing operation the manila towline broke, one X-craft sank with the loss of all aboard, and one other was disabled beyond repair. Admiral Godfrey Place (commanding officer of *X-7*) commented, "If only we had towed the boats [X-craft] for the full eight days we might have known that the manila lines would break."[14]* Repetition hones individual and unit skills, while full-dress rehearsals unmask weaknesses in the plan. Both are essential to success on the battlefield.

Surprise

The *Doctrine for Joint Special Operations* states that surprise is the ability to "strike the enemy at a time or place, or in a manner, for which he is unprepared."[15] Yet in all the special operations examined, the enemy was entirely prepared to counter an offensive action. For example, at the Belgian fortress of Eben Emael, antiaircraft guns were positioned on top of the fort to prevent an airborne assault; the port facility of Saint-Nazaire was ringed with shore batteries and spotlights to prevent British ships from sailing undetected up the Loire River; the German battleship *Tirpitz* and the British battleships HMS *Queen Elizabeth* and HMS *Valiant* were surrounded by antisubmarine and antitorpedo nets; North Vietnam had one of the densest air defense systems in the world; Benito Mussolini was guarded by 250 Italian soldiers; the POWs in Cabanatuan were guarded by 223 Japanese soldiers; and the airport at

---

*There were two types of line used, manila and nylon. Because the manila line had not been tested for the full eight days there was no way of knowing it would part under actual conditions.

Entebbe, Uganda, was surrounded by 100 Ugandan soldiers with two battalions close by. The enemy, in each of these cases, was prepared to prevent an assault on their position, and yet, surprise was achieved in all instances.

Special operations forces do not generally have the luxury of attacking the enemy when or where he is unprepared. Such forces must attack in spite of enemy preparation. Surprise means catching the enemy off guard. This subtle difference is not mere semantics. Like two boxers in a ring, each is prepared to parry the other fighter's punches, but even with preparation, punches are landed. In a special operation surprise is gained through deception, timing, and taking advantage of the enemy's vulnerabilities.

Deception, when it works, either directs the enemy's attention away from the attacking force, or delays his response long enough for surprise to be gained at the crucial moment. For example, during the raid on Son Tay, the navy's Carrier Task Force 77 conducted a three-carrier diversionary strike that "served to deny the enemy the option of concentrating his attention [on the] true and primary mission."[16] This diversion was highly successful. It allowed the heliborne raid force to penetrate North Vietnam's air defense and land undetected in the POW camp. Deception that redirects attention can be risky, and when it fails to gain the appropriate response, it is usually disastrous. At Saint-Nazaire, the Royal Air Force was ordered to bomb the port city to redirect the Germans' attention away from the small armada of boats sneaking up the Loire River. Unfortunately, the air raid served only to heighten the Germans' alert posture and make complete surprise unattainable.

Although deception that redirected the enemy's attention worked well for the Son Tay raiders, in most special operations deception is best used to delay action by the enemy. For example, when the Israelis assaulted Entebbe Airport, they used a Mercedes sedan, similar to the one driven by Ugandan dignitaries, to momentarily delay action by the Ugandan guards. When Skorzeny landed at Gran Sasso to rescue Mussolini, he brought along a high-ranking Italian general. Skorzeny believed that the Italian general's "mere presence would probably serve to create certain confusion . . . a sort of hesitation which would prevent them from resisting immediately or from assassinating the Duce."[17] Skorzeny's assumption proved correct, and the additional confusion provided him with enough time to

reach Mussolini. As several of the cases demonstrate, deception can
be a useful tool in gaining surprise, but overreliance on deception
should be avoided, and it is usually better to delay the enemy's reaction than to divert his attention.

The time of attack is a key factor in gaining surprise. Most attacking forces prefer to assault a target at night, primarily because
darkness provides cover, but also because at nighttime the enemy is
presumed to be tired, less vigilant, and more susceptible to surprise.
But nighttime frequently increases alertness and each mission
should consider the ramifications of a night assault. Several of the
most successful special operations were conducted in daytime and
achieved a high degree of surprise. Skorzeny, for example, landed
at Gran Sasso at 1400. He knew that the Italian guards would have
just finished lunch and would be resting afterward. The Germans
who attacked Eben Emael landed at first light. The morning light
provided the gliders illumination to land, and many of the Belgian
gun crews were still in the nearby town. The midget submarines
that destroyed the *Tirpitz* also attacked in the morning. British intelligence had informed the submariners that the *Tirpitz*'s sonar equipment would be down for repair during the morning of the attack. In
special operations the enemy will be prepared; the question is,
when will he be least prepared and what time of day most benefits
the attacking force?

Every defense has a weak point. Gaining surprise means exploiting this weakness. Although the North Vietnamese had the most
extensive air defense network in Asia, air force intelligence was
able to find a five-minute gap in the radar's rotation cycle. This
allowed the C-130 and the helicopters to insert the Son Tay raiders
undetected into North Vietnam.

A similar problem was encountered by the British during World
War II. The Royal Air Force had made countless attempts to sink
the battleship *Tirpitz* from the air. The battleship, which was anchored in Kaafjord, Norway, was protected by antiaircraft batteries,
and the ship's self-protection included sixteen 4.1-inch, sixteen
37mm, and eighty 20mm antiaircraft guns. Additionally, most of the
ship was encased in 12-inch armor. However, the weak point of the
vessel was its thinly covered keel. It was here, at the soft underbelly, that the British chose to attack. Surprise was gained by two

midget submarines (*X-6* and *X-7*) when they penetrated the German defenses and dropped their explosives. In the case of the *Tirpitz,* weakness in defense was a relative term. The Germans did have several antisubmarine and antitorpedo defenses; however, compared to their antiaircraft defenses, the submarine defenses were considerably weaker.

Many tacticians consider the principle of surprise to be the most important factor in a successful special operation. They mistakenly believe that it is surprise that gives them the decisive advantage over the enemy, as if merely catching the enemy unprepared would assure the attacking force of victory. This is not the case. Surprise is useless and indeed unachievable without the other principles. What good would it do to surprise the enemy, only to be ill equipped to fight him? Relative superiority is gained only through the correct application of all the principles. Surprise is essential, but it should not be viewed in isolation. It is only valuable as part of the complete pyramid of principles.

Speed

In a special operations mission, the concept of speed is simple. Get to your objective as fast as possible. Any delay will expand your area of vulnerability and decrease your opportunity to achieve relative superiority.

Speaking of war in general, the *Fleet Marine Force Manual* (*FMFM 1-3*) states, "As with all things in war, speed is relative."[18] This statement by *FMFM 1-3* may be true in conventional or large-scale warfare where the forces on a battlefield maneuver and adjust to certain tactical advances, but in special operations the enemy is in a defensive position and his only desire is to counter your attack. Therefore, the enemy's will to resist is a given, and his ability to react a constant. Consequently, over time the frictions of war work only against the special operations forces and not against the enemy. It is essential, therefore, to move as quickly as possible regardless of the enemy's reaction.

For example, in the two cases involving submarine attacks, the British X-craft raid on the *Tirpitz* and the Italian manned torpedo attack on the British fleet in Alexandria, the attacking forces were completely clandestine in their approach. The enemy was unaware of their presence and therefore was not trying to counter the will of the attacking force. Nonetheless, speed was not relative; it became a critical factor in mission success. The X-craft midget submarines, which had transited the North Atlantic two days earlier, began to have catastrophic failures in their electrical and ballast systems. As each minute passed, the ballast and trim of one midget submarine became increasingly worse, causing it to list fifteen degrees to port. Time became such a factor that the submarine commander, Lt. Don Cameron, decided not to cut clandestinely through the antitorpedo net but to surface and make a mad dash for the *Tirpitz*. This action was taken at great risk to the mission's success, but Cameron clearly realized that time, not the Germans, was now his worst enemy.

The Italian frogmen who entered Alexandria Harbor on manned torpedoes were constantly exposed to the cold water. They knew that even if the enemy didn't discover them, the forces of nature and physical exertion would overcome them. As he closed in on the British battleship HMS *Valiant,* Lieutenant Durand de la Penne recalled, "I am tormented by thirst . . . I cannot continue working from the extreme fatigue and for the breathlessness."[19] He knew that "speed was essential . . . [if he were forced to surface from fatigue] the alarm would be given, depth charges would be dropped, and [the] operation . . . would be doomed to failure."[20] But because Durand de la Penne worked quickly, he was not discovered until after he had surfaced. Hours later the warhead from the manned torpedo exploded and the HMS *Valiant* sank in Alexandria Harbor. In both of these cases, the enemy was not a factor, but time was still working to prevent a successful outcome.

Most special operations involve direct, and in most cases immediate, contact with the enemy, where minutes and seconds spell the difference between success and failure. Of the successful missions analyzed in this book, only in the Saint-Nazaire raid did the attacker take longer than thirty minutes to achieve relative superiority from the point of vulnerability. In most of the other cases, relative superiority was achieved in five minutes and the missions were completed in thirty minutes.*

---

*There were some cases—i.e., the raid on the Cabanatuan POW camp, the Son Tay raid, and Skorzeny's rescue of Mussolini—where the mission was not over until the return trip was complete.

In order to gain surprise and speed, special forces are generally small and lightly armed, and therefore they are unable to sustain action against a conventional enemy for long periods of time. The raid on Saint-Nazaire illustrates the problems that arise when special forces attempt to prolong the engagement. When the number of objectives at Saint-Nazaire increased from three to eleven, the operation required additional time ashore for the commandos to destroy these targets. In a draft memorandum to the chiefs of staff on Operation Chariot, the Combined Operations Command adviser stated that in order to achieve all the objectives, "the whole force . . . [would require] a maximum period ashore of 2 hours."[21] What advantages the commandos gained in surprise they lost in execution, by actually planning an operation that took two hours of sustained action. This required their lightly armed, and in some cases unarmed, force to fight against a heavily armed German flak brigade of three hundred soldiers. Clausewitz warns: "The more restricted the strength the more restricted the goals must be; further, the more restricted the strength, the more limited the duration."[22] Also during this two-hour period, the seventeen motor launches that had delivered the commandos to Saint-Nazaire were exposed to withering shore fire and within ninety minutes almost all of them were destroyed or had retreated. Had the commandos struck quickly and extracted, the probability of mission completion would have increased dramatically.

Speed in a special operation is a function of time, not, as some imply, a relative factor that is affected by the enemy's will to resist. As I will demonstrate later, relative superiority can be gained, despite the efforts of the enemy, primarily because the attacking force moves with such speed that the enemy's reaction is not an overriding factor.

Purpose

Purpose is understanding and then executing the prime objective of the mission regardless of emerging obstacles or opportunities. There are two aspects of this principle. First, the purpose must be clearly defined by the mission statement: rescue the POWs, destroy the dry dock, sink the battleship, etc. This mission statement should be crafted to ensure that in the heat of battle, no matter what else happens, the individual soldier understands the primary objective. For example, during the X-craft raid on the battleship *Tirpitz*, the midget submarine *X-6* was suffering from major equipment casualties (the attack periscope was broken, the port demolition charge was flooded, the main casing was leaking, and the midget submarine had a fifteen-degree port list), and the commander, Lt. Don Cameron, had to make the decision whether or not to attack. It was conceivable that by attacking and failing, he could compromise the success of the other two X-craft also assigned to attack the *Tirpitz*.* After mentally reviewing the purpose of his mission, as defined by his operational orders, Cameron made the decision to attack. His orders were clear. If the X-craft was still under power and equipped with at least one side charge, then Cameron was directed to complete the mission.

During the assault on the British fleet in Alexandria Harbor during World War II, the Italian frogmen, Gunner Captain Vincenzo Martellota and his swim partner, Petty Officer/Diver Mario Marino, positioned their manned torpedo underneath a large British cruiser before realizing that it was the wrong target. Martellota and Marino had risked their lives avoiding picketboats, depth charges, and pier security, and although sinking the cruiser would have been acceptable, it was not the vessel they were assigned to attack. Martellota subsequently backed away from the ship and continued on. Eventually the Italians reached their assigned target, a large oil tanker. By following their orders, Martellota and Marino not only sank a large tanker, but also severely damaged a destroyer tied alongside. In both the British and Italian cases, the men had clearly defined orders that directed their actions in the heat of battle and focused their efforts on what was important.

The second aspect of the principle of purpose is personal commitment. Lt. Col. Henry Mucci, who commanded the 6th Ranger Battalion and rescued 512 POWs from a Japanese death camp, understood the need for personal commitment. Before the operation

---

X-10, commanded by Lt. Ken Hudspeth, was assigned to attack the *Scharnhorst,* a German cruiser located just a mile from the *Tirpitz.* Hudspeth found himself in similar mechanical difficulty, but his orders clearly forbade him to attack if it could compromise the destruction of the primary target, the *Tirpitz.*

he told his Rangers, "You had better get down on your knees and pray! Damn it . . . don't fake it! I mean . . . PRAY. And, I want you to swear an oath before God . . . Swear you'll die fighting rather than let any harm come to those POWs!"[23]

Similarly, Gen. Joshua Shani, the air commander at Entebbe, stated several years after the raid, "We were absolutely committed to seeing the task completed . . . We were fighting for Israel."[24]

The purpose of the mission must be thoroughly understood beforehand, and the men must be inspired with a sense of personal dedication that knows no limitations. Captain Otto Skorzeny once said, "When a man is moved by pure enthusiasm and by the conviction that he is risking his life in a noble cause . . . he provides the essential elements for success."[25] In an age of high technology and Jedi Knights we often overlook the need for personal involvement, but we do so at our own risk. As Clausewitz warned, "Theorists are apt to look on fighting in the abstract as a trial of strength without emotion entering into it. This is one of a thousand errors which they quite consciously commit because they have no idea of the implications."[26]

The principles of special operations defined above are not merely derivatives of the army's principles of war. They represent unique elements of warfare that only special forces possess and can employ effectively. The next section describes the methodology used to develop these principles.

CASE STUDY METHODOLOGY

To further explain the theory of special operations, I will present eight historical cases and provide an analysis of each. The cases span the entire spectrum of special operations from global conventional war to peacetime engagement. They include missions conducted by United States, British, German, Israeli, and Italian forces, executed from the sea, air, and land. My approach to multiple mission analysis was fostered by the British military philosopher B. H. Liddell Hart, who said, "The method in recent generations has been to select one or two campaigns, and to study them exhaustively as a means of professional training and as the foundation of military theory. But with such a limited basis the continual changes in military means from war to war carry the danger that our outlook will be

narrow and the lessons fallacious."[27] Although eight cases are not
definitive, they are sufficient to demonstrate the validity of the
theory and show how the principles of special operations help reduce the frictions of war and allow the attacking force to achieve
relative superiority.

I conducted interviews with key participants, and, when possible,
visited the actual sites where the operations occurred. In seven of
the eight cases presented, the Mussolini event being the exception,
I was able to interview personnel intimately involved with the mission.* This was unquestionably the most rewarding aspect of my
work. These individuals provided personal insight into the success
or failure of the mission and helped me formulate my theory in a
clear, concise manner. They also verified facts, corrected errors in
documentary sources, provided original documentation and photos,
and in many cases, edited my rough drafts. Where I could not confirm a salient fact by interview or official report, I ensured that at
least three secondary sources were in agreement on the point. It is
from this original research that the principles of special operations,
which subsequently led to the understanding of relative superiority
and the development of the theory, were derived.

Each of the cases is loosely divided into six sections: the background, which provides the military or political justification for the
operation; the objective, including a detailed look at the target and
the enemy order of battle; the commandos, a history of the units
(when available) and biographies of key personnel who led the
missions; the training or preliminary events; the mission, including
a description of the events during the engagement; and an analysis
of the operation.

The analysis begins with an essay on the outcome of the mission,
which is followed by a series of questions designed to flesh out the
merit of the plan and its subsequent execution. These questions are
as follows: Were the objectives worth the risk? Risk in this context

*Although I was unable to interview any of the commandos who partici-
pated in the Mussolini event, I did visit Gran Sasso where Mussolini was
held prisoner and reviewed in depth Lt. Col. Otto Skorzeny's original
(German version) summary of the event.

applies not only to loss of human lives but also to loss of military or political advantage. If the risks are considered acceptable, was the plan developed to achieve maximum superiority over the enemy and minimize the risk to the assault force? If the plan was sound, was the mission executed in accordance with the plan, and if not, what unforeseen circumstances dictated the outcome of the operation? Finally, what modifications to the plan and the execution could have improved the final results? The analysis also includes a relative superiority graph followed by an examination of the six principles of special operations.

The next eight chapters will present the case studies discussed above in great detail. The analysis of these cases will show that relative superiority, although an abstract concept, does exist and that the theory of special operations is a powerful tool to explain victory and defeat.

Notes

1. Joint Chiefs of Staff, *Joint Publication 3-05 (Test): Doctrine for Joint Special Operations* (Washington, D.C.: Office of the Joint Chiefs of Staff, 1990).

2. Carl von Clausewitz, *On War,* ed. and trans. Michael Howard and Peter Paret (Princeton, N.J.: Princeton University Press, 1976), xxx, 358.

3. Ibid., 194.

4. Ibid., 159.

5. The Holloway Commission, "Rescue Mission Report," in *The Iranian Rescue Mission* (Washington, D.C.: Department of Defense, August 1980), 58.

6. Ibid., 59.

7. Clausewitz, *On War,* 198.

8. Thomas Gallagher, *The X-Craft Raid* (New York: Harcourt Brace Jovanovich, 1971), 20.

9. H.M.S.O., *Combined Operations: The Official Story of the Commandos* (New York: Macmillan, 1943), 72.

10. Clausewitz, *On War,* 183.

11. Lt. Gen. Leroy J. Manor, interview by Dr. John Parton and Maj. Dick Meadows, Tampa, Fla., 23 February 1988.

12. Commander, JCS Joint Contingency Task Group, *Report on the Son Tay Prisoner of War Rescue Operation,* Part I (Washington, D.C.: Office of the Joint Chiefs of Staff, 1970), part 1, E-61, E-54.

13. Gen. Joshua Shani, interview by author, tape recording, Washington, D.C., 19 January 1993.

14. RAdm. Godfrey Place, V.C., interview by author, tape recording, Sherborne, Dorset, England, 18 June 1992.

15. JCS, *Doctrine for Joint Special Operations,* E-5.

16. JCS, *Report on Son Tay,* iv.

17. Otto Skorzeny, *Skorzeny's Secret Mission,* trans. Jacques Le Clercq (New York: E. P. Dutton, 1950), 87.

18. Department of the Navy, *Fleet Marine Force Manual (FMFM) 1-3 Tactics* (Washington, D.C.: Department of the Navy, 1991), 63.

19. Luigi Durand de la Penne, "Report on Operation G.A.3: The Attack on HMS *Valiant*," in Dott. Carlo de Risio, compiler, *I Mezzi d'Asssalto* (Rome: Ufficio Storico della Marina Militare, 1991). The report was translated for the author by Lt. Comdr. Paolo Gianetti of the Italian Navy.

20. Juilo Valerio Borghese, *Sea Devils*, trans. James Cleugh (Chicago: Henry Regnery, 1954), 148.

21. Advisor on combined operations, "Draft Memorandum to the Chiefs of Staff: Operation 'Chariot,'" Imperial War Museum.

22. Clausewitz, *On War*, 283.

23. Forrest B. Johnson, *Hour of Redemption: The Ranger Raid on Cabanatuan* (New York: Manor Books, 1978), 171.

24. Shani, interview.

25. Skorzeny, *Secret Mission*, 24.

26. Clausewitz, *On War*, 138.

27. B. H. Liddell Hart, *Strategy*, 2d ed. (New York: Penguin, 1991), 4.

2

The German Attack on Eben Emael, 10 May 1940

BACKGROUND

In January 1933, Adolf Hitler was appointed chancellor of Germany. His rise to power was fueled by his promise to avenge the defeat of World War I and the humiliating Treaty of Versailles. By 1935 Hitler had completely rejected the Armistice of 1918, which limited German arms production. He began to build the most powerful army in Europe, and by the late 1930s there was little doubt the German army was preparing for war.

The small country of Belgium had long been considered a primary axis for a German invasion into France. Before World War I, the chief of the German General Staff, Count Alfred von Schlieffen, developed a plan calling for the encirclement of France by two avenues of approach, through the Swiss Alps and across Belgium. Little had changed during the interwar years to warrant a major modification to the Germans' Schlieffen Plan. The French and Belgians were keenly aware of their geographical predicament. However, cutbacks after World War I significantly reduced the size and effectiveness of both armies and fostered a reliance on defensive warfare. This defensive mentality was manifested in France's Maginot line and Belgium's Albert Canal defenses.

The Maginot line was a system of fortifications built along the eastern French border in the 1930s. It extended from Switzerland to Belgium. The Belgians constructed a similar defensive perimeter along the Albert Canal. The linchpin of their fortifications was the largest single fort of its day, Eben Emael. Between the Albert Canal and the Maginot line stood the massive Ardennes Forest, a seemingly impregnable obstacle for an advancing army. With these fortifications in place the French and British positioned their armies in northern France to take advantage of the only logical German avenues of approach.

The German commander in chief, Gen. Walther von Brauchitsch, and his chief of staff, Gen. Franz Halder, both felt that a German advance must outflank the Maginot line and concentrate the Schwerpunkt (point of the spear) of the attack north of the impassable Ardennes Forest. This would take the bulk of the German army through Holland, then Belgium. A smaller but relatively strong force would attempt to negotiate the Ardennes and cross the Meuse River between Givet and Sedan in eastern France. Although this was the predictable approach, Brauchitsch and Halder were counting on surprise and the superior German forces to rout the enemy.

This plan met with exceptional criticism from two prominent German generals, Erich von Manstein (chief of staff, Army Group A) and Heinz Guderian (XIX Panzer Corps commander). Guderian proposed driving three panzer corps through the Ardennes, across the Meuse, and deep into the heart of France. This would allow the Germans to flank the Allied forces, who were expecting the main thrust to come across Belgium. "Before the attack could succeed," wrote historian Charles Kirkpatrick, "the French mobile forces, along with their British allies, had to be decisively engaged in battle elsewhere, so that they could not swiftly intervene in the developing attack in the south. In essence the trick was to entice the British and French main body into advancing to give battle in Belgium, where German conventional infantry divisions stiffened by a few armored divisions would tie them down."[1]

The Allies were not prepared to commit forces to the north unless the Germans violated Belgian neutrality, and then only if they were certain it was the main German assault. Hitler quickly accepted the Guderian Plan, realizing that its genius lay in the boldness and surprise with which German armor would be deployed.

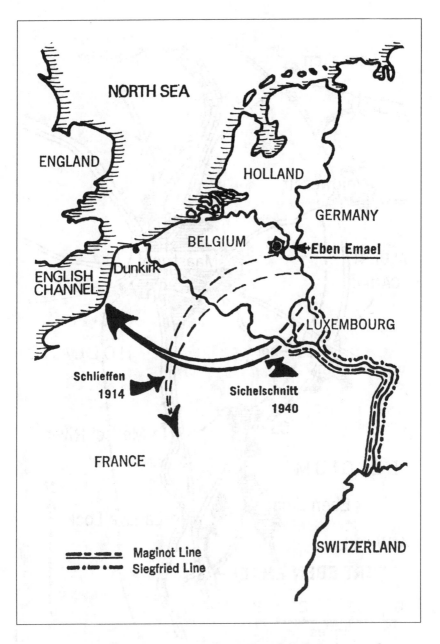

Fig. 2–1. The Importance of Eben Emael in Relation to the Blitzkrieg. From Mrazek, *Eben Emael*, 20

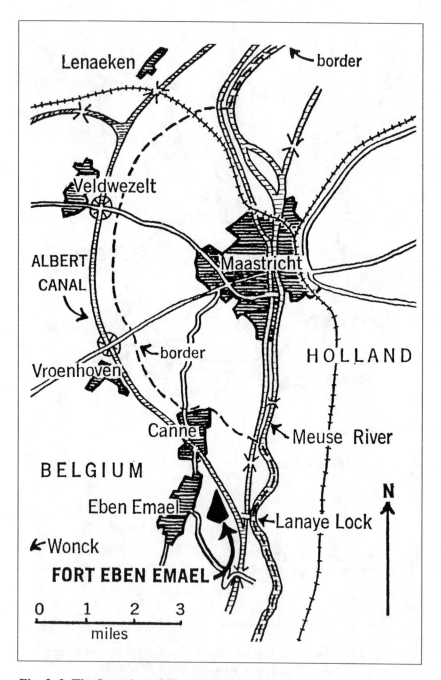

Fig. 2–2. The Location of Eben Emael. From Mrazek, *Eben Emael,* **23**

In order to ensure the Allies committed forces to the north, the Germans had to move swiftly through Holland and into Belgium. This required crossing the Albert Canal and moving two panzer corps through Belgium to engage the British Expeditionary Force and the French First Army. Before the Germans could get deep into Belgium they had to cross fifteen miles of Holland and the Albert Canal. The canal could only be crossed by three bridges at Veldwezelt, Vroenhoven, and Canne. Although the entire campaign hinged on securing the bridges, the defenses surrounding them "were not considered to pose a problem. There were several dropping zones for parachutists [and gliders] close by from which assault parties could quickly overcome the Belgian army defences covering the crossings."[2] The real problem was Fort Eben Emael. Even if the bridges were captured by German paratroopers or glidermen, the guns at Eben Emael could still destroy them from afar and prevent the panzers from entering Belgium.

On 27 October 1939, Gen. Kurt Student, commander of the 7th Airborne Division, was summoned to the Reich Chancellery in Berlin by Adolf Hitler. Student had developed the concept of three-dimensional warfare in which airborne troops could be inserted behind the lines and, using surprise and speed, could attack the enemy where he was least prepared. Hitler viewed Student's concept as a new secret weapon.[3]

Hitler outlined a concept to seize the fort at Eben Emael using gliders to land troops atop the earthen structure and destroy the guns protecting the canal bridges. He directed Student to review his plan and return the following day with an answer. Student was an accomplished glider pilot and had been conducting tests using troop-carrying gliders to insert his airborne personnel. The following day Student returned and told the führer that the mission was possible provided it was done at daybreak or morning twilight. Hitler accepted Student's concept and ordered him to "take Fort Eben Emael!"

FORTRESS EBEN EMAEL

The small town of Eben Emael was located just inside the border separating Belgium and Holland. The fort, which takes its name from the town, was completed in 1935. It was situated on the Albert

Canal adjacent to the Meuse River just three miles south of the city of Maastricht. At the site of the fort, the walls of the canal rose two hundred feet from the water level to the top of the ridge. From the top of the fort the defenders could see miles into the German countryside as well as the three bridges at Canne, Vroenhoven, and Veldwezelt.

The fort itself was roughly diamond shaped with the tip facing north, the east wall along the Albert Canal, and the west wall (fortified with a 450-yard-long antitank moat) bordered by the Geer River. The fort measured eleven hundred yards north to south by eight hundred yards at its widest point. On top were ten casemates, five operational cupolas, and two dummy cupolas. Along the wall of the canal were two additional casemates. The casemates and cupolas were similar in construction to the turrets of a battleship, with guns protruding from apertures in either a six-inch-thick steel dome or a concrete blockhouse. Each fighting position housed a crew of sixteen to thirty men depending on the size and number of guns. The main batteries at casemates 26, 18, and 12 each had three 75mm guns. These guns provided the primary protection for the outlying towns and the three canal bridges. Casement 9 and cupolas 23 and 31 housed twin 75mm guns. Cupola 24 contained twin 120mm guns, the largest at Eben Emael. These guns were capable of ranging twelve miles. The remaining casemates and cupolas housed twin 75mm guns and mitrailleuse machine guns which provided additional anti-infantry defense of the fortress. There were five 60mm antiaircraft batteries situated around casemate 30. The one defensive shortfall of Eben Emael was the lack of fighting trenches and mines on top of the fort. There were, however, five rows of barbed wire strung in strategic positions. Outside the surface of the fort there were rows and rows of barbed wire, steel hedgehogs, and minefields, but the grassy top lay vulnerable.

Below the surface there were three levels that provided support for the fort's main mission as an artillery emplacement. The top level consisted of the machinery for operating the massive guns and the protective steel doors for preventing entry into the belly of the fort. The second level contained a small infirmary, ammunition storage, six 175-horsepower electric generators that provided all the fort's power, a communications center, and the command post. The

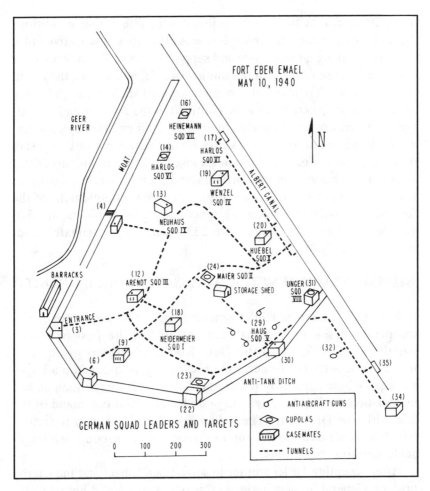

Fig. 2–3. Casemates and Cupolas at Eben Emael and the Squads
Assigned to Destroy Them. From Mrazek, *Eben Emael*, 80, redrawn
with additional material at U.S. Navy Postgraduate School,
Monterey, California

third level housed the barracks for the fort's personnel. The entire complex was designed with the guns in mind. Ammunition hoists serviced
the guns directly, stairs and elevators were constructed to allow
ammo bearers ease of movement, and air-conditioning and heating

units ensured that the troops enjoyed adequate living conditions throughout the year. The entire fort was crisscrossed with five miles of tunnels linking all major gun and support systems. The only exterior entrance into the fort lay on the southwest side, away from the canal.

The troops that manned the guns rotated duty throughout the month. Off-duty personnel were confined to the area around the village of Eben Emael. If they were needed in an emergency an alarm would be sounded by firing twenty blank rounds every thirty seconds. On the day of the German attack, the fort had an authorized strength of twelve hundred officers and men. However, owing to leave, illness, or out-of-area training, the total complement of the fort included only 18 officers, 62 noncommissioned officers, and 570 enlisted. Additionally, there were 233 soldiers approximately four miles away at Wonck.

STORM DETACHMENT KOCH—ASSAULT FORCE GRANITE

In 1935, the German High Command began training its first paratroopers and several months later established the first parachute battalion. In 1938, Luftwaffe Gen. Kurt Student was given command of the airborne forces and quickly began to develop a large-scale parachute capability within the German air force. Soon he had established the 7th Air Division and also received command of the 22d Airborne Division.* These forces included not only parachutists, but all air and ground support necessary to accomplish large-scale airborne operations.

After accepting Hitler's order to seize Eben Emael and the nearby bridges, General Student assigned Capt. S. A. Koch and his 1st Company of Flieger-Jaeger Regiment 1 to conduct the mission. Koch began training his company for the mission on 2 November 1939, and it assumed the name Storm Detachment Koch. The detachment consisted of one company of parachutists (soon to receive the name glidermen), one platoon of parachute-qualified engineers (these men

---

*In an effort to conceal the existence of the airborne forces, the 7th Air Division was assigned to the Wehrmacht but was controlled by the Luftwaffe. All the forces that participated in the assault were German air force.

were eventually tasked with taking Eben Emael), a transport group of Ju 52 aircraft, and over forty gliders with pilots and ground crews.

From these forces Koch divided the detachment into four assault elements. The force assigned to assault Eben Emael was codenamed Granite and commanded by Lt. Rudolf Witzig. It consisted of two officers, eleven glider pilots, and seventy-two enlisted men. The element tasked with capturing the bridge at Vroenhoven was codenamed Concrete and commanded by Lieutenant Schacht. It consisted of five officers including Captain Koch and a small command element, eleven gliders and pilots, and ninety-four enlisted men. The third element was codenamed Steel and was ordered to seize the bridge at Veldwezelt. Commanded by Lieutenant Altmann, it had only one officer, ten gliders and pilots, and eighty-nine enlisted. The last element was codenamed Iron and commanded by Lieutenant Schaechter. Schaechter had one more officer, nine gliders and pilots, and seventy-nine enlisted men. They were assigned to capture the bridge at Canne.

At the outset of the operation, General Student made every effort to conceal the existence of the detachment. "The whole premise behind the operation was that any leak in security could compromise the mission, and the only way for this mission to be successful was to achieve total surprise."[4] They trained at Hildesheim, near Hanover, and took the deceptive title of Experimental Section Friedrichshafen. As the detachment moved to other locations for training they were often renamed. Lieutenant Witzig's engineer platoon once received the title Airport Construction Platoon. The soldiers were not allowed to send personal mail or make calls unless cleared through Koch. Sgt. Helmut Wenzel, the senior enlisted man in Witzig's platoon, recalled, "We couldn't go into bars, but we could go into movies. However, we had to have a guard. Usually by the time the movie was over, the guards had lost interest and gone home . . . Also we didn't wear insignia, and we had other names. Once we ran into some girls we knew and the whole unit had to be transferred."[5]

Each man was also required to sign the following statement:

I am aware that I shall risk sentence of death should I, by intent or carelessness, make known to another person by spoken word or illustration anything concerning the base at which I am serving.[6]

Witzig's engineer platoon had served together for over a year before this mission was conceived. Almost all of the men participated in the Polish campaign but had only seen limited action. "They were honorable men," Sergeant Wenzel recalled, "but they were all a little crazy."[7]

When Witzig first reported to the platoon he was not well received. "They were undisciplined and I was not popular because I changed the standards."[8] Witzig kept his distance from the men. Occasionally he would have a beer with his soldiers, but he never let them get too close. "They never called me by my first name or used informal language."[9] Most of the men expected to be discharged upon return from Poland, but soon found out that their war was just beginning.

The key to a successful mission clearly lay in the ability of the Luftwaffe to deliver Witzig's combat engineers to Eben Emael undetected. Since the early 1930s Germany had been preparing its youth for a future war on the European continent. A large part of this effort was devoted to encouraging the sport of gliding. All across Germany young men and women began learning to fly. This created a sizable pool of talented pilots, fostered competition, and improved the capabilities of existing gliders. In 1933, Dr. Alexander Lippisch developed a large glider capable of carrying heavy loads of meteorological equipment. Although the glider did not soar like the smaller sport gliders, it was able to maintain a gradual glide path from its release point. The Luftwaffe soon saw the military application for this glider and recruited the Deutsche Forschungsanstalt für Segelflug (DFS) aircraft company, which was associated with the Rhoen Research Institute, to build a prototype. By 1939 they had produced the DFS 230. This glider was to have a pivotal role in the operation.

The DFS 230 was approximately thirty-seven feet long, had a wing span of seventy-two feet, and was almost nine feet high at its maximum point. It was capable of being towed at 130 mph with a maximum glide speed of 180 mph. The glider weighed 1,896 pounds and could carry ten combat-loaded troops for a total loaded weight of 4,630 pounds. It was armed with a single flexible 7.95mm MG-15 and two fixed 7.92mm MG-34 machine guns.

Koch had been given a free hand in planning and training for Eben Emael, and it became readily apparent to him that the DFS 230, although an exceptionally capable glider, was difficult for novice glider pilots to fly. He recruited several internationally recognized glider pilots to assist in the training and execution of the mission. The more novice Luftwaffe glider pilots would be used to assault the bridges, where the approach was easier and the landing zone was larger. The seasoned sport pilots would take Witzig's men to the top of Fort Eben Emael. Witzig, who does not dole out praise quickly, said emphatically, "These pilots were the best!"[10]

This infusion of experienced civilian pilots created quite a rift between the civilians and the novice Luftwaffe pilots. The civilians failed to conform to the usual military discipline and constantly berated the less experienced, rank-conscious Luftwaffe. This became a recurring problem for Koch and one that he never fully solved. The morale and esprit de corps evident in the glidermen and Luftwaffe were almost nonexistent in the civilian pilots. However, since the pilots would land with the glidermen, Koch integrated them into the assault element, insuring they participated in the planning and training.[11]

RUDOLF WITZIG—GRANITE FORCE COMMANDER

Rudolf Witzig was born on 14 August 1916, and at the age of twenty-three was placed in charge of the pioneer (engineer) platoon tasked with assaulting Eben Emael. He was young and inexperienced, and most of the platoon sergeants were older than he. Witzig was not well liked by the platoon. He was a strict disciplinarian, and the platoon members, even by Sergeant Wenzel's account, were "bandits." Although disciplined when they fought, they were undisciplined as a matter of routine.

The officer Witzig relieved had allowed the platoon to become lazy. Witzig set out to change that attitude. He was firm in his belief that an officer should be reasonable in his approach to his men. He should have "good nerves . . . be fit . . . be faithful . . . like women, but not be a whoremonger . . . [and above all] be totally convinced that the operation is necessary for the people and the unit."[12] Witzig believed in "meticulous planning and practice."[13] When I interviewed him, Witzig remarked that the reason the Americans failed in Iran (referring to the Iranian hostage rescue attempt) was because the mission "wasn't rehearsed enough."[14]

Although Witzig is often described as a martinet, a rigid, military disciplinarian, he had the highest regard for his enlisted men. The Germans had very few officers by comparison with the Allies. Witzig commented that "attacks led by enlisted men would have been led by officers in other countries. This was allowed because our enlisted men were so good."[15] Witzig stressed that he gave individual squad leaders a great deal of responsibility and the freedom to develop their own plans.

Witzig was an officer with tremendous determination. During the initial journey to Eben Emael, Witzig's glider crashed in Germany. He commandeered a vehicle, got the glider airborne, and arrived at the battle late. Referring to this incident, Wenzel remarked, "It was a testament to Witzig's personality that he was able to get back to the fight."[16] This determination carried Witzig through the remainder of the war. The following year, on 21 May 1941, Witzig parachuted into Crete where, despite being outnumbered three to one, the Germans defeated the Allies and took the island. Although severely wounded there, Witzig recovered and in November 1942 fought in North Africa. In 1943, the 21st Parachute Engineer Regiment, formed under the command of Major Witzig, was sent to Russia and subsequently saw action at Kovno, Lithuania, and Vilna, Poland. In 1944, Witzig commanded the 18th Parachute Regiment and fought in France, Belgium, and Holland, eventually surrendering in April 1945.

After the war he transferred to the German army (the engineers were Luftwaffe) and rose to the rank of colonel, eventually becoming director of the engineer school in Munich. He retired from that assignment and still lives in Munich. His decorations include the Knights Cross with Oak Leaves.

TRAINING

On 3 November 1939, Captain Koch received orders for his company to make preparations to seize and hold the fort at Eben Emael and the three bridges at Vroenhoven, Veldwezelt, and Canne until

German ground forces arrived. The basic plan had already been conceived by General Student and approved by Hitler. On order, the company would depart Cologne from airfields at Ostheim and Butzweilerhof. Separated into four groups (Iron, Granite, Concrete, Steel), they would be transported in gliders towed by Ju 52s to a release point approximately twenty kilometers from their objectives. At an altitude of approximately fifty-five hundred feet the gliders would be released and would proceed to their targets. Upon arrival at Eben Emael, Witzig's engineer platoon would destroy the guns that covered the approaches to the three bridges and with the help of Stuka divebombers attempt to keep the Belgian defenders sealed inside until reinforcements arrived. As Witzig viewed the mission he had three objectives: "The first objective was to take out the machine guns on the surface so we could go in safely. The second objective was to take out the casemates, and the third [objective] was to survive!"[17]

The three bridges would be seized by Koch's other elements, and the permanently emplaced explosive charges would be rendered inoperable.

In order to seize the fort, two phases of the operation had to be rehearsed in excruciating detail, the glider insertion and the actions at the objective. After managing to obtain the requisite number of glider pilots, Koch, with the help of world-class glider pilot Heiner Langer, set out to teach all the pilots the intricacies of the DFS 230. The pilots spent months learning to fly empty and then with a full load. All of the gear in the glider had to be tightly secured. The troops, who straddled a narrow center aisle bench, found that even the smallest unsecured item could become a hazard as the glider rode the shifting air currents. There was some debate as to whether Koch's men actually conducted rehearsals in the gliders. Charles Kirkpatrick, writing for *World War II* magazine, noted that "neither [Koch nor Witzig] attached much importance to having their men actually fly in gliders and make landings in full scale rehearsals. Flying in gliders was inherently dangerous and could easily lead to training accidents that would diminish the force available for the mission."[18]

This, however, is not the case. Both Witzig and Wenzel confirmed the fact that they rehearsed with the gliders. Witzig recalled, "We practiced most of the time in parts, but we did fly twice with the full equipment to ensure that everybody knew exactly how the landing would go and to overcome the fear of flying in the gliders; and to make sure everybody felt secure about the mission."[19]

None of the pilots, even the experienced ones, had spent much time landing on unprepared runways. Initially it was found that the gliders required too much space to effectively land atop Eben Emael. Koch contacted DFS and they modified the DFS 230 with a hand brake that extended below the plywood frame and dug into the ground as the glider touched down. Hanna Reitsch, one of Germany's most renowned aviatrixes, who had set the woman's world record for sustained flight, was called upon to test the device. On her first attempt, she was almost knocked unconscious as the brake dug into the ground, causing the glider to come to a jarring stop. The device was later modified to allow the glider to stop quickly but not so abruptly as to be dangerous.

Most of the experienced civilian pilots were able to master the DFS 230 quickly, and they immediately transitioned to solo flying. However, the Luftwaffe pilots had the advantage of being qualified in both formation and night flying, things the civilians had never practiced. Formation or "daisy chain" flying required the gliders to be tied together and towed by a single aircraft. Eventually, however, the flight plan called for a one-to-one ratio of Ju 52s to DFS 230s. On D day the tow planes and gliders took off in sequence one after the other. "By March [1940] these glider pilots could take off into the night, maneuver into formation, and when cast off from the tow plane land on an unfamiliar field."[20]

During most of the training, Storm Detachment Koch remained near Hildesheim or on the Czech border away from civilian or military observation. In January 1940 the gliders that were to be used on the mission were sent via enclosed truck to their departure airfields near Cologne. Several security measures were taken to conceal the arrival of the gliders and the nature of the training that was to continue in Cologne. A large cyclone fence was constructed around the glider hangars and straw mats were hung from the top to prevent people from seeing inside. Guards were posted and conducted twenty-four-hour-a-day patrols around the compound. On the day the gliders were to be taken from the trucks and reassembled, forty-five smoke generators were activated, creating a cloud over the entire airfield. "Local newspapers, commenting on the incident,

passed it off as an engineer unit exercise designed to provide experience at setting off smoke screens destined to protect Dusseldorf in
case of air raid."[21]

As the glider training progressed, Koch worked with the assault
elements to ensure they were fully prepared to conduct their ground
missions. There were three objectives at Eben Emael that had to be
neutralized in order for the fort to be rendered ineffective: the artillery that covered the bridges, the machine guns and antitank guns
that protected the fort itself, and the antiaircraft guns that could
engage the gliders and prevent the Stuka divebombers from properly supporting Witzig's platoon. Witzig thought the intelligence on
the fort was excellent. "We had flyover pictures, but of course at
that time the detail wasn't as good as today. But I had a picture and
could tell where all the cupolas were, but I couldn't see where the
machine guns were on top of the casemates. I had to look at the
casemates and cupolas and think, 'Where would they put the machine guns?' and I had to estimate where we needed to land and
how to set up defensive positions."[22]

These aerial photos helped determine that the steel cupolas atop
the fort were essential for observing artillery fire. Destroying the
cupolas would blind the observers and render the artillery fire ineffective. Additionally, the Luftwaffe obtained blueprints from a German subcontractor who had helped build the fort.[23] This provided
the assault elements with the exact location of the large guns and
their fields of fire. A tabletop model of both the fort and the bridges
was constructed. This small model was the only reconstruction used
by the glidermen, but according to the model maker's son, "The
whole thing ended up in a rather super size 'Sankastelmodell [sand-
box model], built up in a school's Gymnasium . . . Often paratroopers as well as pioneers came to do intensive practical 'on the spot
training' . . . one even could walk on top respectively through the
artificial landscape built up in this last large scale hall-model."*
Wherever this room-sized model ended up, neither Witzig nor
Wenzel ever saw it.

Practical training began in a small way but quickly developed
into detailed rehearsals. When they practiced at Hildesheim airfield,

---

*Information in a letter from Dr. Gunther Reibhorn of Salzburg to Col.
James Mrazek, author of *The Fall of Eben Emael*. Dr. Reibhorn's father

according to Witzig, "everything was laid out as things were at
Eben Emael. We had markers set up with the exact distances between them. This way the pilots and crew leaders could orient
themselves. I would go to each man and point out his objectives—
'This is yours, this is yours, and this is yours.' "[24]

Witzig sent some of his engineers to school during the workup
period to improve their demolition skills and presumably their understanding of artillery and antiaircraft weapons systems. In February, the remainder of the men from Granite went to German
Sudetenland to work against Czech casemates and cupolas. These
defenses were similar to the fortifications at Eben Emael, but "more
difficult."[25] The engineers and pilots practiced assaulting the casemates and using flamethrowers, bangalore torpedoes, light explosives, and their entire inventory of rifles, machine pistols, and pistols. Even the physical training revolved around the mission. Witzig
recalled later, "It [physical training] was very demanding, and I
tried not to concentrate on soccer and things like that, but on climbing with full gear and running with simulated charges. It was tactically oriented."[26]

The one aspect of the training that was not fully rehearsed was
the use of the new *Hohlladung,* or hollow (shaped), charge. In-
vented in 1888 by Charles Munroe, the shaped charge allows conventional explosives to create a jet of high pressure immediately
upon detonation. This generates a tremendous penetrating capability and allows a relatively small amount of explosives to have a large
effect on both steel and concrete. A 50-kilogram charge was capable
of penetrating both the six-inch steel cupolas and the concrete reinforced casemates. The pressure created by the explosion would generally blow a one-foot hole in the objective and kill everyone inside.
The shaped charges came in two sizes: a 50-kilogram charge in two
pieces (each half came with a leather handle), which required

---

was part of the map-making team that produced the models and maps for
the attack on Eben Emael. Dr. Reibhorn reported that Witzig's assault element was apparently never aware of the supersized model and only relied
on the table model for planning. My interview with Colonel Witzig later
confirmed this fact.

assembly on the target (it could be done in seconds), and a 12.5-kilogram charge, which was used primarily against smaller targets.

Unfortunately, due to the sensitive nature of this new explosive (it was being used as a primer for Hitler's atomic bomb), Witzig was the only man allowed to see the charge detonated before the mission. He was concerned about security. "They [the glidermen] didn't need to know about the charge. They just needed to know exactly what their missions were and trust the charge. Most frogmen who attack ships with mines don't know about [how strong] the charge is. They just know it will work."[27]

By March the platoon had finalized the plan for destroying Eben Emael. Each squad, composed of seven or eight glidermen, had a primary objective and a secondary target in the event all eleven gliders failed to reach the fort. No detail was left to chance. From March to May the platoon continued to train. Several times during the training the detachment was put on alert. The clanging of the hangar bells would summon the glidermen to their positions, but in each case the order to stand down came soon after. By May 1940 Witzig's men were more than ready and anxiously awaiting the moment to attack Eben Emael.

THE ASSAULT—10 MAY 1940

On 1 May 1940, Granite element, now under the cover name of No. 17 Reserve Squadron, was moved to the airfield at Ostheim, where final preparations were made for the assault.[28] At no time during the training had any of Koch's or Witzig's men been told the name of the objective. "They knew that [they] were going to do an attack against a difficult target, but they didn't know exactly where or when the attack would be."[29] Only the element leaders were privy to that information. On 9 May 1940 at 2130 the troops were assembled on the runway and the sealed orders were opened. The men were informed that the objective was a fort in the Belgian defense system. Departure time was 0325, 10 May. In the next few hours the ground crews began positioning the Ju 52s and the DFS 230s. There was one Ju 52 for each glider.

At approximately 0300 the glidermen loaded their planes and began taking off. Even with all the preparation the launches did not go well, but eventually all the gliders were airborne with the last glider, containing Witzig, in the air at 0335. The flight from Ostheim to Eben Emael took exactly fifty minutes as the gliders began to rise to an altitude of eighty-five hundred feet. On the ground German forces lit bonfires to guide the Ju 52s to the release point just northwest of Aachen, Germany.

Shortly into the flight, Witzig's glider broke free from his tow plane when the Ju 52 pilot banked abruptly to avoid colliding with another glider. With only three thousand feet of altitude the glider had no chance of making the fort. Witzig ordered the pilot to "land on the east side of the Rhine so [he] wouldn't have to cross any bridges."[30] Turning the glider back toward Cologne, the pilot managed to land in a field just four miles outside of Cologne. Witzig rushed to the nearest village, commandeered a vehicle, and returned to Ostheim. In the meantime the remaining ten gliders continued on toward Eben Emael. Minutes after Witzig's glider broke free, the glider containing the second squad received the order to unhitch. The glider pilot initially refused to obey, realizing that he was only at sixteen hundred meters. The Ju 52 tried to shake the DFS 230 loose and eventually forced the glider pilot to release. With Eben Emael twenty-five miles away the glider would be forced to land short. The last nine gliders proceeded, unaware that two of their eleven squads were not in the formation. At 0410 (much earlier than scheduled owing to a strong tailwind) the gliders reached their planned release point. The Luftwaffe squadron commander, realizing that the gliders were not high enough to reach the fort, made the decision to continue on until an altitude of eighty-five hundred feet could be reached. This required entering into Dutch airspace and drawing the attention of Dutch antiaircraft guns. Nevertheless, the squadron of airplanes continued on for another ten minutes and released the gliders.

Earlier that morning, at 0030, the Belgians at Fort Eben Emael had been alerted to the movement of German troops toward the border. The commander of the fort, Major Jottrand, received a telephone call and was at his position within minutes of the alert. Standard procedure called for cupola 31 to fire twenty blank rounds every thirty seconds. This was the signal to soldiers living in town to return to the fort immediately. Additionally, it signaled those troops assigned to defend the bridges to muster at their posts. Unfortunately, the gun crew for cupola 31 could not be mustered until 0330. In the interim, it became clear to Jottrand that this was not a false alarm. He could hear heavy antiaircraft fire coming from Maastricht. His orders called for him to evacuate the barracks just outside the main entrance to the fort, move all the bedding supplies into the interior, and destroy the building so it did not obstruct the gun crews' views of their targets. In order to carry out this directive, Jottrand had to use his gun crews to move the supplies and place the demolition. This significantly affected the crews' ability to prepare their guns. Consequently, it was not until 0325 that casemate 23 began firing warning rounds to alert the countryside. This did not overly concern Major Jottrand because he knew German ground troops would have to cross the Dutch border before the fighting actually began, and this would allow ample time for him and his crews to get into position. In order to make the guns ready for firing, the crews were required to clean the rust-preventing Cosmoline from the barrels and bring the ammunition from its storage point to the breech. At 0400 Jottrand received word that thirty to fifty airplanes were headed in the direction of Maastricht.* Moments later his own men reported, "Airplanes are overhead! Their engines have stopped! They stand almost motionless in the air!"[31] High above the fort the gliders were making their final approach.

"Objective 29 [antiaircraft gun position] was under the command of a very determined young lieutenant who, alerted to the gliders' approach by the sentry, reacted swiftly and ordered his men to open fire."[32] The gliders took heavy antiaircraft fire, and although several were shredded by the 60mm rounds, no one was injured. The glider carrying Squad 1 dove steeply to avoid the antiaircraft fire now coming from the fort. The pilot leveled out, touched down, and braked to a crunching stop, leaving the plane a wreck but safely on

---

*The glider assault on Eben Emael was the first event during Operation Yellow (Fall Gelb), the blitzkrieg into Belgium. Roger Edwards, *German Airborne Troops* (New York: Doubleday, 1974), 71, states that the Germans also used *Fallschirmpuppen,* or paratrooper dummies, to distract the Belgians as the offensive began.

the ground. The squad, led by Sergeant Neidermeier, had the responsibility for destroying casemate 18. After scrambling to get out
of the wreckage, Neidermeier ran to casemate 18. With the assistance of Private Drucks, he placed his 50-kilogram shaped charge
in the center of the concrete structure, pulled the fuse, and quickly
extracted. The charge blew the turret to pieces, killing the two Belgians inside. Meanwhile two other members of Squad 1 placed a
12.5-kilogram charge just below the other 75mm gun. The explosion lifted the gun off its stand and killed two of the twenty-one
men inside or directly below the casemate. The wounded tried to
retreat, but Neidermeier and two squad members went through the
breach where the gun had been and killed two more Belgians. The
remaining survivors escaped, but most were severely wounded or
flash burned. Neidermeier donned a gas mask and pulled one of the
wounded Belgians outside away from the caustic smoke-filled interior. The task completed, Neidermeier placed an aircraft-marking
panel on the outside of the casemate to inform the Luftwaffe that
the area was secure. Squad 1 remained inside casemate 18 when
Belgian artillery from a nearby fort began to pound the ground
around them.

The glider containing Squad 2, led by Sgt. Max Maier, never made
the fort. It had been erroneously released early and landed near
Duren in Germany. The squad commandeered a truck and drove toward Canne. They reached the bridge only to find that the Belgians
had destroyed it. Sergeant Maier was killed attempting to cross the
downed bridge, but Cpl. P. Meier continued on, eventually arriving
at the town of Eben Emael. Although he tried several times, Corporal Meier was never able to link up with the other squads at the fort.
The members of Squad 2 who remained at Canne eventually captured 121 Belgian prisoners, but as Wenzel recalls, "Before the
squad would release the prisoners [to the German guards] they
asked for a receipt, so they could prove what they had done."[33]

Squad 3, led by Sergeant Arendt, was assigned to destroy casemate 12. The glider containing the squad released itself from the
tow plane and made a perfect approach. As the glider breezed over
the fort, the Belgians opened fire. The tracers were high and the
pilot landed the DFS 230 just thirty yards east of the objective.

Arendt and his men hurried from the glider and charged the casemate. To their surprise, no Belgians inside the massive 75mm gun
turret attempted to stop them. When they reached the casemate the
squad had trouble affixing the 50-kilogram shaped charge to the
gun, so they elected to place the smaller 12.5-kilogram charge at
the rotating base. They pulled the fuse and ran. As it turned out,
there were several Belgian soldiers inside. They were completely
unaware of the Germans' presence.

The results of the explosion were similar to Squad 1's. The blast
tore the gun from its mount, crushing a Belgian soldier and wounding several others. Smoke and fire, fueled by propellent stacked
inside, engulfed the chamber. The Germans fired their machine pistols through the opening, then cautiously proceeded into the interior. Some of the wounded Belgians had been evacuated by their
comrades, but Arendt found three soldiers left behind. These men
were pulled to the surface.

Arendt continued to move further into the recesses of the fort.
Following voices that led to an elevator shaft, he dropped a 3-kilogram
charge down the shaft and either severely wounded or killed those
Belgians below. Arendt proceeded down a nearby stairwell until he
arrived at another level. A steel door prevented his incursion into
the center of the fort, so he returned to the surface. Squad 3 remained topside, ensuring that no Belgians attempted to break out.
Belgian after-action reports showed that only one of the twelve-
man gun crew had survived the assault uninjured.

Squad 4 was led by Sergeant Wenzel and was assigned casemate
19. The casemate was cut into the side of a hill with four gun openings on the face of the casemate pointing toward the northwest. On
top of the casemate (and flush with the ground) was a steel observation cupola. As soon as the glider landed, it was taken under
machine-gun fire by the Belgians in the cupola. The squad attacked
the Belgians, forcing the machine gunners inside to close the steel
observation doors from which they were firing. Wenzel dropped a
3-kilogram charge down the observation periscope that protruded
from the cupola. The explosion rocked the cupola, but the Belgians
continued firing. Wenzel then placed a 50-kilogram charge on top
of the cupola, but the explosive did not fully detonate and failed to

penetrate the six-inch steel dome. Nevertheless the explosion did render the cupola inoperable and forced the Belgians to retreat into the lower level. Wenzel moved down from the top of the hill until he was even with the gun openings. He placed another 50-kilogram charge on the casemate. This time it blew a large hole through the concrete and killed or wounded everyone inside. Wenzel elected to position his men beside the now abandoned casemate and await further orders. It had been fifteen minutes since Squad 4 had landed.

Squad 5, led by Sergeant Haug, landed and immediately assaulted cupola 23. The charge dislodged the gun mounts and reduced the rate of fire, but it failed to prevent the gun from firing altogether. Haug and his men subsequently attacked casemate 30, although this was not part of the plan. The explosion killed at least two Belgians but again failed to completely neutralize the guns. Throughout Squad 5's assaults, the men received heavy fire from a storage shed located between casemate 30 and cupola 24.*

At the same time that Haug was assaulting his objectives, he noticed Squad 8 was receiving effective fire from the storage shed and casemate 31. Haug and some of Squad 8's men attacked the shed but were repelled and lost two dead and several wounded. About that time Belgian artillery fire from a nearby battery began to rain in on the fort. Haug and his squad took cover in a nearby ditch. Several times they attempted to withdraw to a safer position but were immediately taken under fire. Squad 5 remained in the ditch until later that evening when they slipped out under cover of darkness.

The glider carrying Sergeant Harlos's Squad 6 was hit several times by antiaircraft fire. The pilot was forced to land in a field of concertina wire which brought the airplane to a jarring stop. The squad had difficulty exiting the glider and breaking into open ground owing to the thick barbed wire the Belgians had placed around the northern end of the fort. When they reached their objective, cupola 14, they found another squad had already destroyed it.

*Witzig said later that the small structure was visible on the aerial photos, but it was not determined until after the assault that it was just a wooden storage shed.

As it turned out, the objective was a false cupola. Where the cupola had been, however, there was a machine-gun emplacement dug into the earth. Harlos decided to place a 50-kilogram charge in the hole and detonate. The resulting explosion blew a hole into the inner fortress, causing a cave-in of concrete and earth. His task complete, Harlos established a machine-gun position to prevent reinforcements from coming across either the canal or the moat. During the remainder of the day Squad 6 engaged several Belgian troop movements and kept the north end secure.

Sergeant Heineman's Squad 7 was tasked with destroying cupola 16 at the north end of the fortress. It was not until they arrived and placed their explosive on the cupola that they realized it was a dummy emplacement. Nonetheless the task was completed in a matter of minutes.

The glider carrying Squad 8 had made a harrowing approach to the fort. In an effort to avoid the antiaircraft fire, the pilot had come in below the east wall next to the canal and pulled up at the last minute to settle down just thirty yards from casemate 31. Led by Sergeant Unger, the squad came under immediate small-arms fire from the storage shed and casemate 31. Part of the squad, with help from Squad 5, attacked the shed while Unger and two men ran to the casemate and placed their 50-kilogram charge. After pulling the fuse, Unger placed a 12.5-kilogram charge on a nearby fortress exit, destroying the steel doors and sealing the Belgians' escape route to the surface.

Although the Belgians at casemate 31 were warned of the attack thirty minutes before Unger landed, they were unable to get the guns ready for action. The door to the ammunition locker was locked and no one could find the keys. After the locker was opened, the elevator that carried the ammo to the gun failed to function, so only a limited amount of 75mm rounds could be carried to the breech. As the chief of the section loaded the first round in the chamber, Unger's 50-kilogram charge detonated, killing two Belgians and wounding several others.

Next Unger moved to destroy the cupola on top of the casemate. The 50-kilogam charge appeared to do little damage to the steel dome, but in actuality the penetrating force of the explosion completely destroyed the inner workings of the 75mm guns and rendered them totally inoperable. The squad was then directed to move north to Wenzel's position. As they attempted to extract from their position, they received heavy machine-gun and incoming artillery fire. Unger was killed, and only three men managed to reach Wenzel's position.

The glider carrying Squad 9 received substantial antiaircraft fire and flak but still managed to land within sixty yards of their objective at casemate 13. Like Squad 6 they also landed in a jungle of barbed wire and began receiving ineffective fire from the hangar. Germans from the other squads managed to subdue the Belgians in the hangar, allowing Squad 9 to exit their glider and move to casemate 13. Led by Sergeant Neuhaus, the squad assaulted the target, using flamethrowers to push back the Belgians manning the machine guns inside the casemate. After an unsuccessful attempt to place a 12.5-kilogram charge over the machine guns, Neuhaus placed a 50-kilogram charge on the steel door leading to the interior of the casemate. The resulting explosion blew the door inward and destroyed the supporting wall. Neuhaus stepped in and found the Belgians on the floor in shock. His task completed, he set up a defensive position and sent a runner to find Witzig and report their results. (None of the squads knew that Witzig's glider had failed to reach the fortress.)

Squad 10, led by Sergeant Huebel, had originally been assigned as a reserve force. After landing, Huebel received orders from Wenzel to attack casemate 26. This had been Squad 2's target, but their glider never arrived at Eben Emael. Huebel and one other squad member assaulted the observation dome, placing a 12.5-kilogram charge on top. The resulting explosion either killed or wounded the crew manning the gun, for no further firing occurred for the remainder of the operation.

By this time all the squads had completed their missions. Wenzel stated later, "Our main objective was to take out the guns that could destroy the bridges, and that mission was accomplished in the first fifteen minutes."[34] Now all that remained was to ensure the Belgians did not mount a counterattack before infantry from the German 4th Armored Division arrived.

Wenzel contacted Captain Koch via radio and informed him the fort was under German control. Preplanned bomber support began to arrive almost as soon as the glidermen had completed their missions. "We didn't have radio contact with any of the other groups, only with Captain Koch. So we laid panels on top of the cupolas to let the [Stuka] pilots know we had them."[35]

With the German positions marked by panels, the Stukas began dropping bombs against some of the Belgians still putting up resistance. Also within the hour, more ammunition was air-dropped to Wenzel and his men.

With Witzig still stranded in Germany, command of the detachment was supposed to fall to the next senior officer, Lieutenant Delica. Delica however was a Luftwaffe communications officer with no ground experience. He had been assigned to the detachment to coordinate air support from the Stuka divebombers.[36] Consequently, the major tactical decisions implemented in the first two hours were all the work of Wenzel.

At approximately 0630, two hours after the assault had begun, Witzig arrived, landing near casemate 19. He had managed to requisition another tow plane to get his glider airborne. He arrived late, but much to the delight of his detachment. The initial plan called for the glidermen to hold the fort for approximately four hours until the infantry arrived. By noon, however, it was apparent the commandos would have to defend their position for longer than planned.

Throughout the remainder of the day the Belgians called in artillery from a nearby fort, hoping to force the Germans off the exterior of Eben Emael. Some of the squads remained inside the bombed-out casemates, protecting themselves from incoming rounds and trying to ensure that the Belgians did not gain access to the top of the fort through the openings in the casemates. Other Germans took up defensive positions on the outside, periodically engaging Belgian troops that had managed to surface or that had been in the topside storage shed and barracks. Squad 3 under Sergeant Arendt pursued the Belgians into the fort, destroying exterior access routes as they went. The Belgians attempted several counterattacks, but a lack of infantry weapons (grenades, assault rifles, and squad machine guns) and infantry tactics (all the Belgians were artillerymen) caused them to be no match for the Germans. An infantry unit of forty men from a nearby post (commanded by Captain Wagemans) was called in at 1030 to attempt to evict the Germans. The Stukas curtailed the Belgians' enthusiasm by bombing the infantrymen at each attempted attack. By 1300 the Belgians had repaired casemate 4 and begun to open fire on the glidermen. Witzig ordered Sergeant Harlos's squad to silence the guns by placing a 12.5-kilogram charge against the embrasure. The tactic proved effective, and casemate 4 stopped firing.

In the meantime the commander of Eben Emael, Major Jottrand, contacted another infantry post at Wonck, approximately three miles away. He ordered a force of 233 men led by Lieutenant Levaque to attack the Germans. However, every time the Belgians began their march from Wonck to Eben Emael, they were bombed by Stukas. Consequently, by the time the troops reached the fort they were in no condition to fight, having sustained over 50 percent casualties. The infantry force already at the fort was never able to link up with Levaque. At 1745 Levaque attempted to take a small force of eight men and attack casemate 12. The glidermen spotted the force attempting to reach the casemate and pinned them down with machine-gun fire. Soon afterward, the Stukas began pounding the Belgian position, and after an hour Levaque retreated back to the fort's entrance.

At 2000, Major Jottrand decided to mount a counterattack of his own. He mustered sixty men and planned to sneak to the surface through an emergency exit. Unbeknownst to the Belgians, the Germans had already discovered the exit, and just as Jottrand's men were approaching the surface the Germans detonated another charge. The blast left a gaping hole in the fort. Jottrand, realizing he had lost the element of surprise, elected to stay inside and fortify his position to prevent German incursion into the interior.

Throughout the remainder of the early evening the Germans came under constant but ineffective fire from various Belgian positions. Witzig decided to consolidate his position. "I pulled my forces back in anticipation of a counterattack on the north end."[37] It was then that Witzig realized that casemate 17, which was positioned alongside the Albert Canal, could still engage advancing German infantry.* Although the glidermen tried three times to destroy the guns, they were

---

*Casemate 17 wasn't a primary objective because it couldn't destroy the bridges, but it could fire in the general direction of the advancing troops, so Witzig wanted the casemate silenced.

unsuccessful each time. Wenzel said later, "We tried to lower charges down on a rope, but the gun kept firing."[38]

At 2030 Jottrand issued defensive orders for the fort. Throughout the night incoming artillery from both Belgian and German batteries, along with periodic explosions from Witzig's men, kept the defenders of Eben Emael in a constant state of fear. The men inside the fort were afraid that the Germans would breach the makeshift defenses they had erected. The interior of the fort was a shambles. The explosions had cut off power to many areas. There was minimal lighting and no air-conditioning or heat, and smoke permeated the majority of the spaces. All of these conditions added to the Belgians' apprehensions. Additionally, "the Belgians didn't know how many Germans there were [on the surface of the fort]."[39]

Throughout the night, Witzig's men continued to assault those casemates and cupolas that were still harassing the Germans. By morning the fort was virtually out of commission, although Stukas continued to bomb the heavy guns until approximately 1200. At 0830 Witzig was officially relieved by elements of the 151st Infantry Regiment. He buried his six dead and departed Eben Emael at approximately 0930. At 1215 Major Jottrand sent Captain Vamecq to meet with the Germans and arrange a surrender of the fort. Before Vamecq could discuss details of the surrender, Belgians from inside Eben Emael came pouring out with their arms raised in defeat. At exactly 1227, Jottrand officially surrendered the fortress at Eben Emael. The Belgians had lost twenty-five killed and sixty-three wounded, and the Germans had destroyed ten of the seventeen casemates and cupolas. Before they surrendered, the Belgians destroyed casemate 33 and the 120mm guns, leaving only five operational defenses.

ANALYSIS

Critique

There is little debate that the assault on Eben Emael was one of the most decisive victories in the history of special operations. Sixty-nine German glidermen engaged and soundly defeated a Belgian force ten times their size protected by the largest fort of its day. It is the best example in modern times of a well-defined plan thoroughly rehearsed and flawlessly executed.

Were the objectives worth the risk? Hitler felt it was absolutely necessary to check the Anglo-French forces in Belgium and northern France by convincing them that the main German attack was coming through Holland, across the Albert Canal, and down from the north. In order for this deception to work, the Germans had to get two corps (Schmidt's 39th Panzer and Hoepner's 16th Panzer) into Belgium as soon as possible. The failure to check the Anglo-French forces would allow those units to reinforce the French Ninth and Second Armies, which were guarding the axis of the real main assault coming through the Ardennes. The only access into Belgium was across the Albert Canal. Securing the three bridges guarded by the fortress at Eben Emael was the key to German success in that region. Had the bridges fallen and Eben Emael survived the glidermen's attack, the Belgians could have delayed the German advance long enough for the Anglo-French forces in the north to be redeployed to the south. Consequently, there should be no question that destroying the fort was necessary and the risks worth the effort.

Was the plan developed to maximize superiority over the enemy and minimize the risk to the assault force? In the case of Eben Emael it is reasonable to ask if the Luftwaffe alone could have rendered the fort inoperable, thereby minimizing the risk to ground forces. Discounting the three bridges, which had to be seized quickly by ground forces to defuse the explosives, could Stuka divebombers have destroyed the fort's guns, which threatened the German armored advance? As the case study shows, the Stukas were very successful at deterring the Belgian infantry from reinforcing and counterattacking the glidermen. However, they had little effect on the steel and reinforced concrete casemates and cupolas. The defenses had been designed to withstand aerial bombing both in the way they were built and in where they were positioned. Casemate 33 withstood more than twenty-four hours of constant bombing before the guns eventually failed. It was the introduction of the shaped charges, which were able to penetrate the hardened gun positions, that made the fort vulnerable. Additionally, speed in destroying the guns was essential. Had the glidermen failed to render the guns inoperable within the first half hour, the Belgians could have fired on their own bridges to halt the German advance.* No other force offered the advantages of surprise, speed, and destructive capability that the glidermen did.

Was the mission executed according to plan, and if not, what unforeseen circumstances dictated the outcome? The plan to seize Eben Emael did not change much from its original conception. It was rehearsed in various forms from November 1939 to May 1940, and with a few notable exceptions it was executed exactly as planned. As mentioned, neither Lieutenant Witzig nor Sergeant Maier's squad arrived with the other elements. However, the plan had foreseen such contingencies. Witzig's role was command and control. When he failed to arrive, Wenzel ably took over. Later Wenzel remarked, "The officers had trained all of the men so well that the officers were expendable."[40] The plan also called for one squad in reserve. When Maier's squad failed to arrive, Wenzel ordered Sergeant Huebel to attack casemate 26. Resupply and close air support were both coordinated ahead of time and were instrumental in allowing the glidermen to sustain their positions and prevent Belgian counterattacks.

The raid appears to have been executed as planned and within the scope of possible contingencies. The only shortfalls were the squads' failure to destroy casemate 17 and the apparent lack of coordination on the glider launch. Although casemate 17 had been targeted as a secondary objective for Squad 6, the casemate was not in a position to destroy the bridges; it could only harass the German infantry. Therefore, failing to render it inoperable did not impinge on the initial success of the mission. Nonetheless it was a target, and no viable plan was devised to render it inoperable.

A full-scale rehearsal of the glider launch was never conducted for fear of compromising the operation. Had Koch been able to secure a discreet landing field he should have conducted at least one launch sequence involving all gliders and accompanying tow planes.

What modifications could have improved the outcome? Considering the magnitude of the problem and the fact that all the primary

---

*Although not well documented, cupola 23 fired upon and destroyed a lesser-known bridge at Lanaye.

objectives were destroyed within twenty minutes, it is doubtful that any modifications to the plan would have improved upon success.

Relative Superiority

The assault on Eben Emael may be the best representation of relative superiority in modern-day special operations. The attacking force was numerically inferior—outnumbered ten to one. The fortifications surrounding Eben Emael were some of the finest of their day. And yet a small, lightly equipped force destroyed the fort's main batteries in twenty minutes and eventually compelled the fort's commander to surrender the entire garrison. Figure 2-4 shows that the attacking force became vulnerable as they began their final approach to the fort. The machine guns tasked with antiaircraft duty actually hit six of the nine gliders as they descended. The Germans' vulnerability was minimized by surprise, and the probability of mission completion curve rose sharply as each glider made its landing. With all the gliders on the ground, relative superiority was achieved, that is, a condition existed where the Germans had a decisive advantage over the Belgians. The Germans' probability of mission completion strongly outweighed their probability of failure. On the graph this is shown as a significant rise above the relative superiority line. The Belgians didn't realize the precarious position they were in; they viewed the fortress as invulnerable to infantry attack. Even with no one manning the casemates, it would have been difficult for a conventional force to destroy the thick concrete bunkers. With the 50-kilogram shaped charges, however, all the German glidermen had to do was place the charges, pull the nine-second fuses, and stand back. Clearly the glidermen were vulnerable between achieving relative superiority and mission completion. However, by using prerehearsed tactics and moving quickly, they were able to subdue the machine gunners in the casemates and place their charges. Within fifteen minutes of landing, all the primary casemates that threatened the three bridges were destroyed.

Even if we define mission completion as the surrender of the fortress and extend the graph out twenty-four hours, the additional area of vulnerability would be negligible owing to the close air support provided by the Stukas and the bombers' ability to suppress any Belgian counterattack.

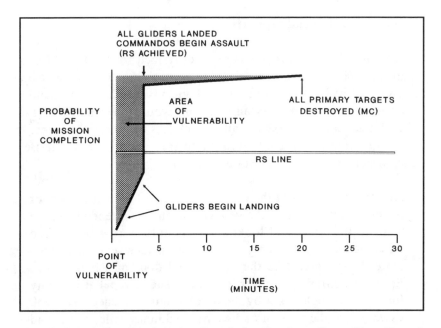

Fig. 2–4. Relative Superiority Graph for the Assault on Eben Emael

Could a large conventional force have achieved the same results? No. The fort was designed to repel ground forces, both armored and infantry. Had the Germans attempted a conventional assault they may have been able to destroy the fortress, but not before the Belgian guns destroyed the bridges. A parachute assault would not have been possible for a large force for the same reasons it was discounted for a small force: the parachutists would be too widely dispersed, and they couldn't carry enough ordnance. And, although the surface of Eben Emael was sufficient to handle nine gliders, a large gliderborne force would not have had enough room to land.

In the end, relative superiority was achieved because the attacking force had superior technology, national-level intelligence, excellent security, realistic and detailed training, and highly motivated troops. These factors reduced the frictions of war to a manageable level and provided the Germans a decisive advantage over the entrenched Belgians. In the next section we will see how adhering to the principles of special operations allowed the Germans to gain relative superiority and sustain it until mission completion.

Principles of Special Operation

Simplicity. Although Hitler is often criticized for his lack of strategic and tactical acumen, his plan for seizing the fort at Eben Emael was brilliant both in its strategic vision and in its tactical simplicity. Prior to the assault no one would have believed that Eben Emael could be taken at all—much less by so small a force. In 1938, Lt. Albert Torreele toured the fortress, and later, as the Belgian attaché to the United States, he stated:

> An officer member of the garrison of the fort led us to many of the outer defences and showed what each was intended for. We went to the walls and looked over countless rows of barbed wire. He led us to the only door on the surface set deep in concrete. It appeared like the heavy steel door of a bank vault. From here infantry in reserve would issue to repel any enemy fortunate enough to get by the tough ground defences. He took us deep into the interior and we trudged many miles to the end of the tunnels, visiting the crews and the guns of emplacements we had seen on the surface . . . I got the impression of tremendous power and first rate efficiency. I was convinced nothing could happen.[41]

The problem of seizing the fort seemed insurmountable. But by limiting the objectives, using good intelligence, and devising innovative tactics and technology, the Germans were able to simplify the problem significantly.

Witzig, who developed the specifics of the plan, knew that only certain casemates or cupolas had guns capable of reaching and destroying the three bridges, and this was Hitler's main concern.[42] Other casemates could still lob 75mm rounds on the advancing infantry regiment and panzer division; but by attempting to destroy all nineteen casemates and cupolas, Witzig would have had to either increase the size of his assault force or give each squad multiple targets. The assault on Eben Emael already required Witzig's entire engineer platoon. Consequently, additional forces would have had to come from outside the platoon; and to break unit integrity on a mission this critical was considered unacceptable. Giving each squad an additional target would also have significantly complicated the operation. As it was, each squad of seven or eight men carried two 50-kilogram shaped charges, two 12.5-kilogram shaped charges, three bangalore torpedoes, a flamethrower, and a host of other ordnance and assault equipment—all for one casemate or cupola.* Adding one more target to each squad would have complicated the command and control, required additional fire and movement training, and increased the number of gliders to handle the added weight of twice the ordnance.† After consultation with Koch, Witzig chose to forgo some of the smaller casemates and concentrate on the real threat.

Intelligence for the operation helped simplify the plan by reducing the number of unknown factors. Witzig knew exactly how many casemates and cupolas there were and where they were located. He knew the dimensions of the landing area and what surface obstacles could impede a glider assault. He had blueprints that showed the inside of the fortress and the emergency exits used for conducting a counterattack. All of this intelligence allowed Witzig to plan his training around a realistic scenario: the demolition training was against casemates that resembled Eben Emael's bunkers, the gliders learned to land in an area comparable to the surface of the fort, and even the physical training (running the exact distances, climbing the casemate walls) was based on intelligence provided to Witzig.

Innovation played a major role in simplifying the plan to assault Eben Emael. Although the surface of Eben Emael had a large enough drop zone for a small number of parachute troops, the Germans, after conducting several test drops, concluded that the platoon would be too widely dispersed to be effective. Additionally, parachutists could not carry enough ordnance, and the sound of propeller-driven jump aircraft would have prevented surprise.

*Sergeant Harlos and Squad 4 were the only ones who had two targets: cupola 14, which turned out to be a false target, and casemate 17, which was positioned along the Albert Canal.

†During an interview, Helmut Wenzel stated that some of the DFS 230 gliders were over their maximum takeoff weight of 4,630 pounds. This he concluded was "why later some of the tow ropes broke."

Although gliders had been around for quite some time, they had never been used in actual combat. Their unique capability to land troops and their equipment within fifteen to thirty yards of the target was an undeniable advantage owed to new technology. The DFS 230 was newly designed and modified specifically to meet the demands of landing on a grassy strip. Even today there are very few air insertion techniques that can deliver ten men and their equipment with that level of accuracy.

The most significant technological innovation was, of course, the shaped charge. This was the first time this explosive device had ever been used in combat. The shaped charge's ability to penetrate both the six-inch-thick steel cupolas and the reinforced concrete of the casemates was unquestionably the single most important factor in the success of the mission. Within the first twenty minutes the glidermen had destroyed casemates 18, 12, 19, 13, and 26, and partially immobilized casemate 30. Additionally, they destroyed cupolas 14, 16 (false cupolas), 23, and 31. The Belgians were so stunned by the swiftness with which their defenses were incapacitated that they never recovered. The glidermen continued to inflict severe damage on additional cupolas and machine-gun embrasures with both the 50-kilogram and 12.5-kilogram shaped charges.

The more difficult a plan is the longer it will take to execute, and consequently the greater will be the area of vulnerability. By limiting the objectives and using good intelligence and innovation to overcome the obstacles, a plan can be reduced to its simplest terms. And a simple plan is the base upon which rests the remainder of the operation.

Security. The Germans' operational security throughout the planning and preparation for the assault on Eben Emael was extensive but not overbearing. From the time Koch received his orders until the day of the attack, only the assault element leaders (the officers) were told the exact name and location of the objectives. Security was considered paramount to achieving surprise. Assault Force Granite changed its name each time it moved to a new location. The troops were given cover stories and cover names. Guards were assigned to each unit to ensure no "inadvertent" information was divulged. Letters were censored by Captain Koch's staff. In the last days prior to the assault, all personnel were restricted to the base and, when necessary, transported in covered furniture vans to hide their presence. An operational deception plan placed phoney news stories in local papers to conceal the glidermen's activities, and special units set off smoke makers to hide the force from aerial observation. But even with all these measures, the operational security never inhibited proper preparation. With only one exception, a full-scale launch of all gliders, all phases of the mission were rehearsed again and again.

It is important for security personnel to understand what aspects of the mission absolutely have to be concealed. This allows operational security to be more effective and less restrictive overall. Even with all the Germans' operational security, the Belgians at Eben Emael were prepared to halt an attack, even a gliderborne attack.

The "Phoney War" had been brewing since 1939, with anticipation of a German full-scale attack into Belgium and Holland. On the days preceding 10 May, the fort at Eben Emael had several false alarms and all the soldiers in the fort were recalled to their stations. The Belgians realized that the Germans might attack at any moment. They just were not worried because the fort seemed indestructible, particularly to an airborne assault. The surface of the fort had barbed wire, antiaircraft guns, a tank moat, and infantry fighting positions. Had the Germans attempted a parachute drop, the parachutists would have been cut to pieces. So it was important for operational security to hide the glider insertion method and to conceal the time of the assault. Although it was important to conceal the name of the unit, the personnel involved, and the demolition training on the casemates, it is doubtful it would have dramatically affected the outcome of the mission had any of this information leaked out. Even if the Belgians had found out about the glider training, it is arguable whether they would have altered the surface defenses of the fort. Why should they have? What could gliderborne infantry forces expect to achieve against concrete casemates and steel cupolas surrounded by machine guns and barbed wire? Even if the Belgians had learned about the shaped charges, it is doubtful that they could have developed countermeasures to protect the casemates. It was the timing of the mission that was most crucial to conceal. Had the Belgians known the time of the attack, they

could easily have prevented the Germans from succeeding, even
with their ineffective surface defenses. A couple of well-manned
machine guns could have held the glidermen at bay and prevented
them from ever gaining relative superiority. Consequently, operational security must take into account the nature of a special operations mission; it is the method of insertion and the timing that are
the most crucial. The fact that a mission is pending should be concealed, but not at the expense of proper preparation.

Repetition. Sergeant Wenzel remarked during our interview that "at
first the plan to assault Eben Emael didn't look good. I thought,
'we've really gotten ourselves into it this time.' But as we practiced
more and more on the bunkers, it became apparent it would
work."[43] This comment speaks volumes about the importance of
realistic rehearsals.

On 3 November 1939, Koch received his mission orders. From
November until May, Storm Detachment Koch, which included
Witzig's Granite Force, prepared for the assault on Eben Emael.
Although some of this time was spent recruiting glider pilots and
sending Witzig's engineers to advanced demolition school, at least
four months' time was used in direct preparation for the attack.
Witzig was known as a detail man, and during the planning and
preparation phase he ensured no detail was left unaddressed. The
glider pilots, both the Luftwaffe and the more skilled civilians, flew
dozens of flight profiles that corresponded to the landing on Eben
Emael. At first these flights were done without full loads, but eventually all Witzig's engineers and their equipment were placed in the
DFS 230 and "flown many, many times."[44] Before 10 May, every
pilot could take off at night, fly the profile, and land on a grassy
surface within fifteen to thirty yards of his target. Witzig even ensured that all the glider pilots were capable of using the weapons
and shaped charges carried by the engineers.

While the pilots were flying, the engineers were conducting
mock drills: first in a large field with nothing but markers to signify
the casemates, and then on actual casemates and cupolas on the
Czech and Polish borders. Witzig's men conducted hundreds of
partial drills and at least two full-dress rehearsals with the gliders
and full equipment. As previously noted, the only aspect of the

mission the Germans didn't conduct was a full glider launch of the entire Storm Detachment Koch. Unfortunately, since they had practiced only in individual elements, the logistic problem only became clear when it came time to orchestrate the entire launch sequence. Although Witzig's group launched without difficulty, the remaining gliders were several minutes late taking off when the tow planes and gliders began to stack up. This time delay cost precious minutes and was responsible for the failure of Assault Force Iron to gain surprise at Canne, which resulted in the bridge's destruction and the loss of several German lives.* Repetition as manifested in realistic rehearsals is the litmus test of simplicity. Concepts that seem easy on paper may in fact be difficult in practice. Consequently, it is imperative that all facets of an operation be rehearsed prior to the mission.

Surprise. Most historians view the raid on Eben Emael as a classic example of employing surprise to gain a tactical advantage over the enemy. They cite Belgian unpreparedness to defend against a glider assault as the main reason for the fort's demise. It is interesting to note just how prepared the Belgians were and what the element of surprise really contributed to the Germans' success.

On 10 May at 0030, the local Belgian command headquarters at Liège notified the fort at Eben Emael of German movement across the Dutch border. This was the third alert that month, and it received an unenthusiastic response from the troops stationed in the nearby town. Nonetheless most of the available Belgian defenders were at their posts by 0300. At 0315, one hour before the gliders appeared in the sky, Lieutenant Longdoz reported that his crews were manning the four pairs of multiple-mount antiaircraft guns. At approximately 0400 Belgian outposts reported inbound aircraft at an altitude of four to five thousand feet.

---

*Assault Force Iron, under the command of Lieutenant Schaechter, was tasked with capturing the Canne bridge intact. The Belgians had wired the bridge with explosives, and when Schaechter's assault force failed to gain surprise and then had difficulty exiting the gliders, the Belgians destroyed the bridge. Assault Force Iron lost four dead and six seriously wounded.

When the gliders cast off from the tow planes at 0415, many of the Belgian gun crews stood dumbfounded as the silent aircraft descended on the fort. There was a momentary delay before the antiaircraft and light machine guns began firing; nevertheless six of the nine gliders were hit by gunfire, although none were seriously damaged. As the gliders landed, most were immediately taken under fire by machine guns from the cupolas or the nearby storage shed. Although there were no built-in defenses against glider assault (like the triangular steel obstacles that protected against tanks), the surface of the fort was ringed with barbed wire (which many of the gliders landed in) and fighting positions to counter enemy infantry troops. There is no doubt that the Belgians were surprised by the glider assault, and I would argue that they were unprepared to deal with the situation.

The real surprise, however, was not the manner in which the Germans inserted; it was the swift employment of the 50-kilogram shaped charges that caught the Belgians completely unprepared. Although the casemates were constructed to withstand both enemy artillery and aerial bombardment, the shaped charge was new technology, and there were no countermeasures available. To the Belgian defenders, the gliders and their German commandos presented an insignificant threat provided that the Belgians could retreat into the safety of the hardened fortress. From their steel cupolas, they could employ overlapping fields of fire to decimate any infantry on the surface of the fort. The Belgians were prepared to deal with both air and ground assaults. What they were not prepared to deal with was the sudden and complete destruction of their fortified casemates and cupolas. This was the real surprise.

Speed. It was 0425 when the first glider landed atop the fortress at Eben Emael. Within the first twenty minutes all squads had reported back to Wenzel that their missions were complete, well before the allotted sixty minutes. Had the glidermen extracted from the fort at that moment, they still would have achieved their major objective of destroying the main guns covering the bridges at Canne, Vroenhoven, and Veldwezelt. The special operations aspect of the mission was complete. However, the original plan called for Witzig to hold the fort for four hours until he was relieved by the engineer battalion of the 151st Infantry Regiment. Consequently, he was prepared to "go conventional" immediately following the accomplishment of the main objective. His men, under the guidance of Wenzel, dug in and positioned themselves to repel Belgian counterattacks. Even with preparations for an extended stay, problems began to arise as the glidermen were forced to hold the fort longer than planned.

Special operations forces, by virtue of their insertion methods, are generally unable to sustain operations for an extended period. Whether they insert by glider, parachute, or C-130 aircraft, commandos are limited in their firepower by what they can carry. Speed is essential to minimize time on target and maximize available resources. Witzig's company had the advantage of being within range of continuous air support, a luxury not normally available to behind-the-lines operations. Nevertheless, as time passed, several counterattacks were attempted, first by Captain Wagemans and his forty Belgians, then by Lieutenant Levaque and his reinforced company from Wonck. Additionally, Major Jottrand tried several times to oust the glidermen from the surface of his fort. Without Luftwaffe support, Witzig would not have been able to receive ammunition resupply nor the fire support he clearly needed to accomplish the holding action.

Even with this prolonged action there can be little doubt that the first several minutes dictated the outcome of the entire mission. Witzig spent six months of training to ensure every aspect of the initial phase, from exiting the glider to assembling the shaped charge to reporting the results, was completed as quickly as possible. Unfortunately for the Belgians his training paid off.

Purpose. How important is being personally committed to a mission? Corporal Alefs of Squad 7 remarked after the battle, "We had been cooped up for months and had been transformed into killers. Everything we had done was in preparation for this hour . . . There was unyielding determination in each man's eyes. Those who are our friends, are our strong loyal friends; those who are our enemies will find us unyielding enemies. With this feeling we could search out the devil in hell!"[45]

The principle of purpose is always viewed from two directions: the purpose of the mission as stated in the operation order and the sense of purpose or personal commitment that each soldier brings to the battle. First, the individual soldier must understand the purpose of the mission so that, if required, he can react without supervision, knowing that his actions are consistent with the mission directive. As Wenzel said later, "They [the troops] must be able to recognize the situation and act accordingly."[46] This ability to "act accordingly" requires the plan to be clearly articulated to the troops. In the case of Eben Emael the individual soldier had a simple task: exit the glider, place the charge on the casemate, pull the fuse, extract, and then survive until relief arrives—that was it! Understanding the purpose of his individual mission was easy. However, understanding the overall picture while being counterattacked by the Belgians also needed to be simple. Fortunately, it was. When Witzig failed to arrive to control the actions at the objective, Wenzel quickly took command. He knew exactly what had to be done. He notified Koch that the casemates were destroyed and then consolidated his forces and set up defensive positions. Wenzel had a clear understanding of where all the squads were, even though he could not see them from his position. When it became apparent that Max Maier's squad had not arrived, Wenzel quickly redirected an available squad to destroy Maier's assigned target. Wenzel could also visualize the Belgians' situation and was prepared to counter their efforts, which he did successfully several times. Although Wenzel became the "hero of Eben Emael," the purpose of the mission was so clearly understood by most if not all of the participants that any of them probably could have commanded the actions at the fort.

There are countless reasons to be personally committed to a mission. Whether the commitment is for God, country, or self, a sense of purpose must be instilled into each soldier. It may never be needed if the operation goes according to plan, but when the frictions of war are at their peak, and the enemy is threatening to repel the attack, a sense of purpose is absolutely necessary. There are several examples of this sense of purpose during the assault on Eben Emael. To Rudolf Witzig, a sense of purpose was instilled through the knowledge that Hitler had personally planned and directed the operation and that Witzig, as the mission commander, was responsible for its outcome. Witzig was so committed to the purpose that even though his glider was forced to land short of the fortress, he managed to arrive at Eben Emael three hours later, in the middle of the battle. Wenzel, although shot in the head by a sniper (causing a scar that he still bears today), continued to direct his portion of the operation. After destroying casemate 12, Sergeant Arendt, leader of Squad 3, seized upon the opportunity to enter the fortress. Without regard for his own life, he proceeded deep into the fort, dropping 3-kilogram charges as he went. This act of boldness frightened the Belgians so badly that they reconsidered any attempts to counterattack through that opening. The Germans were "merciless" in their attack,[47] while, according to Witzig, "[the Belgians] didn't have the fighting courage."[48] Without a sense of purpose it will be difficult to overcome the "stronger form of warfare." In the case of the assault on Eben Emael the Germans had purpose, and the Belgians apparently did not.

Notes

1. Charles E. Kirkpatrick, "Simple Deceptions Pay Off," *World War II* (July 1991): 44.

2. Anthony Farrar-Hockley, *Student* (New York: Ballantine, 1973), 66.

3. "Student and the Capture of Crete," in John Westwood, Patrick Jennings, and Judith Steeh, *Strategy and Tactics of the Great Commanders of World War II and Their Battles* (New York: Gallery, 1990), 43.

4. Rudolf Witzig, interview by author, trans. Colin J. Kilrain, tape recording, Munich, Germany, 26 June 1992.

5. Helmut Wenzel, interview by author, trans. Colin J. Kilrain, tape recording, Celle, Germany, 24 June 1992.

6. James E. Mrazek, *The Fall of Eben Emael* (Novato, Calif.: Presidio, 1991), 49.

7. Wenzel, interview.

8. Witzig, interview.

9. Ibid.

10. Ibid.

11. James Lucas, *Storming Eagles: German Airborne Forces in World War Two* (London: Arms & Armour, 1988), 20. Lucas alludes to the fact that the landing area of Eben Emael was "very small" and therefore required exceptional pilots. Although the area is relatively small compared to a conventional glider landing strip, it was well within the capabilities of the average pilot. Compared to the landing area atop Gran Sasso, where Mussolini was rescued, Eben Emael was massive.

12. Witzig, interview.

13. Ibid.

14. Ibid.

15. Ibid.

16. Wenzel, interview.

17. Witzig, interview.

18. Kirkpatrick, "Simple Deceptions," 47.

19. Witzig, interview.

20. Mrazek, *Eben Emael,* 54.

21. Ibid., 60.
22. Witzig, interview.
23. Russell Miller, "The Storming of Eben Emael," in *The Commandos, World War II* (Alexandria, Va.: Time-Life, 1981), 10.
24. Witzig, interview.
25. Ibid.
26. Ibid.
27. Ibid.
28. James Lucas, *Kommando* (New York: St. Martins, 1986), 56.
29. Witzig, interview.
30. Ibid.
31. Mrazek, *Eben Emael*, 83.
32. Lucas, *Kommando*, 64.
33. Wenzel, interview.
34. Ibid.
35. Witzig, interview.
36. Lucas, *Kommando*, 23. Lucas reports that Lieutenant Delica had communications with the Stukas and was directing the air strikes on the Belgians.
37. Witzig, interview.
38. Wenzel, interview.
39. Witzig, interview.
40. Mrazek, *Eben Emael*, 111.
41. Ibid., 31–32.
42. Witzig, interview.
43. Wenzel, interview.
44. Ibid.
45. Mrazek, *Eben Emael*, 65.
46. Wenzel, interview.
47. Ibid.
48. Witzig, interview.

3

The Italian Manned Torpedo Attack at Alexandria, 19 December 1941

BACKGROUND

On 10 June 1940, Germany invaded France, and Italy subsequently declared war on France and Britain. In the Mediterranean Sea the British had secured vital ports at Gibraltar, Malta, and Alexandria. From these ports the British fleet controlled key lines of supply between Europe and North Africa. In March 1941, the Italian navy lost three cruisers to the British in the Battle of Cape Matapan. Until they could build more ships, the Italians had to limit their naval activities to convoy escort duty. In the meantime, the British ruled the Mediterranean, and there seemed to be little the Italians could do. Mussolini knew that the key to success in the Mediterranean involved restoring Italian naval power. With control of the Mediterranean "beleaguered Malta would fall like a ripe plum. Erwin Rommel's flying squadrons in North Africa would be sure of a flow of supplies and the small British Army [in Egypt] would wither for lack of the same."[1] The assault on the British fleet took many forms including aerial bombing from the Italian air force and German U-boat attacks. The greatest success achieved by the Axis, however, came from an unlikely source, Italian frogmen.

In 1938, the fledgling Italian 1st Light Flotilla was tasked with interdicting British shipping at sea and in port. This mission was to become the focus of the Italian frogmen for the next three years. By the end of the war, the Italians had sunk over 265,000 tons of British shipping. The most famous of these operations occurred on 19 December 1941, when six Italian divers riding manned torpedoes entered Alexandria Harbor in Egypt and sank two British battleships, HMS *Valiant* and HMS *Queen Elizabeth,* and the tanker *Sagona,* and badly damaged the cruiser HMS *Jervis.* The attack on the ships at Alexandria was one of the most successful special operations of any kind during World War II, and it shows the value of well-executed underwater operations.

Even before World War II, the Italians had a history of naval commando operations, but one mission in particular inspired two young naval engineers to develop the manned torpedo that would be so successful in the Mediterranean. In October 1918, two Italians traveled from Venice to the mouth of Pola Harbor in a sixty-five-foot torpedo patrol boat and attached mines to the vessel *Viribus Unitis.* The following day the mines exploded, and the vessel sank in place. Years later, Teseo Tesei and Elios Toschi developed the capability of clandestinely placing mines on a ship by using an old torpedo to deliver divers to the target. Toschi described the new weapon system as follows: "The new weapon is in size and shape very similar to a torpedo but it is in reality a miniature submarine with entirely novel features, electrical propulsion and a steering wheel similar to that of an aeroplane. The innovation of greatest interest is the point that the crew, instead of remaining enclosed and more or less helpless in the interior, keep outside the structure."[2]

In 1935, plans for the manned torpedo were sent to the Naval Ministry and two prototypes were authorized. Thirty mechanics from the Submarine Weapons Station at La Spezia spent several months constructing the torpedoes, and by January 1936 the prototypes were ready for testing. The tests were conducted under the watchful eye of Admiral Falangola of the Naval Ministry, who, after observing the demonstration, authorized further testing and construction of additional torpedoes. By the year's end a small cadre of manned torpedo pilots assembled at La Spezia and began training with the new weapon.

This concept of attacking ships in port was well received by the Italian Naval Staff, if not the entire navy, and in addition to the manned torpedoes, high-speed motorboats loaded with explosives were developed for the same purpose. The motorboats, the brainchild of the Italian general of aviation, Duke Amedeo of Aosta, were originally wooden framed with a waterproof canvas cover. The engine was positioned as far in the rear as possible to allow the maximum space in the bow for the placement of explosives. The pilot of the motorboat would guide the craft on a collision course with the target ship and at the last moment jump off and attempt to escape. The pilot had a float that kept him above the water during the explosion. In 1938, these high-speed motorboats, along with the manned torpedoes, were placed under the command of Comdr. Paolo Aloisi and designated the 1st Light Flotilla.

In 1939, as the possibility of war became greater, the Naval Staff ordered the production of twelve manned torpedoes and recruited more volunteers to pilot these secret weapons. The recruitment and subsequent training proceeded slowly at first, for although the Naval Staff supported the initiative, some elements within the Italian navy were suspicious of this new organization and helped only reluctantly. Nevertheless, by January 1940 the first launch of a manned torpedo from a submarine was conducted in the Gulf of La Spezia from the Italian submarine *Ametista*. In command of the *Ametista* was Comdr. J. Valerio Borghese. Borghese later became commander of the *Scire* and was a prominent player in operations with the Italian frogmen.

During the exercise, the *Ametista* surfaced with the deck just slightly awash. Three manned torpedoes were launched over the side, and the divers proceeded submerged into the entrance of the harbor. Once inside the harbor they "attacked" the Italian vessel *Quarto,* exited the harbor, and began their return to the submarine. While returning to the submarine, the frogmen tried a new rendezvous and docking system which used shortwave underwater signals to guide the manned torpedoes back to the *Ametista*. Although the rendezvous with the submarine was completed, the shortwave docking system proved unsuccessful. This, however, made no difference, for a decision was made that precluded the need to use the rendezvous system. There would be no more rendezvous. From that moment onward the Italians planned their operations based on a one-way insertion by the manned torpedoes. This provided the maximum standoff distance for the parent submarine and allowed the divers to use all their energy for the insertion and engagement. Escape came only after completing the mission and required the frogmen to swim to land and link up with agents or partisans. The success of the exercise added momentum to the weapons program, new prototypes were developed, and the older manned torpedoes were upgraded. The 1st Light Flotilla was soon ready for war.

ALEXANDRIA HARBOR, EGYPT

Alexandria Harbor is located on the west side of the Nile Delta in Egypt. During World War II the British occupied the harbor, using it as their primary operating base in the eastern Mediterranean. The harbor was almost fully enclosed by a long quay that extended from the old fort batteries on the northern peninsula across the entrance to the southern flank. The channel leading into the harbor was on the southern end, and access was controlled by use of an antisubmarine net. The net was only opened when authorized vessels were entering. Intelligence reports transmitted to the Italians at La Spezia noted the following fixed and mobile defenses:

(a) minefield 20 miles NW of harbour; (b) line of "lobster-pots" arranged at a depth of 30 fathoms in a circle with a radius of about six miles; (c) line of detector cables closer in; (d) groups of "lobster-pots" in known positions; (e) net barriers relatively easy to force; (f) advanced observation line beyond minefield.[3]

Lobster pots were small explosive devices that detonated on command. From the northern battery, a line of these devices extended out in a westerly direction for two thousand yards. Inside the harbor the British battleships and cruisers were on a wartime alert status, and watch standers were constantly cautioned about the danger of saboteurs. The possibility of saboteurs, although real, was not considered a serious threat to the heavily armored battleships that lay anchored in the middle of the harbor. The night of the operation there were two battleships in port, the HMS *Queen Elizabeth* and the HMS *Valiant*. Both ships were of the *Queen Elizabeth* class and crewed by approximately 1184 officers and men. The *Queen Elizabeth,* commissioned on 16 October 1913, was 643 feet long and 104 feet wide, drew 35 feet, and displaced 35,000 tons fully loaded. It had four shafts driven by Parsons geared turbines that propelled it in excess of twenty-four knots and gave it a combat radius of forty-four hundred miles. Topside the *Queen Elizabeth* was equipped with eight 15-inch guns mounted two apiece on two turrets forward and two turrets aft, eight 6-inch guns mounted forward of the midsection, eight 4-inch antiaircraft guns, four 3-pounders, five machine guns, ten Lewis antiaircraft machine guns, four aircraft, and twenty 4.5-inch guns as secondary armament.

To protect against air, surface, and subsurface attack, the *Queen Elizabeth* was one of the most heavily armored ships of its time. On the waterline thirteen inches of armor plating surrounded the ship. Other critical areas (i.e., torpedo rooms, gunhouses, and battery storage rooms) had from four to eleven inches of armor plating. On deck there was between one and three inches of armor to protect from aerial bombardment. Unfortunately for the British, the flat bottom of the battleship was virtually unprotected and offered an exposed target for the Italian frogmen. The *Valiant* was virtually identical to the *Queen Elizabeth,* except that it was shorter by four feet. Surrounding all the high-value targets were anti-torpedo nets. Strung in a circle thirty yards from the vessels, these nets were made of steel mesh suspended by large buoys and hung down to a depth of forty feet. Designed to keep air-dropped torpedoes from hitting the ships, these nets could be circumvented by the Italian frogmen either cutting them or going over or under them.

Also in port the evening of 19 December were the French battleship *Lorraine* and several smaller British cruisers and tankers. The Italian frogmen also had to contend with countless small boats motoring between piers and ships as a part of the normal in-port routine. The security surrounding the port was extensive, but the Italians had learned their lessons from several previous operations and were prepared to make the attack on Alexandria a success.

THE 10TH LIGHT FLOTILLA

With the advent of war in the Mediterranean, the Italian navy quickly began to increase the number of manned torpedoes and high-speed boats with the idea of attacking the British navy at anchor. To man these new weapons Italy established a recruiting and training program at the Training Center of Sea Pioneers at Leghorn near the Italian Naval Academy. All the men chosen for the 1st Light Flotilla were volunteers. At the training center they were screened to ensure they met the physical and moral standards necessary to join this unique outfit.* Each man's moral standards were assessed as good only after an extensive search into his background. This search included a financial background check, a review of the applicant's family history, and a look into recent romantic involvements that might impact his ability to function under stress. After a thorough check the applicant was interviewed by the commanding officer of the training center to gauge "his spirit, ideas, stamina and mental formation."[4] In addition to this screening process, each applicant received physical training and extensive instruction in the use of the underwater breathing apparatus. Spartaco Schergat, one of the Italians who participated in the attack on Alexandria, thought the six-month class was going to teach him to be a frogman. (Schergat was under the impression that frogmen only used fins and swam on the surface.) He was surprised when he got to Leghorn for training. "They tricked me! Instead of swimming with flippers they taught me to use the Belloni aqualung. They made me walk on the bottom for four hours carrying a big heavy drum to simulate a bomb."[5]

If the volunteer passed all the physical and academic examinations and met the subjective criteria of the commanding officer,

*When the war started the Italian navy recognized the need for more assault swimmers and attempted to recruit nationally ranked athletes from the Italian Swimmers' League. Unfortunately most of the world-class swimmers had already been conscripted by the army. Consequently, the 1st Light Flotilla bypassed normal procedures and became a joint venture with swimmers from the navy, army, and Alpine Corps.

then he was assigned to one of the special branches, either manned torpedoes or high-speed motorboats. The diver's training continued for a year until he could master his assault weapon.

The Italians were exceptionally strict about secrecy. No member of the 1st Light Flotilla was ever to reveal the nature of his work to anyone other than his immediate supervisors. This rule even extended to the other men within the 1st Light Flotilla who were not intimately involved with a member's work. Commander Borghese, in his book *Sea Devils,* makes it clear that this was not an easy undertaking for most Italians. "When one considers the extent to which most Italians feel a communicative urge, to show that they are well informed and to boast, one can realize what exceptional qualities were required in these young men; for it is sometimes easier to get an Italian to lay down his life than to make the sacrifice of holding his tongue."[6]

Between 1936 and 1940 the Italian engineers at La Spezia developed several prototypes and production model submersibles, manned torpedoes, motorboats, and ancillary equipment that would be used by the 1st Light Flotilla. These included the following:

- The SCL—a slow-speed human torpedo. This was an improved version of the original manned torpedo. It was 6.7 meters long and manned by two divers. Maximum speed was 2.5 mph with a range of ten nautical miles and a submersion depth of thirty meters. The SCL was propelled by a battery-powered motor, and the pilot maintained buoyancy through forward and aft trim tanks. The tanks were blown dry with air from bottles positioned in the midsection. The pilot steered the torpedo using a magnetic compass and a depth gauge, both luminescent. The warhead, contained in the bow, was a 300-kilogram explosive. It was detachable and could be slung under the ship like a mine. In the midsection, behind the second diver, was a tool chest containing net cutters, air net lifters, clamps for attaching the explosives, and plenty of line.
- The MTM—a modified touring motorboat. This was an explosive motorboat (E-boat) that was 5.2 meters long and 1.9

meters wide. It was powered by an Alfa Romeo engine and had a speed of 32 mph. The bow contained three hundred kilograms of explosives that separated upon impact with the target and then detonated hydrostatically at a prearranged depth.

- The MTB—a light touring motorboat. This motorboat was similar in construction to the MTM but was small enough to fit inside the chambers aboard the transport submarines.
- The MTSM—a torpedo touring motorboat. This craft was designed to attack ships at sea. It was larger than the MTM with a length of 7 meters and a width of 2.3 meters. The MTSM was propelled by two Alfa Romeo engines and contained a torpedo launch tube situated aft. When fired the torpedo turned 180 degrees underneath the MTSM and then began to pursue its target. It had a crew of two.
- The CA—a midget submarine. This was a twelve-ton dry submarine crewed by two men. It held two 450mm torpedoes and was later modified to carry eight one-hundred-kilogram charges. The CA2, a later version, was part of an operation to attack United States ships in New York Harbor. The defeat of Italy in 1943 canceled the mission.
- The CB—a larger version (thirty tons) of the CA with a crew of four and an increased range. The CBs were used extensively in the Black Sea and were responsible for sinking three Soviet submarines.

In addition to the inventory of submersibles and motorboats, the Italians developed diving rigs and explosives to augment the diver's bag of tricks. These innovations included the following:

- An underwater breathing apparatus that used two high-pressure oxygen bottles and was good for six hours underwater. The oxygen traveled from the bottles into a rubber breathing bag and then through a reduction regulator to the diver. The diver expelled air into a canister of soda lime that eliminated the carbon dioxide and allowed the oxygen to be recycled into the breathing bags for further consumption.

- A rubber dry suit which covered the diver from neck to toe leaving only the head and hands exposed. Underneath the dry suit the divers wore thick underwear. The suit was called a Belloni suit after its designer, Commander Belloni.
- The leech or bug, a 2-kilogram, time-fused explosive charge that attached to the hull of a ship by means of air-cushion pressure. A free-swimming assault swimmer could carry five of these charges around his waist.
- The limpet, a 4.5-kilogram explosive charge that was clamped to the hull and detonated by a space fuse. The space fuse had a small propeller that activated the detonator only after the ship got under way and attained a speed of five knots.

By August 1940, while training for some of the frogmen was just beginning, the 1st Light Flotilla received its first mission: sink the aircraft carrier *Ark Royal* and the battleships *Queen Elizabeth* and *Valiant* in port at Alexandria. The submarine *Iride* was chosen to be the delivery platform for the mission. The plan was for the *Iride* to sail from La Spezia in northern Italy to the vicinity of Tobruk in Libya. Outside Tobruk the submarine was to rendezvous with a support vessel carrying four SCL manned torpedoes. The torpedoes would be lashed to the deck, and the *Iride* would transit to a point four miles outside Alexandria.* There the manned torpedoes would be launched to conduct their mission.

The *Iride* arrived outside Tobruk on the morning of 21 August, and that afternoon, British bombers returning from a mission noticed the support vessels in the isolated waters. The next day the support vessels transferred the torpedoes to the *Iride.* As the submarine was beginning to conduct a test dive to check the lashing of the torpedoes, three British torpedo-carrying aircraft bombed and sank the *Iride* in fifteen meters of water. After the aircraft departed, twenty hours of salvage operations ensued. Eventually the Italians succeeded in rescuing twenty members of the submarine crew along

---

*Because the manned torpedoes were only pressure tested to thirty meters, the submarine *Iride* was required to transit at that depth, making the submarine easier to detect from the air.

with some of the embarked frogmen. The first attempt to attack the British had ended in disaster, but it was not to be the last misfortune.

The loss of the *Iride* was due, in part, to the need for the torpedoes to be transferred and then lashed on deck. The *Iride* had not been equipped with chambers to house the manned torpedoes. Consequently, the two submarines that succeeded the *Iride*, the *Gondar* and the *Scire,* were fitted with three chambers apiece, one forward and two aft. Once alterations were completed, the *Gondar* received orders to renew the attack on Alexandria. The *Scire* received orders to attack the British navy at Gibraltar at the same time.

Gondar arrived outside Alexandria on 29 September 1940. Soon after arriving the submarine received orders to return to La Spezia, since the British navy had departed Alexandria. While returning to Italy, *Gondar* was spotted by British warships and sunk after twelve hours of hide-and-seek. Although most of the crew survived, several key members of the 1st Light Flotilla were captured, including Elios Toschi, one of the original founders of the organization. The *Scire* meanwhile had arrived at Gibraltar only to receive similar orders to return to Italy. The British had sailed from Gibraltar as well.

On 15 October 1940, the 10th Light Flotilla, which had been a branch under the 1st Light Flotilla, was formed as a separate organization under the command of Commander Belloni. It retained its cover as a subaquatic research center for the study of problems of human life underwater.

Later in October the *Scire* returned to Gibraltar and launched three manned torpedoes that successfully penetrated British defenses. Unfortunately, the divers experienced trouble with their torpedoes. Petty Officer Emilio Bianchi, one of the divers, recalled later, "The defenses at Gibraltar were very simple. We got through nets with no problem, but then there was an explosion inside the pig [manned torpedo]. The gases that came out of the batteries caught fire. Operation BG2 [the attack on Gibraltar] was a fiasco, but it was useful because it allowed our technical staff to understand what went wrong in the pig and fix it."[7]

One of the three swim pairs was captured, but the other four men escaped to Spain and returned to La Spezia. Bianchi and his officer, Luigi Durand de la Penne, escaped and would later spearhead the attack against Alexandria. Unfortunately for the Italians, the British were now fully aware of the capabilities of the Italian divers.*

On 25 May 1941, the *Scire* made its third attempt against Gibraltar. Again the manned torpedoes penetrated the harbor but found no warships at anchor. Mechanical difficulties with the manned torpedoes required all three swim pairs to scuttle their torpedoes and escape to Spain. Fortunately no personnel were lost, and the Italians viewed this experience as realistic training for the divers. Over the next three years, however, the Italians conducted seven operations against Gibraltar with a high degree of success. "At the cost of three men killed and three captured," according to Frank Goldsworthy, "Italian naval assault units sank or damaged fourteen Allied ships of a total tonnage of 73,000. The constant threat of silent attack in the night demanded tens of thousands of hours of vigilance by Naval and Army personnel."[8]

Later that summer, in July, the Italians had their greatest setback since forming the 1st Light Flotilla. They were operating against the British fleet at Malta. The plan called for a combined force of two manned torpedoes and nine explosive boats (E-boats). One manned torpedo, piloted by Lt. Teseo Tesei, was to destroy the steel net barriers that hung below the Sant' Elmo Bridge and protected the entrance to the harbor. Once the barrier was destroyed, the E-boats, which had been transported to the target area aboard the Italian destroyer *Diana,* would speed into the harbor and attack the fleet. The other manned torpedo was assigned to attack nested British submarines in an adjacent harbor. All of these attacks would be preceded by air raids designed to divert British attention.

At the scheduled time, the manned torpedoes and E-boats were launched from their respective platforms. Unfortunately for the Ital-

---

*Spartaco Schergat was apparently unaware that the British had gathered extensive information on the capabilities of the manned torpedoes. During his interview with the author, Schergat stated that one of the reasons the attack on Alexandria was so easy was that the British had no idea the Italians had such a weapon. The British in fact knew quite a bit about the Italian pigs.

ians, the British radar operators spotted the unidentified launch craft and tracked the E-boats from the beginning of their mission. The British alerted their four main batteries guarding the harbor. At 0430 Tesei reached the net barrier and remained with his torpedo while he detonated the warhead. A letter found after the operation revealed that he had committed suicide, in his words, "[to] attain the highest of all honors—that of giving my life for my King and my flag. This is the supreme desire of a soldier, the most sublime joy he can experience."[9] The E-boats began their assault only to be caught in British crossfire from the defensive batteries. All nine E-boats were destroyed. As the launch platforms attempted to escape, they were attacked by British aircraft and destroyed. The remaining manned torpedo had mechanical difficulties, and the crew was later captured. By the end of the Malta operation fifteen Italians were killed, eighteen were captured, and all the manned torpedoes, E-boats, and support platforms had been destroyed.

The Malta operation was destined to fail from the beginning: the plan was too complicated, intelligence was inadequate, the rehearsals were only partially successful, and the execution phase lacked surprise and speed. Borghese, who was not directly involved in the operation, identified these problems early in the preparation phase. He commented that the combined operation had assumed "a new, more extended and complex aspect . . . The idea of employing . . . weapons so different in nature [torpedoes and E-boats] . . . was an extremely hazardous one."[10] Additionally, the intelligence was "very sketchy . . . It was incredible but true [that the Italians] had no agent at Malta who could furnish . . . intelligence."[11] The rehearsals for the mission, which were executed near Malta over a seven-day period, resulted in several damaged and sunken E-boats. Following these rehearsals Vittorio Moccagatta, the commander of the 10th Light Flotilla, wrote in his diary, "I was never a believer in bad luck but now I had 99 reasons out of a 100 for believing in it."[12] To make matters worse, during the execution phase, the diversionary air raid had put the British on alert and subsequently led to the detection of the approaching E-boats.

Nevertheless, the Italians continued to aggressively pursue the British and finally achieved their first success in Gibraltar on 21 September 1941. Launching from the submarine *Scire*, three manned torpedoes entered Gibraltar and, using their detachable warheads, sank three vessels: the naval tanker *Denby Dale* (15,893 tons), the British motorship *Durham* (10,900 tons), and the British tanker *Fiona Shell* (2,444 tons). The crews scuttled their torpedoes and diving rigs and swam to Spain where they met Italian agents and were returned to La Spezia.

This success marked the culmination of intensive modifications to the manned torpedoes, which now constituted "an absolutely efficient and trustworthy weapon, capable of achieving the most brilliant success in war."[13] Three months later the opportunity to achieve that brilliant success presented itself at Alexandria. The men who volunteered for Alexandria did so with the understanding that their success could change the balance of naval power in the Mediterranean. Alexandria, however, was unlike Gibraltar. There was no place to find refuge, and volunteering meant agreeing to a one-way trip with the best result being imprisonment.

PRELIMINARY EVENTS

Since the beginning of the war, the Italians had put considerable effort into sinking the British fleet at Alexandria. Italian bombers had made routine runs against the port facility with no success. The heavy British air defense and the long flight time from Italy made this a dangerous and expensive proposition for the Italian air force. With the formation of the 1st Light Flotilla, the navy took the lead in attempting to destroy the British fleet; however, after the disaster with the *Iride* in August 1940, it was over a year before another mission was attempted. The Italians literally went back to the drawing board and modified the transport submarines and manned torpedoes to minimize their detectability and improve their range and reliability.

In the fall of 1941 the 10th Light Flotilla asked for volunteers for a one-way mission.[14] A dozen men volunteered. Those who were eventually chosen were: Durand de la Penne and Bianchi, Gunner Captain Antonio Marceglia and Petty Officer/Diver Spartaco Schergat, and Gunner Captain Vincenzo Martellotta and Petty Officer/Diver Mario Marino. There were also two spare crews in the event that one of the primary divers became ill or was injured in training.

Most of the men had been members of the 10th for some time, but Spartaco Schergat, who was working at the Italian Naval Academy when he volunteered, had had no previous combat experience or training with the torpedoes. (By the time the Alexandria operation began, Schergat had been part of the reserve crew on one previous mission to Gibraltar, but the primary crews launched as scheduled, and Schergat never got the opportunity to participate.)

Over the next several months the mission was planned out in detail, and the training of the crews continued unabated week after week. Commander Borghese was assigned to lead the operation and later remembered how they approached the planning and training:

> This kind of operation, if it were to have any decent chance of success, had to be thought out to the last detail; . . . from the collection of hydrographic and meteorological data to intelligence as to enemy vigilance; from the taking of aerial photographs of the harbour, to the arrangement of safe and extremely rapid channels of radio liaison with the submarine . . . to the training of operators so as to bring them to the maximum of physical efficiency by the pre-arranged day . . . nothing was to be left to chance, all impulsiveness was to be held in check; on the contrary, everything was to be coolly calculated and every technical and ingenious resource was to be exploited to the fullest extent possible.[15]

While agents in Alexandria fed the Italian navy information about the harbor patrols, reaction forces, and net defenses, aerial photos showed the physical layout of the port including the locations of piers, pilings, mooring buoys, and gun emplacements. From this collection of intelligence the 10th Light Flotilla was able to plan the exact route and distances that would be traveled by the manned torpedoes. Exercises were conducted in the La Spezia operating area that duplicated the mission profile. Schergat later recalled, "We did some very specific training for the mission in Alexandria. One day Commander Borghese ordered an exercise. We left the port and traveled many miles in a profile that resembled Alexandria. We sailed to La Spezia. [The manned torpedoes] entered port and attacked the ship at anchor. At the time we didn't know the reason for that particular training—Borghese told us about that later."[16]

As the training continued and the intelligence picture became clear, a plan was finalized and forwarded to the Supermarina in Rome. The *Scire,* carrying three manned torpedoes, would leave La Spezia and sail to the island of Leros. The five crews and technicians would be flown to Leros and would link up with the submarine. This would allow the crews some additional time to plan and conduct physical training. The *Scire* would depart Leros and sail directly to Alexandria, arriving at a point approximately one thousand meters from the northern battery. The Italian air force would conduct a diversionary bombing raid both the night before and the night of the mission. Once on station, the *Scire* would receive final intelligence on the position of the British ships in port. This information would be passed to the torpedo crews just prior to launch. Upon launch the three manned torpedoes would proceed to their assigned targets, place their ordnance, scuttle their torpedoes and diving equipment, and swim to shore. Once ashore the crews would attempt to find a small boat and sail ten miles out to sea to rendezvous with the submarine *Zaffro.* This escape and evasion plan was quite weak and Bianchi later said, "We knew that even in the best case there was no chance to avoid capture. There was an escape plan, but it was just for psychological comfort."[17]

The Supermarina approved the plan, and after two more months of mission-specific training, the manned torpedo crews of the 10th Light Flotilla were prepared to attack Alexandria Harbor. Durand de la Penne and his men were anxious to begin the operation. He later recalled, "We knew it was to be a dangerous mission because this was the third attempt for a submarine to go into Alexandria. But, we felt, the third time never fails."[18]

THE ATTACK ON ALEXANDRIA

On 3 December 1941, the *Scire* departed La Spezia on a "routine" patrol; her oblong chambers were empty. Soon after she left port, the sun set and the *Scire* came to all stop approximately three

miles out from the harbor. A small vessel came alongside and transferred three manned torpedoes, hull numbers 221, 222, and 223.
The torpedoes had just been refurbished at San Bartolomeo and
were in excellent condition. The torpedo crews eased the submersibles into their chambers and gave them one final inspection. That
evening, after all the equipment was checked and double-checked,
the torpedo crews left the *Scire* and returned to port aboard the
small vessel that had brought them out. They would rendezvous
with the submarine in six days on the island of Leros.

The *Scire* began the initial leg of her transit by hugging the
coastline to avoid the Italian minefields and then proceeded around
Sicily and into the open sea. As scheduled, six days later, after only
a single enemy encounter, *Scire* reached Leros and entered Port
Lago. Although Lago was under Axis control, Borghese took every
precaution to maintain secrecy. A cover story was circulated that
the *Scire* was a submarine from another command damaged while
on patrol and in need of repair. Huge tarpaulins were placed over
the transport chambers ostensibly to protect ship repair personnel
from the weather. Additionally, "technicians" arrived from La
Spezia to help with repairs. These were, in fact, engineers from La
Spezia who conducted the final inspection on the torpedoes.

On 10 December, the four crews left Italy. They had been on premission leave, and Bianchi recalled later, "When we left Italy my
thoughts at first went to my family, but then those thoughts van-
ished, because we had many things to do."[19] They arrived at Port
Lago and were placed aboard the transport vessel *Asmara*. Durand
de la Penne and his men spent the next three days making final
preparations and reviewing the intelligence that came in daily from
agents in Alexandria and from Italian aerial reconnaissance. The
commander of the 10th Light Flotilla, Comdr. Ernesto Forza (who
had relieved Moccagatta), had been sent to Athens to coordinate
intelligence and overhead photography, provide weather reports,
and maintain radio contact with the Scire throughout the operation.
On the thirteenth, Admiral Biancheri, commander in chief of the
Aegean Naval Sector, arrived in Leros and wanted Borghese to conduct one final rehearsal prior to getting under way for Alexandria.
Borghese refused, citing his orders, which gave him full authority
to conduct the operation as he saw fit. The admiral was disap-

pointed, and chastised Borghese for not wanting to train until the last possible minute.

On 14 December, the *Scire* departed Leros and proceeded on course towards Alexandria. Borghese, remembering the plight of the *Iride* and *Gondar,* remained submerged almost the entire transit, surfacing only at night to recharge batteries. The final aerial reconnaissance flight was conducted on the eighteenth, and the intelligence was forwarded via coded message to Borghese. The *Scire* had stayed in constant contact with Forza, who was in Rome and then Athens, coordinating aerial overflights and providing updated intelligence. Schergat remembered that "Commander Forza radioed us before entering port [at Alexandria]. He told us how many ships were in port and which ones we were supposed to attack."[20] The message also congratulated Petty Officer Bianchi, who was a new father. Everyone agreed that this was a good sign.

Later that evening, as the *Scire* approached the designated manned torpedo launch point, Borghese ordered all quiet and brought the submarine to sixty feet. At this depth he hoped to avoid the moored minefields. At 1840 the *Scire* arrived at its launch point, approximately 1.3 miles at 356 degrees from the Ras el Tin Lighthouse on the northern end of the harbor. Borghese surfaced to outcrop level (transport chambers submerged), came out of the conning tower, and surveyed his surroundings.* He reported, "The weather was perfect: it was pitch-dark; the sea very smooth and the sky unclouded. Alexandria was right ahead of me, very close. I identified some of its characteristic buildings and determined my position; to my great satisfaction I found that we were within a meter of the pre-arranged point."[21]

Navigating from Leros was no easy feat. The *Scire* had traveled more than seventeen hundred miles through enemy-patrolled waters; she had encountered a severe storm on the sixteenth that forced her to stay submerged well beyond the normal limits of the

---

*Most reports indicate that the *Scire* had planned to come to outcrop level. In his interview with the author, Schergat stated that Borghese had to bring the conning tower above the surface because the hatch normally used by the divers to reach the manned torpedoes was broken.

crew; and with constant enemy air and sea patrols, the navigator had had few opportunities to get a daytime fix. But despite all this, and even though they spent the final sixteen hours completely submerged, Borghese brought the submarine to within one meter of the launch point.

At approximately 2100, the reserve crews of the manned torpedoes went on deck (which was fully submerged). Equipped in full dive gear, they had the task of opening the chamber doors. This was a physically exhausting job, and it would have reduced the efficiency of the operational crewmembers had they been required to undertake this endeavor. Once the chamber doors were open the operational crews, which were fully suited up, arrived to take command of their torpedoes. One by one the manned torpedoes eased away from the *Scire* and headed slowly toward the entrance of the harbor. The launch was very smooth. Bianchi recalled, "I felt a sense of satisfaction, because everything was going so well. It seemed like an exercise."[22] Borghese monitored their departure on the submarine's hydrophones, and when he concluded they were safely on their way, he submerged.

An interesting side note: During the launch process, one of the reserve crewmen (who was also the diving medical officer) drowned when he overexerted himself opening the chamber doors. This was not noticed for several minutes and when the doctor was brought aboard, he showed no sign of life. Borghese injected a vial of stimulant into the doctor's chest and then began artificial respiration. At the same time he issued orders for the *Scire* to depart the immediate vicinity on a reciprocal course. Unfortunately, the doctor had left the chamber door ajar, and the submarine was taking on water, making it difficult to maintain trim. As soon as the submarine was out of range of the lighthouse, Borghese surfaced and closed the chamber door. Miraculously, after three and a half hours the doctor began to breathe again. By the time the *Scire* arrived back in Leros, the doctor was out of medical danger. Several days later the *Scire* returned to La Spezia after covering thirty-five hundred miles in twenty-seven days.

The three manned torpedoes departed the submarine and proceeded together on the surface toward the antisubmarine gate at the south end of the harbor. They had traveled approximately two miles

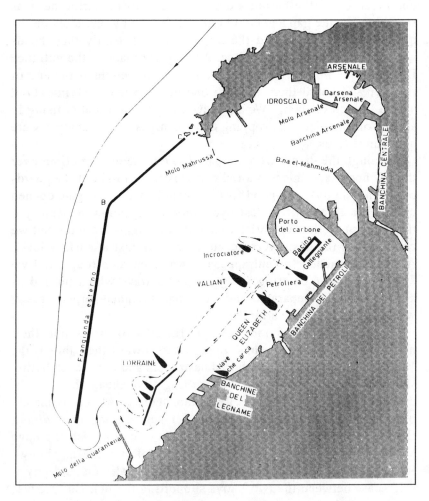

Fig. 3–1. Routes of the Three Manned Torpedoes
(Petroliera is the tanker *Sagona*.) From de Risio,
***I Mezzi d'Assalto*, 123**

when Durand de la Penne ordered the torpedoes to stop. Floating on the surface barely five hundred yards from the Ras el Tin Lighthouse, the frogmen decided to take a break. They broke out their rations and Durand de la Penne passed out small bottles of cognac. "Things [had] been going too easy," he later reported, so he decided to "relax a bit before going in."[23] After finishing the meal, they continued on to the harbor's entrance. An antisubmarine net was strung across the gap and could only be opened by operators on the quay. The divers trimmed the torpedoes so that only their heads were exposed above the surface. As they approached the entrance Durand de la Penne reported, "We saw some people at the end of the pier and heard them talking; one of them was walking about with a lighted oil-lamp. We also saw a large motorboat cruising in silence off the pier and dropping depth charges. These charges were a nuisance to us."[24]

Although the divers were prepared to cut the nets or climb over them if necessary, this was a risky proposition in light of the guards patrolling the quay. As good fortune would have it, the gate opened up to allow three British destroyers through. Schergat remembered the incident well. "We noticed the entrance lights were on, but we couldn't see the destroyers because we were just at surface level. As we approached the entrance, the water became rough and we knew ships were entering. They created a wave which pushed us apart . . . we got separated and each man [manned torpedo crew] went toward his destination."[25]

Durand de la Penne and Bianchi cruised into the harbor, their heads barely visible. As they maneuvered toward their target, the *Valiant*, they passed two anchored destroyers and the French battleship *Lorraine*. Realizing that a larger target lay ahead, they continued, ignoring the temptation of a certain success. At approximately 0219 they reached the antitorpedo net surrounding the *Valiant*. Bianchi stated later: "It was not difficult to distinguish the huge shape of the *Valiant*. As we arrived at 50 meters from the ship we found as expected an obstruction net. I saw that we could physically pass between the two buoys supporting the net. But because we were so close to the ship I suggested to de la Penne that we pass under the net. He decided to check it out and left the pig and dove down. He came back and said we would pass over the buoys. I didn't agree, but he said he was tired and his dry suit was leaking."[26]

Durand de la Penne's dry suit had been leaking since he had departed the *Scire,* and the cold water was beginning to sap his strength, so instead of taking time to submerge and cut the net he elected to go over the top.* Once inside the net, he was fifty meters from the *Valiant.* He drove the torpedo slowly into the side of the ship, bumping his way down to the keel. For some unexplained reason the torpedo took on water and began to sink quickly. Durand de la Penne and Bianchi rode the torpedo to the bottom of the harbor, seventeen meters below the surface. The two divers, realizing that they were not directly under the *Valiant,* struggled to move the torpedo toward the British battleship. The effort was exhausting, and Bianchi began to feel faint. "I was going to go up to the surface, get some fresh air and return and continue my work. At that moment I don't remember what happened. When I regained consciousness I was floating near the ship and illuminated. I thought my surfacing had caused a lot of noise, so I took off my aqualung [which didn't work] and sunk it. Then I headed for a nearby buoy."[27]

Moments later, Durand de la Penne realized that Bianchi was not with the torpedo. Leaving the submersible, he surfaced to find his partner. After a brief look around with no success, Durand de la Penne returned to the torpedo.

Grabbing the bow of the torpedo, he began dragging it underneath the battleship.

Speed was essential, because I was so weak and not able to last much longer . . . The pig is moving a few centimeters; I cannot distinguish the compass due to the mud clouds that I raised while working. My mask is dim and I cannot see anything anymore . . . During the operation I flood the mask. I try to eliminate the water from inside but it is impossible. I must drink it . . . At that moment it seems that I cannot continue

---

*The Belloni suit was made of light rubber and according to Schergat frequently broke at the wrists and neck. Schergat confirmed that this is what happened to Durand de la Penne's dry suit.

working because of the extreme fatigue and for the breathlessness. I go to the surface. The target nearness gave me strength;
I am not worried about the bomb, but only for the thought of
not being able to reach the hull.[28]

For the next forty minutes Durand de la Penne pulled the torpedo
inch by inch until he had positioned it directly under the keel, in the
middle of the ship. He was now completely exhausted. He set the
timers on the charge and swam to the surface. Almost immediately
he was spotted by pier security and fired upon with an automatic
weapon. The sentry directed him back to the *Valiant* where he
climbed out of the water onto the mooring buoy only to find
Bianchi hiding in the shadows. At 0330 a motorboat picked up the
two Italians from the buoy, and a guard escorted them to the *Valiant*. They were briefly interrogated aboard the ship and then taken
to the base security hut near the Ras el Tin Lighthouse. The officer
in charge of the interrogation reported the following actions:

> Early that same morning [18 December] I was sleeping peace-
> fully in a pension in Alexandria when the telephone rang and
> I was summoned immediately to Ras el Tin; a car was on its
> way to fetch me. Two Italian frogmen had been caught sitting
> on the bow buoy of the *Valiant* and had been sent across from
> the other side of the harbour for interrogation by RAF's inter-
> preter. What questions were to be asked? An attack by sabo-
> teurs had been expected for some time, and the harbour en-
> trance was protected by heavy nets and explosive charges. We
> wanted to know
>
> (1) Had they completed their missions?
> (2) Were they alone?
> (3) How did they get into the harbour?

They strenuously denied the first two questions and said they
had got into difficulties outside the harbour and had to abandon their equipment and swim ashore. Of course we did not
believe them and I rang the battleships and suggested they
should drag chain bottom lines to try and dislodge any limpets.
They were already doing this and C in C [commander in chief,

Alexandria] ordered them [Durand de la Penne and Bianchi] to be returned to *Valiant* where they were put below on the lowest deck in the fore part of the ship.[29]

Aboard the *Valiant* their British escorts behaved very nicely and gave them rum and cigarettes. It was only then, when Durand de la Penne spotted the ship's name embroidered on the escort's shirts, that he knew he was aboard the *Valiant*. At 0550, with ten minutes remaining until the charge was scheduled to explode, he asked to see the captain. "I told him that in a few minutes his ship would blow up, that there was nothing he could do about it and that, if he wished, he could still get his crew into a place of safety."[30] The captain demanded to know where the bomb was located. When Durand de la Penne refused to answer, he was placed, once again, in the forward hold, this time without Bianchi and without escorts.

At approximately 0600 the charge beneath the *Valiant* detonated, lifting the battleship out of the water and severely damaging the port side. The ship immediately settled on the bottom and began to list to port. All the electricity went out, and the room Durand de la Penne was in began to fill with smoke. After several attempts, he finally forced his way out a hatch and climbed up to the main deck. After a few minutes, he found the captain and demanded to know the whereabouts of Bianchi. Moments later the charge beneath the *Queen Elizabeth* exploded, sending oil and debris skyward and soaking all those on the deck of the *Valiant*. Durand de la Penne was sent back to the hold, but after thirty minutes he was escorted up to the officers' mess where he found Bianchi. The two were held in the mess for a short while, then transferred by motorboat back to the security hut at Ras el Tin Lighthouse. By that evening they were both in a POW camp in Alexandria.

The second crew consisted of Engineer Captain Antonio Marceglia and Petty Officer Diver/Spartaco Schergat. Their target was initially the HMS *Eagle*. After losing sight of Durand de la Penne at the harbor's entrance, the second crew came under attack from precautionary depth charges that were being dropped two hundred to five hundred yards away. The explosive force caused strong contractions in the divers' legs, and it felt "as though [the manned torpedoes] had crashed against some metallic obstacle."[31] It bothered the two divers, "but not too much."[32]

The second crew followed the British ships on through the entrance only to have three other destroyers almost run them over half an hour later. After evading the ships, Marceglia returned to his preplanned course and proceeded onward. During the planning phase Marceglia had decided to plot a course parallel to shore, allowing the background lights to silhouette the vessels at anchor.

The *Eagle* was a large target and within minutes the second crew spotted what they thought was their objective. They did not know until later that the ship was in fact the *Queen Elizabeth*. They closed rapidly and had no problem negotiating the antitorpedo net. At approximately 0230 they were within striking distance of the largest battleship in the British fleet. Schergat recalled later, "We entered the antitorpedo net which was approximately fifty or sixty meters from the *Queen Elizabeth*. Marceglia took the pig in at 90 degrees perpendicular to the ship. We dropped to five or six meters going forward, and we hit the hull. This was quite a difficult phase. We tried to hit the ammunition deposits, but we ended up under the engines."[33]

Once securely underneath the vessel, Marceglia pumped out a small amount of ballast water and buoyed up underneath the ship. Schergat got off the torpedo and secured a loop-line from the port to the starboard bilge keel. Marceglia disconnected the warhead from the bow of the torpedo and attached it to the line that was hanging four feet below the hull. He set the fuse and the two divers remounted the torpedo, ballasted to neutral, and returned to the surface. The time was 0315.

As the torpedo surfaced, a roving patrol spotted the exhaust bubbles and shined a light on their position. The two Italians remained motionless and averted their faces to prevent any reflection from the glass in their masks. The patrol moved on, and the second crew continued its extraction. The escape and evasion plan called for the divers to make for shore, destroy their torpedo and equipment, and attempt to find a boat from which to rendezvous with the Italian submarine *Zaffro*. Marceglia and Schergat executed their extraction according to the plan, reaching shore by 0430. Unfortunately, while posing as French sailors they were picked up by the

Egyptian police for suspicious behavior and eventually turned over to the British. While being held in the British Port Authority building, the two Italians discovered the ship they had sunk was the *Queen Elizabeth* and not the aircraft carrier *Eagle,* as they had originally thought. In his after-action report submitted upon release from prison, Marceglia reported: "As you can see, Sir, our performance had nothing heroic about it; its success was due solely to the preparations made, the specially favorable conditions under which it took place and above all the determination to succeed at all costs."[34]

The third crew consisted of Gunner Captain Vincenzo Martellotta and Petty Officer/Diver Mario Marino. They had been ordered to attack the sixteen-thousand-ton tanker *Sagona.* After attaching their demolitions, the crew was to release floating incendiary mines that would explode after the *Sagona* blew up to light the oil on fire. It was hoped the fire would spread throughout the harbor and destroy several other ships. In port at the time were twelve loaded tankers with a total weight of 120,000 tons. Although Martellotta understood the need to destroy the oilers before leaving the *Scire,* he complained to Borghese about not getting a chance to sink a combatant. Borghese subsequently modified the orders to allow Martellotta to attack the HMS *Eagle* if it was in port.

Like the other two crews, Martellotta and Marino approached the harbor entrance while being subjected to constant depth charging. In an effort to lessen the pain the two divers "ducked in such a way as to lie low in the water, but with heart, lungs and head above the surface."[35] As the British destroyers entered the harbor, their wake threw the tiny submersible against a mooring buoy used to secure the antisubmarine net. After pushing off from the buoy Martellotta followed the second destroyer through the entrance, passing within twenty yards of the small guardship that was dropping the depth charges. The time was 0030.

Martellotta and Marino were now inside the harbor and began to search for the aircraft carrier. In the course of their search the two divers spotted a large vessel they believed to be the *Eagle.* After taking a bearing on the center stack, Martellotta dove the torpedo and came up underneath the vessel. It was only then that he realized that it was not the *Eagle* or even a battleship but a much smaller cruiser. Adhering to his prescribed orders, Martellotta backed off and reluctantly returned to the surface. As he broached the surface, a sentry on the cruiser flashed his light on the divers' position. The two Italians remained motionless for several moments, and eventually the sentry returned to his patrol.

By this time the cold water and the pure oxygen from their diving rigs were beginning to have an adverse effect on Martellotta. He began to vomit and was unable to keep his mouthpiece securely between his lips. Fortunately upon surfacing, the two divers spotted their assigned target, the *Sagona*. Unable to submerge because of his illness, Martellotta drove the torpedo on the surface, positioning it aft of the tanker underneath the stern.* He reported later, "I went toward the stern of the oil tanker and ordered Marino to go under the hull and establish a connection nearest to the bilge keel. He tried at first, but [the torpedo] was too light. I put on more ballast and Marino tried again. This time he succeeded . . . I told him to take off the head, start the fuse, and bring the charge to the other end of the connection. Marino carried out my orders exactly . . . I made sure the fuses were started."[36]

At 0255 Marino set the timer for three hours and pulled the fuse. After Marino surfaced the two divers remounted the torpedo and proceeded to set the incendiary mines around the tanker. When this was done they headed toward the shore.

Once the two divers reached the shore, they destroyed their diving rigs, set the destruction device on the torpedo, and entered the city. Unfortunately for the Italians they were stopped at a control point and arrested by Egyptian police. Eventually they were turned over to the British and spent the rest of the war in a POW camp in Cairo.

By 0600 the charges beneath the targets began to detonate, and within a few minutes the six Italian divers had sunk two battleships and a tanker and seriously damaged the destroyer *Jervis,* which was alongside the *Sagona*. The *Valiant* suffered severe internal damage and had an eighty-foot gash in her side. Three boiler compartments aboard the *Queen Elizabeth* were destroyed, and her hull was torn

---

*According to Schergat, Martellotta was supposed to hit the tanker amidships where the oil was held. The resulting explosion would rupture the tanker and then the oil could be ignited by incendiary bombs.

open. It was several months before either ship was repaired, and the extent of damages was such that neither vessel ever contributed to the war effort again. On 23 April 1942 Prime Minister Winston Churchill spoke before a secret session of the House of Commons and reported the following:

> On the early morning of December 19 half a dozen Italians in unusual diving suits were captured floundering about in the harbour of Alexandria. Extreme precautions have been taken for some time past against the varieties of human torpedo or one-man submarine entering our harbours. Not only are nets and other obstructions used but underwater charges are exploded at frequent irregular intervals in the fairway. None the less these men had penetrated the harbour. Four hours later explosion occurred in the bottoms of the *Valiant* and the *Queen Elizabeth* produced by limpet bombs fixed with extra ordinary courage and ingenuity, the effect of which was to blow large holes in the bottoms of both ships and to flood several compartments, thus putting them both out of action for many months. One ship will soon be ready again, the other is still in the floating dock at Alexandria, a constant target for enemy air attack. Thus we no longer have any battle squadron in the Mediterranean. *Barham* [is] gone and now *Valiant* and *Queen Elizabeth* are completely out of action. Both these ships floated on an even keel, they looked all right from the air. The enemy were for some time unaware of the success of their attack, and it is only now that I feel it possible to make this disclosure to the House even in the strictness of a Secret Session.[37]

As it turns out the Italians were aware of the damage they had done to the British fleet; nevertheless, they did not pursue their advantage in the Mediterranean. With overwhelming naval power the supply lines to Rommel would have been assured and the "occupation of Egypt would only have been a question of time, bringing with it incalculable consequences for the outcome of the war."[38] Borghese was bitter throughout the war, placing the blame for "losing this opportunity" squarely at the feet of the German High Command, which refused to provide fuel to the Italian navy and "again displayed its underestimation of sea power in the general conduct of the war and in particular of the importance of the Mediterranean in the general picture of the entire conflict."[39] The lost opportunity notwithstanding, the attack on the British fleet at Alexandria was strategically the most important and successful operation of the war for the Italian navy. Luigi Durand de la Penne and his five teammates received the Italian Gold Medal for gallantry, which is equivalent to the Medal of Honor. It was the only time in Italian history that all participants in an operation were so decorated.

ANALYSIS

Critique

Were the objectives worth the risks? The Italian navy, although beaten badly in the months prior to the attack on Alexandria, was in the process of commissioning three new battleships, *Doria, Vittorio Veneto,* and *Littorio.* The British had also suffered several naval defeats with the loss of the aircraft carrier *Ark Royal* and the battleship *Barham* in November 1941. If the Italians could destroy the remaining two battleships, *Queen Elizabeth* and *Valiant,* they, along with the Germans, could dominate the Mediterranean. As it stood, however, even with its numerical superiority, the Italian fleet was insufficient to challenge the British in the eastern Mediterranean. With the British still controlling the vital sea-lanes, the Italians had to struggle to resupply Rommel's forces in North Africa. By using the manned torpedoes to conduct underwater guerrilla warfare, the Italians were able to make maximum use of their maritime resources. With the destruction of two battleships and a destroyer, the Italians had an opportunity to control the maritime playing field and propagandize about the "weakness" of the British. Unfortunately, they did neither. Nevertheless, when one considers that only six men and three manned torpedoes were used to destroy the targets, the objectives were undeniably worth the risk.

Was the plan developed to maximize superiority over the enemy and minimize the risk to the assault force? The development of the manned torpedoes was a technological revolution in underwater warfare. It allowed the Italians to circumvent the conventional submarine defenses protecting the capital ships and to bypass the picketboats that were specifically designed to stop frogmen and divers. Superb operational intelligence allowed the planners to tailor the rehearsals to the mission and thereby ensured that the manned torpedo crews were properly prepared to overcome most obstacles. Although the plan maximized the possibility that the battleships would be destroyed, it did not minimize the risk to the divers. Unlike the attacks on Gibraltar, in which the divers could hit the target and swim to neutral Spain, there was little chance the Alexandria divers would return from a trip deep in enemy territory. The *Scire*, which would have provided the best extraction platform, departed immediately after launching the torpedoes. This reduced the submarine's vulnerability, but certainly did not help the manned torpedo crews. There was an escape and evasion plan, but it was not well thought out and the divers did not truly expect to return.* Although this one-way trip may seem unacceptable by today's standards, the Italians were able to maximize their combat effectiveness by eliminating the extraction phase. The torpedo's battery power, the air in their Belloni rigs, and their physical endurance were all dedicated to mission accomplishment and not saved for escape.

Was the mission executed according to the plan, and if not, what unforeseen circumstances dictated the outcome? With some minor exceptions, the plan was executed exactly as rehearsed. Schergat said later, "From my point of view, the mission looked just like further training."[40] However, several problems arose that typify the frictions of war. Durand de la Penne lost his second diver, Bianchi, when the petty officer fainted and floated to the surface. One of the three manned torpedoes took on too much ballast and sank to the bottom of the harbor. One of the officers, Martellotta, got violently ill and had to direct the actions of his torpedo from the surface. All of these incidents were happenstance, but that is the nature of war.

*The divers had been given British pounds to use as currency while in Alexandria. Unfortunately for the Italians, the Egyptians were still using the local currency, and as soon as the divers attempted to buy something they were arrested by the police.

Regardless of how well the planning and preparation phases go, the environment of war is different from the environment of preparing for war. But, by being specially trained, equipped, and supported for a specific mission, special forces personnel can reduce those frictions to the bare minimum and then overcome them with courage, boldness, perseverance, and intellect—the moral factors.

What modifications could have improved the outcome of the mission? The success of the mission speaks for itself. However, it is conceivable that had a more thorough escape and evasion plan been arranged, two of the crews might have escaped. By prepositioning an agent and a small boat outside the harbor, the evading crews could have quickly linked up and sailed away from the scene before the demolitions exploded. Apparently, this was never addressed. The Italians did have an agent in Cairo who was supposed to assist the divers in their escape, but the Italians, being unfamiliar with the city and unable to speak the language, had little chance of reaching this individual. This part of the plan notwithstanding, the operation was extremely well planned and coordinated, and there are very few modifications that could have improved the outcome.

Relative Superiority

Operations that rely entirely on stealth for the successful accomplishment of their mission have inherent weaknesses; however, they have one overwhelming advantage. As long as the attacking force remains concealed, they are not subject to the will of the enemy. Therefore their chances of success are immediately better than 50 percent because the inherent superiority of the defense is lost.[41] The attacking force has the initiative, choosing when and where it wants to attack, and if the mission is planned correctly, the force will attack at the weakest point in the defense. Consequently, if the will of the enemy is not a factor, only the frictions of war (i.e., chance and uncertainty) will affect the outcome of the mission. Clearly the frictions of war can be detrimental to success, but through good preparation and strong moral factors, the frictions can be managed. The inherent problem with special operations that rely entirely on stealth is obvious. If that concealment is compromised, the mission has little or no chance of success.

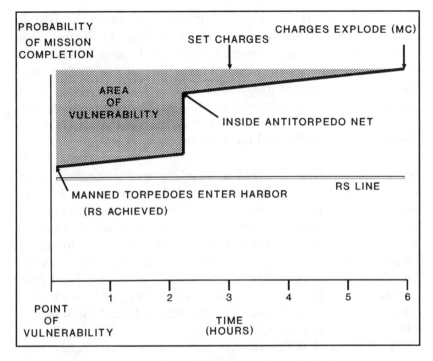

**Fig. 3–2. Relative Superiority Graph for the
Italian Frogman Attack on Alexandria**

Figure 3-2 represents a composite graph of all three manned torpedo operations. Although there were some differences in the individual profiles, basically all three torpedoes reached the critical points at approximately the same time. At midnight on 19 December 1941, all three torpedoes entered the harbor and passed by the antisubmarine net. This was the point of vulnerability, but because the British did not know the torpedoes were in the harbor, the Italians began with relative superiority, albeit not very decisively. As the manned torpedoes continued into the harbor, circumventing the picketboats and pier security, their probability of mission completion improved marginally. Their decisive advantage came when they penetrated the antitorpedo nets. After this point, there were no other defenses that could prevent them from successfully fulfilling their mission. However, as the graph depicts, there was still an area of vulnerability even after overcoming the antitorpedo net. Had the Italians been detected (for instance, when Bianchi floated to the surface), the British crews could have dropped concussion grenades and possibly stopped the attack. Fortunately for the Italians, they were able to set their charges before the British detected them. Three hours later the charges exploded, and the mission was complete.

The Principles of Special Operations

Simplicity. This mission had several advantages not normally associated with a special operation. Although the target was clearly strategic, with the balance of the naval forces in the Mediterranean hinging on the mission success, the execution was almost an extension of routine training and wartime operations. Under Borghese's command the *Scire* had previously conducted three missions that paralleled the attack on Alexandria. Durand de la Penne and Bianchi were also veterans of a previous attempt to attack the British. This experience helped mold the approach the Italians took in planning and preparing for Alexandria.

The lessons of the disaster at Malta convinced Borghese, who was the overall mission commander, not to create a complex plan of operation. Borghese limited the objectives by reducing the forces assigned to attack Alexandria. He could just as easily have incorporated another three manned torpedoes and several E-boats to overload British defenses and ensure the Italians of some success. Additionally, although each manned torpedo had only one warhead, it was possible, and often rehearsed, for each crew to hit multiple targets by placing the smaller limpet mines on as many ships as feasible. Borghese chose to avoid both these pitfalls and limit each manned torpedo to only one target with "all other targets consisting of active war units to be ignored."[42] Although not involved in the planning, Bianchi recognized the need to limit the number of targets. He said later, "In limiting the attack to one objective [per crew] the commander considered having the offensive power increased."[43] Even attacking one target became difficult. In each of the three cases the frogmen were able to execute their assigned tasks, but only after overcoming significant physical problems (vomiting, unconsciousness, headaches) and equipment failures (dry suit leaks, flooded torpedoes). Had the mission called for more than one target per dive pair, it is unlikely the divers would have had the physical or technical resources to complete it. Also, with multiple targets, the fuses on the charges would have to have been set for more time to allow the divers time to attack their other targets and escape. Arguably this might have allowed the British to find the charges or move the vessels from their anchorage (in Durand de la Penne's case, moving the vessel would have prevented any damage to the *Valiant*). In either case, limiting the objectives clearly simplified the plan and allowed maximum effort to be applied against the primary targets.

Borghese knew the value of accurate intelligence, and he consistently used it throughout the operation to reduce the unknown variables and improve the divers' chances of success. Knowing the physical limitations of divers exposed to cold water, Borghese insisted on getting his submarine as close to the harbor entrance as possible. Italian agents in Alexandria provided the 10th Light Flotilla with a clear picture of the British defenses and in particular the minefields off the coast. Borghese wrote later, "I had therefore decided that as soon as we reached a depth of 400 meters [which was probably where the minefield started], we would proceed at a depth of not less than 60 meters, since I assumed that the mines, even if they were anti-submarine, would be located at a higher level."[44]

This information eventually allowed the *Scire* to maneuver to a point only 1.3 miles from the entrance of the harbor. So close, in fact, that after launching the torpedoes, Durand de la Penne stopped his assault crews for a sip of cognac and a tin of food.

The torpedo crews were also provided the latest human intelligence and aerial reconnaissance photos to allow them to plot courses and find the simplest approach to the target. Borghese noted during the preparation phase that the divers' desks "were covered with aerial photographs and maps . . . daily examined under a magnifying glass and annotated from the latest intelligence and air reconnaissance reports; those harbours, with their moles, obstacles, wharfs, docks, mooring places and defences, were no mysteries to the pilots, who perfectly knew their configuration, orientation and depths, so that they, astride the 'pig', could make their way about them at night just as easily as a man in his own room."[45]

The accurate intelligence had simplified the problem of negotiating minefields and navigating in an enemy harbor. Alexandria Harbor was thirty-five hundred miles from Italy. It was ringed with antiaircraft guns and supported by Spitfires from the Royal Air Force. It seemed impenetrable from the air. On the other hand, the Italian navy, which had almost no presence in the eastern Mediterranean, posed no significant threat to the more than two hundred vessels (merchant and warships) tied up in Alexandria. The only major fears the British had were from submarines and saboteurs, and extensive precautions had been taken to overcome both these possibilities.Until the establishment of the 10th Light Flotilla and the innovations that followed (i.e., the manned torpedoes, diving rigs, limpet mines, Belloni dry suits, and submarine transport chambers), the difficulty of penetrating the static defenses of Alexandria was not worth the risk in human lives or equipment.* These innovations allowed the Italians to reconsider the possibility of a direct assault.

The most significant tactical innovation was the use of disposable torpedoes. Having to plan for only a one-way trip meant enhanced time on target for the divers and reduced the threat envelope for the submarine *Scire*. Obviously one-way trips have their drawbacks for the individual operators, but from a mission accomplishment standpoint they improve the possibility of success by reducing the extraction variables. The technological innovations allowed the divers to completely bypass the British defenses. The small visual signature of the manned torpedo provided the Italians a host of tactical advantages. It allowed them to surface unobserved and ride out the depth charges. They were able to navigate around the harbor undetected by ballasting the submersible just under the surface. These actions would not have been possible with either a midget submarine or a conventional submarine. The ease of handling the torpedo also allowed the crews to climb over antitorpedo nets and allowed Durand de la Penne to physically move his flooded machine to a position under the

*The possibility of using a conventional submarine to penetrate the harbor was remote, particularly in light of the shallow depth of the water inside Alexandria Harbor. Additionally, once inside the harbor the submarine would have had to fire torpedoes to attack its target, thereby immediately condemning itself to death.

Valiant's keel. Innovation simplified the assault plan by eliminating the defensive threats posed by the nets and depth charges, and it was without question the dominant factor in the success of the mission.

Security. The raid on Alexandria again demonstrates how the importance of security was not a function of hiding the intent of the mission but of the timing and the insertion means. By December 1941 British intelligence was fully aware that the Italians had manned submersibles capable of penetrating their harbors. The second Italian attack on Gibraltar had provided the British with one torpedo and its crew. The attack on Malta had also resulted in the capture of Italian frogmen. And the sinking of the *Gondar* resulted in the capture of Elios Toschi, the designer of the original manned torpedo. With all this information, the British unquestionably knew the kind of operations they could expect from the 10th Light Flotilla. As Winston Churchill later said in his speech to the House of Commons, "Extreme precautions had been taken for some time past against the varieties of human torpedo or one-man submarines entering our harbours."[46] Even with all these precautions, however, the Italians still managed to sneak in and destroy the fleet.

The security employed by the Italians was tight but not overbearing. It did not prevent Borghese from asking for volunteers from among all the members of the 10th Light Flotilla, nor did it prevent the crews from conducting several full-mission profiles in and around La Spezia Harbor, although in both cases it is believed that the actual target was not made known to the general participants.

Borghese was, however, cognizant of the need to conceal the timing of the operation. Upon departing La Spezia for the final voyage, he ensured that the *Scire*'s transport chambers were visibly empty, and he did not load the manned torpedoes until he was out of sight of the harbor. He took these actions to convince possible onlookers that the *Scire* was out for just another routine operation. Borghese kept up pretenses when he arrived in Leros. While in port he had the transport chambers covered to reduce speculation about the submarine's mission, and he refused an admiral's order to conduct another exercise for fear of compromising the impending mission.

Borghese also understood that all things being equal, operational needs were more important than security. Throughout the mission he maintained radio contact with Athens and Rome. Although interception of the message traffic could have compromised the mission, Borghese obviously felt the need for updated intelligence outweighed that concern. In the end, Italian security was instrumental in preventing the enemy from gaining an advantage by knowing the timing of the mission. A good special operation will succeed in spite of the enemy's attempt to fortify his position, provided security prevents the enemy from knowing when and how the attack is coming. In the case of the Italians' attack on Alexandria, security achieved its aims.

Repetition. The principle of repetition as it applies to the attack on Alexandria can be viewed in both the macro and the micro senses of the word. The manned torpedoes of the 10th Light Flotilla had a very limited role: to conduct attacks on ships in port. Every mission profile was similar: launch from the submarine, transit to the objective, cut through the nets, place the charge, and withdraw. Because of this narrowly defined role every training exercise added to the base of knowledge of the operator regardless of what specific mission he would eventually undertake. If one considers that each of the six divers had been on board the 10th Light Flotilla an average of eighteen months (Durand de la Penne and Bianchi almost two years), during which time they had dived at least two times a week, then each man had over 150 dives. In addition, three of the divers (Durand de la Penne, Bianchi, and Marceglia) had previously conducted wartime missions, and all of the divers had at one time or another been designated as reserve crewmembers and undergone a complete mission workup. So, in the macro sense, the only aspect of the Alexandria mission that had not been rehearsed well over one hundred times was the exact course the divers would take.

The operational and reserve crews for the Alexandria mission were assembled in September 1941 to begin mission-specific training. It was during this preparation that the crews conducted exact profiles of the Alexandria mission. Borghese reported that this training "became highly intensified, this being the key to secure the greatest possible efficiency in the men and materials composing the unit. The pilots of the human torpedoes . . . travelled to La Spezia twice a week and were there dropped off from a boat or, in all-around tests, from one of the transport submarines, and then performed a *complete assault exercise,* naturally at night; this consisted of get-

ting near the harbour, negotiating the net-defences, advancing stealth-
ily within the harbour, approaching the target, attacking the hull,
applying the warhead and, finally, withdrawing."[47]

Although exact numbers are not available, Spartaco Schergat
indicates that a total of ten full-mission profiles were conducted
by all three crews and the reserves. Other limited dives concentrated
on specific aspects of the mission, such as net cutting or charge emplacement. In the end, however, it was repetition that provided the
divers familiarity with their machines and their environment. The
training became so routine that Schergat later remarked, "Being in
Alexandria or La Spezia was the same. For me it didn't make any
difference."[48]

The raid on Alexandria presents a broader view of the principle
of repetition. It shows that repetition must be measured in terms of
both experience and mission-specific training. Special operations
forces that are multidimensional will require more rehearsals and
more time during the preparation phase than a unit whose sole mission encompasses this training on a daily basis.* However, no amount
of experience can obviate the need to conduct a minimum of two
full-dress rehearsals prior to the mission.

Surprise. In an underwater attack, unlike other special operations,
surprise is not only necessary, it is essential. As illustrated in the
relative superiority graph, special operations forces that attack underwater have the advantage of being relatively superior to the enemy throughout the engagement as long as they remain concealed.
Owing to their inherent lack of speed and firepower, however, once
surprise is compromised, underwater attackers have little opportunity to escape. Although many commanders may find this risk unacceptable, experience shows that this type of operation is mostly
successful. During World War II the Italians sank over 260,000 tons

---

*This statement is not intended to deny the need for special operations
forces that are flexible enough to respond to a variety of threats. It is obvious, however, that units will perform better when they can focus their
attention on one mission area. The need for repetition in the preparation
phase will also be reduced if the event is one for which the unit consistently trains.

of shipping and lost only a dozen men, while the British had similar successes in both the European and the Japanese theaters.* The reason for this paradox is that it is relatively easy for divers or submersibles to remain concealed, up to a certain point. Alexandria was a huge harbor with approximately two hundred vessels anchored out, and wartime conditions called for all vessels to be at darken ship. Consequently, a small black submersible, even on the surface of the water, would have been detected only by chance. However, once the manned torpedoes got within close proximity of the target, the chance of detection was greatly increased. This is true of all underwater attacks. The fatigue of the divers, the vigilance of the crew, and the uncertainty of the situation combine to make the actions at the objective exceedingly difficult. This is why relative superiority remained only marginal in this operation until the Italians actually overcame the final obstacle, the antitorpedo net. Beyond the antitorpedo net the British were least prepared to defend themselves, and now the Italians had all the advantages.

The antisubmarine and antitorpedo defenses at Alexandria also show that, contrary to the accepted definition of surprise, the enemy is usually prepared for an attack.[49] To be effective, special operations forces must either attack the enemy when he is off guard or, as in the Italians' case, elude the enemy entirely. But to assume that the enemy is unprepared to counterattack is foolhardy and might lead to overconfidence on the part of the attacker. It is the nature of defensive warfare to be prepared for an attack. Consequently, if the attacker is compromised, the enemy will be able to react rapidly and the attacker's only hope for success lies in quickly achieving his objective.

Speed. Underwater attacks are rarely characterized by speed. A quick review of the relative superiority graph shows that it took the manned torpedoes over two hours from the point of vulnerability until they reached the antitorpedo net. Throughout this time they

---

*The British used both manned torpedoes (chariots) and midget submarines (X-craft). The X-craft had great success against the German battleship *Tirpitz* in Norway and the Japanese cruiser *Takao* while she was anchored in the Johore Strait near the Malay peninsula.

were subject to the frictions of war, and by moving slowly and methodically they only increased their area of vulnerability. However, as long as the will of the enemy is not infringing on the relative superiority of the attacker, speed is not essential, although it is still desirable. Speed becomes essential when the attacker begins to lose relative superiority. Two of the torpedo crews reached their objectives and calmly proceeded to attach the explosives and depart. Durand de la Penne, however, reached his target and immediately began to have difficulties: his torpedo sank to the bottom, he lost his second diver, his dry suit filled with cold water, and he was fatigued to the point of exhaustion. As he said in his after-action report, at that point speed was essential. Durand de la Penne was rapidly losing his advantage and knew that if he didn't act quickly "the operation . . . would be doomed to failure."[50] The closer an attacker gets to the objective, the greater the risk. Consequently, speed is still important to minimize the attacker's vulnerability and improve the probability of mission completion.

Purpose. Commander Borghese, who was in overall charge of the attack on Alexandria, ensured that the purpose of the mission was well defined and that the divers were personally committed to achieving their objectives. This was a straightforward mission without any complicated command and control issues; therefore, defining the goals and objectives—the purpose—was relatively easy. Each manned torpedo had only one warhead and one target. Therefore it was essential not to waste the warhead and the effort on an undesirable objective. Borghese ordered Martellotta and Marino to attack the aircraft carrier *Eagle* if she were in port, and if not, the tanker *Sagona*. Once inside the harbor, however, the pair accidently attacked a cruiser. Fortunately, before they could detach the warhead, they realized it was not their target, and as Borghese notes, "with great reluctance, in obedience to orders received, abandoned the attack."[51] Their orders were clear; they understood the purpose of the mission. They were not to waste their effort on a small cruiser, but instead were to seek out a larger target, which they eventually found and destroyed.

Men who volunteered for the 10th Light Flotilla were typical of special forces personnel everywhere. Each was a combination of adventurer and patriot. They understood the risks involved in penetrating the enemy's harbor and fully accepted the consequences. They did so out of a love for excitement and the understanding that their missions were important to the country. Teseo Tesei, who, at Malta, detonated his torpedo underneath himself in order to achieve his objective, said, "Whether we sink any ships or not doesn't matter much; what does matter is that we should be able to blow up with our craft under the very noses of the enemy: we should thus have shown our sons and Italy's future generations at the price of what sacrifice we live up to our ideals and how success is to be achieved."[52]

Although Tesei, who had died three months earlier, did not participate in the Alexandria attack, his inspiration was apparent in the attitudes of the Alexandria crews. All six divers knew they would be either captured or killed, and yet Borghese says the difficulties and dangers merely "increased their determination."[53] This personal commitment to see the mission completed at any cost is, as Tesei said, how success is achieved.

Notes

1. Bruce Williamson, *by Sea and by Stealth* (New York: Coward-McCann, 1956), 39.
2. J. Valerio Borghese, *Sea Devils*, trans. James Cleugh (Chicago: Henry Regnery, 1954), 14.
3. Risio, *I Mezzi d'Assalto*, 117.
4. Borghese, *Sea Devils*, 32.
5. Spartaco Schergat, interview by author, trans. Lt. Comdr. Paolo Gianetti, tape recording, Monterey, Calif., 4 November 1992.
6. Borghese, *Sea Devils*, 33.
7. Emilio Bianchi, letter to author, trans. Lt. Comdr. Paolo Gianetti, 22 May 1993.
8. As quoted in Borghese, *Sea Devils*, 57.
9. William G. Scofield and P. J. Carisella, *Frogmen: First Battles* (Boston: Branden Publishing, 1987), 97.
10. Ibid., 101–2.
11. Borghese, *Sea Devils*, 98.
12. Ibid., 100.
13. Ibid., 129.
14. Schergat, interview.
15. Borghese, *Sea Devils*, 135.
16. Schergat, interview.
17. Bianchi, letter to author.
18. Carisella, *Frogmen*, 179.
19. Bianchi, letter to author.
20. Schergat, interview.
21. Borghese, *Sea Devils*, 144.
22. Bianchi, letter to author.
23. Carisella, *Frogmen*, 127.
24. Risio, *I Mezzi d'Assalto*, 118.
25. Schergat, interview.
26. Bianchi, letter to author. Passing under the antitorpedo net would have required cutting the net and this is what Durand de la Penne felt would take too much time.
27. Bianchi, letter to author.
28. Risio, *I Mezzi d'Assalto*, 120.

29. Report on the events of 18 December 1941 by the HMS *Jervis* antisubmarine officer, 14th Destroyer Flotilla, Imperial War Museum.

30. Risio, *I Mezzi d'Assalto,* 120.

31. Borghese, *Sea Devils,* 152.

32. Schergat, interview.

33. Ibid.

34. Borghese, *Sea Devils,* 153.

35. Ibid., 154.

36. Risio, *I Mezzi d'Assalto,* 127.

37. Winston Churchill in a secret session of the House of Commons on 23 April 1942.

38. Borghese, *Sea Devils,* 158.

39. Ibid.

40. Schergat, interview.

41. Carl von Clausewitz, *On War,* ed. and trans. Michael Howard and Peter Paret (Princeton, N.J.: Princeton University Press, 1976), 357.

42. Borghese, *Sea Devils,* 154.

43. Bianchi, letter to author.

44. Risio, *I Mezzi d'Assalto,* 117. After-action report of Commander J. Borghese.

45. Borghese, *Sea Devils,* 53.

46. Churchill's Report to the House of Commons.

47. Borghese, *Sea Devils,* xx.

48. Schergat, interview.

49. Joint Chiefs of Staff, *Joint Publication 3-05 (Test): Doctrine for Joint Special Operations* (Washington, D.C.: Office of the Joint Chiefs of Staff, 1990), E-5.

50. Borghese, *Sea Devils.*

51. Borghese, *Sea Devils,* 155.

52. Ibid., 97.

53. Ibid., 142.

4

Operation Chariot:
The British Raid on Saint-Nazaire,
27–28 March 1942

BACKGROUND

In July 1940 Winston Churchill established the Combined Operations Command and appointed Admiral of the Fleet Lord Roger J. B. Keyes as its first commander. The organization was tasked with planning and conducting raids against the Germans. Lord Keyes was given command of the special service brigades and parachute troops along with the landing craft to transport them. It was his responsibility to organize and train this new amphibious strike force called the commandos.[1]

One year later after only limited success, Keyes was replaced by Lord Louis Mountbatten. In the months immediately following Mountbatten's appointment, the commandos of Combined Operations conducted several major raids, most notably harassing attacks against the Germans at Lofoten Island and Vaagsö in Norway.

The planners at Combined Operations had looked at the French port facility of Saint-Nazaire several times. It contained the largest dry dock on the Atlantic as well as fourteen submarine pens. The initial studies discounted the port as a viable target because "the difficulties they thought were insurmountable. The shoal waters in the approaches were unnavigable, the ships would be unlikely to survive the long sea passage [250 miles from Falmouth, England] without detection, and the raiding force would have to be impossibly large, perhaps 300 men, to destroy the targets envisioned."[2]

As the war continued, several events began to alter the decision to attack Saint-Nazaire. The raids conducted by the British from 1941 to early 1942 had met with only limited success and had failed to significantly impact the German war effort in the Atlantic. In May of 1941 the British sank the German battleship *Bismarck,* but by early 1942 Hitler had completed construction of her sister ship, the *Tirpitz,* and sailed her to safe harbor in Kaafjord, Norway.

The Germans planned to use the 45,500-ton *Tirpitz* in conjunction with the battle cruisers *Scharnhorst* and *Gneisenau,* the cruiser *Prinz Eugen,* and the pocket battleships *Scheer* and *Lutzow* to attack and destroy the British merchant fleet in the North Sea. The *Tirpitz* became the focus of the Royal Navy's attention and the primary reason for the raid on Saint-Nazaire. In 1942 Winston Churchill wrote: "The whole strategy of the war turns at this period to this ship, which is holding four times the number of British capital ships paralysed, to say nothing of the two new American battleships retained in the Atlantic. I regard the matter as of the highest urgency and importance."[3]

From the safety of the fjords, the *Tirpitz* could strike at will against both British and Russian merchant convoys as well as stifle an Allied landing in Norway. The admiralty made every effort to lure the *Tirpitz* from her lair in attempts to destroy the giant battleship. As these efforts failed, concern grew stronger that the *Tirpitz* might break out into the Atlantic through the Strait of Dover or around Scotland. Once in the Atlantic the *Tirpitz,* with the support of the German navy and the dominance of Hitler's U-boats, could wreak havoc on the British fleet. The long-term success of this endeavor, however, rested in the capability of the *Tirpitz* to receive proper maintenance and repair. Already the battleship was suffering from defects in her "gun mountings and fire control systems, boilers and main turbines, and various electrical installation," all requiring maintenance if she were to remain battleworthy.[4] The British knew there was only one port in the Atlantic that could provide the necessary services, the French port of Saint-Nazaire.

SAINT-NAZAIRE, FRANCE

Saint-Nazaire was a French port city of fifty thousand situated on the banks of the Loire River six miles inland from the Atlantic. At the north end of the port was the Penhouet Basin. The basin, which could hold ships of up to ten thousand tons, could be reached through either the Normandie dry dock or the Saint-Nazaire Basin.

The Normandie dry dock, or as the French called it the Forme Louis Joubert, was over eleven hundred feet in length and was originally built to house the liner *Normandie*. It was the primary target for the raid force. The two caissons (situated on the north and south ends) that sealed the dry dock were each 167 feet long, 54 feet high, and 35 feet thick. Destroying these caissons would flood the dry dock from the Loire River and render it unusable. The Saint-Nazaire Basin housed nine completed submarine pens with five under construction. In 1942 the completed pens had been made bombproof.

Although the Saint-Nazaire Basin could be accessed from the east side through the Old Entrance, most of the traffic came through the newly constructed deep-water entrance, a canal 350 yards long at the south end of the basin. This main entrance connected the Saint-Nazaire Basin with the outer harbor or Avant Port. The canal contained a series of four locks that kept the basin free from the tide.

Other important features of the facility included: four underground fuel storage containers at the north end adjacent to the Normandie dry dock; the Old Mole pier, which rose twenty-five feet above the water and was situated south of the Old Entrance; and the Old Town area, a small commercial and residential section adjoining the Old Mole pier. This vast array of maintenance and support facilities meant that "only Brest and Lorient rivaled the importance of Saint-Nazaire as a German naval base for enemy forces engaged in the Battle of the Atlantic."[5] Consequently both the German coastal and port defenses were formidable. Four 105mm howitzers guarded the entrance to Charpentiers Channel, the main estuary leading from the Atlantic to Saint-Nazaire. Once in the channel, vessels could be engaged by twenty-eight different 170mm or 70mm coastal batteries. In addition, the 280th Naval Artillery Battalion, which commanded the guns, also had a rail-mounted 240mm gun. The final approach was ringed with ten 20mm guns, four 37mm guns, and six large search-lights that ensured incoming ships were well illuminated to deter-mine their identity.

Defenses inside the harbor were equally formidable. They in-cluded one 20mm gun with an accompanying 40mm gun at the south end of the Avant Port. As a vessel proceeded up the river, it could be engaged by two 37mm guns, one at the north end of the Avant Port and the other at the base of the Old Mole. The Old Mole also had a 20mm gun positioned midway down its length and a search-light at the far east end.

The Normandie dry dock was surrounded by four 20mm guns and two 37mm guns. Additionally, the Germans had placed an anti-torpedo net at the entrance to the dock. All of these port defenses were complemented by four harbor defense boats and over twenty mobile guns mounted on trucks and manned by three battalions of the Naval Flak Brigade.

THE COMMANDOS

In June of 1940 there were no personnel in the British army trained or equipped for raiding operations. All available troops were being used for the defense of the British Isles. When the idea of amphibious guer-rilla warfare was proposed to Churchill, he quickly embraced the concept and ordered the formation of the commandos. The term *commando* was derived from the Afrikaans word meaning military unit. During the British war with the South Africans, Lord Kitchener, after dispersing the main Afrikaner army, found himself fighting individual units that used guerrilla tactics to inflict severe damage on the British army. The Boers called these units commandos.

The prospective British commandos were selected from the spe-cial service battalions. All trainees went through a twelve-week basic selection course. This training included cliff assaults, close-quarter combat with rifles, knives, and garrotes, assault courses, survival training, river crossings, and live-fire exercises. Strong emphasis was placed both on perfecting amphibious raiding skills and on having the confidence and initiative to use those skills when confronted with a difficult situation. *Combined Operations: The Official Story of the Commandos* says:

To get in and out of a small boat in all kinds of weather, to swim—if necessary in full equipment with firearms held above the water, to be familiar with all the portable weapons of the soldier from the rifle and the tommy gun to the three-inch mortar and the anti-tank rifle, to be able to carry and use explosives, to hunt tanks, and their crew—here are some of the things a Commando soldier must learn . . . he must master his mind as well as his body and become not only a specially trained soldier but a trained individual soldier. In other words, self-reliance and self-confidence . . . It is not for them to await orders from their officer or N.C.O. They must do the sensible, obvious thing just because it is the sensible, obvious thing.[6]

The commando training conducted at Achnacarry, Scotland, rivaled present-day selection courses in combat skills training and exceeded today's regimen in discipline and realism. During the war, over forty trainees were killed, most in live-fire exercises. After graduation the commandos received the coveted green beret and were assigned to commando units. At these units the training continued. Weekly marches exceeding fifty miles were routine. "One troop marched in fighting order 63 miles in 23 hours and 10 minutes covering the first 33 miles in eight hours dead."[7]

Teamwork was constantly emphasized. During basic training, groups of eight men were required to carry an eight-inch log around on their shoulders and exercises like "Me and My Pal" were conducted to emphasize the need for pairs of men to overcome obstacles together. Because the primary focus of the commandos was amphibious guerrilla warfare, much of their time was spent learning to insert from the water and fight at night. These skills were to prove particularly useful to the men of No. 2 Commando who later comprised the majority of the men participating in the raid on Saint-Nazaire.

Number 2 Commando was established in March 1941 from components of No. 3 Independent Company. Some of the soldiers already had limited combat experience in Norway, including the commanding officer, Lt. Col. A. C. Newman. The outfit was absorbed into the Special Service Battalion for a short time but then reconstituted when the size of raiding parties was reduced. Newman chose his men based on brains and common sense; there were schoolmasters, business executives, bank clerks, and salesmen. His emphasis lay clearly on intelligence and not on muscle. This should not be taken to mean that these men were physically unfit. On the contrary, Newman ensured his men were at peak physical efficiency. They conducted record-breaking marches, spent most of their time in the field, and continually improved on the infantry skills they had learned at Achnacarry. Newman also ensured they spent ample time at sea, much to the chagrin of Lord Mountbatten, who initially had difficulty accepting the idea of soldier-sailors.

From the time it was reconstituted until the beginning of the Saint-Nazaire raid, No. 2 Commando relocated several times. The personnel started in Devonshire where they conducted long marches in the country and then spent time with the 5th Destroyer Flotilla getting their sea legs. In the summer of 1941, No. 2 Commando returned to Ayr, Scotland, for cliff assault training and small-boat handling. Early in 1942 Newman took the unit to the Outer Hebrides to practice amphibious guerrilla warfare in a cold, wet environment. Throughout these training sessions Newman continued to stress the fundamentals of good soldiering: "affection for [one's] unit, fighting spirit, discipline, bearing and integrity."[8]

Number 2 Commando would eventually comprise the bulk of the assault force for the raid on Saint-Nazaire. There were also, however, personnel from Nos. 1, 3, 4, 5, 9, and 12 Commandos on the demolition teams. In all, 44 officers and 224 enlisted soldiers participated. Their amphibious counterparts in the raid were men from the Royal Navy. The navy would crew eighteen craft and supply 62 officers and 291 enlisted.* These eighteen craft were instrumental to the success of the operation. Their combat specifications are as follows:

- HMS *Campbeltown,* formerly the U.S. destroyer USS *Buchanan,* was modified to resemble a German *Mowe*-class destroyer. Her four funnels were reduced to two raked-back stacks. The *Campbeltown* was armor plated around the bridge

*These figures do not include the personnel from the destroyer escorts HMS *Atherstone, Tynedale, Cleveland,* and *Brocklesby,* nor those from the submarine *Sturgeon,* none of whom were directly involved in the raid.

and amidships to protect the commandos (1/4-inch plate designed to withstand 20mm rounds). Her draft was reduced from fourteen to twelve feet in order to negotiate the shallow waters around the entrance to Saint-Nazaire. The 4-inch guns, torpedo tubes, depth charges, and depth charge throwers were all removed. This left only a twelve-pounder light automatic high-angle gun forward, a single .50-caliber on each bridge wing, four 20mm Oerlikons positioned amidships, and two more 20mm guns mounted in echelon on the aft deck. Lastly, twenty-four Mark VII depth charges, weighing four and one-quarter tons altogether, were enclosed into steel tanks, placed over the forward fuel compartments, and encased in cement. The twenty-four depth charges were linked together with cordtex, a waterproof detonation cord, and primed with an eight-hour delay fuse. With all the modifications, the maximum speed available was approximately twenty knots. The embarked personnel included seventy-five Royal Navy and eighty commandos.

- Motor Gunboat 314 was 110 feet long with three 850-horsepower supercharged engines capable of twenty-six knots. Armament included a 3-pound Vickers forward (120 rounds per minute), a Rolls Royce 2-pound gun aft, and two twin 1/2-inch machine guns amidships. The crew consisted of twenty-six men plus Lieutenant Colonel Newman, the commander of No. 2 Commando, and Comdr. R. E. D. Ryder, commander of the naval surface forces.
- Motor Torpedo Boat (MTB) 74 was sixty-eight feet long with three Isotta-Fraschini engines capable of forty-three knots fully loaded. This particular hull, however, had frequent engine problems and alternated between seven knots and forty knots. Armament included two 21-inch torpedo tubes and two 20mm Oerlikon cannon. The torpedo tubes were remounted forward and special time-delay torpedoes with 1800-pound warheads were incorporated. The crew consisted of ten men.
- Four torpedo motor launches (TML), including hull numbers 270, 160, 156, and 177. They were 112 feet long with two 650-horsepower gas engines capable of speeds up to eighteen

knots. Two five-hundred-gallon fuel tanks were added to
increase the range from six hundred to one thousand miles.
Armament included two 18-inch torpedo tubes and two
20mm Oerlikon guns. Each TML was crewed by two or
three officers and ten enlisted.
• Twelve motor launches (ML), including hull numbers 192,
262, 267, 268, 298, 306, 307, 341, 443, 446, 447, and 457.
Each ML carried a crew of ten and fifteen commandos. They
had the same characteristics as the TMLs without the 18-
inch tubes.

LT. COL. A. C. NEWMAN AND COMDR. R. E. D. RYDER

The man with the most effect on the outcome of the raid was Lt.
Col. A. C. Newman, commanding officer of No. 2 Commando. Newman was an officer who had spent the sixteen years before the war
serving in the Territorial Army, 4th Battalion of the Essex Regiment. In civilian life he was a building contractor and at the age of
thirty-eight was married with several children.

When the war broke out Newman was called to active duty and
assigned as the commanding officer of No. 2 Commando, which
was one of twelve commando units forming the Special Service
Brigade. An avid boxer and rugby player, he earned the troops' respect through hard work, discipline, and a desire to make them the
best commandos in the brigade. Eric de la Torre, the secretary of
the Saint-Nazaire Society and a former member of No. 3 Commando, remembered that Newman "had a warm outgoing personality, and everybody liked him."[9] He could, however, be very stubborn and direct when it came to getting the task accomplished.
During Newman's first meeting with Lord Mountbatten, Newman
requested that his men be allowed to spend time at sea with the
destroyer squadron to gain experience. Mountbatten dismissed the
idea, encouraging Newman to leave the sailing to sailors. Newman
refused to back down. He protested to Mountbatten that sailing
would be a large part of any amphibious operation and that it was
necessary to get his commandos familiar with life at sea. Mountbatten continued to resist the idea, "suggesting rather unkindly that
perhaps Newman wanted to train his men to be seasick like gentle-

men." Newman fired back without hesitation, "The aim is to train them not to be seasick at all."[10] Newman's persistence paid off, and Mountbatten agreed to support his request.

Although Newman had seen some limited action in Norway, it could not have prepared him for the bloody engagement at Saint-Nazaire. Nonetheless, throughout the chaotic struggle for survival that characterized the raid, Newman remained poised and optimistic and frequently interjected his dry sense of humor to calm the troops. At one point, when the chance of escape from Saint-Nazaire was virtually hopeless, Newman ordered the remaining seventy men to break up and attempt to make their way to Spain. They would have to evade the Germans in town and push through to the open countryside. Unshaken by their dilemma Newman looked up and pronounced, "It's a lovely moonlight night for it."[11] Newman was captured hours after this incident and imprisoned for three years in a German POW camp. For his actions at Saint-Nazaire he received the Victoria Cross.

Commander R. E. D. Ryder was placed in command of the naval forces assigned to support the commandos in their raid on Saint-Nazaire. At thirty-four years old, Ryder was an exceptionally experienced sailor. He had served with the Royal Submarine Force during his early years in the navy, taking leave once to sail a ketch from China to England. After the outbreak of war he received command of a navy Q-ship. The Q-ships plied the waters of the Mediterranean disguised as merchant vessels. Their mission was to attract German U-boats. As the U-boat approached, the Q-ships would drop their exterior screens and open fire with a battery of guns. Although the program as a whole was successful, Commander Ryder's Q-ship was sunk by two U-boats on its first outing. Ryder survived at sea for four days, clinging to a piece of wood before he was rescued.

Ryder was later given command of two more vessels, a frigate and the transport ship *Prince Philippe*. Unfortunately for Ryder, the *Prince Philippe* was rammed and sunk off Scotland. After losing his second ship, Ryder understandably fell out of favor with the admiralty. He was subsequently assigned as the Southern Command naval adviser for anti-invasion plans.

When the need arose for an officer to command the naval raid forces, Ryder was the obvious choice. His experience, coupled with his availability, was perfectly suited for the mission. Ryder was the consummate professional. De la Torre described him as "an old style Naval Captain who leads a sort of lonely life. Doesn't really mix with people. Completely different character to Colonel Newman. Ryder was very reserved, a very shy man. He was never at ease with the ordinary chap. But he was the sort of officer you would follow anywhere. You could trust him. He was a chap who would never let you down."[12] For his actions at Saint-Nazaire, Ryder also received the Victoria Cross.

Louis Lord Mountbatten, although not involved in the raid, was the commander of Combined Operations Command and therefore had some direct impact on the planning decisions that were made. Mountbatten was one of the best-liked and most respected men in England. "His father was a Hessian prince and his mother a granddaughter of Queen Victoria, making him kin to half the crowned heads of Europe."[13] Yet for all his royalty, Mountbatten had the common touch. He started his naval career as a cadet and worked his way up through the officer ranks. During the war he commanded a destroyer squadron and eventually was assigned to head Combined Operations.

The commandos liked Mountbatten's style. He personally would inspect the troops before each major operation, giving them a pep talk and ensuring they had all the resources they required.* When shortfalls in equipment or assets came to his attention, Mountbatten would use his influence with Churchill or his cousin, the king, to resolve them quickly. This was done often at the expense of other naval commanders, and although it displeased his peers greatly it endeared him to the commandos.

Mountbatten's most significant impact on the raid was his determination to see it succeed at any cost. He felt that by denying Saint-Nazaire's repair facilities to the *Tirpitz*, the commandos could alter the course of the naval war in the Atlantic. Mountbatten refused to acknowledge any possibility of defeat. He was intimately involved in the planning phase of the raid and frequently overruled tactical objections by both Ryder and Newman. In two incidents he

---

*Although Mountbatten was well known for his premission pep talks, interviews with several of the Saint-Nazaire raiders indicate that contrary to legend Mountbatten never inspected the troops prior to the raid.

called in experts to rebut both men and substantiate his position. In retrospect Mountbatten's decisions were both correct.

It was apparent from the beginning that this operation was exceptionally risky and that the odds for success were slim. During the planning a senior naval officer had warned Mountbatten, "'We may lose every man.' With a slight grimace, Mountbatten had agreed, but he added, 'If they do the job, we've got to accept that.'"[14]

TRAINING

It was exactly one month from the time Ryder and Newman received their first briefing on Saint-Nazaire to the commencement of the operation. During this time several changes occurred in the plan, but the basic scheme remained the same. On 26 March 1942, No. 2 Commando and certain elements from other commando groups would sail via a surreptitious route from Falmouth, England, to the entrance of Charpentiers Channel on the French coast, arriving at 2300 on 27 March.

Twenty vessels, including the HMS *Campbeltown* and the escorts *Atherstone* and *Tynedale,* would rendezvous with the submarine HMS *Sturgeon.* Using the submarine as a landmark, they would take their final bearing to Saint-Nazaire. The escorts would return to England, leaving the small boats and the *Campbeltown* to negotiate the heavily defended estuary into the port. At 2200 on the twenty-seventh, the Royal Air Force would conduct an air raid on Saint-Nazaire. The air raid was intended to divert attention and to draw the dual-purpose guns away from the approaching vessels.

Once in the inner harbor, the *Campbeltown,* loaded with four and one-quarter tons of explosives (with an eight-hour time fuse), would ram the southern caisson of the Normandie dry dock. On board were eighty commandos who would disembark across the caisson and destroy other vital targets with explosives. These targets included the winding house, pumping house, north caisson, and German gun positions.

The eighty commandos would be divided into demolition, protection, assault, and headquarters elements. Each demolition man had to carry ninety-five pounds of explosives, so it was necessary to assign certain troops the sole role of party protection.

At the same time the *Campbeltown* rammed the dry dock, some of the 180 commandos embarked on eleven motor launches would land at the Old Mole pier while the rest landed at the Old Entrance. From the Old Entrance the commandos were assigned to destroy the Penhouet Basin swing bridge, the Old Entrance lock gates, and key German gun positions. The commandos disembarking at the Old Mole were to destroy the main entrance lock gates, the power station, and German gun positions.

Upon completion of their missions, but no more than two hours later, all commandos would return to the Old Mole, reembark on the launches, and return to England. After all commandos were retrieved, MTB 74, under the command of Sublieutenant Mickey Wynn, would fire her time-delayed torpedoes at the Old Entrance and retract. Ryder later reported in the after-action report, "We all hoped to get well in undetected and then hoped to bluff the enemy for just sufficient time to achieve our object. We had to realize, however, that though we might get in unseen and by bluff, there was no question of employing these on the way out. For this purpose we hoped that smoke would help."[15] Upon hearing the plan, one officer at Combined Operations Headquarters remarked, "Anyone who even thinks of doing such a thing deserves the Distinguished Service Order."[16]

The man in charge of the demolition teams was a reserve officer, Capt. William Pritchard. Pritchard had been instrumental in developing the plan for destroying Saint-Nazaire. While on leave in 1941, he visited his father who was the dockmaster at Cardiff, England. Lieutenant Colonel Robert Montgomery, the second officer in charge of the demolition teams, recalled what Pritchard said upon his return. "While he was there the Germans bombed the dock. He came back [off leave] and said, 'You cannot put the dock out of operation by bombing it. The warehouses were burned, Cardiff was plastered, it looked absolutely awful, but within forty-eight hours the dock was operating as a dock again. The only way to demolish a dock is to place the charges in the vital spots.'"[17]

So Pritchard and Montgomery put together a plan for destroying docks. This was under the assumption that the Germans might invade, and the British would be forced to destroy their own facilities. The plan was forwarded to the Transportation Department of the War Office and subsequently shelved. When the Saint-Nazaire mission was being considered, someone in the War Office remembered Pritchard's plan, and he and Montgomery were subsequently summoned to train and lead the demolition parties.

In civilian life Pritchard was a dockyard engineer, but his active-duty time was spent as a Royal Engineer with the Territorial Army. During the Dunkirk evacuation Pritchard, assigned to the British Expeditionary Force, won the Military Cross for thwarting a German advance by blowing up a bridge while under heavy enemy fire.

Pritchard gathered ninety men from No. 2 Commando and other units under the guise of a training course in explosives. He taught them all about demolitions and showed them how a dock functions and how it could be rendered useless. At the end of February, the demolition teams separated, and some went with Pritchard to the docks at Cardiff, while the others went with Montgomery to Southampton. These ports closely resembled the Saint-Nazaire facility, with the King George V Dock at Southampton being very similar to the Normandie dry dock. Pritchard and Montgomery conducted countless drills at Southampton and Cardiff. They ensured that each team, while loaded with a full complement of explosives, could move to their assigned targets day or night and destroy them in minimal time.

In another part of England, the assault and protection parties from No. 2 Commando were being assembled. Newman insisted each man be in the peak of physical condition. Consequently the troops conducted daily marches and physical training. "Every one of them knew that when the time came to put their training into operation sheer physical fitness could make all the difference between survival and failure."[18] Newman also continued to insist his troops put to sea to get accustomed to life on a motor launch. On one cruise to the Scilly Isles, all the men aboard got severely seasick. Newman even went so far as to send his troops to a local slaughterhouse and a hospital emergency room to prepare them for the sight of blood.

Up until then the specifics of the mission had been kept secret from the troops, but on 18 March, Newman laid out the plan in detail and the training continued at an accelerated pace.

As David Mason worte in *The Raid on St. Nazaire,* "Every stage of the operation was separated out and analyzed, every movement plotted in fine detail. However daring the nature of the raid, however debonair and carefree the soldiers and sailors who went on it, the only hope of success lay, ultimately, in the detailed thoroughness with which it was planned."[19]

A scale model of Saint-Nazaire was constructed from overhead photos, and the details of the facility were ingrained into each man's head. Special recognition signals were assigned, and the commandos were issued rubber-soled shoes to reduce noise and make the German footfalls more recognizable. Assault and protection parties developed special load-bearing equipment to maximize the amount of ammunition they could carry. It appeared that the only detail the commandos could not plan for was the will of the enemy.

Two weeks before the mission, overhead photos revealed four new coastal defense guns in the middle of the dock. The decision was made to add an additional thirty commandos to the force.

With time getting short a full-dress rehearsal was planned at the Devonport dockyard under the guise of an exercise to test the dockyard defenses. The Devonport security forces were augmented by the local Home Guard and practically everything went wrong. Later LCpl. Eric de la Torre recalled, "After doing the dress rehearsal it didn't seem like we would come out alive."[20]

During the rehearsal, the motor launches had difficulty in coming alongside a jetty and landing commandos in the glare of the searchlight. Although the record shows this was of great concern, no measures were taken to alleviate the problem. The failure to address this problem was to have disastrous effects on the success of the mission and the men who attempted it.

THE RAID ON SAINT-NAZAIRE

On 26 March 1942, "in accordance with the Operational Orders for 'Chariot,' the 10th A/S Striking Force sailed from Falmouth at 1400/26. M.L.s were sailed in advance so as to form up outside."[21] It was the first time the entire force had been assembled. The weather was good for the launch with a slight swell rolling over the port quarter.

"The cruising order was in three columns: the port and starboard columns consisted of the motor launches, and the midships column

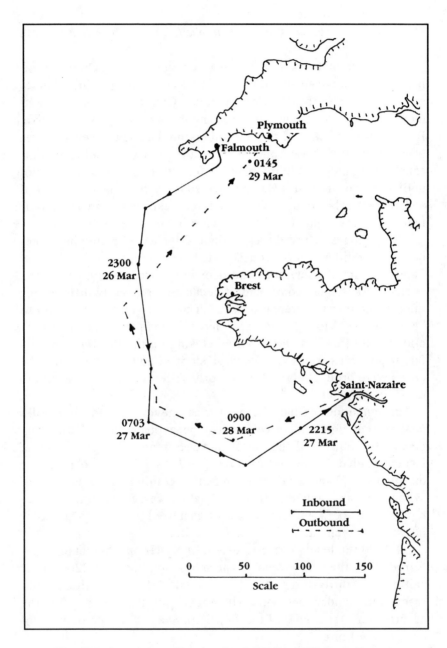

**Fig. 4–1. Operation Chariot Outbound and Return Routes,
27–28 March 1942**

of the two *Hunt*-class destroyers, *Campbeltown,* and the motor torpedo boat in tow."[22]

The transit on the twenty-sixth was without incident. On the morning of the twenty-seventh, the weather was clear with visibility unrestricted. At 0720, the *Tynedale* spotted a German submarine at four thousand yards and opened fire, causing the submarine to crash-dive. Initially it was believed that the submarine had sunk. Nevertheless, Commander Ryder was concerned that the submarine had communicated its sighting to the mainland before it disappeared. It was not until after the war that it was discovered the submarine had survived and in fact relayed by radio that three destroyers and ten motor launches were sighted at 0720 moving in an easterly direction.

The Germans believed these British ships were conducting minelaying operations and never associated them with a possible raid on Saint-Nazaire. Ryder made the decision to continue on with the mission. As the day continued, it became increasingly difficult for the flotilla to evade French trawlers. These trawlers were known to be manned by Vichy French or to have German soldiers aboard. At midday two trawlers were spotted closing on the flotilla from different positions. Both vessels were stopped and searched, and the crews were brought aboard the escorts. After a brief discussion the trawlers were sunk.

The remainder of the afternoon was uneventful and the flotilla continued at eight knots to effect its rendezvous with the HMS *Sturgeon.* At 1830 one of the motor launches reported engine trouble. Ryder decided to leave a torpedo motor launch behind to assist the disabled vessel and have the main flotilla continue on as scheduled. When it became apparent that the disabled vessel was unable to be repaired, the crew and commandos transferred to the torpedo motor launch and eventually rejoined the flotilla.

At 2000 the headquarters element of Ryder and Newman transferred from the *Atherstone* to the motor gunboat. At 2200, after sailing for thirty-three hours and over 450 miles, the flotilla reached the rendezvous point. Upon receiving the final bearing, the escorts were released and the flotilla proceeded up the outer right bank of the Loire.

At midnight the flotilla could see antiaircraft guns firing at the incoming bombers. Owing to security, the Royal Air Force was never told the reason for the bombing raid. Their orders were to bomb only if the dockyard targets were visible from the air. This was to reduce civilian casualties. Unfortunately, when the airplanes arrived, low clouds prevented them from identifying their targets. Consequently, the raid was very short and the bombers returned home. The commandos knew that the lack of bomber support was going to impact their ability to get in undetected. Sergeant Dick Bradley of No. 2 Commando had planned on a continuous bombing attack throughout the commando raid. Later he commented, "We thought things had gone wrong. We didn't have the air raid we should have been getting. Anybody whose been in an air raid knows what muddle there is in the town. We reckoned that we would be there doing our demolitions and out before anyone realized what happened."[23] Instead of creating a diversion with a sustained air raid, this bombing effort only succeeded in waking the Germans and piquing their interest in other possible British attacks.

Captain Mecke, commanding officer of the Naval Flak Brigade guarding Saint-Nazaire, became increasingly suspicious of the limited air raid. At midnight he signaled all Wehrmacht command posts with the following message: "The conduct of the enemy aircraft is inexplicable and indicates suspicion of parachute landings."[24]

Meanwhile the flotilla had entered the estuary and was proceeding as scheduled. Soon after entering the outside of the channel the *Campbeltown* ran aground. After a few minutes she pulled free only to ground again moments later. Once again she broke free and was able to continue on unabated. By 0030 the entire flotilla was into deeper water and entering the outer approaches of the port. At this time Lieutenant Tibbets, the officer in charge of the ordnance aboard the *Campbeltown,* activated the eight-hour time fuse. Interestingly enough only a few people aboard the *Campbeltown* knew of the demolitions' existence.

Soon thereafter the German coastal radar picked up the inbound vessels. Captain Mecke was informed by his command post, and he subsequently ordered all units to beware landing. The time was 0120. Two minutes later the flotilla was challenged by flashing lights from a shore battery. The official British after-action report stated the following:

During this time we made our bogus identity to the shore signal station at No.3 battery and signalled in German that we
were "proceeding up harbour in accordance with instruction."
On receipt of this signal some of the searchlights switched out
but we were then called up from the South entrance and passed
a similar message. While this was in progress however the
force was fired on by light flak from one position so we made
the signal for "a vessel considering herself to be fired on by
friendly forces." This stopped him for a bit. At this time we
must have been recognized as definitely hostile as we were
suddenly fired on heavily and the action became general. It is
difficult to describe the full fury of the attack that was let
loose on both sides, the air became one mass of red and green
tracer travelling in all directions, most of it going over.[25]

Aboard the *Campbeltown,* Lt. Comdr. Sam Beattie ordered the bogus German ensign pulled down and the white British ensign hoisted
up. From the shore came fire from all the coastal defense guns including 75mm, 150mm, 170mm, 6-inch howitzers, Oerlikons, and
Bofors. Fortunately, the darkness and distance from shore precluded
accurate fire except by the close-in 20mm and 37mm guns. All the
British vessels returned fire and sailed virtually unscathed through
the blanket of rounds. Initial casualties included the *Campbeltown*
coxswain and quartermaster who were killed on the bridge.
    At this point the flotilla had reached the east jetty. Anchored off
to their starboard was the German ship *Sperrbrecker,* which commenced firing as the vessels approached. A gunner aboard the British motor gunboat raked the ship with counterfire and promptly silenced the German batteries.
    With the motor gunboat leading the way, the *Campbeltown*
headed straight for the Normandie dry dock at eighteen knots. At
the last second the motor gunboat veered away, and the *Campbeltown* struck the southern caisson of the dry dock at exactly 0134,
only four minutes later than initially planned. "The main objective
of the raid had been achieved before a single Commando soldier
had set foot ashore."[26] The force of the collision crushed the bow of
the *Campbeltown* for thirty-six feet and drove her up onto the caisson a full twelve inches into the steel gate.

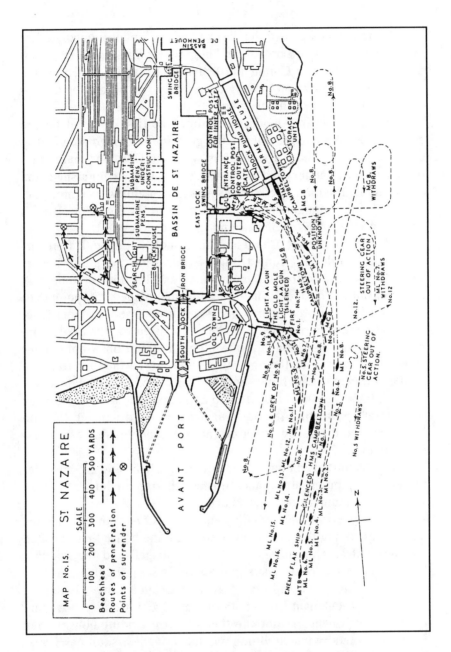

**Fig. 4–2. Action of HMS *Campbeltown* and
Motor Launches at Saint-Nazaire. From HMSO**

The commandos aboard the destroyer came under immediate fire as they struggled to disembark and begin their missions. Lieutenant Stewart Chant (No. 5 Commando) said later that 75 percent of the commandos on deck had already been hit by fire before the *Campbeltown* ever reached the dry dock.

Climbing down iron ladders and rope, the first group of twelve commandos attempted to silence the guns in the immediate vicinity of the dry dock. Their first victims were the Germans manning a light gun in a sandbagged nest. After this was extinguished, the commandos assaulted a concrete bunker containing a 37mm gun. Although four commandos were wounded in the fight, the British had established a perimeter around the insertion point.

With a perimeter set, Chant and his demolition crew of four sergeants moved down a long flight of stairs into the pump house. Their task was to destroy the pumps that raised and lowered the water level in the dry dock. Chant and his men placed 150 pounds of explosives around the pumps and set a ninety-second time fuse. They immediately returned topside and waited for the explosion. As they mustered up outside the pump house, Bob Montgomery showed up to oversee the operation and ordered the men to move further away. "It was lucky he did," Chant recalled. "For a few seconds later there was a deafening explosion and the large blocks of concrete protecting the building from air-raid damage flew up into the air and crashed down on the quayside where we had just been standing."[27]

After the initial charge had detonated, Chant and his men returned to the pump house and finished the remainder of the task with sledgehammers and incendiaries.

Lieutenant Christopher Smalley and four NCOs were assigned the task of destroying the southern caisson winding house that operated the lock gates. This mission was accomplished and the winding house was destroyed almost simultaneously with the pump house.

Two additional demolition teams commanded by Lieutenant Purdon and Lieutenant Brett, both of No. 12 Commando, moved up the west side of the dry dock to the northern winding house. They were supported by ten surviving members of the assault party who had cleared the initial entry point. As they moved the five hundred yards from the southern caisson to the northern caisson, the assault team had to clear a German position and suppress heavy fire from a nearby stronghold. In the process, Brett was wounded and was replaced by Lt. Bob Burtenshaw and some of his men.

Upon reaching the northern winding house, Purdon's men smashed in the door and set the charges. Several commandos were wounded by advancing German troops and effective fire from nearby ships moored in the Penhouet Basin. Meanwhile Burtenshaw found he was unable to enter the northern caisson through the locked steel door and elected to lower twelve 18-pound charges over the north side of the caisson. This entire time he and his men were receiving 20mm fire from the Penhouet Basin ships. After tying off the explosives to a nearby guardrail, "Burtenshaw realizing they must at least silence the ships lying inside the dry-dock, south of the caisson, took several men with him along the wall, firing their pistols down into a tanker undergoing refit. More effective was the rush by two of the protection squad firing their tommies as they ran down the ship's steep gangplank. When Germans appeared on the west dockside, Bob Burtenshaw—still humming 'There'll always be an England'—ran at them firing his pistol, despite his wounds. The Germans scattered, but the Lieutenant and a corporal were killed."[28]

Although the assault and demolition crews sustained heavy casualties, all the targets in the dry dock area had been destroyed as planned.

In the meantime Newman and his command element had come ashore at the Old Entrance. They were attempting to locate the building they had designated as their command headquarters. As they arrived at the proper location (just adjacent to the swing bridge at the Old Entrance), Newman captured two German soldiers who informed him that his designated headquarters building was in fact the Wehrmacht's headquarters building.

Newman intended to capture the Germans inside the building but came under intense fire from several ships in the Saint-Nazaire Basin. Newman was soon joined by Troop Sergeant Major Haines, who had come ashore from Lieutenant Rodier's motor launch. Equipped with a 2-inch mortar, Haines was able to quiet the guns in the basin, but almost immediately thereafter another group of German sailors engaged the commandos with machine guns. Again

Haines returned fire with a Bren gun and silenced the sailors. Newman returned to the task of securing the headquarters building and, after a few well-placed hand grenades, was in command of the facility.

At the other end of the Saint-Nazaire Harbor, the motor launches had timed their assaults to coincide with the ramming of the *Campbeltown*. Their formation sailing into the harbor had been two lines abreast just to the rear of the *Campbeltown*. The port line broke off and attempted to land commandos at the Old Mole while the starboard line continued on to the Old Entrance.

The port line motor launches were led by Lieutenant Irwin's torpedo motor launch. It carried no commandos and was assigned only to escort the other motor launches and attack targets of opportunity. Irwin continued on past the Old Mole. His boat was eventually hit by a shell, and the steering mechanism was damaged. Soon after, he retreated back to the open sea.

Immediately following Irwin was Lieutenant Platt, whose embarked commandos had the mission of attacking the gun positions on the Old Mole and seizing the area between the Old Mole and the southern entrance to the Saint-Nazaire Basin. As Platt approached the Old Mole his motor launch ran aground and came under fire from the shore. His boat was set ablaze, and he gave the order to abandon the craft. The commandos attempted to swim the three hundred yards to shore, but the weight of their clothes and equipment caused many to drown. Twelve of the commandos and four of the motor launch's crew were killed or drowned in the river. The lead motor launch in the starboard line, having seen Platt's predicament, managed to rescue the remaining survivors.

Behind Platt's motor launch came Lieutenant Collier with the two demolition teams embarked, including Captain Pritchard, the explosives expert who had trained the commandos. Collier weaved around Platt's stalled motor launch and started off-loading his commandos at the Old Mole steps. One of the navy men, Len Ball, "was firing up his gun . . . enjoying himself and exhorting [the commandos] come on you Limeys."[29] The fire was so intense that only three men managed to disembark. Collier pulled away and after several minutes attempted to land once again. Collier was unaware at this point that Platt was beached and in fact believed he had successfully off-loaded his commandos. After accomplishing his mission,

Collier returned to his loiter point in the middle of the river. The Germans continued to pepper the small boat. De la Torre, who had gotten ashore and then returned with a wounded commando, remembered that "shells were coming inside one end of the motor launch and coming out the other. There were bodies lying all around the mess deck . . . I cut loose a Carley float and jumped in after it . . . bullets were hitting all around us."[30]

Next in sequence was Lieutenant Wallis who was carrying a small demolitions team with orders to destroy the central lock gate of the main entrance. Wallis came in at eighteen knots and missed the Old Mole landing, beaching the motor launch momentarily. The Germans on the pier began tossing grenades at the boat and engaged the craft with small-arms fire. The commandos aboard attempted to suppress the fire, but eventually Wallis was forced to withdraw.

The three remaining motor launches, under the command of Lieutenants Horlock, Henderson, and Falconar, were all driven off by heavy enemy fire as they approached the Old Mole. None of their commandos were landed. The end result was that of the six motor launches, only Collier's succeeded in landing any troops.

At the Old Entrance, Lieutenant Boyd, commanding a torpedo motor launch, had broken off from the starboard column as planned to make room for the commandos to land. His orders were to provide covering fire for the troop-carrying motor launches and attack targets of opportunity. As Boyd ran between the Old Entrance and the Old Mole, he came under intense fire, which disabled his engines for ten minutes. As soon as they were repaired, Boyd proceeded to Platt's burning motor launch and recovered the remaining survivors from that craft. Boyd began to head toward midstream but stopped to pick up three more commandos from the river. In the process, his motor launch was hit again and several men aboard were killed. Boyd eventually managed to extract and headed to the open ocean under a hail of shells from coastal defenses.

Following Boyd was Lieutenant Stephens with an embarked commando assault element. Stephens's motor launch was hit and severely damaged before it reached the Old Entrance. Out of control, the motor launch crashed into the east jetty, and Stephens ordered the craft abandoned. Some of the men made it to rafts while others attempted to swim ashore. Only five of the commandos survived; four of them were captured immediately. The other commando, Captain Burn, made it ashore and with the help of a navy enlisted man reached his objective (two gun towers three-quarters of a mile away at the northern end of the submarine pens). During the excursion, Burn and the enlisted man killed two Germans and captured four others. Burn unfortunately found the gun towers empty, so he decided to set fire to the control room with incendiary grenades.

The next two motor launches, commanded by Lieutenants Burt and Beart, overshot the Old Entrance landing. By the time they swung around to try again, the Old Entrance was covered with Germans. Burt landed his troops on the north side of the Old Entrance, but several were killed instantly. Burt extracted into midstream, but effective fire from the shore killed more men on deck. Burt's motor launch was eventually destroyed as he drifted downstream. The few remaining survivors made it into rafts and were eventually captured.

At the same time, Beart was again attempting to land at the Old Entrance. As the motor launch nosed in, heavy fire from the Saint-Nazaire Basin killed Beart and several commandos. The remaining commandos fought ashore momentarily and then struggled back to the motor launch. The motor launch, however, was soon set ablaze. The commandos and crew abandoned the boat and attempted to take rafts or swim ashore. Eventually all but three of the twelve commandos were shot or drowned.

During the ten minutes that it took for Burt and Beart to reapproach the Old Entrance, three other motor launches had attempted to land. The first of the three, commanded by Lieutenant Tillie, was hit and immediately burst into flames. Fifteen of the seventeen commandos aboard and most of the crew were killed.

The second motor launch, commanded by Lieutenant Fenton, was also hit and failed to land any troops. It maneuvered to midstream and continued to fight at a distance, eventually withdrawing to the open ocean. The third motor launch was commanded by Lieutenant Rodier. He managed to successfully negotiate the heavy fire and land his commandos. One of the commandos, Sgt. Dick Bradley, remembered, "We had a perfect landing. It couldn't have been nicer. We got off, tied the thing up as cool as if nothing had happened."[31]

Rodier then returned to the *Campbeltown* to assist in the removal of her remaining crew, including the commanding officer, Lieutenant Commander Beattie. After embarking fifty men, Rodier began to move downstream. His motor launch was soon hit by fire from the 75mm coastal defense guns. Rodier was killed and the motor launch eventually destroyed. "Most of the men on board, including all the officers of the *Campbeltown* except Beattie and one other man, were killed or died in the water, and the few survivors were picked up at about 9.30am by a German patrol boat."[32]

The last boat in the starboard column was a torpedo motor launch commanded by Sublieutenant Nock. Like the other torpedo motor launches, Nock was assigned to draw fire and provide support to the motor launches. Nock had the additional mission of helping to off-load the *Campbeltown*'s crew, but he never got the chance. Nock managed to subdue some of the fire from ashore but was eventually hit and his boat lost.

In the first sixty minutes of the battle, over half the assault force, including eight launches, had been hit or destroyed. The Loire River was burning from the oil and debris of damaged boats. Everywhere German defense guns pounded away at targets in the water and ashore. Smoke from the explosions at the pump and winding house lingered over the city, and searchlights darted from point to point chasing real and imaginary commandos.

Back on shore the commandos from Collier's motor launch had succeeded in getting away from the Old Mole and were proceeding to their target. Those commandos consisted of Lieutenant Walton's demolition team, Captain Pritchard's roving demolition team, and Second Lieutenant Watson's protection team. These elements were directed to destroy the bridge over the main entrance to the Saint-Nazaire Basin.

Walton's party was hit almost immediately after departing the Old Mole. Walton was wounded, and the team separated in the action. Walton eventually died after attempting to lay his explosives at the dock gate. The explosives never detonated.

Watson's team rendezvoused with the members of Newman's headquarters element and the remains of Walton's team. Watson made several attempts to reach the main entrance bridge but was turned away by heavy fire from an armored tanker moored in the basin. Eventually a runner from headquarters ordered them to return to Newman's location.

Pritchard's roving demolition team managed to reach the bridge but elected to leave that target for Walton and destroy two ships tied up at the quay instead. Slipping over the side of the quay, the commandos placed their charges below the waterline and sneaked away. Moments later the demolitions detonated and the ships sank. Pritchard and Corporal Maclagan departed the basin in search of other targets. Pritchard later died as a result of wounds received sometime in the action.

Having completed their missions, commandos from the *Campbeltown* were beginning to assemble at the headquarters building. Newman decided that most of the objectives had been achieved and it was time to withdraw. Unfortunately, the Very pistol needed to fire the withdraw signal had gone down with Sergeant Moss, the No. 2 Commando regimental sergeant major, while he was aboard one of the motor launches. Consequently, Newman sent Lance Corporal Harrington to retrieve Captain Roy's blocking force and other elements that were positioned in the vicinity. Eventually Newman had seventy officers and men at his location. It was then that he learned that withdrawal was impossible owing to the fate of the motor launches. Chant later recalled, "Colonel Newman told us, 'This is where we walk home. All the boats have been blown up or have gone back.' "[33]

Several escape options were discussed, but Newman's final plan called for the men to split up and attempt to make their way through town and eventually to the Spanish frontier. "He ordered them not to surrender until all their ammunition had been used up, and not to surrender at all if they could help it."[34]

The commandos left the headquarters building as a group and attempted to move from the Old Town area across the bridge over the main entrance and into the city of Saint-Nazaire. They encountered heavy resistance, and several men fell wounded or dead. Upon reaching the bridge, Troop Sergeant Major Haines laid down a base of fire, and the remaining commandos dashed across, firing as they moved. Upon reaching the town of Saint-Nazaire the group split up. Roy and twenty men went into a home and waited for a while. Soon they decided to depart and met Lieutenant Hopwood and ten of his men. Together the group was eventually captured when it sought refuge in a police station.

Newman's group went from house to house, encountering Germans at every turn and eventually ending up in an air-raid shelter. Not long afterward, a German party arrived. Newman, out of ammunition and with several wounded men, surrendered. By the end of the evening, all the commandos who had departed the headquarters building were either dead or captured.

Back on the Loire River, seven launches managed to make it out of the harbor. Lieutenant Henderson, who had been forced to withdraw from the Old Mole, was the first to reach the open ocean. His boat was separated from the remaining six. At approximately 0545 Henderson's motor launch came under attack from a German destroyer, the *Jaguar*. The British fired every available weapon, inflicting serious casualties on the Germans. Refusing to surrender, the British fought until only a few survivors remained. Eventually however the motor launch was overpowered by the heavily armed destroyer and forced to surrender. The after-action report read, "Surrendered after unequal fight and many casualties including C.O. killed."[35] The remaining men were brought aboard the German destroyer and given prompt medical attention. Those who survived were later transferred to a POW camp.

Three other motor launches (Irwin, Fenton, Falconar) and Ryder's motor gunboat managed to escape from the river and rendezvoused with the *Atherstone* and *Tynedale*. The dead and wounded were transferred, and Irwin's, Falconar's, and Ryder's boats were scuttled. At 0730, a German Heinkel 111 appeared and sank Fenton's abandoned motor launch but elected not to attack the escorts.

Ten minutes later a Royal Air Force fighter arrived to provide air cover and was met by a German Junker 88. The air-to-air combat ended in a midair collision, killing both pilots. Later the Royal Air Force sent additional air support to cover the return trip, and the navy added two additional destroyers, the *Cleveland* and the *Brocklesby,* to the convoy.

The remaining three motor launches, commanded by Horlock, Wallis, and Boyd, also escaped the coastal defense guns but failed to rendezvous with the *Atherstone* and *Tynedale*. The three boats were attacked several times from the air but managed to return unharmed to Falmouth.

At approximately 1030 on Saturday, 28 March, the four and a quarter tons of explosives aboard the *Campbeltown* detonated, destroying the southern caisson and rendering the dry dock unusable. Aboard the *Campbeltown* at the time of the explosion were dozens of German officers and enlisted who were apparently looting the vessel of all its liquor and candy bars. Montgomery later recalled the incident: "There is a lovely little story of Sam Beattie [commanding officer of the *Campbeltown*] being interrogated and the German chap saying, 'Surely you didn't think that a silly little boat like that ramming the caisson would smash it up?' and then the detonation went 'whoom' and all the windows blew out, and Sam said, 'No we didn't.' "[36]

Reports indicated that as many as two hundred people were killed when the charges ignited. "The remains of torsos, detached limbs, bits of flesh, and daubs of blood hideously adorned the dock for several days, sticking to walls, resting on rooftops, and staining the ground."[37]

The Germans were thrown into a state of panic and began firing at imaginary commandos. By afternoon some order was being restored, when, at 1600, the first time-delayed torpedo fired from Wynn's torpedo motor launch exploded at the Old Entrance. This was followed one hour later by a second explosion from the number two torpedo. Again panic ensued, and by the following morning another forty-two French civilians and Germans had been killed by friendly fire.

The casualties on the British side included 169 dead and 200 captured out of the 611 who participated. The primary goal of destroying the Normandie dry dock was achieved. The British often refer to Saint-Nazaire as the "greatest raid of all," but in retrospect, how successful was this mission? What could have been done to improve the survivability of the men and the effectiveness of the raid?

ANALYSIS

Critique

In wartime the success of an operation is judged almost solely on the achievement of the objectives. The cost in lives, although regrettable, lies within the realm of the necessary. In the case of Saint-Nazaire, the destruction of the dry dock was the primary objective and from a strategic and operational perspective the objective was achieved. Eric de la Torre commented after seeing the plan, "I thought it was a very good plan, but I thought all of us would be killed. When you saw where all the [German] guns were, you thought, well, we're not going to come out alive."[38] In the end 169 British soldiers and sailors were killed and 200 captured.

Were the objectives worth the risk? No! The *Tirpitz* clearly was a formidable threat and warranted every effort to sink her. Denying the battleship access to maintenance facilities in the Atlantic, however, would not and did not preclude her from operating in the North Sea against Allied convoys bound for Russia, and this was her primary mission. Hitler was obsessed with cutting the vital Anglo-Russian convoy link that supplied Russian forces at Murmansk. By January 1942 (three months before Saint-Nazaire), all available German ships, including the *Tirpitz,* were stationed in Norway for this express purpose. Not only did the Norwegian fjords provide excellent protection for the *Tirpitz,* but the port city of Foettenfjord near Trondheim was able to conduct a complete refit of the battleship beginning in October 1942.* This obviated the need for the *Tirpitz* to seek repairs elsewhere. Additionally, the Royal Air Force kept constant aerial surveillance on the *Tirpitz* and actually hoped the ship would sail south so it could be attacked by bombers—the fate to which it eventually succumbed.

Was the plan developed to maximize superiority over the enemy and minimize the risk to the assault force? Even if we accept the rationale for the raid, the merit of the plan warrants questioning. Early in the establishment of the Combined Operations Command, the idea of conducting a raid on Saint-Nazaire was dismissed owing to the shallow waters of the Loire, the heavy coastal and port defenses, and the anticipated size of the assault force. (The initial size of the force was 300 men. Operation Chariot eventually required 611 soldiers and sailors.) Even after the initial plan was formulated there was disagreement about the tactics to destroy the dry dock.

*Although Trondheim was not comparable to Saint-Nazaire as a maintenance facility, all the necessary repair work was completed in a matter of months by staggering the tasks so that the battleship was never completely immobilized.

Interestingly enough, the most successful aspect of the mission, the *Campbeltown* operation, was not considered the best approach. Commander Ryder, in a memorandum entitled "Considerations of the Advantages and Disadvantages of Using or Not Using an Expendable Destroyer," stated, "I think the destroyer would certainly hazard the element of surprise and would be plastered by all the coastal batteries at ranges of one to two miles and generally speaking block ships [ships used to block the exit of a harbor] have always failed really to get into the correct position . . . As a means of destroying the lock gate, I prefer the idea of firing 8 torpedoes at it to the idea of trying to blow it up from the bows of a destroyer."[39]

In retrospect, Ryder may have been correct. The *Campbeltown* mission, although successful, may in fact have jeopardized the element of surprise for the rest of the flotilla. The real question is, was it necessary to have eighteen assault craft and 257 commandos to do the mission?

After I spent several hours on the ground at Saint-Nazaire, it was clear to me that the decision to attack several targets instead of just the dry dock was fatally flawed. Once that decision was made, however, the tactical plan to implement that decision was fundamentally sound. Had the commandos gotten ashore as planned at the Old Mole and the Old Entrance the outcome could have been different. The air raid was scheduled to continue throughout the commando assault. This would have created chaos within the city, allowing the British to slip in undisturbed, as they almost did anyway. Once ashore the commandos were relying on massing combat power quickly and using the assault teams to subdue the Germans until the objectives were destroyed. There would have been casualties; however, the plan clearly made every effort to minimize losses.

Was the mission executed according to the plan, and if not, what unforeseen circumstances dictated the outcome? Once the mission was launched, it adhered very closely to the original plan until the enemy situation forced the support craft to withdraw and the commandos ashore to scatter. The Germans from the new town area quickly reinforced those Flak Brigade personnel in the dry dock area. The British lost fire superiority when they were forced to slow down the assault. Additionally, because the British were divided into assault, protection, and demolition teams, some of the commandos ashore were only lightly armed and didn't stand a chance against the better-armed German troops. One other aspect of the German defenses that received only scant consideration in the planning was the armed sailors aboard the vessels in port. When the firefight began many of these sailors took up guns, killed several of the commandos, and disrupted the commandos' ability to move to their assigned objectives. These actions by the Germans disrupted the entire flow of the assault and subsequently undermined the success of the operation.

What modifications could have improved the outcome? Either of two approaches might have improved the outcome. The *Campbeltown* could have rammed the dry dock, off-loaded her commandos, and picked them up within twenty minutes by high-speed boat. This would have accomplished the primary mission and reduced the loss of life. Or, as Ryder suggested, the commandos could have used a motor torpedo boat to attack the dry dock. Unfortunately, this second option would only have damaged the dry dock temporarily. In order to render the dry dock completely inoperable, the commandos had to get ashore and enter the pump house and winding house. Still, the ashore missions could have been accomplished with a minimum of personnel.

The mission of the Combined Operations Command was to "be offensive." In that respect Saint-Nazaire was an attempt to take the fight to the enemy. Irrespective of the reasons, an assault force was assembled, and a plan was formulated to destroy the dockyard area. Let's now examine where relative superiority was achieved and how the principles of special operations were used to improve the probability of mission completion.

Relative Superiority

Special operations forces, because of their limited sustainability and requirement for either quick egress or rapid reinforcement from conventional forces, must achieve relative superiority quickly. By increasing the number of primary objectives, the British essentially were attempting multiple engagements in a single area of operation and therefore were required to achieve relative superiority several times in order for the overall operation to succeed. Relative superiority, instead of occurring at a point in time, had to occur at several points in time and therefore the speed of execution was decreased and the opportunity for failure was dramatically increased.

The British did gain relative superiority when the *Campbeltown* struck the dry dock and, owing to the concealed nature of the four and one-quarter tons of demolition, were able to sustain that relative superiority until the ordnance exploded the next morning.

Figure 4-3 shows that the point of vulnerability occurred when the *Campbeltown* and the rest of the flotilla entered the mouth of the Loire River. It was here, along the coastline, that the Germans had positioned their batteries to engage enemy ships. Although the crossing of the Atlantic was not without risk, the flotilla had the destroyers *Atherstone* and *Tynedale* for protection. It was not until the flotilla left the safety of the destroyer escorts that the success of the mission hinged on avoiding the German defenses. From mid-

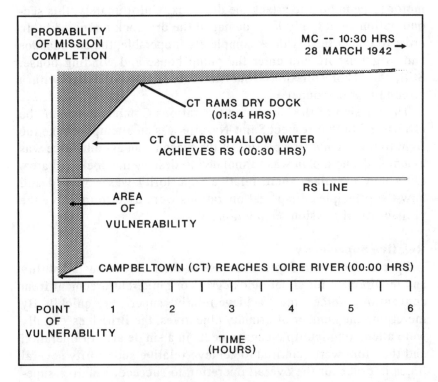

**Fig. 4–3. Relative Superiority Graph for the Raid on
Saint-Nazaire (HMS *Campbeltown*)**

night on 27 March until thirty minutes after, the *Campbeltown* was in an area of vulnerability. The ship had to cross the shallow waters to avoid the coastal batteries. If she had run aground the mission would have failed. Fortunately, the hull modifications reduced her draft and the shoal waters caused only momentary delays. At 0030 hours the entire flotilla entered deep water. It was at this point that the *Campbeltown* achieved relative superiority. With the *Campbeltown*'s improved speed, modified hull, armor plating, and hold full of demolition, the British had gained a decisive advantage over the Germans protecting the dry dock. The frictions of war now affected the Germans more than the British. The Flak Brigade would have to react quickly to prevent the *Campbeltown* from completing her mission. Fortunately for the British, and as planned, the close-in harbor defenses were inadequate to stop the armor-plated "war wagon." At 0134 the *Campbeltown* struck the dry dock. That morning at 1030 the mission was completed when the *Campbeltown* exploded, destroying the Normandie dry dock. The total area of vulnerability for the *Campbeltown* portion of the raid did not exceed 5 percent of the mission. It is interesting to compare this aspect of the raid with the failed attempt to land the commandos at the Old Mole and Old Entrance.

Figure 4-4 graphically illustrates the motor launches' attempts to land the commandos. From the point of vulnerability there is a sharp rise in the probability of mission completion. The motor launches were able to use surprise and speed to negotiate the shoal waters and enter the harbor undetected. Unfortunately, once they were engaged by the Germans, the thin-hulled motor launches were ill equipped to withstand the 20mm rounds. Their inability to quickly land the commandos caused the area of vulnerability to expand and eventually made it impossible to gain relative superiority. After two hours, most of the motor launches either were destroyed or had retreated to open water.

Had the British achieved relative superiority at each necessary point throughout the engagement, they probably could have sustained that superiority long enough to place their demolitions and destroy the targets. The plan, however, did not adequately address the withdrawal. Regardless of the outcome ashore, relative superiority could not have been maintained during the extraction, and casualties upon the return would have been high.

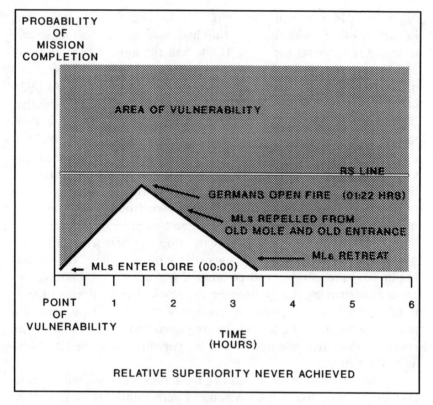

**Fig. 4–4. Relative Superiority Graph for the Raid on
Saint-Nazaire (Motor Launches)**

The Principles of Special Operations

Simplicity. On paper Operation Chariot sounded relatively simple.
The concept of operation stated,

> The troops will be divided roughly equally between the destroyer
> and the M.L.s, approximately 15 men going in each M.L. The
> whole force will proceed in company so as to approach St.-
> Nazaire after dark on a moonlight night . . . On arrival the de-
> stroyer will ram the outer gate of the big lock, and the troops on
> board will disembark over her bows, then proceeding to carry out
> their demolition tasks. The remainder of the force will disembark

from their M.L.s at selected points in the dockyard area . . . The whole force will withdraw in the M.L.s after a maximum period of 2 hours.[40]

The staff planners at Combined Operations had succeeded in clearly defining the mission objectives; they had gathered extensive intelligence on the port facility and the German defenses, and armed with this knowledge they had devised a bold and innovative means of countering most of the obstacles.

Nevertheless, the plan was not simple. Operation Chariot involved 611 men, sixteen motor launches, the destroyer *Campbeltown*, two escort destroyers (the *Tynedale* and the *Atherstone*), and the submarine *Sturgeon*. The plan called for the destruction of eleven major targets, using 257 commandos, from eight different units, most of whom had never met prior to the final weeks of training. Once ashore at Saint-Nazaire, the commandos were divided into three elements for each target, and the destruction of a target relied heavily on all three elements doing their assigned tasks, (i.e., assault, protection, and demolition). At any one point in the operation there could have been fifty separate elements (sixteen motor launches, thirty-three commando elements, and a headquarters element), all required to act independently during the engagement and then reassemble at the designated time for extraction. This "simple plan" was exposed as difficult at the dress rehearsal (in which most of the commandos did not participate). However, the mistakes identified were not corrected and the plan went basically unchanged.

What aspects of the principle of simplicity were ignored and what effect did they have on the operation? Primarily, the planners failed to limit the objectives. "In the plan as finally agreed upon, it was decided to make the destruction of the lock gates and mechanism of the forme écluse [Normandie dry dock] by H.M.S. *Campbeltown* the principal objective, while the destruction, first of the smaller South Lock gates and their installation, secondly of other key points such as pumping machinery for the Bassin, and thirdly of any accessible U-boats and shipping, were to be subsidiary objects in that order of priority."[41]

In actuality by the time the plan was completed there were eleven primary targets assigned to the commandos. These included: the two winding houses at the northern and southern caissons, the northern caisson pumping house, the fuel storage tanks to the east of the dry dock, the swing bridges at the Penhouet Basin and the Old Entrance, the lock gates at the Old Entrance, and the two bridges and two lock gates at the main entrance. These objectives did not include the assault parties' targets, which consisted of: "forty-three guns of 20 mm, 37 mm, and 40 mm calibre . . . skillfully (positioned) on the jetties at each side of the Avant port, on the Old Mole, on the southern caisson of the Normandie dock, and at the northern end of the submarine basin. Many of them were stationed on the top of concrete block houses, making it difficult to attack and even more difficult to shoot at from water level."[42]

By increasing the number of objectives from one to eleven, the assault force was required to add fifty more soldiers and over two hundred naval support personnel. More importantly, it required ten additional small craft for transportation, added training for the demolitions, assault, and protection elements, and most importantly required a modification of the tactics. This increased scope in the mission compounded the command and control problem to an unmanageable level. Had the planners reduced the objectives to the dry dock alone, the commandos would never have needed to set foot ashore. Those aboard the *Campbeltown* could have rammed the destroyer into the southern caisson and extracted by a single high-speed motor launch. Even if the requirement to destroy the pumping house and winding house remained, the training, logistics, and implementation would have been much simpler. As we will see, expanding the objective increases the potential for problems in other areas and was the overriding factor in the disaster at Saint-Nazaire.

The intelligence on Saint-Nazaire was superb. The planners had aerial photography, blueprints of the dock area, and detailed agent reports showing the exact location of all the coastal and harbor defenses.* Armed with this information, the planners developed a scheme to avoid the coastal batteries by modifying the *Campbeltown* and sailing her across the shoal waters. Once inside the inner

*Lieutenant Colonel Robert Montgomery, who helped develop the demolition plan, stated in an interview with the author that the contractors who built the British dry dock King George V were the same ones who built the

ring of defenses, the armor-plated old destroyer could withstand the 20mm harbor guns. The *Campbeltown* mission is an excellent example of how intelligence can be used to develop a plan that avoids or neutralizes the enemy's defensive advantage. As previously shown, the *Campbeltown* gained relative superiority very early in the operation, primarily because good intelligence allowed the British to plan around the Germans' natural defensive superiority, but also because the British used innovation to overcome obstacles.

Considering the massive size of the Normandie dry dock and the seemingly impenetrable nature of the caissons, the plan for destroying the target was excellent. The Combined Operations staff's ingenious use of the *Campbeltown* is an excellent example of using innovative technology to gain relative superiority.

Under normal circumstances an old destroyer with a crew of fifty men would have been unable to negotiate the outer banks of the Loire River and destroy a heavily defended target. By significantly modifying the *Campbeltown,* the British were able to reduce the draft from fourteen to eleven feet, increase speed from eighteen to twenty knots, and improve the destroyer's survivability by adding quarter-inch armor. This allowed the *Campbeltown* to steam across the shallow outer banks and survive the pounding of German harbor defense guns.

The most important modification was the addition of four and one-quarter tons of high explosives in the *Campbeltown*'s bow. The demolition experts accurately calculated how far the bow would compress upon impact with the southern caisson. With this in mind they arranged the twenty-four depth charges to achieve maximum destructive potential. The results were impressive. The explosion completely unhinged the caisson, sending the *Campbeltown* and millions of gallons of water into the dry dock. The dock remained out of commission for the rest of the war.

The other technological innovation that had profound effects on the outcome of the mission was the modification to Sublieutenant

---

Normandie dry dock. These contractors were questioned by British intelligence and their report was made available during the planning for Saint-Nazaire.

ᵃᵃᵃᵃᵃᵃᵃᵃᵃᵃᵃ

Wynn's motor torpedo boat. The torpedo tubes, which were normally situated in the rear, were remounted on the forecastle and loaded with special torpedoes equipped with eighteen hundred pounds of explosives and a delayed-action time fuse. During the final stages of the action, Wynn fired his torpedoes at the Old Entrance gate and departed. Hours later the torpedoes exploded as planned.

In addition to these innovations, the commandos gained some limited advantage through the use of the Bren submachine gun, which held a thirty-two-round magazine and had a rate of fire of five hundred rounds per minute. With a weight of 6.62 pounds and a length of only thirty inches, the Bren allowed the commandos to move quickly and carry more ammunition to sustain their activity ashore. The Bren of course was no match against protected machine guns, but it gave the commandos a decided advantage over the individual German soldier.

In retrospect, the plan for Saint-Nazaire made excellent use of good intelligence and innovative technology; however, it was far from simple, and as the number of objectives and the level of participation increased, so did the level of difficulty.

Security. David Mason in *The Raid on St. Nazaire* said that "because of a passion for security, they [the bomber pilots] had been told nothing of the nature of the raid going in below them, and were flying under orders which severely restricted their bombing activity . . . As one of them later pleaded: 'Why didn't you tell us what was going on in St.-Nazaire that night? We would have taken our bombers down to zero altitude to help with the landing.' "[43]

The failure of the bombers to provide continuous cover for the landing party resulted in the Germans' directing their attention toward the river and eventually detecting and destroying the flotilla. Although this aspect of overbearing security was the most glaring, it was not isolated. During the planning and preparation, only a handful of men knew the details of Operation Chariot, and most of these men did not participate in the actual mission.

The demolition teams trained for months at various docks around England but never knew the ultimate goal of their training. Later, Eric de la Torre, who was in the demolition party, said that each man had too much equipment. "We could have done a lot more with less. It was a pity too, we'd have been much faster."[44] Had the demolition parties known ahead of time that they were going to run five hundred yards through a hail of German bullets wearing over ninety-five pounds of equipment, the plan might have been changed, for the better.

The dress rehearsal that was conducted at Devonport only included a portion of the force for fear that a full-scale rehearsal might reveal the intent of the mission. Consequently, the majority of the commandos never had an opportunity to off-load from the motor launches onto the mole pier under simulated combat conditions. And, the demolition teams, who were not included in the rehearsal, never exercised their missions in conjunction with the protection and assault parties. In fact, the various units that were involved in the raid had little or no contact with each other until just days prior to launch.

Even during the actual operation, Robert Montgomery recalled that security continued to remain tight. He said, "Not many of the crew of the *Campbeltown* even knew it [the four and one-quarter tons of demolition] was down in the hold. And I don't think any of our chaps knew. Now you might say that that was for security reasons. But it wouldn't have been necessary to have security at that time."[45]

The passion for security that surrounded the raid on Saint-Nazaire proved to be detrimental to success. It prevented effective planning by isolating personnel who could help identify tactical problems and contribute ideas to improve the mission. Overbearing security limited effective preparation by reducing the scale of the dress rehearsal, which thereby failed to adequately test the plan prior to launch. Keeping the various commando and naval units separated also prevented any cross-pollination of ideas and methods, which could have improved the execution. Finally, a failure to "trust [the bomber pilots] with at least an outline briefing on the raid" caused the air raid deception plan to fail, and the element of surprise was lost.[46] Security is important, but not at the expense of good planning, preparation, and execution.

Repetition. As I stated before, large forces are unable to use the principles of special operations to achieve relative superiority because they cannot fully assimilate the principles during planning, preparation, or execution. The raid on Saint-Nazaire is an excellent example of this dilemma and of how the problem of large forces impinges on success.

The plan for Operation Chariot, by virtue of the size of its raiding force and complexity of the mission, was not simple. And the security surrounding the preparations for the raid was overbearing and limited individual dialogue that could have improved the tactics. Both of these factors compounded the problem when it came time for a rehearsal. First, with 611 men and a host of support platforms, most of which were not located at the same base, it was difficult to organize and then conduct a rehearsal. Furthermore, once a limited rehearsal was arranged, there was concern about the inadvertent disclosure of the operation, so many of the key elements did not participate.

How did this lack of a full-dress rehearsal affect the outcome of the mission? The mission suffered from two major shortcomings: first, the inability of the motor launches to land the commandos quickly, and secondly, a disjointed assault resulting from too many targets and too little unity. Both of these problems could have been identified in a full-dress rehearsal. Had all the commandos and all the motor launches participated in the rehearsal, it would have been apparent that landing in sequence was a slow procedure that required modification. Additionally, if during the dress rehearsal all 257 commandos had gotten ashore, it would have become obvious that "unity of command was a big problem."[47] Directing that many men over a two-hour period and then extracting under fire was more than a small headquarters element could hope to accomplish.

Again, owing to the size of the force and concern about security, the plan was rehearsed only once. The few problems that were identified never had the opportunity to be resolved in a simulated environment. The value of repetition cannot be overemphasized. Although individual skill training (i.e., demolition placement, small-boat handling, and weapons firing) was exceptionally thorough for all phases of the mission, the failure to conduct a full-dress rehearsal prevented the commandos from understanding how these individual skills needed to dovetail in order to be effective in combat. These shortfalls in the preparation phase eventually surfaced in the execution phase with disastrous results.

Surprise. The planners of the raid on Saint-Nazaire suffered from a common problem among special operations personnel. They equated surprise to relative superiority. They assumed that gaining the element of surprise would immediately provide them with a decisive advantage. In a ground engagement, surprise alone cannot overcome defensive warfare. Surprise is only a prelude to a longer battle, and the enemy generally has the advantage the longer the battle continues. Had the Combined Operations staff approached the raid from the position that there would be no surprise, or at best minimum surprise, the plan would have been considerably different.

Overreliance on surprise placed the small craft in an untenable position. Like submersibles that rely solely on stealth, small craft have virtually no protection from the enemy once their coup de main is compromised.* This was particularly true in the case of Saint-Nazaire, where the target was ringed with shore batteries, and the only escape route was back to the Atlantic through a gauntlet of coastal guns. By overestimating the value of surprise, the planners falsely assumed that the motor launches could land the commandos and then somehow loiter until extraction time. Had they planned for no surprise, they could have used the speed and agility of the motor torpedo boats to outrun the shore batteries and fire on the Old Entrance as well as the dry dock. This would have negated the use of the commandos, but it would have improved the chances of achieving relative superiority by making better use of the other principles of special operations, innovation and speed.

The *Campbeltown* aspect of the mission did not rely entirely on surprise. The planners knew that the ship "would be an excellent target for coastal battery No. 3 at a range of 3200 yards."[48] Consequently they planned around the defensive strong points and relied on the armor plating to sustain the vessel until impact. This proved to be an effective plan, for even when the *Campbeltown* was plastered by shore batteries five minutes from the target, she still sailed to victory.

The importance of the principle of surprise should be neither understated nor overestimated. Surprise generally provides only a momentary advantage, and although it is usually necessary for success, it alone is not sufficient for success.

*Some of today's small craft have the advantage of speeds in excess of sixty knots; nonetheless, it is still difficult to outrun fixed- or rotary-wing alert aircraft.

Speed. In a raid more than in seizing an objective, speed is vitally important. The raiding party is at a tremendous disadvantage because it must destroy its objective and escape the danger area before reinforcements arrive. Nevertheless the planners at Combined Operations Headquarters stated, "[The raiders] should be ashore no longer than 1-1/2 hours, landing at 0130 and reembarking at not later than 0330 hours on the 28th of March."[49] At Saint-Nazaire the German defenders numbered approximately three hundred with a reinforcement of six thousand men within a few miles. This number does not include the sailors aboard the seventeen vessels in the immediate vicinity.

Those commandos who got ashore quickly from the *Campbeltown* did an excellent job of destroying the German gun positions and moving to their targets. Unfortunately, they began to be overwhelmed within thirty minutes.

Had all the 257 commandos gotten ashore as planned, it is conceivable they could have destroyed the small bridges that connected the city of Saint-Nazaire to the dock area and prevented German reinforcements from overrunning their positions. This would have allowed the demolition parties time to carry out their assigned tasks and reembark the motor launches. The flaw in the plan was the assumption that they could get sufficient combat power ashore quickly enough to prevent immediate reinforcement by the Germans.

Again the approach used aboard the *Campbeltown* was simple and well conceived. As soon as the old destroyer impacted the southern caisson, the commandos stormed ashore. Even with heavy German resistance the soldiers were ashore in under five minutes. This eventually led to a successful attack of the dry dock targets.

The same logic was not applied to the soldiers' disembarking from the motor launches. The plan called for a staggered landing of the commandos at both the Old Mole and the Old Entrance.* Even under the best of circumstances, it would have taken fifteen minutes

---

*The commandos were fully aware of the off-load problems but were constrained by the lack of good landing sites. The Old Mole and the Old Entrance provided the only quick access to the dock area that did not involve climbing the quay with full equipment.

for the last commando to set foot ashore. As it was, the British failed to quickly seize the shoreline and eventually were forced off their landing site by overpowering German gunfire.

The plan also called for the motor launches to loiter in the river for one and a half hours after landing the commandos. This extended time in conjunction with the lack of cover on the river placed the motor launches in an impossible position. Of the seventeen boats that participated in the operation, eight were destroyed in the river. Of these eight motor launches, four—those of Platt, Stephens, Beart, and Tillie—were hit while attempting to land the commandos. However, the other four motor launches—those of Irwin, Burt, Rodier, and Nock—were hit while maneuvering in the river, at least two of these boats being destroyed by coastal-defense guns.

Therefore, even if the commandos had gotten ashore and isolated the objective area, the ninety minutes of loiter time would have allowed the Germans ample opportunity to range and engage the boats with coastal-defense and naval guns. Those motor launches that did escape left within sixty minutes of the initial engagement, and most suffered personnel casualties from coastal gunfire.

This raid provides the best example of differences in the application of speed in an operation. When speed was properly used, the commandos aboard the *Campbeltown* were able to successfully accomplish their mission. When the decision was made to add more targets at the expense of speed (and simplicity) the plan broke down and disaster resulted.

Purpose. In 1942, the British had been at war with the Germans for almost two years. The British Expeditionary Force had suffered a humiliating defeat on the continent and been forced to retreat unceremoniously from Dunkirk. At home the British had had to endure continuous bombings by the Luftwaffe that cost thousands of English lives. Consequently, it was not hard for the raiders of Saint-Nazaire to develop a sense of purpose for this mission. Eric de la Torre stated later, "It had been so impressed upon us, 'You must get to your target, doesn't matter how many of you are killed. Don't stop to help anybody. Just get to that target and lay your charges.' "[50]

Although I have continually faulted the planners for not limiting their objectives, at least when the objectives were identified, each commando knew exactly what was expected of him. There was no dispute over the purpose and assigned roles of the individual units. Each unit, including the demolition, the assault, the protection, the headquarters, and the naval parties, understood its objectives and trained extensively, albeit separately, for its missions.

Personal commitment was also not an issue. Captain Robert Montgomery, who helped plan the mission, understood the consequences ahead of time. "I knew I wasn't going to get back," he said.[51] Nevertheless, he accepted that fact and enthusiastically pressed onward. De la Torre thought, "All of us would be killed . . . we [weren't] going to come out [alive]." But even with this premonition, de la Torre concluded, "I wouldn't have missed [the raid on Saint-Nazaire] for the world."[52]

As expected, where a sense of purpose was not instilled, the plan failed. The pilots, who for security reasons had not been advised of the plan, never developed a sense of purpose for the mission. They flew to Saint-Nazaire, dropped a limited number of bombs, and then, owing to low cloud cover and light flak, returned to England. Had the Royal Air Force been informed about the raid and understood the need for the air cover, there is no doubt that they would have gone to any lengths to support the commandos.

Without purpose, a plan must be virtually flawless and able to overcome the disparity between the will of the enemy and the lack of personal commitment on the part of the attacking force. But, as the great Prussian chief of staff Helmut von Moltke said, "No plan survives first contact with the enemy." Therefore, a sense of purpose is essential, and what limited success the commandos did have can be directly attributed to understanding their tasks and being fully committed to seeing them completed.

In conclusion, the raid on Saint-Nazaire represents the best and worst of special-operations planning, preparation, and execution. The use of the *Campbeltown* to destroy the Normandie dry dock was a stroke of military genius. It maximized relative superiority by effectively utilizing all the principles of special operations. It was a simple plan with a single objective that made good use of innovation and intelligence. Security prevented the enemy from knowing the ship's mission and that the old destroyer contained four and one-quarter tons of demolition. Although a ramming exercise was never conducted, the Captain of the *Campbeltown,* Lt. Comdr. Sam Beattie, had thousands of steaming hours, thereby repeating the process of sailing in a straight line countless times. Surprise was achieved through deceptive signaling, and after surprise was lost, time to the target was under five minutes. Finally, the sailors and commandos aboard the ship had a clearly stated purpose with a personal commitment to see the mission completed.

On the other hand, the operation of the motor launches and commandos at the Old Mole and Old Entrance shows the limitations of a large force. The plan was complicated, security was overbearing, rehearsals were inadequate, surprise was minimal and basically ineffective, and the speed on target was insufficient. In the end, only a sense of purpose and the indomitable spirit of the British commandos allowed for any success at all.

Notes

1. Roger J. B. Lord Keyes, *Amphibious Warfare and Combined Operations* (New York: Macmillan, 1943), 10.

2. David Mason, *The Raid on St.-Nazaire* (New York: Ballantine, 1970), 10.

3. Thomas Gallagher, *The X-Craft Raid* (New York: Harcourt Brace Jovanovich, 1971), 11.

4. David Brown, *Tirpitz: The Floating Fortress* (London: Arms & Armour, 1977), 26.

5. H.M.S.O., *Combined Operations: The Official Story of the Commandos* (New York: Macmillan, 1943), 71.

6. Ibid., 5–6.

7. Ibid., 7.

8. Mason, *St.-Nazaire,* 22.

9. Eric de la Torre, interview by author, tape recording, London, 19 June 1992.

10. Mason, *St.-Nazaire,* 22.

11. Peter Young, *Commando* (New York: Ballantine, 1969), 100.

12. De la Torre, interview.

13. Russell Miller, *The Commandos* (Alexandria, Va.: Time-Life, 1981), 168.

14. Ibid., 37.

15. Saint-Nazaire raid report by naval force commander, 1942, Imperial War Museum.

16. Young, *Commando,* 92.

17. Lt. Col. Robert Montgomery, interview by author, tape recording, Mere Warminster, England, 19 June 1992.

18. Mason, *St.-Nazaire,* 43.

19. Ibid., 48.

20. De la Torre, interview.

21. "Narrative/Report on Operation Chariot," in Saint-Nazaire raid report, Section B.

22. H.M.S.O., *Combined Operations,* 74.

23. Dick Bradley, interview by author, tape recording, London, 19 June 1992.

24. Mason, *St.-Nazaire,* 76.

25. Saint-Nazaire raid report, Section B, 3.

26. Young, *Commando,* 98.

27. Stuart Chant-Sempill, *St.-Nazaire Commando* (Novato, Calif.: Presidio, 1985), 43.

28. James Ladd, *Commandos and Rangers of World War II* (London: David & Charles, 1978), 47.

29. De la Torre, interview.

30. Ibid.

31. Bradley, interview.

32. Mason, *St.-Nazaire,* 108.

33. Young, *Commando,* 100.

34. Ibid.

35. "Summary of Narrative of the M.L.," in Saint-Nazaire raid report, Section C, 2.

36. Montgomery, interview.

37. Mason, *St.-Nazaire,* 134.

38. De la Torre, interview.

39. Comdr. Robert Ryder, "Considerations of the Advantages and Disadvantages of Using or Not Using an Expendable Destroyer." Undated but believed to be part of the minutes from a meeting held at Combined Operations Headquarters on Thursday, 26 February 1942, Imperial War Museum.

40. Adviser on Combined Operations, "Most Secret Draft Memorandum to the Chief of Staff: Operation 'Chariot,'" Imperial War Museum, 1.

41. H.M.S.O., *Combined Operations,* 72.

42. Mason, *St.-Nazaire,* 61.

43. Ibid., 148–49.

44. De la Torre, interview.

45. Montgomery, interview.

46. Mason, *St.-Nazaire,* 148.

47. Montgomery, interview.

48. Most Secret Memorandum.

49. Mason, *St.-Nazaire,* 43.

50. De la Torre, interview.

51. Montgomery, interview.

52. De la Torre, interview.

5

Operation Oak:
The Rescue of Benito Mussolini,
12 September 1943

BACKGROUND

On 25 July 1943, Benito Mussolini, the Fascist dictator who had ruled Italy since 1922, was dismissed by King Victor Emmanuel after Italy suffered military disasters in North Africa and Greece. Mussolini was subsequently arrested by the Badoglio government and secretly confined in a prison on Maddalena Island. A few weeks later he was moved to a hotel on top of Gran Sasso Mountain in central Italy. Hitler knew that without Mussolini, Italy would soon fall into the hands of the Allies. It was essential that Mussolini be found quickly and returned to the seat of Italian government. The führer ordered his staff to identify the best commando leaders in the German armed forces and have them report to him immediately. One of these officers was Capt. Otto Skorzeny.

OTTO SKORZENY

Otto Skorzeny was born on 12 June 1908 in Vienna, Austria. His father, Anton, was a successful engineer who tried to raise his son with an appreciation for the arts and music. Skorzeny showed no interest in cultural activities, but he did follow his father's advice and enrolled in the University of Vienna as an engineering student.

Skorzeny was not a particularly good student, but he managed passing grades in those subjects needed to graduate. Skorzeny's real passion was dueling, and he earned a reputation as the finest swordsman in the school. Prior to graduating Skorzeny had engaged in fifteen saber combats, winning each one. In one duel, the opponent's sword sliced Skorzeny's face, giving him a distinctive scar on his left cheek. Later during World War II, when Skorzeny's reputation grew, the Allies nicknamed him "Scarface." Dueling taught Skorzeny a valuable lesson: he said later, "My knowledge of pain, learned with the sabre, taught me not to be afraid and just as in duelling when you must concentrate on your enemy's cheek, so, too, in war. You cannot waste time on feinting and sidestepping. You must decide on your target and go in."[1]

Skorzeny eventually graduated from the university in December 1931. He worked for several engineering firms and then started his own company. The year prior to graduating, Skorzeny joined the National Socialist Party (Nazis). During postwar interrogations, Skorzeny admitted his early affiliation with the Nazi party but claimed it was his interest in road racing that enticed him into the organization. Each weekend the Nazis held road races around Germany, and it appears that Skorzeny's passion for racing did indeed outweigh his interest in politics—initially.

On 12 February 1938, the chancellor of Austria, Kurt von Schuschnigg, succumbed to pressure from Hitler and signed the *Anschluss* (union) that paved the way for a Nazi takeover of Austria. On 12 March 1938, after several attempts by the Austrians to derail Hitler's plan, German soldiers were sent into Vienna. During a rally of the Austrian Nazi party, the ousted Austrian president, Wilhelm Miklas, attempted to retake the royal palace by force. When the Nazis found out about the plot, they intercepted the Austrian president and bloodshed seemed inevitable. Skorzeny, who was attending the rally, intervened between the two groups and demanded calm. Claiming he was a representative of the new chancellor, he brokered a peaceful resolution, and the crisis ended. This act of bravado did not go unnoticed by the head of the Austrian SS, Ernst Kaltenbrunner, who was also attending the rally. Kaltenbrunner would later recommend Skorzeny to command the führer's special troops.

A year later when the war broke out, Skorzeny requested assignment to the Luftwaffe, but at thirty-one years of age he was considered too old for flight training. Instead, he was ordered to a communications outfit but soon received a transfer to the Waffen SS. As an officer-cadet Skorzeny was assigned to the Das Reich Division where he was responsible for maintaining all the division's mobile equipment, including tanks, wheeled artillery, and trucks.

Skorzeny was constantly in trouble and received several official reprimands. Once while drinking in a cafe in the Netherlands, Skorzeny demanded that a portrait of Prince Bernhard of the Netherlands be removed. When the cafe owner refused, Skorzeny shot the picture off the wall. The local Dutch citizens became furious, and Skorzeny was confined to his barracks for six weeks. His efforts to become an officer seemed to be in serious jeopardy, but all that was forgotten when he captured fifty-seven soldiers while fighting in Yugoslavia. He was promptly promoted to lieutenant. When the Germans invaded Russia, Skorzeny's Das Reich Division suffered heavy casualties. Skorzeny was wounded in December of 1941, when shrapnel from an artillery shell hit him in the head. In January 1942, he returned to Germany to recover from his wounds.

Several weeks after receiving treatment for his shrapnel wounds and a recurring gallbladder problem, Skorzeny was assigned to the 5th Panzer Regiment in France. During this tour Skorzeny saw duty in the Netherlands and Russia, but by the following year his gallbladder problem was so severe that he was discharged from combat duty and transferred to a repair depot in Berlin.

That same year Admiral Canaris's Abwehr, the organization within the German High Command responsible for covert operations, was falling out of favor with Hitler. The führer rightly suspected that Admiral Canaris was attempting to betray the Reich, so Hitler formed his own commando force under the auspices of the Reich Main Security Office (RSHA). The branch responsible for the commandos was the Amt VI-S. Skorzeny's old friend from the *Anschluss* days, Ernst Kaltenbrunner, recommended Skorzeny be placed in charge of the new unit, and on 20 April 1943, Skorzeny assumed command of Amt VI-S and was promoted to captain.

In September 1943 Skorzeny and his commandos from Amt VI-S rescued Mussolini from Gran Sasso Mountain and Skorzeny was awarded the Knight's Cross to the Iron Cross. The rescue was used

by the Reich propaganda leader, Joseph Goebbels, to elevate
Skorzeny to the level of national hero. Goebbels named Skorzeny
"the most dangerous man in Europe." Skorzeny was subsequently
promoted to major. His exploits during the remainder of the war
were almost as legendary.

In October 1944, Skorzeny kidnapped Miki Horthy, the son of
the Hungarian regent, Adm. Miklós Horthy de Nagybanya. The regent was planning to sign an alliance with Russia, and Hitler hoped
that the regent would reconsider his actions if his son was in German hands. When the kidnapping failed to change the regent's
mind, Skorzeny developed a plan to seize the citadel on the Burberg
River, Horthy's castle. In another show of pure bravado, Skorzeny,
convinced that the Hungarians would not resist, took a column of
German soldiers directly to the well-protected citadel and seized it
without a shot being fired.

As the war wound down to its final stages, Skorzeny was tasked
with organizing a special brigade of English-speaking Germans to
disrupt Allied activities in the Ardennes. The Germans, disguised as
American soldiers, tried to take the Meuse bridgehead and hold it
until they could be relieved by conventional forces. The attempt fell
well short of its main goal; however the German commandos did
create considerable confusion and fear among Allied units. By the
war's end, Skorzeny was a divisional commander and in charge of
all special operations forces in the Third Reich.

Skorzeny surrendered to the Americans on 15 May 1945 and was
tried at Dachau for war crimes committed during the Ardennes offensive.* He was acquitted on 9 September 1947, but the Germans
forced Skorzeny to stand trial as a Nazi. Under mysterious circumstances, Skorzeny escaped from the internment camp at Darmstadt
and later surfaced in Argentina.†

---

*The prosecution charged that Skorzeny had violated the Law of Armed
Conflict when he ordered his men to disguise themselves as American
soldiers. Skorzeny's defense counsel argued that this was common practice among the Allies as well and, using testimony from a British agent,
was able to get Skorzeny acquitted.
†On 27 July 1948, three "American" military police arrived at Darmstadt
to take Skorzeny to Nuremberg for a scheduled hearing on the denazifi-

While in Argentina, Skorzeny helped recover millions of dollars of Third Reich money that had been sent to Juan Peron for safe-keeping. The money, which was part of the Bormann treasure, was used to establish the Organization for the Release of Former SS Members (ODESSA).*

In 1951 Skorzeny returned to Madrid, and under the protection of the Spanish government he opened an import-export company. He used the company as a conduit to move SS officers from Germany to all parts of the world. He was also heavily involved in supplying money, passports, and escape routes to the Waffen SS veterans' association, HIAG, and the Federation of German Soldiers. ODESSA and a similar organization, Die Spinne, consumed the remainder of Skorzeny's life. Glenn Infield, in his book *Skorzeny: Hitler's Commando,* stated: "The 'feeding and caring' of former SS members by Skorzeny and his associates since the end of the Third Reich has been a marvel of patience, intrigue, and meticulous planning, as well as a display of brutality and terrorism learned under the Fuhrer. Hitler left a legacy of violence to the world; Skorzeny made certain it was preserved."[2] Otto Skorzeny died of cancer in Madrid on 5 July 1975.

JAGDVERBANDE 502—THE COMMANDOS

On 20 April 1943 Skorzeny reported to the chief of political information of the Reich Main Security Office and was given command of section Amt VI-S. His immediate supervisor was Maj. Walter Schellenberg, head of Amt VI. The first day on board Schellenberg briefed Skorzeny on his new assignment: "He told me [Skorzeny]

---

cation trial. The German guard, intimidated by the "American" officer, released Skorzeny into his custody. When Skorzeny was asked where his rescuers stole their American uniforms, he responded, "They weren't stolen. They were provided by the Americans." (Otto Skorzeny interviewed by Glenn Infield, Rome, 1973.)

*Martin Bormann was the head of the party chancellery and Hitler's private secretary. Toward the end of the war, Bormann withdrew an estimated $127 million. According to Glenn Infield, who wrote a biography of Skorzeny, it is widely suspected that Skorzeny helped Bormann ship the money in armored trucks to Spain, where it was taken by U-boat to Argentina.

he wanted me to take charge of the schools being established to instruct agents of the new unit and to convert an SS battalion called Oranienburg into a sabotage and subversive organization renamed Jagdverbande 502 [Hunting Group]. All orders were verbal. Nothing was on paper."[3]

Skorzeny quickly found that the lack of clear written directions and a convoluted chain of command created considerable confusion. In theory, Amt VI-S worked for Amt VI, under Major Schellenberg. Schellenberg worked for RSHA, which was headed by Skorzeny's friend Kaltenbrunner, and RSHA came under the command of the SS. In practice, however, the head of the SS, Heinrich Himmler, frequently bypassed the chain and went directly to Skorzeny. Additionally, for political reasons, the Abwehr, headed by Admiral Canaris, also had oversight of the Amt VI-S's operations. Admiral Canaris detested the SS and was therefore constantly attempting to thwart Amt VI-S's efforts to establish a viable organization.

Skorzeny's initial attempts to define his unit's role and missions and procure facilities and equipment for training proved frustrating. He states in his autobiography, "I had to wrestle with an infinite number of bureaucrats in order to wrench from them the minimum I needed."[4] Eventually, however, Skorzeny's tenacity paid off. His first recruit was Karl Radl, an old college acquaintance. He and Radl scoured the German army for the finest personnel available. This included men from the Brandenburg Battalion, the Waffen SS, and the SS Parachute Battalion. Himmler also ordered that Kampf Geschwader 200, an elite aviation squadron, be assigned directly to Skorzeny to provide aircraft for insertion and extraction. Kampf Geschwader 200 was equipped with gliders, piloted V-1s, Storks, and a variety of remote-controlled bombs and aircraft.

Skorzeny established his commando headquarters in a small castle at Friedenthal, near Oranienburg. Here he erected barracks, hangars, and a gymnasium, installed a drill field, and began to develop his training regiment. Skorzeny had always been enamored of the British commandos. Using documents and information from captured British agents, Skorzeny studied the selection, training, and employment of Louis Lord Mountbatten's Combined Operations Command forces. By using a double agent net, Skorzeny was even able to obtain a British silenced pistol and the suppressor for a Sten gun, both of which he used in the training of his commandos. Additionally, at the prompting of Kaltenbrunner, Skorzeny studied the successful operations of the Abwehr's Brandenburg Battalion.*

In November 1943, Skorzeny finally began to train in earnest, consciously avoiding the fact that Germany was losing badly and that the war might end any day. "'Too late!' should not figure in the vocabulary of a soldier," he later recalled.[5] The training required each commando to be well versed in a number of areas. "Each man was first to be trained thoroughly as an infantryman and an engineer; next, he was to gain at least a rudimentary knowledge of rifle grenades, field pieces and tanks. Obviously, he was to know how to handle not only a motorcycle and an automobile but also a motorboat and a locomotive. [Skorzeny] also encouraged all manner of athletics, especially swimming. A course for parachutists was also in prospect."[6]

The commandos spent much of their time exercising against mock Soviet and Anglo-American targets in the hopes that they would be deployed behind the lines in a sabotage role. A certain number of the men also received instruction in English and Russian for the same purpose. By July 1943 there was little doubt that Skorzeny's special unit was in fact the best-trained, best-equipped, and best-led commando outfit in the German armed forces. All they needed now was an opportunity to prove it.

PLANNING AND PREPARATIONS

On 23 July 1943, Otto Skorzeny was relaxing at the Hotel Eden in Berlin when he received a message to telephone his headquarters. Over the phone Skorzeny's secretary told him that the führer wanted to see him and that a plane would be waiting for him at Tempelhof Airport.

---

*While being interrogated at Nuremberg, Skorzeny stated that he had hoped Kaltenbrunner would provide him clear guidance in establishing the commandos. Instead Kaltenbrunner said, "You are an SS leader. You are supposed to know how to organize and lead such a battalion. Use the British commando and the Brandenburg Battalion as an example."

When Skorzeny arrived at the airport his executive officer, Karl Radl, met him with a suitcase and news that Mussolini had been overthrown. But neither Skorzeny nor Radl "dreamed of associating this event with [Skorzeny's] orders to report to G.H.Q."[7] Traveling aboard a specially configured Ju 52, Skorzeny flew to Hitler's "Wolf's Lair" situated in Rastenburg, East Prussia.

Skorzeny arrived at the Wolf's Lair at approximately 2000 and was immediately escorted to the Tea House, a one-story building with two wings joined by a covered passageway. Inside the lightly camouflaged building, Skorzeny met five other officers apparently summoned for the same reason. Soon afterward, a Waffen SS captain announced that the six men would be meeting with the führer and each man was to give a brief summary of his career, which would be followed by questions from Hitler. Skorzeny later wrote: "At first I thought I must be mistaken. Then an unreasoned fear almost swept my legs from under me. In a few moments, for the first time in my life, I was to stand in the presence of Adolf Hitler, Führer of Greater Germany and Supreme Commander of the German Armed Forces! Talk about your surprises, here was one to end them all! Moved as I was, I felt sure I would make some unpardonable break or behave like an idiot."[8]

Hitler entered the room and was presented to each of the six officers. The führer wanted to know which of the men knew the terrain around Italy. Skorzeny replied that he had driven through the countryside from one end to the other on his motorcycle. Then addressing all the officers, Hitler asked, "What do you think of the Italians?" The first five officers responded with an obligatory statement about the strength of the Axis relationship and how good an ally the Italians were. When it was Skorzeny's turn to reply he stated firmly, "I am an Austrian, my Leader, and our attitude toward Italy is prejudiced by the happenings in the previous World War and by South Tyrol."[9]

Hitler dismissed the other officers and ordered Skorzeny to remain. He told Skorzeny:

I have a mission of the highest importance for you. Yesterday Mussolini, my friend and our loyal partner in the struggle, was betrayed by his king and arrested by his own compatriots.

Now I cannot and will not abandon the greatest of Italians in his hour of peril. For me Il Duce represents the personification of the last of the Roman Caesars. Italy, or rather her new government, will no doubt join the enemy camp, but I shall not go back on my word: Mussolini must be rescued, and speedily, otherwise they will deliver him up to the Allies. I therefore intrust you with this mission: its successful outcome will be of incalculable bearing upon the development of future military operations.[10]

Hitler told Skorzeny that the operation must be absolutely secret and that only five people would know the details of the mission.

As of that moment, Skorzeny's special group was detached from the Luftwaffe and would report directly to Gen. Kurt Student, commander of the XI Air Corps. Student was an expert in airborne operations, having also been instrumental in planning the glider attack on the fortress at Eben Emael. Hitler also directed Skorzeny not to discuss the operation with the German embassy in Rome. Hitler believed that Field Marshal Albert Kesselring, commander of the German armed forces in the Mediterranean, and his staff "listen[ed] completely to the monarchy" and had "gone soft in the southern sun," becoming "half-Italians themselves."[11]

After a final word of encouragement from Hitler, Skorzeny was dismissed and directed to another room where he met with General Student and the head of the Gestapo and Waffen SS, Reichsführer-SS Heinrich Himmler. Himmler gave the two men a brief on the political situation in Italy. When Skorzeny began to take notes, Himmler flew into a rage, reminding Skorzeny that this mission was top secret.

Himmler was certain that Italy's defection was assured with the transfer of government. Italian diplomats were currently in Portugal negotiating with Allied emissaries. The question was not if but when the government would leave the Axis camp. Around midnight Himmler departed, and Skorzeny and Student began to plan the basics of the mission. The first problem was to find Mussolini. Once Il Duce was located, the details of the mission could be worked out. In the meantime, Student arranged to have the XI Air Corps sent to Italy from their base in southern France. Skorzeny contacted Radl and ordered him to identify fifty commandos and have them prepared to depart for Italy the next day. When Radl asked for amplifying information, Skorzeny responded, "I cannot give you more exact details over the telephone . . . tonight no sleep for anybody . . . have all the trucks ready because we must pick up equipment . . . I am taking fifty men with me, our best men, that is all those who can more or less speak Italian . . . I shall draw up a list, you do the same thing, and we will talk over whom to choose . . . everything must be done by five in the morning."[12]

An hour later Skorzeny called Radl and gave him a list of equipment he wanted prepared prior to the next day's departure. It included two machine guns per nine men, tommy guns for all the rest, grenades, tracers, rocket launchers, sixty-five pounds of plastic explosives (British made), detonators, helmets, underwear, radios, medical supplies, civilian clothes, and rations for three days. Radl informed Skorzeny that the troops were in rebellion. No one wanted to stay behind. Skorzeny directed Radl to immediately post the names of those who were going on the mission. This way the decision would be quickly finalized, and it would minimize the troops' discontent.

At three in the morning Skorzeny was shown to his room, a small cabin in an air-raid shelter. With the excitement of the mission on his mind, Skorzeny did not sleep. He eventually got out of bed and drew up his last will and testament. Later that morning, posing as General Student's aide-de-camp, Skorzeny departed East Prussia with Student and flew to Rome's Pratica di Mare Airport, landing at approximately 1330.

From Rome, the two men were driven to Marshal Kesselring's headquarters at Frascati. That evening over dinner Student subtly inquired about the possible location of Mussolini. Student was careful not to seem overanxious about Kesselring's answer. Kesselring, however, had heard nothing and believed that the Italian General Staff was equally in the dark about Mussolini's imprisonment.

Two days later Skorzeny's men arrived with the XI Air Corps and established a base camp close to the Pratica di Mare Airport. Skorzeny informed his men that they were ordered to conduct a very important mission, but he gave no specifics. He detailed his senior enlisted men to keep the troops in top physical condition, and Skorzeny personally inspected all the commandos' equipment to ensure it was ready for immediate use. After providing instructions to the men, Skorzeny and Radl departed for Frascati.

According to Skorzeny, Radl was informed of the nature of the mission upon arriving in Frascati. "He showed himself as surprised and stirred as I had been to hear the Führer's orders. From the beginning we were agreed on one point; it would be extremely difficult to discover the place where the Duce was being held prisoner. As for our action, in other words his actual liberation, we did not ever dream about it because zero hour still seemed to us to be very far off."[13]

Skorzeny was right: zero hour was indeed far off. For the next four weeks he and Radl made every effort to find Mussolini. All rumors, no matter how fantastic, were investigated. Fortunately for Skorzeny, there were still officials within the Italian government who supported the Fascist dictator and were willing to come forward with bits of information. On a tip from a fruit vendor, Skorzeny and Radl learned that Mussolini had been moved by the carabinieri to the island of Ponza. Before this was confirmed, Mussolini was moved again to La Spezia, on the Ligurian coast of northwest Italy. At La Spezia, Mussolini was imprisoned aboard an Italian cruiser. When this intelligence was received by the German High Command, Skorzeny was ordered to mount an immediate rescue attempt. "Luckily we learned [the] next day that the Duce had once more changed prisons . . . No doubt at G.H.Q. they imagined nothing was easier than to make a man vanish from under the eyes of the crew of a cruiser on war footing."[14]

After several more unfounded rumors, it was suspected that Mussolini had been moved to the naval fortress on Maddalena Island, a small island north of Sardinia. Skorzeny, accompanied by Lieutenant Warger (an Italian-speaking German commando) and Commander Hunaus, the German liaison to the Italian navy, conducted a visual reconnaissance of the area by sailing along the coastline and into the small port facility. The security in the port, at the naval fort, and at nearby Villa Weber was heavier than usual. The villa was guarded by 150 men with a twenty-four-hour police patrol on the surrounding streets and alleys. Additionally, temporary telephone lines had been installed at the house, apparently to allow the guard commander in the villa to call for immediate reinforcements.

The following day, Lieutenant Warger, disguised as a German sailor, returned, rented an apartment, and reconnoitered the villa and the naval fort.* At night Warger visited the local bars trying to determine if the Italian sailors knew where Mussolini was interned. In three days, Warger returned to Skorzeny with a detailed report on the guard routine and exterior gun emplacements of the villa and the fort. By now Skorzeny was convinced that Mussolini was indeed being held at Villa Weber.

On 18 August 1943, while Radl began to develop the basic plan for rescuing Mussolini from Maddalena Island, Skorzeny commandeered a Heinkel 111 to conduct an aerial reconnaissance of the fort. After taking off from Rome, the aircraft made several intermediate stops and then headed for Maddalena Island. Unfortunately, as the Heinkel flew out over the Tyrrhenian Sea, two British fighters appeared and shot down the plane. Skorzeny recalled later that he "was still taking pictures when the plane suddenly jerked violently and started a sharp descent."[15] Miraculously none of the crew was killed, and Skorzeny suffered only three broken ribs. Within two days he was rescued and returned to Rome.

Upon his return, Skorzeny was informed that the Abwehr had determined that Mussolini was not on Maddalena Island, but on Elba. Convinced that the Abwehr's intelligence was wrong, Skorzeny asked for, and received, another audience with Hitler. The next day Student and Skorzeny flew back to East Prussia and upon landing were immediately ushered in to brief Hitler. In Hitler's company were Joachim von Ribbentrop, the minister of foreign affairs; Field Marshal Wilhelm Keitel, chief of staff of the High Command; Gen. Alfred Jodl, chief of the operations staff of the High Command; Grand Admiral Karl Dönitz, commander in chief of the German navy; Marshal Hermann Göring, commander in chief of the Luftwaffe; and Himmler. After receiving an introduction from Student, Skorzeny was directed to state his position. Skorzeny later

*Italy was still officially an Axis power and had not broken diplomatic ties with Germany. Across the channel from Maddalena Island, on the island of Sardinia, was a German naval base. The German sailors frequently visited the port city of La Maddalena when on liberty.

recalled how nervous he was to be briefing so influential an audience. "In the beginning I had terrible stage fright; the glances of
these eight men so flustered me that I forgot to consult the notes I
had prepared during my trip from Berlin."[16]

Gradually, however, Skorzeny regained his confidence and convinced the führer that Mussolini was not on Elba, but on Maddalena.
Using a map he had sketched out on the flight to the Wolf's Lair,
Skorzeny explained his plan. It involved the use of a squadron of
swift boats and six minesweepers. On the minesweepers a company
of SS troops and Skorzeny's fifty commandos would be embarked.

On D day minus one, the squadron of swift boats, which was
normally based in Sardinia, would make an official port visit to Maddalena. The minesweepers, with SS troops and commandos embarked, would cross the straits from Corsica and anchor out one
thousand yards from the fort. The following morning at dawn, the
SS troops would land, surround the villa, cut telephone lines, seize
the cannon that guarded the port, destroy several naval vessels, and

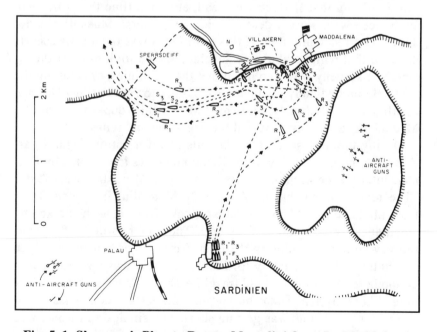

**Fig. 5–1. Skorzeny's Plan to Rescue Mussolini from La Maddalena.
Adapted from National Archives**

act as a blocking force against reinforcements from the fort. Skorzeny and his fifty commandos would march in formation from their landing spot directly to the villa. Once at the villa Skorzeny would demand the release of Mussolini. Skorzeny felt that marching his commandos to the villa would be an act of such boldness that it "would increase the effectiveness of [the] surprise attack."[17] Hitler was exceptionally pleased with the plan and granted Skorzeny permission to conduct the mission. However, he warned Skorzeny, "If the mission is a failure . . . I will find myself obliged to repudiate you in public and state that you acted on your own initiative."[18]

The mission began exactly as planned. Radl departed for Corsica to direct the onload of SS troops, and the swift boats arrived at Maddalena on schedule. Skorzeny decided to make one last reconnaissance of the port. Dressed as German sailors, he and Warger wandered into town and struck up a conversation with a lone carabiniere. Skorzeny maneuvered the discussion around to Mussolini, implying that Il Duce was dead, at which time the policeman announced with a great deal of pride, "Of course Mussolini is not dead! Why I saw him myself this morning. I was one of his escorts down to that white ambulance seaplane which took him off the island."[19] Skorzeny was convinced that the carabiniere was telling the truth. He immediately contacted Radl, only to find out that German intelligence had already confirmed Mussolini's departure from La Maddalena. Skorzeny canceled the operation and returned to Rome.

During the next several weeks, bits of information began to arrive at Skorzeny's headquarters. Radio messages intercepted by German intelligence pinpointed the area where Mussolini was held.[20] "The report stated that on August 27 Mussolini had been flown from Maddalena to Vigna di Valle on Lake Bracciano then taken by ambulance to the village of Assergi. There he boarded a funicular railway which took him up the Gran Sasso—where he was hidden in a hotel."[21] Unfortunately for Skorzeny, there was no information on the hotel other than an old travel brochure. Prior to serious planning, Skorzeny knew that he had to conduct a reconnaissance of Gran Sasso, but time was getting short. The situation in Rome was deteriorating daily. On 7 September, Gen. Maxwell Taylor had secretly arrived in Italy to discuss an armistice with the Badoglio government. Italian divisions were withdrawing from the front and surrounding the capital city. If the Germans hoped to rescue Mussolini, it had to be now.

On the morning of 8 September, Skorzeny, Radl, and another staff officer boarded a German reconnaissance airplane at Pratica di Mare and took off for Gran Sasso. In order to maintain security within the German ranks, the pilot was informed that the purpose of the flight was to clandestinely photograph ports on the Adriatic Sea. To conceal this reconnaissance mission from the Italians, Skorzeny ordered the pilot to fly over the Abruzzi Mountain Range at an altitude of eighty-five hundred feet, well below the normal flight patterns of the Italian air force.

The aircraft, which was equipped with an automatic camera, began to set up for the photo test run twenty miles west of Gran Sasso. Unfortunately, the camera, which was in the belly of the plane, was covered with frost and wouldn't advance the film. Skorzeny moved to the rear of the plane and cut out a window in the aft gunner's turret. Using a handheld camera, which he had brought along for just such an emergency, Skorzeny leaned out of the aircraft with Radl holding his feet. At this altitude, the outside temperature was so cold that Skorzeny could only snap a few pictures before he had to retreat back into the aircraft. As the plane rose to clear the mountain range, Skorzeny noticed a small triangular meadow adjacent to the hotel. He determined this would be the best, and possibly the only, place to land his commandos.

The pilot continued on toward the Adriatic. After pretending to photograph an Italian port facility, Skorzeny ordered the pilot to return via Gran Sasso at an altitude of twenty-one thousand feet. This time Radl was held outside the plane, and he proceeded to finish the photo reconnaissance.

On the return trip to Rome, Skorzeny looked out the window and saw the sky was filled with American bombers. He was witnessing the beginning of the Allied invasion of Salerno. Three waves of bombers attacked the German strongholds around Rome, but upon landing Skorzeny found his headquarters still intact. The Italians had signed the armistice, and the Germans now stood isolated in the ancient capital.

Over the next few days, chaos reigned around Rome. General Student, who had been placed in charge of most German forces in the area, conducted a magnificent series of maneuvers and managed to stabilize the situation.[22] This effort to secure German positions required Student's full attention, and the operation to rescue Mussolini was delayed until German reinforcements could be brought in from southern Italy.

In the meantime, Skorzeny made one final attempt to verify Mussolini's location. He arranged to have an unwitting German medical officer travel to Gran Sasso to determine the hotel's suitability as a malaria clinic. The doctor traveled through Italian lines and managed to reach the funicular railway at Gran Sasso before he was turned away. Upon his return the doctor told Skorzeny that there were a number of carabinieri outposts all along the road from L'Aquila to Gran Sasso and that the funicular railway was heavily guarded. The townspeople, with whom the doctor had talked, informed him that a number of high-ranking Italian officers had stayed in L'Aquila and that all the civilians in the Campo Impertore Hotel had been dismissed.

On 10 and 11 September, Skorzeny continued to refine his plan of attack. It was clear that an assault up the mountain was not feasible. If the rescue was not conducted swiftly, Mussolini could be spirited away or killed if necessary. The small patch of grass that Skorzeny had spotted on the aerial reconnaissance seemed to have potential as a landing site. The idea of conducting a parachute operation was also quickly ruled out; the air was too thin and the drop zone too small to insert parachutists.

Skorzeny proposed using gliders and landing adjacent to the hotel. Student, who had successfully employed gliders at Eben Emael and was a glider pilot himself, clearly knew the risks of attempting to land in a small area at high altitude. Skorzeny recalled, "After three almost sleepless nights of crisis . . . the general was in no mood for hare-brained escapades. He sent for two technical officers of the Airborne staff, and [I] had to expound the scheme again in detail."[23]

The experts were dead set against the idea and told Student that based on the terrain and rarefied air, only 20 percent of the gliders would survive the flight. Skorzeny made one final plea, "There are

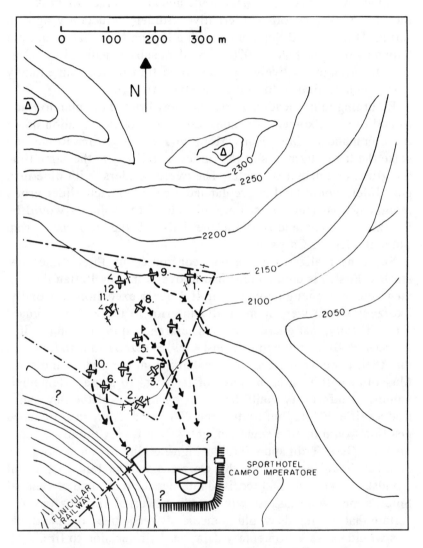

Fig. 5–2. Skorzeny's Plan to Rescue Mussolini from Gran Sasso. Adapted from National Archives

some things you can't work out with a slide rule. That's just where
our experts may be wrong; and the Italians too. The safer the enemy
feel, the better our chances of catching them unawares."[24] Skorzeny
also reminded the general that the new DFS 230 gliders were now
equipped with braking rockets in the nose and parachute brakes in
the tail. Seeing no other alternative, Student reluctantly agreed,
setting D day for 12 September with a launch time that would put
Skorzeny over the hotel at 0700.[25] Student subsequently directed his
staff to arrange for twelve gliders to be transported immediately
from southern France to Pratica di Mare Airport.

Returning to his headquarters, Skorzeny briefed the plan to Radl.
In addition to Skorzeny's commandos, a parachute battalion under
the command of Maj. Hans Mors would drive from Rome and
seize the lower terminus of the funicular railway at the same time
the gliders landed at the hotel. The twelve gliders, with nine men
per glider, would land in preplanned areas with each glider group
assigned a particular mission. Only 26 of the soldiers would be
Skorzeny's commandos, with the bulk of the 108 men from
Student's XI Air Corps.

Skorzeny realized that he was confronted by three major obstacles. First, his commandos had to overcome the Italian detachment quickly enough to prevent Il Duce's execution. Secondly,
Skorzeny's men were numerically inferior to the 250-man guard
force. Thirdly, that guard force was "entrenched in the hotel as in a
fortress."[26] To overcome these obstacles, Skorzeny and Radl agreed
that their commandos had to disembark from the gliders and seize
Mussolini within three minutes of landing. To some extent their
numerical inferiority could be offset by the use of the new paratrooper rifle, FG-42, but routing out 250 guards from an entrenched
position would require some thought.[27] Radl finally proposed "convincing" Gen. Ferdinando Soleti, a high-ranking Italian carabiniere,
that he should accompany the Germans on the raid to prevent
bloodshed. Skorzeny had received intelligence that some of General
Soleti's men were tasked with guarding Mussolini. Skorzeny felt
certain that the guards would immediately recognize Soleti and that
this would cause a momentary delay in their decision to fire.

Once Mussolini was rescued there were three plans for extracting
him. The most desirable plan was to move Mussolini from the ho-

tel, down the funicular, and to L'Aquila Airport. From L'Aquila he would be returned to Rome. If the L'Aquila Airport was controlled by Italian troops, a Stork—short takeoff and landing aircraft—could land in the valley. The third and least desirable plan was to have Captain Gerlach, Student's personal pilot, land on top of Gran Sasso and embark Mussolini for the return flight.

The chances of actually succeeding on the mission seemed slim indeed. At one point in the planning, as Skorzeny began to calculate the possibility of success, Radl interrupted, "My dear Captain, please do not use a table of logarithms to evaluate our chance of success. We already know how infinitesimal they are. But we also know that we are going to undertake this operation at all costs."[28]

CAMPO IMPERATORE HOTEL—GRAN SASSO

Campo Imperatore Hotel was a seventy-room hotel located on top of Gran Sasso Mountain, a sixty-three-hundred-foot peak in the Central Apennines Range. Situated on a small plateau, the hotel was surrounded on the north and east by several higher peaks that rose to an elevation of seventy-five hundred feet. To the south of the hotel, the plateau dropped off into a small narrow valley. The hotel could only be reached by taking a funicular railway (tram) from the base of Gran Sasso to the plateau. The plateau itself was strewn with large- and medium-sized rocks, not visible from the air, which created a hazard to Skorzeny's gliders and somewhat hampered the movement of the commandos. Below the mountain to the west lay the valley of L'Aquila, which extended in a southeasterly direction from Terni to Sulmona and was bordered on the northeast by Gran Sasso and on the southwest by the Abruzzi Mountains.

In the valley, the Italians had positioned carabinieri outposts along the road leading from the town of L'Aquila to the base of Gran Sasso. At the hotel there were an estimated two hundred Italian soldiers and carabinieri. They were commanded by Inspector Giuseppe Gueli, a carabiniere officer. Additionally, a high-ranking Italian general and his bodyguards were present at the hotel. The Italians had only loosely positioned their troops around the hotel, never expecting any type of airborne assault. They assumed that the only weak point in the mountain defense was at the funicular railway. The Italians who were guarding Mussolini, however, were not necessarily loyal to the new Badoglio government. Although Skorzeny had no fore-knowledge of the Italian soldiers' political allegiance, their lack of the will to fight, coupled with the surprise and speed with which Skorzeny's commandos assaulted the hotel, proved to be pivotal to the success of the mission.

ASSAULT ON GRAN SASSO

On 12 September at 0500, Skorzeny and his men departed for Pratica di Mare Airport. Student, in control of the operation, had set up a command post from which to direct the action. It was not long before problems in the plan started to develop. The gliders, which were set to land early that morning, were delayed until 1100. The Italian general did not arrive, and Radl was required to go to Rome, find the carabiniere officer, and forcibly bring him to the airport. It was explained to General Soleti that Hitler had personally asked for his assistance in this matter, after which the general became more accommodating.

At 1100 the gliders arrived and all preparations were made to launch at 1300. The commandos and paratroopers loaded their gear, and Skorzeny gave them a final brief. Pulling out a large map, he plotted all glider ground checkpoints, showed key terrain features, and briefed individual glider groups on their responsibilities. Skorzeny and Soleti would be positioned in the third glider. The first two gliders would be used as guide aircraft and, after landing, the commandos aboard them would provide cover for Skorzeny as he moved to the hotel. Student, who was following the instructions closely, told the pilots that under no circumstances were they to conduct a vertical or controlled crash landing. If the terrain did not permit a horizontal landing, then the gliders were to abort.

Toward the end of the brief, Allied aircraft suddenly appeared and bombed the airport, causing minor runway damage. Fortu-nately, none of the gliders were hit. Shortly before 1300, the com-mandos and paratroopers loaded the aircraft, and on signal from Skorzeny the tow planes and their gliders began to lift off. Inside the canvas-covered glider the commandos were packed tightly be-tween their equipment and each other. The small cellophane windows that bordered the cockpit were too dirty to see out of, so only the pilot had any idea of the glider's location.

During the hour-long flight to Gran Sasso, Skorzeny periodically came forward to the cockpit to check his bearings. Although the weather was good, large cloud banks obscured visibility to the ground, making navigation difficult. Additionally, the clouds created severe updrafts, causing the gliders to make erratic pitching motions. Several minutes into the flight Skorzeny noticed that the two lead tow planes and gliders were missing. He did not know until later that the gliders had hit bomb craters upon takeoff and were unable to get airborne.

Pulling a knife from his assault gear, Skorzeny cut a hole in the canvas fuselage. This enabled him to look out and judge his location. Below he could see the small town of L'Aquila, only minutes by air from Gran Sasso. Major Mors and his paratroopers, who had driven from Rome an hour earlier, were proceeding to the funi-

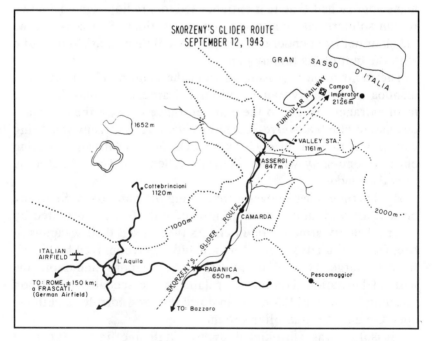

Fig. 5–3. Skorzeny's Glider Path from Rome to Gran Sasso.
Adapted from National Archives

cular railway at the base of the mountain. From his altitude of eighty-five hundred feet, Skorzeny could see the small triangular patch of grass that he had identified as the landing zone. Unfortunately, what had appeared flat and smooth from twenty-one thousand feet was in reality a steep incline covered with large- and medium-sized rocks. Skorzeny knew that to land horizontally as ordered was impossible. He made up his mind quickly and yelled at the pilot, "Dive—crash-land as near to the hotel as you can!"[29]

The glider went into a "fantastic tailspin" before the pilot released the parachute brake and plowed into the small field, thirty yards from the hotel. Skorzeny's men jumped from the mangled glider and immediately proceeded toward the hotel.

Skorzeny had previously ordered the commandos not to shoot unless fired upon. This silence added to the element of surprise. Pushing General Soleti before him, Skorzeny followed his men toward the hotel, past an Italian guard who stood stunned as the Germans approached. The rear entrance led to a radio room where two Italian soldiers sat monitoring communications. Skorzeny kicked the chair out from under one of the men and then smashed the radio with the butt of his tommy gun.

The radio room was isolated from the main hotel, so the commandos immediately exited and circled around the outside to the main entrance. To get to the main entrance quickly the commandos had to climb a twelve-foot terrace wall. As Skorzeny was being helped over the wall by one of his NCOs, he saw Mussolini peering out a second-story window. Skorzeny yelled to Il Duce, "Get away from the window!"[30]

By this time other gliders were making their approach. Skorzeny pushed his way into the main entrance only to be confronted by several heavily armed carabinieri. As they raised their weapons to fire, General Soleti stepped forward and was recognized by the officer in charge. The Italians lowered their weapons, and Skorzeny, without hesitation, continued upstairs to the second floor. Upon reaching the second floor, he ran down the long corridor and threw open the door to Mussolini's room.

Mussolini was surrounded by two Italian officers. Skorzeny ordered them against the wall, and then with the help of Lt. Otto Schwerdt, his third officer, he ushered the Italians out of the room.

Skorzeny then approached Mussolini and introduced himself. "Il Duce, the Fuehrer has sent me to free you."[31] Mussolini hugged Skorzeny and said, "I knew my friend Adolf Hitler would not leave me in the lurch."[32]

Two of Skorzeny's men suddenly appeared at the window. Unable to force their way through the lobby full of carabinieri, they had climbed up the lightning rod and were preparing to enter the room from the outside. Within three to four minutes of their landing, Mussolini was securely in German hands.

Meanwhile Radl had landed in glider 4, and his men were taking up positions on the ground floor. Soon afterward gliders 5, 6, and 7 touched down, and those commando groups also moved to their assigned positions. Glider 8 was not so fortunate. Upon final approach a downdraft forced the glider into the side of the mountain where most of the men were killed or critically injured.

Outside the hotel several shots were fired and Skorzeny realized that the situation was deteriorating quickly. Major Mors's men had still not made their way up the mountain, and without reinforcements Skorzeny and his men were severely outnumbered. Skorzeny demanded to see the Italian officer in charge. Police Inspector Giuseppe Gueli arrived within minutes. Skorzeny gave the Italian sixty seconds to surrender. Gueli left the room momentarily and returned with two glasses of wine. "To the victor!" he said and surrendered the hotel to the Germans.[33] Within minutes of the surrender, Major Mors and his paratroopers arrived at the mountain station. As the Germans gained numerical superiority, the Italians became more and more cooperative, so much so that Skorzeny allowed most of the carabinieri officers to retain their side arms.

With the situation under control, Skorzeny and Mors reviewed the options for returning Mussolini to Rome. "Both he and I considered that it would be too dangerous to travel 150 kilometers by road through an area which had not been occupied by German troops since the defection of Italy. I had therefore agreed with Generalleutnant Student that Plan A should be the sudden coup de main against the Italian airfield of L'Aquila di Abruzzi, at the entrance to the valley."[34]

Unfortunately Plan A was canceled when the radio operator could not raise Rome to request the transport aircraft be sent to L'Aquila.

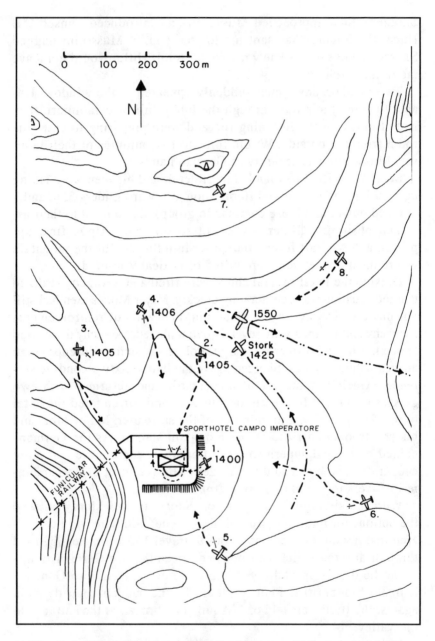

**Fig. 5–4. Glider/Stork Landing Positions on 12 September 1943.
Adapted from National Archives**

Plan B was subsequently aborted when the Stork aircraft that was to land in the valley damaged its landing gear. Finally, it was decided to bring in Captain Gerlach's Stork and land beside the hotel. After several minutes, during which the carabinieri and Germans cleared a makeshift airstrip, Gerlach landed his plane. Although the Fieseler 126 Stork was only built for two passengers, Skorzeny insisted on flying with Gerlach and Mussolini. Gerlach argued vehemently against the idea. It would endanger the entire mission. Skorzeny realized, however, that Mussolini was solely his responsibility. He wrote later about the episode, "Suppose the take-off resulted in catastrophe, my supreme consolation could only be to blow out my brains. How could I ever face Hitler to announce that my mission had succeeded but Mussolini had died shortly after being freed?"[35]

Gerlach relented. "Well, for God's sake come!"[36] After a few moments, Gerlach got in and started the engines. Mussolini crawled into the second seat, and Skorzeny wedged in behind the dictator. Skorzeny's men and some of the carabinieri held the wings and tail section until the engines achieved the appropriate revolutions per minute. At the right moment, Gerlach signaled for the soldiers to release the aircraft. At full power the small plane bumped down the rocky slope, occasionally catching a soft spot in the soil. As the Stork reached the edge of the plateau it fell toward the valley below, gaining airspeed and eventually leveling out. The rescue from Gran Sasso was complete.

Within half an hour the Stork landed at Pratica di Mare Airport where Mussolini was met by Student. Student informed Il Duce that Hitler was expecting him in Vienna. Reluctantly, the Italian dictator boarded a Heinkel 111 for the flight to Austria. Skorzeny, who knew that glory, and his wife, awaited him in Vienna, insisted that he accompany Mussolini. The last leg of the rescue almost turned tragic when the pilot of the Heinkel got lost in the darkness and clouds and flew around aimlessly until midnight before he and his passengers finally landed in Vienna.

Skorzeny checked into the Imperial Hotel. Early that morning a full colonel came to Skorzeny's room. He took off his own Knight's Cross to the Iron Cross and presented it to Skorzeny. Immediately afterward Hitler called to congratulate Skorzeny, saying, "Today, you have carried out a mission that will go down in history. You have given me back my old friend Mussolini. I have given you the Knight's Cross and promoted you to Strumbannfuhrer [major]."[37] This officially ended the mission to rescue Benito Mussolini.

ANALYSIS

Critique
Were the objectives worth the risks? Hitler hoped that by rescuing Mussolini and returning him to the seat of power, he would return Italy to the Axis camp. This never occurred. Although Mussolini was the puppet head of government in northern Italy, he never regained support in Rome. Less than two years later, in April 1945, Italian partisans captured and executed Mussolini, hanging his body in the town square in Milan. One doubts, after reading Skorzeny's post–World War II account of the Mussolini event, that even Skorzeny believed that rescuing Mussolini would really make a difference. He noted several times in his writing the dissatisfaction of the Italian people with fascism and Il Duce. One of the reasons Skorzeny elected not to take Mussolini back to Rome via the roadways was fear of Italian reprisals.

Nevertheless, the mission was well worth the risk. First, it demonstrated that Hitler was prepared to take extraordinary steps to save his friends and allies. Secondly, conducting such a raid showed the professionalism of the German armed forces. Thirdly, the mission may actually have forestalled some Italian resistance in the last two years of the war. Goebbels, the minister of propaganda, used the operation to promote the image of German superiority and instill fear among the Allies, in both of which endeavors he appeared to have succeeded. The mission also set the precedent for future commando operations, including the kidnapping of Miki Horthy, the attempts to assassinate Marshal Tito and General Eisenhower, and the deception operations during the Battle of the Ardennes. Finally, considering that only ten men were killed or wounded (in the glider landing) at a time when thousands of soldiers were losing their lives daily, the risks appear well justified.

Was the plan developed to maximize superiority over the enemy and minimize risk to the assault force? In the Mussolini rescue operation, maximizing conventional superiority would not have improved the chances of rescuing Mussolini. Massing forces at the base of Gran Sasso would only have provided the Italians ample time to kill Mussolini. Gaining relative superiority through the use of a bold plan was the only viable alternative. The Campo Imperatore Hotel was located at sixty-three hundred feet with no approachable avenues on any side. The use of gliders, although risky, was certainly preferable to parachutes. With the drop zone at sixty-three hundred feet, the parachutists would have jumped from a minimum altitude of sixty-eight hundred feet. A low-level drop of this sort presents innumerable problems. For instance, the jumpers would have lost the element of surprise by inserting in a propeller-driven jump aircraft, and the winds at that altitude would have dispersed the jumpers across the drop zone and possibly off the mountain. Even at low levels, the jumpers would have lingered in the air for ten to fifteen seconds. Finally, once on the ground the jumpers would have had to exit their parachutes quickly. In light of the problems of a parachute operation, the use of gliders clearly was the best choice, and it maximized surprise and speed.

The plan took into account the limited sustainability of Skorzeny's glider force by adding Major Mors's parachute battalion. These troops not only reinforced Skorzeny's commandos but provided a large escort force for the return overland trip to Rome.

Even with all these troops, the Italians still could easily have spoiled the rescue. The brilliance of the plan was the use of General Soleti to momentarily confuse them. This deception was the great equalizer and helped Skorzeny minimize the risk to his assault force.

Was the mission executed according to the plan, and if not, what unforeseen circumstances dictated the outcome? The operation was executed according to plan with two exceptions. Only nine of the twelve gliders landed at Gran Sasso. Two were damaged on takeoff and one crashed into the side of the mountain. This did not appear to affect Skorzeny's execution of the mission. With Mussolini in Skorzeny's custody and Mors's paratroopers reinforcing the commandos, Skorzeny was able to carry out his plan. The real dilemma came when both initial extraction plans fell through. Fortunately, the tertiary plan, landing Captain Gerlach's Stork, proved workable.

What modifications could have improved the outcome? Even though the Stork proved a successful extraction platform, Skorzeny could have directed Captain Gerlach to land in the valley and consequently reduced the risk of taking off from a small plateau. Otherwise, the plan was well conceived and well executed. The mission was dominated by security, surprise, and speed but relied heavily on the moral qualities of boldness and courage for the Germans to face down the Italians and quickly seize the objective.

Relative Superiority

The relative superiority graph (Figure 5-5) shows that Skorzeny was able to achieve a decisive advantage over the enemy within minutes of landing by using gliders to gain surprise and the presence of General Soleti to confuse the Italian guards long enough to reach Mussolini. This is particularly impressive considering there were only 9 men in Skorzeny's glider as against 250 guarding Mussolini. Eventually the other gliders arrived to help sustain the advantage, but not until after relative superiority was achieved. Relative superiority was supported throughout the mission by the paratroopers and Skorzeny's acts of boldness, which were so audacious that they reduced the frictions created by the Italians and increased his speed on target.

Gaining relative superiority did not guarantee mission success. Mussolini still had to be returned to Rome, and the first two alternative extraction means were thwarted. Had Skorzeny attempted to return Mussolini to Rome via the overland route, it is conceivable that the Germans could have been intercepted by Italian troops and Mussolini retaken.

Skorzeny's decision to fly Mussolini off Gran Sasso, via the Stork, could have jeopardized the entire mission. But with Mussolini's departure, the tenseness between the Germans and the Italians was immediately relaxed, and the Germans were able to return to Rome by vehicle, unhindered by Italian intervention.

The graph shows the point of vulnerability to be the gliders' final approach to Gran Sasso. This was the first line of defenses the Italians had against an airborne attack. Prior to this time the glider force was in no danger of being engaged by the Italians. Although friction came into play (two gliders were damaged on takeoff), these actions were not imposed by the enemy.

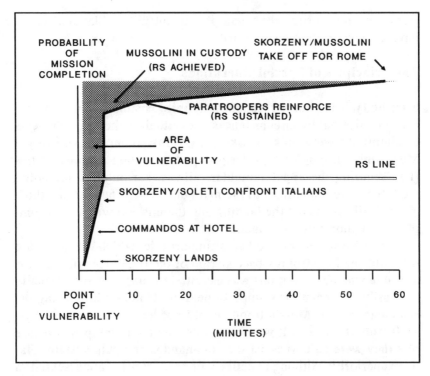

PROBABILITY OF MISSION COMPLETION

MUSSOLINI IN CUSTODY (RS ACHIEVED)

SKORZENY/MUSSOLINI TAKE OFF FOR ROME

PARATROOPERS REINFORCE (RS SUSTAINED)

AREA OF VULNERABILITY

RS LINE

SKORZENY/SOLETI CONFRONT ITALIANS

COMMANDOS AT HOTEL

SKORZENY LANDS

POINT OF VULNERABILITY

10   20   30   40   50   60

TIME (MINUTES)

Fig. 5–5. Relative Superiority Graph for the Rescue of Mussolini

The X-axis shows a total time of one hour. This was the length of time between Skorzeny's glider landing and Mussolini's departure in the Stork. Conceivably one could extend the time frame to two hours to include the return trip from Gran Sasso to Rome. Reaching relative superiority only took four minutes and sustaining it was fairly easy; consequently the area of vulnerability was extremely small. In length of time, the area of vulnerability did not exceed 12 percent of the entire mission. On a graph, Mussolini's rescue is an ideal representation of how the principles of special operations helped achieve success. However without the intervention of the moral factors of boldness, courage, and intellect, the mission would probably have failed. Additionally, the frictions of war, which normally work against the attacking force, worked primarily in Skorzeny's favor. Had gliders 1 and 2 arrived before General Soleti as scheduled, it is highly probable that the Italians would have fought the

Germans. Once a firefight began, it is doubtful that Skorzeny could have achieved relative superiority.

The Principles of Special Operations

Simplicity. The plan to rescue Mussolini was simple, not necessarily by choice but by circumstances. Nevertheless the three elements of simplicity were present. Skorzeny's only objective was to get Mussolini. Although the glider groups had certain responsibilities (i.e., securing the upper funicular railway, surrounding the hotel, etc.), these were ancillary to the main objective. The fact that three gliders failed to make the landing and the mission was still accomplished supports this argument.

Mors's paratroopers also had a support role, which was to secure the valley and control the base station of the funicular railway. It is arguable whether or not this was essential to success.* It is virtually impossible to reach the Campo Imperatore Hotel without using the funicular rail, so Mors's troops could not have conducted the assault from the valley. It was only after the mountaintop was secure that they were able to assist the commandos and help sustain relative superiority. Although ancillary or support roles are essential in most special operations, they should be held to a minimum to reduce the level of command and control.

Intelligence for the raid was far from ideal. However Skorzeny did have an opportunity to conduct a personal reconnaissance of the target prior to execution. Without this aerial reconnaissance, Skor-

---

*There is considerable debate about who was the actual hero of Operation Oak. After the mission was completed Major Mors and General Student both complained that Skorzeny's role was overstated and that the real accolades should have gone to Mors and his parachute battalion. Clearly Mors played a significant role in both the planning and execution of the mission. But it was Skorzeny who conducted the aerial reconnaissance, it was Skorzeny who was the first to land at Gran Sasso, it was Skorzeny who controlled General Soleti, and it was Skorzeny who first reached Mussolini. Whether Skorzeny was a straphanger or the mastermind of the operation is inconsequential. Ultimately, success resulted from Skorzeny's actions at Gran Sasso and not from Mors's.

zeny would have been limited to a travel brochure and a small-scale map of the L'Aquila Valley area, neither of which could have given him the insight needed to develop a simple plan. By seeing for himself the location of the hotel, the triangular landing zone, and the funicular railway, Skorzeny crafted the best plan possible. Not knowing the floor plan of the hotel did cost Skorzeny a minor delay; however, he made up for this loss by storming the main entrance and intimidating the Italians who guarded the hotel.

As discussed earlier, the use of gliders seemed to be innovative, but the alternative options were actually nonexistent. General Student, as head of the XI Air Corps, was well aware of the limitations of parachutists. And Student had used gliders on several other occasions with reasonable success. Although Student's biography implies that he was reluctant to approve a glider assault, he probably realized there were no other viable alternatives.[38]

What was innovative and significantly improved the simplicity of the plan was the use of General Soleti to delay the Italians. This ruse prevented the Italians from engaging the commandos and thereby reduced the obstacles the commandos had to overcome. Had the commandos been required to fight their way into the hotel, the operation might not have succeeded. It is worth noting that this was the first deployment of the paratrooper rifle, FG-42, which was not used, but which if required would have given the commandos a small edge in firepower over the Italians.* The plan to rescue Mussolini used the three elements of simplicity—limited objectives, good intelligence, and innovation—to reduce the frictions of war and improve the opportunity for success.

Security. Throughout the operation to locate and rescue Mussolini, all the participants were conscious of the need to maintain the utmost secrecy. During Skorzeny's first meeting with Hitler at the Wolf's Lair, the führer said, "Your mission to free Il Duce must be

---

*The FG-42 was a 7.92mm gas-operated automatic rifle with a twenty-round magazine, collapsible bipod, and weight of only 9.93 pounds. Also used by Skorzeny's commandos and the paratroopers was the MP-38 9mm submachine gun that had a thirty-two-round magazine and weighed 9.5 pounds.

kept particularly secret. I have ordered, and I give the order to you expressly, that only a total of five persons may know of this plan."[39] Although the number of people privy to the search grew larger than five, it was still confined to those who had a need to know. Even Marshal Kesselring, the theater commander, was not informed.

Skorzeny states in his account of the Mussolini event that every effort was made to disguise the nature of the mission. There were three levels of cover. On the surface, Skorzeny's commandos entered Italy disguised as an element of the XI Air Corps. When this cover was exposed, Student gave Marshal Kesselring another story, claiming Skorzeny's men were on a special commando mission having nothing to do with Mussolini. Satisfied that this story was the "real" reason for the commandos' presence, neither Kesselring nor Italian spies pursued the issue further.

A problem arose, however, when Skorzeny needed to access the intelligence community without exposing the reason for his questions. Even with the assistance of a high-ranking German intelligence officer, intelligence requests had to be vague. Consequently, Skorzeny and Radl had to sift through volumes of information to isolate the location of Mussolini. Even after Mussolini was located, Skorzeny had to keep up pretenses. His flight over Gran Sasso would have been more productive had he informed the German pilot of his reconnaissance needs. And the unwitting doctor who traveled to Gran Sasso, if informed, could have gathered more detailed intelligence on the Italians' position in the valley. Fortunately, these minor inconveniences did not affect the outcome of the mission. Security was tight, but not pervasive. The Italians, who were fully prepared to ward off an attempt to rescue Mussolini, did not gain an advantage through lax German security.

Repetition. There is little historical information on the extent of premission rehearsals. However it is doubtful that Skorzeny's men conducted a full-dress rehearsal prior to landing on top of Gran Sasso. The various aspects of the mission—in particular, the glider and Stork takeoffs and landings and the building assaults—were routine for both the pilots and the ground troops. It is dangerous to single out this mission as an exception to the theory. Although it was indeed successful, there was no enemy resistence. Had there been opposition to the assault, a rehearsal might have made all the difference between success and failure.

Surprise. The Campo Imperatore Hotel rested on a plateau that was no larger than four or five acres. On that small parcel of land were approximately 200 to 250 Italian carabinieri and soldiers. The strength of the Italians' defense was the location of the hotel. The Campo Imperatore appeared to be in the perfect defensive position. It was sixty-three hundred feet above the valley and unapproachable from any direction except by the funicular railway, which was guarded top and bottom by over a hundred soldiers and police. It was probably inconceivable to the carabinieri that any force would attempt an assault from the air, particularly a gliderborne attack into such a small landing zone. Skorzeny effectively exploited the Italians' defensive weakness by using the gliders. However, the real value of surprise was not the glider assault but the use of General Soleti to mentally disarm the carabinieri.

The gliders gained Skorzeny rapid access to the area surrounding the hotel. However, considering that for the first four minutes it was Skorzeny and his eight men against 250 Italians, it is arguable whether the surprise landing achieved any tactical advantage. It must be remembered that only days earlier the Germans and the Italians were allies. The Italians' first instincts were not to shoot the German soldiers. When the carabinieri saw General Soleti with the Germans, they stopped resisting. This allowed Skorzeny time to reach Mussolini and provided time for the remaining gliders to land. Once Skorzeny's men were in control of Mussolini and the funicular railway, the operation was essentially over.

Throughout his military career Skorzeny used tactical deception and acts of extreme bravado to throw the enemy off guard and gain an advantage. Arriving undetected at the objective is not the only way to use surprise to gain relative superiority. An innovative commander will view the entire operation as an opportunity to exercise surprise with the goal of keeping the enemy off balance.

The rescue of Mussolini demonstrates all three elements of surprise: timing, deception, and exploiting the weak points in the defense.

Speed. Skorzeny planned to reach Mussolini within three to four minutes of landing at Gran Sasso. He felt that speed was imperative to ensure Mussolini's survival. As soon as the glider came to a stop, the commandos were moving for the hotel. Unfortunately, premission intelligence did not provide an accurate layout of the hotel, and Skorzeny and his men incurred a short delay in the communications room. This may have proved to be fortunate, for Skorzeny was able to destroy the radio and prevent the Italians from calling for reinforcements.

Skorzeny soon found the main entrance and bullied his way past the Italian guards stationed in the lobby. Approximately four minutes into the mission, Mussolini was in Skorzeny's custody. A minute later, Radl and the remaining gliders began landing and securing their assigned positions. Additionally, Mors and his paratroopers were gaining control of the funicular railway. All of this action transpired within ten to fifteen minutes of the initial landing. Within thirty to forty minutes, the Italians had surrendered, and Mussolini was preparing to depart for Rome. Speed not only reduces the area of vulnerability, it prevents the enemy from raising the level at which relative superiority is achieved. But speed in the face of an uncertain enemy requires a genuine commitment to the purpose of the mission.

Purpose. When Hitler first met with Skorzeny, the führer made it clear that the rescue of "the savior of Italy" was essential to the survival of the Axis.[40] Whether this was the case or not is a moot point. Skorzeny had been ordered by "Adolf Hitler, Führer of Greater Germany and Supreme Commander of the German Armed Forces,"[41] to save "his friend Mussolini."[42] Skorzeny was so moved by Hitler's request that it "almost swept [his] legs from under [him]."[43] When he told his executive officer, Radl, that Hitler had personally entrusted him to rescue Mussolini, Radl was awestruck. These were two young officers who had just been given the mission of their lives, and both knew that failure meant not only personal and professional shame but probably death. Radl told Skorzeny that if they failed, the two SS officers "could always share a padded cell in one of Himmler's special sanatoria."[44]

Skorzeny's sense of purpose is evident from the beginning. He went to unusual lengths to see the mission succeed. While reconnoitering La Maddalena, his plane crashed and Skorzeny broke three ribs. Later, he personally conducted reconnaissance of La Maddalena and Gran Sasso, at great risk to himself. Even after the experts stated that it was folly to attempt a glider landing on top of the mountain, Skorzeny convinced General Student that it was the only way. Had Skorzeny's sense of purpose been any less intense, it is possible the mission may never have begun. General Student, who was a brilliant officer, knew that the possibility of a success- ful glider insertion was slim and that the whole rescue mission rested on the landing's success. Risking an elite German commando unit and his finest paratroopers for what, by now, was an exercise in futility was not Student's way of doing business. It took consider- able persuasion on Skorzeny's part before Student realized "there was no other course."[45]

Once the mission was under way, Skorzeny's determination was evident throughout. He crash-landed on a small patch of turf cov- ered with boulders and then, with his eight men, proceeded to as- sault a hotel guarded by more than two hundred Italians. Skorzeny's sense of purpose, coupled with his extraordinary boldness and cour- age, were without question essential to the success of the mission.

In conclusion, an analysis of the Mussolini rescue clearly demon- strates the principles of special operations and their relationship to relative superiority. However, in this case success was significantly bolstered by the intervention of the moral factors and benevolent frictions of war.

Notes

1. Charles Whiting, *Skorzeny* (New York: Ballantine, 1972), 17.
2. Glenn B. Infield, *Skorzeny: Hitler's Commando* (New York: Military Heritage, 1981), 230.
3. Testimony of Otto Skorzeny at Nuremberg, taken by Lt. Col. Smith W. Brookhart Jr., RG 238, National Archives.
4. Otto Skorzeny, *Skorzeny's Secret Mission*, trans. Jacques Le Clercq (New York: E. P. Dutton, 1950), 50.
5. Skorzeny, *Secret Mission*, 21.
6. Ibid.
7. Ibid., 36.
8. Ibid., 40.
9. "Mussolini Event," Foreign Military Studies, RG 338, National Archives. South Tyrol was annexed during World War II by the Italians and the Austrians never fully forgave them for this act.
10. Ibid., 29.
11. Infield, *Hitler's Commando*, 31.
12. Skorzeny, *Secret Mission*, 48.
13. Ibid., 54.
14. Ibid., 57. It was later confirmed that Mussolini had been aboard the Italian cruiser *Panthere* and then transferred to the naval base at La Maddalena under the custody of Adm. Bruno Brivonesi.
15. "Mussolini Event," 103.
16. Skorzeny, *Secret Mission*, 65.
17. Ibid., 69.
18. Infield, *Hitler's Commando*, 36.
19. Charles Foley, *Commando Extraordinary* (New York: Bantam, 1979), 43.
20. James Lucas, *Kommando: German Special Forces of World War II* (New York: St. Martin's, 1985), 99. It was also learned after the war that Skorzeny and his men had captured two carabinieri officers and tortured them until they confirmed the intercepted radio report.
21. Infield, *Hitler's Commando*, 37.
22. Roger Edwards, *German Airborne Troops* (New York: Doubleday, 1974), 116. The 2d Parachute Division and the 3d

Panzer Division were made available to General Student to help protect Rome and keep vital communication lines open to German divisions in the south of Italy.

23. Foley, *Commando Extraordinary,* 47.

24. Ibid., 48.

25. A. H. Farrar-Hockley, *Student* (New York: Ballantine, 1973), 121.

26. Skorzeny, *Secret Mission,* 86–87.

27. Farrar-Hockley, *Student,* 124.

28. Skorzeny, *Secret Mission,* 87.

29. "Mussolini Event," 311.

30. Ibid., 314.

31. Ibid., 315.

32. Ibid., 316.

33. Ibid.

34. Winston G. Ramsey, "It Happened Here: The Rescue of Mussolini," *After the Battle,* no. 22 (1978): 23.

35. Skorzeny, *Secret Mission,* 102.

36. Infield, *Hitler's Commando,* 44.

37. "Mussolini Event," 138.

38. Farrar-Hockley, *Student,* 121.

39. "Mussolini Event," 24.

40. Ibid., 25.

41. Skorzeny, *Secret Mission,* 40.

42. "Mussolini Event," 25.

43. Skorzeny, *Secret Mission,* 40.

44. Foley, *Commando Extraordinary,* 43.

45. Farrar-Hockley, *Student,* 121.

6

Operation Source:
Midget Submarine Attack on the
Tirpitz, 22 September 1943

BACKGROUND

On 27 March 1942, British commandos attacked and destroyed the Normandie dry dock at the French port of Saint-Nazaire. This action was undertaken to prevent the German battleship *Tirpitz* from sailing from her anchorage in Norway into the Atlantic and then seeking refuge at Saint-Nazaire. The Normandie dry dock was the only facility in the Atlantic capable of repairing the fifty-three-thousand-ton vessel, and the Germans would not risk exposing the *Tirpitz* to action without being assured of adequate repair facilities. Nonetheless, the *Tirpitz,* the sister ship of the *Bismarck,* still threatened the North Sea and required constant attention by both British and American forces to keep her in check.[1]

After the raid on Saint-Nazaire, several plans were formulated to sink the *Tirpitz* in Norway, but by early 1943 Winston Churchill was getting impatient and wrote to his chief of staff, General Ismay, "Have you given up all plans for doing anything to *Tirpitz* while she is in Trondhjem? We heard a lot of talk about it five months ago, which all petered out. At least four or five plans were under consideration. It seems very discreditable that the Italians should show themselves so much better at attacking ships in harbour than we do . . . It is a terrible thing to think that this prize should be waiting and no one be able to think of a way of winning it."[2]

Unbeknownst to Churchill, the British admiralty had been working for two years on developing a midget submarine capable of penetrating the Norwegian fjords and winning the prize. In early May 1941 volunteers were recruited "for special and hazardous duty." These men, including Lt. Don Cameron, who would later participate in Operation Source, were instrumental in the development and construction of the first operational X-craft. Originally conceived by Cromwell Varley of Varley Marine, Ltd., the X-craft midget submarine was constructed by three different shipbuilders who independently built the bow, center, and tail sections. Twenty other contractors were responsible for the internal workings of the craft. This distribution of effort resulted in a submarine whose "design was a little unsound in many respects."[3]

The first submarine available for trial was the *X-3*, built under extreme secrecy and launched on 19 March 1942. Upon completion of *X-3*'s trials, the midget submarine was sent by rail to the submariners' new base at Port Bannatyne, Scotland, subsequently renamed HMS (His Majesty's Station) Varbel. In the meantime, additional volunteers were recruited and began to be screened for suitability. They were sent to the submarine base HMS Dolphin at Gosport, England, where they underwent six weeks of screening that included physical training, six one-hour dives in a nearby lake, and "theoretical" courses on the *X-3* submarine. Most of the men were unaware of the nature of the operation.

In mid-January 1943 six more midget submarines designated *X-5* through *X-10* were delivered. The 12th Submarine Flotilla was formed under Capt. W. E. Banks to coordinate with RAdm. C. B. Barry (whose title was Rear Admiral, Submarines) on the "'training and material of special weapons'; and to his flotilla *X-5–X-10* were attached, with *Bonaventure* [Acting Capt. P. Q. Roberts, R.N.] as their depot ship."[4]

The *X-5* series was larger and better designed than the prototype *X-3*. It was fifty-one feet long and weighed thirty-five tons fully loaded. It had an external hull diameter of eight and one-half feet except directly under the periscope, where it extended an additional few inches. The internal space was significantly shorter and more cramped with a diameter of five feet, nine inches. The only place a man could stand up was underneath the periscope.

The craft was divided into four compartments. The forward space was the battery compartment that provided power for all electrical equipment in the X-craft, including the pumps, lights, and main motor. The second compartment was the wet/dry chamber and head (bathroom). This space was used to lock out the diver who would be tasked with cutting antisubmarine or antitorpedo nets. The third compartment was the control room. Inside this small space the crew piloted the X-craft by a simple system of wheels and levers that controlled the helm, hydroplanes, and main ballast tanks. The control room had two periscopes used by the conning officer; a short wide-angle periscope for night operations while surfaced, and a slender, telescopic attack periscope for while submerged daytime operations. The control room also served as the galley where the crew could heat up tin cans or boil a pot of water for tea or coffee. The aft compartment contained the main motor used for submerged propulsion and a London bus engine that normally propelled the X-craft on the surface but could be used for submerged operations at periscope depth.

Submerged, the craft cruised at two knots with a top speed of five and one-half knots. On the surface it could make six and a half knots depending on the sea state. Being a diesel submarine, the X-craft submerged only when absolutely necessary and spent most of the night surfaced to recharge batteries. When surfaced the captain would normally trim the craft so that it barely protruded above the water. This reduced the visual signature and radar cross section and allowed the captain to lie along the outer casing of the submarine and conn the craft from the surface. This technique, however, was seldom used for a variety of reasons.*

---

*Commander Richard Compton-Hall, the curator of the Royal Submarine Museum and a former X-craft commanding officer, stated in a letter to the author that the captain would only lie down on the casing when "in extremis." The induction mast, which also served as a voice pipe to the control room, had to be lowered for the captain to talk with the helmsman. When this happened there was always the possibility of water going down the mast. Additionally, the captain was prone to being washed overboard in such an exposed position.

The X-craft was capable of conducting dives to over three hundred feet, but most of the submerged cruising was around sixty feet.* The midget submarine was equipped with two viewing ports that allowed the captain to observe the diver, who would normally stand on the X-craft while cutting through antitorpedo nets. These ports had steel shutters that could be closed during deep dives or depth charge attacks.

The X-craft was specifically designed to attack the *Tirpitz* at her berth in Norway, so it had no torpedoes, rockets, or surface guns. These weapons would be useless in a confined area like the fjord. The X-craft did come equipped with two side charges (referred to as side cargos), one on each side, each composed of two tons of amatol high explosive. The charges were contoured to the outer hull and made neutrally buoyant.

Thomas Gallagher explained in *The X-Craft Raid* that "when a side charge was released [by turning what looked like an ordinary steering wheel inside the X-craft], a copper strip between the hull and the charge peeled off, unsealing the buoyancy chamber and allowing enough water to enter to make the charge negatively buoyant."[5] The charge, now negatively buoyant, would sink to the bottom of the fjord below the *Tirpitz*. A timer was installed to allow the X-craft crew to dial in the desired delay and extract before the explosive detonated.

Admiral Godfrey Place, commander of *X-7*, was not completely satisfied with this configuration. "We at the time really thought . . . if we made the charge positively buoyant to go upwards it would stick to it [the *Tirpitz*] without any problem . . . we would really have preferred to have the charges floating upward, but the explosive experts claimed that it was better to send it [the side charge] down to the seabed to make the sort of tamping effect to create a vast explosion over a longer area. Our outlook was a little doubtful. We'd rather have blown a darn great hole in the thing."[6]

---

*Admiral Place, in a letter to the author, stated that the hull could withstand depths of 300 feet or more; however, the rate of blowing would make it fairly "dicey" to come up from even 150 feet.

The biggest drawback of the midget submarine was its limited endurance. The published specifications indicated that the range was fifteen hundred miles at four knots, but in reality the range was limited by human duration. Although a crew of four was able to exist inside the craft for extended periods, they were not able to actually operate the controls for much farther than three hundred miles while submerged. The conditions were just too physically taxing. This forced the Royal Navy to tow the X-craft (with passage crews inside that merely maintained the depth) for the first twelve hundred miles from Scotland to the release point off the Norwegian coast. This towing effort presented several problems during the actual mission, but it was still felt to have been an effective way of getting the X-craft from Scotland to Norway.

During the course of the next several months, plans were prepared for attacking German shipping in three separate operational areas of Norway. This would allow for any change in German berthing plans. On 11 September 1943, six conventional submarines would tow the six X-craft from Loch Cairnbawn, Scotland, to a position 75 miles west of the Shetland Islands and then follow routes 20 miles apart until they were approximately 150 miles from Altenfjord. At this point the submarines would navigate to their assigned release points off Soroysund (Soroy Sound) and prepare to detach the X-craft. A change from passage to operational crew was authorized for any time past 17 September when the weather and tactical conditions allowed. The entrance to Soroysund was extensively mined by the Germans. Nevertheless, the Royal Navy planned the following:

"The X craft were to be slipped in positions 2 to 5 miles from the mined area after dusk on D Day [20 September], when they would cross the mined area on the surface and proceed via Stjernsund to Alten Fiord, bottoming during daylight hours on 21st September. All were to arrive off the entrance to Kaa Fiord at dawn 22nd September and then entering the Fleet anchorage, attack the targets for which they had been detailed. These would be allocated by signal during the passage, in the light of the most recent intelligence."[7]

The conventional submarines were to return to their patrol sectors and await the return of the X-craft. If no rendezvous were effected, the submarines were to proceed to one of the bays on the north coast

of Soroy and attempt a link-up on the nights of 27–28 and 28–29
September. As a tertiary plan the X-craft crews were authorized to
proceed to the Kola Bay in Russia, and a British minesweeper would
be looking out for them between 25 September and 3 October.

THE BATTLESHIP *TIRPITZ*

The *Tirpitz* was commissioned in December 1940, but not actually completed until February 1941. She was the largest battleship
of her time with an overall length of 822 feet and a beam of 118
feet. Fully loaded, the *Tirpitz* displaced fifty-three thousand tons
with a draft of thirty-six feet. The ship was powered by twelve boilers in six separate compartments. These boilers produced 163,000
shaft horsepower, allowing the battleship to reach speeds in excess
of thirty knots. Topside the *Tirpitz* was equipped with eight 15-inch
guns and twelve 5.9-inch guns for surface action. For air defense
she had sixteen 4.1-inch, sixteen 37mm, and eighty 20mm antiaircraft guns. Additionally, the *Tirpitz* carried four Arado reconnaissance and light-bomber aircraft.

Although the topside armament was impressive, it did not unduly
concern the X-craft crews. What did matter to the planners of Operation Source was the *Tirpitz*'s hull, which was encased in twelve-
inch steel at some locations. This steel band protected the battleship
in strategic areas including her control room amidships, boilers and
turbine rooms, gunnery control rooms, electrical controls, and
magazines. This steel protection coupled with the interior steel
bulkheads made the *Tirpitz* invulnerable to torpedo attack, and 5.9-
inch steel decks protected her vital areas from high-altitude bombing. However, thirty-six feet below the waterline, the *Tirpitz* keel
remained a soft underbelly. It was this weakness that the British
hoped to exploit.

The *Tirpitz* and her battle group, which included the twenty-six-
thousand-ton *Scharnhorst* and several destroyers, were berthed in
Kaafjord, Norway, which was located well above the seventieth
parallel and over twelve hundred miles from Scotland. Surrounded
by steep, virtually treeless mountains, the fjord was fed by waters
from the Gulf Stream, which kept it ice-free year around. For most

of the year the ground was covered with snow, and the sun remained high on the horizon. When the snow did melt, it sent mountainous slabs of ice crashing into the water, creating a brackish environment of fresh and salt water.[8]

Using the terrain as a natural fortress, the Germans placed radar stations and antiaircraft batteries on the mountaintops and flew fighter aircraft to protect the fleet from British bombers. In the fjords, the three islands of Stjernoy, Altafjord, and Altenfjord funneled intruders into a channel where antisubmarine nets were placed and picketboats patrolled the waters. As extra protection in the unlikely event that a submarine negotiated the channel or a dive-bomber attempted a suicide run in the Kaafjord Valley, an antitorpedo net surrounded the high-value targets preventing any possible damage. The net, which completely surrounded the *Tirpitz,* was constructed of woven steel grommets and was capable of stopping a torpedo moving at fifty knots. Based on aerial photos and reports from Norwegian resistance, British intelligence believed that the net only extended sixty feet down from the surface. It was not apparent that the Germans had actually constructed three nets, one that extended from the surface to 40 feet beneath the surface and two more that reached to the seabed 120 feet below. To augment all these precautions, the Germans added smoke screen equipment to conceal the battle group and patrolled the surrounding roads and villages to prevent Norwegian resistance from conducting reconnaissance or sabotage operations.

Intelligence on the target area was difficult to obtain. Kaafjord was well outside the combat radius of British-based aircraft. Consequently, the Royal Air Force (RAF) arranged to have the Soviets construct an airfield outside Murmansk. From here Mosquito reconnaissance planes, flown by the RAF, could photograph the fjord and develop the film immediately upon return to Russia. The processed film was returned to England via Catalina long-range aircraft. Norwegian resistance based at Kaafjord collected detailed intelligence on the daily habits of the officers and crew. They were able to determine picketboat patrol routes, identify net defenses, watch general-quarters drills, and most importantly ascertain the maintenance schedules of the guns and sonar equipment. The two main Norwegian agents were Torstein Raaby and Alfred Henningsen. After the war Raaby joined Thor Heyerdahl and the crew of *Kon Tiki* on their famous voyage across the Pacific, and Henningsen later became a member of the Norwegian parliament. Together these men compiled an accurate description of the target area and secretly transmitted the information back to England.

LIEUTENANTS DONALD CAMERON AND GODFREY PLACE

There were several men who distinguished themselves throughout Operation Source, but the two officers who received most of the credit for the mission's success were Lts. Don Cameron and Godfrey Place. Both men received the Victoria Cross for the actions against the *Tirpitz.*

Cameron, after serving a year with the merchant navy, joined the Royal Navy Reserve on 22 August 1939. He spent another year in general service and then on 19 August 1940 received orders to HMS Dolphin, the submarine school in Gosport, England. Upon completion of submarine training, he reported to HMS *Sturgeon* at Blyth, spending the next nine months conducting operations in the North Sea. In May 1941, a call for volunteers sent Cameron back to HMS Dolphin where he joined in the development of the first X-craft, eventually commanding *X-6* during the attack on the *Tirpitz.*

Throughout Operation Source Cameron kept a personal diary that provides a chronological account of the training and actual mission. Cameron was exceedingly dedicated to the cause for which the X-craft were built and employed, and he worried that during the course of the mission he might somehow fail that cause. He wrote, "I have that just-before-the-battle-mother feeling. Wonder how they [the crew)] will bear up under fire for the first time, and how I will behave though not under fire for the first time . . . I can't help thinking what the feelings of my next of kin will be if I make a hash of the thing."[9]

His close friend Comdr. Richard Compton-Hall later said, "Like all of us, he was afraid of the unknown and especially of possible failure, of letting people down, rather than of being afraid of the enemy."[10]

Cameron and his crew, Lt. W. S. Meeke and Chief E. R. A. Richardson, were caught during the operation and imprisoned in a German POW camp for the remainder of the war. Cameron was repatriated in May 1945 and was subsequently assigned to HMS *Surf* as additional lieutenant. Following duty on the *Surf,* Cameron was assigned to several other submarines before he received command of the HMS *Tiptoe* in May 1947. Three years later he returned to HMS Dolphin and in 1951 took command of another submarine, the HMS *Trump.* In 1955 Cameron returned to HMS Dolphin for the final time and was assigned as Commander, Submarines. Although Cameron served many tours after the war with the submarine service, he never fully recovered from his wartime internment. His health, which had been poor prior to Operation Source, deteriorated in the POW camps. He died unexpectedly in 1962.

Godfrey Place was graduated from the Royal Navy's college at Dartmouth and commissioned in September 1938. He received posting to submarines after serving on the cruiser HMS *Newcastle.* His initial submarine training began at HMS Elfin and upon completion in 1941, he was assigned as the spare officer at Saint Angleo. Later in 1941, Place received orders to the Polish submarine *Sokol* out of Malta. Upon his departure from *Sokol,* Place was awarded the Polish Cross of Valor for combat service. After several short tours, Place joined the crew of the HMS *Unbeaten* in February 1942. While on combat patrol in the eastern Mediterranean, Place brought *Unbeaten* to periscope depth only to find a German submarine directly off his bow. He later recalled, "I called the Captain and we went to diving stations. I think it was something like 45 seconds from first sighting to firing the torpedo, under continuous wheel [constantly maneuvering] and in fact we got two hits."[11] German airplanes escorting the submarine converged on *Unbeaten* and began to pursue her. The submarine lay on the bottom for twenty-four hours before she escaped. Place was awarded the Distinguished Service Cross for his actions.

In August 1942, he joined the 12th Submarine Flotilla and began training with the X-craft. One year later, as commander of *X-7,* he attacked and disabled the *Tirpitz.* Like Cameron, Place was captured during the action and was interned until May 1945. While in the POW camp, he was awarded the Victoria Cross. Upon his return to England, Place left submarines and went on to become a pilot in the fleet air arm of the Royal Navy. He had a distinguished military career, being promoted to rear admiral on 7 January 1968. He retired in 1970 and was made a Companion of the Bath (C.B.).

X-CRAFT TRAINING

By August 1942, most of the volunteers had been screened, and those that met the standards were sent to HMS Varbel at Port Bannatyne, Scotland, to begin training. Varbel was the old Kyles Hydropathic Hotel and shooting lodge.* Prior to the war it was a health spa with numerous baths for rheumatic patients. Although Loch Striven, which formed Port Bannatyne, had always been restricted for submarine use, there was some concern about the lack of security surrounding the X-craft training effort. There were no guards or barbed wire, and the X-craft were moored in plain sight of local townspeople. This business-as-usual approach seems to have prevented tourists or townsmen from becoming overly curious as to the base's operations. Nevertheless, the submariners tried to remain as inconspicuous as possible. The locals thought the X-craft was a newly designed, high-speed craft, so during daily operations the crew would wait until they were completely out of sight before diving the X-craft. Their support ship, initially the HMS *Alecto* and then the HMS *Bonaventure,* remained anchored in Loch Striven away from prying eyes, and while in town all the officers and crew stayed in civilian attire. Additionally, a cover story was developed to coincide with their daily routine. The X-craft crews were instructed to tell the townspeople they were testing a new rough-water speedboat.

Within a few months HMS Varbel began to be filled with prospective X-craft crews, including four Australians and two South Africans. The trainee officers learned how to conn and navigate the

---

*Varbel was actually a fabricated name derived from Commander Varley, who designed the original X-craft, and Commander Bell, the training commander.

craft as well as to simultaneously operate the hydroplanes, wheel, pumps, and main airline. The conditions inside the X-craft were so cramped that from the control room the captain could touch any of the four crewmen without taking a step in any direction. Navigation was exceedingly difficult as condensation built up inside the midget and the charts became soggy. The captain learned to navigate based on time and used shaft revolutions to determine his speed and distance. Although all of the crew learned to use the wet/dry chamber, an enlisted man was assigned as the primary diver. The diver practiced exiting and entering the two-foot hatch, and he learned to cut every conceivable antitorpedo and antisubmarine net known to the British. This procedure required the diver to exit the midget and, using a hydraulic cable cutter attached to the X-craft, begin cutting the net from the bottom up with the final cut done while standing on the bow of the midget. After extensive practice, the crews could cut a net in under seven minutes.

During the early months, *X-3* was the only midget available for training, and she was used by all the crews to conduct day and night dives. In November, John Lorimer, one of the first X-craft volunteers, was conducting a day dive with two new officers when the snorkel jammed open upon diving, allowing water to rush in. The wheel spanner used to blow the main ballast tanks was accidentally dropped into the bilges, and the *X-3* immediately began to fill with water, taking on an eighty-five-degree down angle. Within a minute the *X-3* was at the bottom of Loch Striven in 110 feet of water. The flooded battery compartment began to give off chlorine gas and soon after, the midget submarine lost all electrical power.

Lorimer, who was only twenty years old at the time, quickly directed the two officers to don their emergency breathing apparatus. The oxygen in the breathing apparatus was limited to forty minutes, and at one hundred feet it would be some time before the X-craft flooded completely and the three men could exit. With only minutes to spare the aft hatch was forced open and the men escaped. On the surface the diver-support vessel, *Present Help,* picked up the three officers. Upon returning to HMS Varbel, the two new officers involved in the accident requested orders back to the regular navy. Later that evening, the HMS *Tedworth,* a salvage ship, arrived and raised the *X-3.*

The *X-3* was sent off for repairs, and *X-4* arrived soon after with Lt. Godfrey Place as the commander. In December 1942, Place was conducting endurance trials in Inchmarnock Water, to the north of the Isle of Arran. Topside was Sublieutenant Morgan Thomas, *X-4*'s first lieutenant. Without warning, an ice formation broke off from the cliffs surrounding the loch. The resulting wave washed Thomas overboard and he drowned. Additionally, the wave flooded the escape compartment, causing *X-4* to take on a ninety-degree down angle. Although almost perpendicular in the water, the *X-4* remained afloat with Place and the other crewman, W. M. Whitley, separated by the wet/dry compartment and unable to communicate. Four hours later at the routine communication time, Place managed to transmit an emergency signal to the *Present Help,* located nearby in Loch Ranza. It took another two hours before the *Present Help* could tow *X-4* to safety, bail out the wet/dry compartments, and release Place and Whitley. As a result of the accident, several modifications were made to the X-craft, including a buckle for the topside watch stander and a device for closing the hatch from inside the control room.

In late December, *X-5* was launched at Faslane, Scotland, and *X-6* arrived on 11 January 1943. These new production boats were built from scratch and were significantly better designed than the prototypes. By March, *X-7* was finished, and the three X-craft were placed aboard the support vessel HMS *Bonaventure* and sent to Loch Cairnbawn to conduct tow training with the passage crews.[12]*
Warren and Benson in *The Midget Raiders* observed:

> It is not often realized how big a part these men [the passage crews] play in the success of an operation. Towing at high speed [it was sometimes as much as eleven knots] is far from being an easy or even a particularly safe job and it is very far from being a comfortable one. It calls for a high degree of alertness under trying conditions for several days [ten days] at

---

*Towing training was done by any vessel that could be commandeered into service. This included the occasional submarine and the vessels *Present Help* and *Fidele.*

a time. In addition it calls for constant attention to the vital routine duties of mopping up moisture, testing, and if necessary, repairing every item of equipment in the craft. To a considerable extent the success of an operation depends upon the condition in which the craft is turned over to the operational crew . . . The best analogy that can be given is that they correspond to a diving watch in a large submarine [except that they are continuously on watch for days, without a break] and like the diving watch of a big submarine they are relieved when the crew goes to action stations.[13]

The tow training was exceedingly arduous and therefore rarely extended beyond a day or two. The procedure called for the passage crew to submerge and then level out at about forty feet below the parent submarine's keel depth. Unfortunately the speed of the tow and the size differential caused the midget to porpoise constantly and made life inside the X-craft miserable. The way to avoid this constant depth change was to set the hydroplanes at the correct angle and ballast the craft a little heavily. However, if the towline broke, the ballast and the weight of the towline could cause the X-craft to plunge before the passage crew could correct the problem. Throughout all the extensive workups the X-craft were never towed for the full duration of the expected mission. Admiral Place later regretted this oversight.

What we never tried, though, really, was the length of tow, which was actually the best part of the mission. It was over a thousand miles and . . . the longest [tow] took nearly ten days. So that was our fault . . . We couldn't really spare ten days just towing the boats out to sea to do the approach. But that was the trouble. In those small boats there are so many things that can go wrong. You have an odd valve or two go bad, or be unlucky, and it gets damp inside and you get shivering . . . It never occurred to us that the tows could part . . . we didn't discover until afterwards . . . those [towlines] weren't tow tested.[14]

During every six hours of a tow, the midget would surface to replace the stale air and recharge the air bottles. This normally was limited to about half an hour. Depending on the sea state, the time on the surface could be more unpleasant than porpoising. In either case, the tow would be an exceptionally challenging aspect of the mission.

In April, the newly launched *X-8* through *X-10* replaced *X-5, X-6,* and *X-7* in Loch Cairnbawn. *X-5* through *X-7* returned to Port Bannatyne to continue training new crews and conduct advance exercises with the designated operational crews. In May, the crew of *X-7* was conducting net-cutting training when Sublieutenant David Locke was lost at sea while attempting to cut through an antisubmarine net. Locke was a submariner but not a qualified diver. After this incident the decision was made to add a fourth man to the X-craft crew, specifically for this task.

Throughout the summer of 1943 the passage and operational crews continued training. All six midgets were now fully incorporated into the plan and exercises were conducted simulating the actual mission. Success during these exercises bolstered the confidence of the crews.

Godfrey Place recalled, "I think we were quite confident. It seemed to be quite simple really. All six boats attacked the harbor in Loch Cairnbawn in the north of Scotland . . . and going through a fictitious channel . . . that more or less approximated the fjord—all six boats got into the harbor, attacked, and weren't detected at all."[15]

On 30 August 1943, all six X-craft, the *Bonaventure,* the *Titania* (submarine tender), and the six towing submarines arrived in Loch Cairnbawn for final training. Between 1 and 5 September, each parent submarine was paired off with its midget for towing exercises that included transferring the crews at sea and recovering the X-craft. Following these exercises the midgets conducted a final calibration of the compass and were then hoisted aboard the *Bonaventure* for loading of the side charges. While aboard the *Bonaventure,* the crews received their final briefings. As the official battle summary recounts, however, "At this stage of course, it was by no means certain where the enemy would be found, but the indications were that Alten Fiord was the most probable spot, and in order to reach this area by D Day it was necessary for the submarines to leave 11th–12th September."[16]

Rear Admiral Barry, Commander, Submarines, arrived at Loch Cairnbawn on 10 September to conduct an inspection of the X-craft and parent submarines. It was not a cursory inspection but an exacting look at the midgets and their crews. Barry concluded that the midget submariners were

> like boys on the last day of term, their spirits ran so high. Their confidence was not in any way the outcome of youthful daredevilry, but was based on the firm conviction, formed during many months of arduous training, that their submarines were capable of doing all that their crews demanded of them, and the crews were quite capable of surmounting any difficulties or hazards which it was possible for human beings to conquer. It was in this spirit that they went out into the night in their tiny craft to face a thousand miles of rough seas before they reached their objective, which itself, to their knowledge, was protected by every conceivable device which could ensure their destruction before they completed the attacks.[17]

THE ATTACK ON THE *TIRPITZ*—11–22 SEPTEMBER 1943

The battle summary noted that "at 1600, 11th September, the *Truculent* towing X-6, and the *Syrtis* with X-9, sailed from Loch Cairnbarn, followed at intervals of about two hours by the *Thrasher* with X-5, the *Seanymph* with X-8, and the *Stubborn* with X-7. The *Sceptre* with X-10 did not sail till 1300, 12th September."[18]

As each craft departed Loch Cairnbawn, cheers from the support vessels *Bonaventure* and *Titania* encouraged them onward. Barry, his staff, and the commanding officer of the 12th Submarine Flotilla, Capt. W. E. Banks, were also on hand as the X-craft set sail. This launch culminated eighteen months of training—training that had resulted in the death of three men. But if the X-craft were successful, it could save thousands of Allied lives.

After departing Cairnbawn, the submarines traveled independently until they were approximately seventy-five miles west of the Shetland Islands. Once at the Shetlands they proceeded on parallel courses ten miles apart. They were to maintain this relative position until 150 miles from Altenfjord.

The first four days of the transit were relatively uneventful. The weather remained clear and the seas calm. The parent submarines had paid out about two hundred yards of towline, but even with this separation the X-craft ascended and descended as much as sixty feet on a routine basis. The passage crew had to keep a constant vigil on the midget to ensure it did not lose control and suddenly plummet downward. As Gallagher recounted in *The X-Craft Raid*:

> In addition to seasickness, the three men in each X-craft had to endure appalling discomfort during passage. Dampness penetrated their clothing, wet their hair, and seemed to narrow the already cramped space they shared. Able to sleep only in snatches, they had to work constantly to keep the craft in condition for the operational crew. There were electrical insulations to be checked, motors to be tested, machinery to be greased and oiled, bulkheads and hull plates to be wiped of condensation, records to be written, readings to be made on all the electrical circuits, and meals to be prepared.[19]

The X-craft surfaced three or four times a day for periods of fifteen minutes, during which time the parent submarine would slow to three knots. Communications between the midget and parent was maintained (usually at two-hour intervals) through a telephone cable inserted into the towline. This unique feature required the towlines to be handmade. Consequently, when nylon lines were introduced late in the workups, there was not enough time to outfit each midget with a nylon tow. The older manila towlines were attached to *X-7*, *X-8*, and *X-9*.

On the fifth day of the transit, 15 September, at 0100, the manila towline separated and the crew of *X-8* lost communications with their parent submarine, the *Seanymph*. *X-8* immediately surfaced but was unable to locate the *Seanymph*. At 0430, the commander of *X-8* decided to proceed on the original course of 029 degrees. The *Seanymph* did not discover the parted line until two hours later when she surfaced to allow *X-8* to ventilate. At 0600 the *Seanymph* reversed her course in an attempt to find the missing X-craft.

The *Stubborn*, towing *X-7* and running on the adjacent parallel path with *Seanymph*, surfaced around noon to ventilate. After several minutes on the surface, the watch sighted a "U-boat," and both parent and midget submerged to avoid detection. Unbeknownst to the *Stubborn,* the U-boat was the lost *X-8.* An hour later the *Stubborn* surfaced and the U-boat appeared to have departed. At 1550, the watch aboard *Stubborn* noticed the manila line used to tow *X-7* had parted as well. Fortunately, the passage crew noticed the break and surfaced. Although the weather was "rough to very rough," the crews had trained for such a contingency, and the towline was quickly refastened.

After securing the line and testing the tow, *Stubborn* prepared to submerge. But moments before diving, the watch spotted *X-8,* "flogging around on the surface." *Stubborn* proceeded to the midget's location and directed *X-8* to follow. By 1900 the weather was too bad to remain surfaced, so the three submarines, *X-7, X-8,* and *Stubborn,* submerged and began to transit to *Seanymph's* location.* Before submerging, the commander of *Stubborn* had shouted the course to *X-8.* Unfortunately, the commander of *X-8* misunderstood the course and steered 146 degrees instead of 046 degrees. At dawn, when *Stubborn* surfaced, *X-8* was nowhere to be found. Fourteen hours later, however, *X-8* managed to effect a rendezvous with *Seanymph,* ending their troubles for a while.

Meanwhile the *Syrtis* and *X-9* were conducting an uneventful passage, even though they had lost communications the previous day. Every six hours the X-craft would surface and pass or receive any vital information. At 0920 on 16 September, when *Syrtis* surfaced, the *X-9* was not attached to the towline. *Syrtis* executed a search for a day, but *X-9* was never found. Although the cause of the accident was unknown, it was suspected that the crew ballasted the *X-9* too heavily. When the towline broke there wasn't enough "spare boat-blowing capacity" to bring it to the surface. The towline, which was exceptionally heavy, was attached to the bow of the X-craft and very difficult to release from the inside, particularly during an emergency descent. Although the midget was never found, the *Syrtis* sighted a "well defined" oil slick paralleling the track the *X-9* had been steering. For years there was some hope that

---

**Stubborn had radioed Rear Admiral, Submarines, and requested that they contact *Seanymph.* All messages to Rear Admiral, Submarines, were made in individual one-time pads and therefore could not be deciphered.

the crew had made the Norwegian coast and rendezvoused with the resistance. This, however, was not the case. *Syrtis* signaled Rear Admiral, Submarines (Barry), with the news and was directed to proceed in company with the other parent submarines to assist where possible.

On the morning of 17 September, *X-8* began to have difficulty maintaining trim. The starboard side charge was taking on water, and it was decided to jettison the ordnance and proceed with only the portside charge. At 1635 the commander of *X-8* set the charge on safe and released the two tons of explosives. Fifteen minutes later, when the *X-8* and *Seanymph* were approximately one thousand yards away, the ordnance detonated. The explosion damaged the seal between the port charge and the X-craft. This caused the midget to list to port. After agonizing over the decision, the commander elected to release the second side charge with a two-hour delay. Nevertheless when the charge detonated on time at 1840, the ensuing concussion badly damaged the *X-8,* flooding the wet/dry compartment, fracturing pipes, and buckling the watertight doors. The X-craft was finished. The crew disembarked on the morning of the eighteenth and the *X-8* was scuttled. Earlier, on 16 September, when the fate of *X-8* seemed precarious at best, "the Rear-Admiral, Submarines, had signalled to the *Seanymph* and *Stubborn:*—'Should at any time you consider it necessary to sink X 8 in order not to prejudice the operation, this step would have my full approval. 162208A.' Rear-Admiral Barry subsequently remarked:—'I consider that the Commanding Officer of X 8 acted correctly in releasing the side charges when it became apparent that they were flooded, and that the Commanding Officer, H.M.S. *Seanymph*'s decision to sink X 8 to avoid compromising the mission was the correct one.' "[20]

On 19 September only four X-craft remained operational. During the transit Rear Admiral, Submarines, had transmitted their attack orders. The *X-5, X-6,* and *X-7* would attack the *Tirpitz, X-8* would attack the pocket battleship *Lutzow,* and *X-9* and *X-10* would attack the battle cruiser *Scharnhorst.* With *X-8* scuttled, the *Lutzow* was no longer a viable target, and with *X-9* lost, *X-10* would have to attempt the *Scharnhorst* alone.

That evening the *Truculent,* towing *X-6,* arrived at its release point off Soroy Island, which was well inside the Arctic Circle. The poor weather subsided, and the seas were good for transferring the passage and operational crews. There was a sense of excitement and fear among the operational crew. John Lorimer, second in command of *X-6*, wrote, "I can almost remember losing my nerve. Then the dingy came alongside the stern of Truculent and . . . I felt much better, the seamen wishing me 'Good luck,' and 'See you in two days' time sir.' "[21] When the operational crew boarded the *X-6*, they found that one of the ballast tanks was cracked, the starboard side charge was beginning to take on water, and the periscope gland was leaking. These "minor" problems did not unduly disturb the operational crew and after the transfer of personnel, *X-6* began its two-day voyage toward Kaafjord. Two other X-craft, *X-5* and *X-10*, also transferred their operational crews and began their passage up the fjord.

Stubborn, towing *X-7,* was delayed a few hours owing to the incident with *X-8.* While they were transferring the operational crew, a floating mine lodged on the bow of *X-7* a few feet from the starboard side charge. Lieutenant Place exited the midget and made his way to the bow. Once on the bow, he calmly dislodged the mine by kicking it free. The commander of *Stubborn* later relayed this story to Admiral Barry, and it became a bit of submarine legend. Place, however, is quick to point out that he noticed the horn on the mine had been crushed, indicating it was inoperable.

By 2000 on 20 September, all four X-craft had slipped their tows and were proceeding to their assigned targets. The tracks for *X-5, X-6,* and *X-7* were almost identical (*X-10* proceeded along an alternate path toward the *Scharnhorst*), yet the midgets never caught sight of one another. The X-craft negotiated the minefield off Soroy Island and entered the Stjernsund Channel without much trouble. By daylight they were cruising on the surface toward Altafjord. The weather was bright and sunny with a light breeze, and the channel was free of traffic.

Intelligence indicated that the best place for the X-craft to lie up during the night of the twenty-first was Brattholm Island, a small isolated outcrop that was within ten miles of the *Tirpitz.* As the midgets approached the island, the traffic began to increase. The midgets were required to dive frequently to avoid detection. At 1630, *X-7* sighted the *Scharnhorst,* and although he was tempted to attack, Place proceeded as ordered to Brattholm Island.

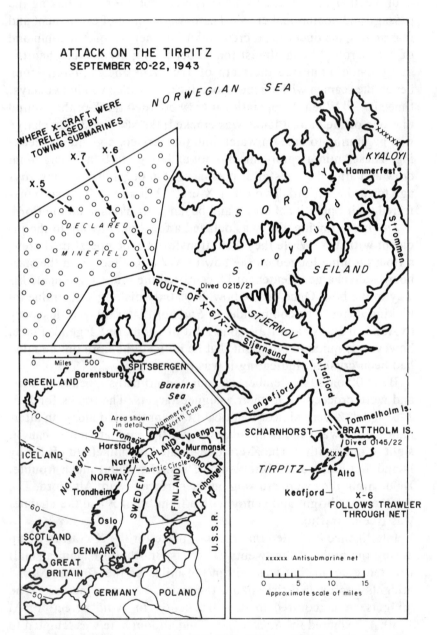

Fig. 6–1. Route of *X-6* and *X-7* from Release Point to Kaafjord

The *X-6,* which also made Brattholm by evening, was experiencing difficulties with her periscope. The packing gland was leaking severely and required maintenance throughout the voyage. This attack periscope would be essential during the final approach on the *Tirpitz.* Without it the crew was blind and any attack would have to be conducted by gyroscope alone. Additionally, *X-6* had "a nasty list to starboard" compounded by a flooded side charge. The crew of *X-6* attempted to repair the problems but had limited success. That night the two X-craft remained surfaced in secluded areas of the island and charged batteries before the final leg of the attack. Periodically, the midgets submerged to avoid detection, but it was more precautionary than required.

On 22 September at 0145, *X-6* departed Brattholm and began the ten-mile approach on the *Tirpitz.* With a partially flooded periscope, the commander, Lieutenant Cameron, dived to sixty feet and dead reckoned toward Kaafjord, the site of the *Tirpitz.* The weather was perfect for an attack. There were low clouds and rough seas punctuated by occasional rain showers. The first obstacle was the submarine net located at the mouth of Kaafjord. Cameron planned to approach the net at forty feet, lock out his diver, and maintain his position there until the diver cut an opening. Once the craft was through, the diver would be retrieved, and the X-craft would proceed into the inner harbor.

As *X-6* approached the antisubmarine net, the diver, Dick Kendall, suited up and prepared to enter the wet/dry chamber. Kendall had practiced this procedure dozens of times, but it was never a pleasant experience. He said later, "You're shut up in a space about the size of a water main with a lid over your head. You sit there, cold and lonely, waiting for the water to come up. You long for it, but you can't let it in too fast because there's a limit to what the body can stand. It takes about four minutes, and then when you're completely covered and all the air is gone, the force on your body terminates in a sudden, final squeeze as the pressure inside equalizes with the pressure outside. It's like a nasty kick in the head from a mule."[22]

It was now 0400 and the sun was just up. Less than half a mile from the net, Cameron ordered the midget to periscope depth to get one final look. As he looked through the periscope he realized his chances for success were diminishing quickly—the periscope was fully flooded. He wrote in his diary, "We had waited and trained for two years for this show and at the last moment faulty workmanship was doing its best to deprive us of it all. There might be no other X-craft within miles. For all I knew, we were the only starter, or at least the only X-craft left. I felt very bloody minded and brought her back to her original course . . . It might not be good policy, we might spoil and destroy the element of surprise, we might be intercepted and sunk before reaching our target, but we were going to have a very good shot at it."[23]

Cameron dove to sixty feet. Inching his way along, he removed the periscope eyepiece and cleaned it once again. As he approached the antisubmarine net he brought the X-craft to thirty feet. The crew was prepared to cut their way through the net when Cameron heard the propellers of a ship overhead. In a very risky move, he ordered the X-craft to the surface and proceeded "full ahead on the diesel." X-6 passed right through the parted net in the wake of a small coaster. No alarm was raised, and after-action reports indicate X-6 went undetected. Had Cameron come to periscope depth instead of surfacing, the X-craft would have been too slow to pass through the nets before they closed.

Earlier in the evening at just past midnight, X-7 had left Bratt-holm and by 0400 had slipped through a large boat passage in the antisubmarine net. Now both X-6 and X-7 had only one more obstacle to overcome, the antitorpedo net. Place and Cameron had two different plans for overcoming the net. Place intended to dive deep and go under the net. Cameron's initial plan was to cut through the net.

Once through the antisubmarine net, X-6 was only three miles from the Tirpitz. Cameron slowed the boat to two knots and maintained a depth of seventy feet. A final check of the periscope showed it had flooded again. Cameron stripped down the lens and dried the prism for the last time. Unfortunately the leak was on the outer casing and no amount of cleaning would last for long. After refitting the lens, Cameron came to periscope depth. There he could see a tanker refueling two destroyers and beyond them the Tirpitz. He took a bearing on the Tirpitz and dove to thirty feet. The water in the fjord was a mixture of fresh and salt, and it made it difficult to maintain proper depth. Even with this problem the crew was reluctant to operate the pumps for fear of being detected by hydrophones.

From the submarine net to the stern of the tanker took *X-6* over an hour. Coming up for one final look, Cameron almost collided with the cable connecting the destroyer to her mooring buoy. Diving quickly he avoided the cable and remained undetected. Moments later an electrical fire broke out in the control room, filling the small space with smoke. The crew reacted instantly and extinguished the fire. Cameron looked around the control room and took stock of his crew and X-craft. It had been almost thirty-five hours since *X-6* had released from the parent submarine. The crew was physically exhausted from the cold and lack of sleep. The periscope was almost completely flooded, the hoisting motor was burned out, they were listing fifteen degrees to port, and a steady stream of bubbles followed them throughout their transit.

Cameron did not know the status of the other two X-craft assigned to attack the *Tirpitz*. If he decided to continue with the attack, it would have to be completed no later than 0800. This was the time when the side charges would explode if the other X-craft had succeeded. He realized that *X-6* and her crew would not survive eight tons of explosives at close range. If he turned back now there was a chance of scuttling the midget and escaping across the mountains toward Sweden. The Royal Navy had provided escape and evasion equipment necessary to exist for a short while. This included boots, clothing, compasses, maps, medical supplies, handguns, food, and money. Cameron knew, however, that beyond the mountains lay a vast expanse of arctic wilderness in which the submariners would probably not survive. Cameron consulted the crew as to whether they wanted to continue the mission with the X-craft in such poor condition. There was very little discussion and the decision was made to continue on.

Godfrey Place, in *X-7,* had crossed the antisubmarine net and was proceeding toward the *Tirpitz* when the X-craft was forced deep by a picketboat on patrol. While avoiding detection, *X-7* ran afoul of a discarded section of antitorpedo netting once used to protect the *Lutzow.* Place spent an hour executing a series of pumping and blowing maneuvers before *X-7* finally broke free. Unfortunately, the actions damaged the gyroscope and trim pump, and within minutes the X-craft was caught again on a stray cable. Finally, by 0600 *X-7* was free from the entanglement and heading toward the anti-torpedo net and the *Tirpitz*.

At 0707 *X-6* reached the northern end of the antitorpedo net and luckily found the small boat gate open. According to Comdr. Richard Compton-Hall, "This gate was guarded by hydrophones and a special guard boat but, unwisely, the Germans stood down the guard at 0600. At 0700 [actual time 0707] Cameron slipped through the narrow entrance, keeping just shallow enough to see the surface through the glass scuttles in the pressure hull."[24]

Once through the gate the X-craft was within a hundred yards of the now-unprotected *Tirpitz*. Unknown to Cameron, *X-7* arrived at the southern end of the antitorpedo net at 0710. Place, having been informed that the net only extended to sixty feet, dived to seventy-five feet and attempted to go under the obstacle. The intelligence estimates on the net defenses had been wrong. There were actually three nets, each forty feet long. In his after-action report Place wrote:

Seventy-five feet and stuck in the net. Although we had still heard nothing, it was thought essential to get out as soon as possible, and blowing to full buoyancy and going full astern were immediately tried. X.7 came out, but turned beam on to the net and broke surface close to the buoys . . . We went down immediately . . . and the boat struck again by the bow at 95 feet. Here more difficulty in getting out was experienced, but after five minutes of wriggling and blowing she started to rise. The compass had gone wild and I was uncertain how close to the shore we were; so we stopped the motor, and X-7 was allowed to come right up to the surface with very little way on. By some extraordinary luck we must have passed under the nets or worked our way through the boat passage for, on breaking the surface, I could see the *Tirpitz* right ahead, with no intervening nets, and not more than 30 yards away . . . '40 feet.' . . . 'Full speed ahead.' . . . We struck the *Tirpitz* on her port side approximately below 'B' Turret and slid gently under the keel. There the starboard charge was released in the full shadow of the ship . . . '60 feet.' . . . 'Slow astern.' . . .

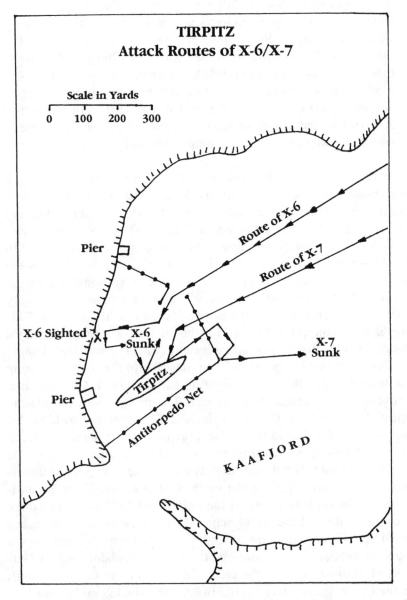

Fig. 6–2. X-Craft Attacks on the *Tirpitz*

Then the port charge was released about 150 to 200 feet farther
aft—as I estimated, about under 'X' turret . . . After releasing
the port charge [about 0730] 100 feet was ordered and an al-
teration of course guessed to try and make the position where
we had come in. At 60 feet we were in the net again . . . Of the
three air-bottles two had been used and only 1200 pounds [less
than half] was left in the third. X-7's charges were due to explode in an hour—not to mention others which might go up
any time after 0800 . . . In the next three-quarters of an hour
X-7 was in and out of several nets, the air in the last bottle
was soon exhausted and the compressor had to be run.[25]

In the meantime, the watch aboard the *Tirpitz* had spotted *X-6*
and shouted the alarm. Fortunately for the X-craft, the *Tirpitz* was
constantly conducting antisubmarine and antiswimmer drills, and
the crew had become complacent. The chief of the watch questioned the crewman's sighting, and it was not until 0712, when
X-6 broke the surface eighty yards abeam of the battleship, that the
Tirpitz's crew was energized. Even with this sighting, the actual
alarm did not sound until 0720. When the alarm was eventually
sounded, the crewman on the bridge issued five short blasts. This
signal was incorrect and called for the crew to man their watertight
doors, as if the *Tirpitz* had hit an iceberg. This created considerable
confusion and added to the delay in reacting to the X-craft. During
the time between the second sighting and the alarm, Cameron maneuvered *X-6* underneath the *Tirpitz*. The midget got entangled in
wires dangling from the port side, and Cameron had to blow his
way out. As *X-6* shot to the surface, the craft was engaged by small
arms and hand grenades from the crew of the *Tirpitz*.

Cameron submerged immediately and backed the X-craft underneath the *Tirpitz*'s hull, in the vicinity of B turret. There he jetti-
soned his two side charges, set the timers for 0815, then ordered the
crew to destroy all the secret material. It was clear now that escape
was impossible. Cameron surfaced for the last time, opened the sea
cocks to scuttle *X-6,* and ordered the crew to abandon ship. A German picketboat captured the crew and attempted to tow the X-craft
to the beach. Fortunately for the British, the sinking midget was too
heavy, and the Germans had to cut the towline. *X-6* sank to the bot-

tom. Cameron and his men were taken aboard the *Tirpitz.* They felt certain the Germans would have them shot. Instead, however, the crew of the *Tirpitz* was relatively hospitable and offered the British coffee and schnapps. At 0812 when the charges detonated, however, the captain immediately ordered the four crewmen of *X-6* shot as saboteurs. Fortunately, he changed his mind.

Meanwhile *X-7* was attempting to escape. Lieutenant Place stated in his after-action report:

> At 0740 we came out while still going ahead and slid over the top of the net between the buoys on the surface. I did not look back at the *Tirpitz* at this time as this method of overcoming net defenses was new and absorbing . . . We were too close, of course, for heavy fire, but a large number of machine-gun bullets were heard hitting the casing. Immediately after passing over the nets all main ballast tanks were vented and we went to the bottom in 120 feet. The compressor was run again, and we tried to come to the surface or to periscope depth for a look so that the direction indicator could be started and as much distance as possible put between ourselves and the coming explosion. It was extremely annoying, therefore, to run into another net at 60 feet. Shortly after this [0812] there was a tremendous explosion. This evidently shook us out of the net, and when we surfaced it was tiresome to see the *Tirpitz* still afloat.[26]

The explosion left *X-7* "a bit of a mess inside" with water rushing in quickly, the compass and periscope broken, and only one light functioning. Place sat on the bottom of the fjord momentarily, trying to decide the best course of action. He wanted to beach the X-craft but was concerned about "giving the enemy full knowledge of the boat."[27] Place later recalled, "We all decided that we weren't really going to do any good at all by going on. So I thought the safest thing was for us to try to [surface and] get out . . . If we were being shot at it was up to me to go outside [and risk being shot by the Germans]."[28]

Place exited the X-craft first, waving a white sweater to signal surrender. As he jumped from the midget into the water, the force of his weight pushed the small X-craft underwater. The inrush of water forced the crew to secure the hatch, and *X-7* sank to the bottom. Place didn't know why the midget sank. "Whether they, the first lieutenant took the boat down or whether it hadn't got enough buoyancy lift, I don't know."[29] Place was taken to the *Tirpitz* and fully expected the crew of *X-7* to exit the craft using the emergency lock-out procedures.

"See," Place told the author, "I'd briefed them carefully on doing an [emergency] escape . . . They'd practiced diving and things . . . We tried so many submarine escapes I think what went wrong was they were too slow flooding up and on oxygen if you're slow flooding up you get oxygen poisoning."[30]

Unfortunately, the deep depth of the fjord forced the crew to wait for forty-five minutes before the internal pressure could equal that of the sea. During that time, the oxygen in their breathing apparatuses was exhausted, and only one crewman, Sublieutenant Robert Aitken, escaped.

The eight tons of amatol that exploded underneath the *Tirpitz* did not sink the battleship, but it did severely damage all three main engines, all lighting and electrical equipment, one generator room, the hydrophone station, antiaircraft control positions, port rudder, range-finding equipment, and both B and X turrets. One German was killed and forty wounded as over five hundred tons of water rushed into the interior compartments of the battleship. As a result of the action, the *Tirpitz* never went to sea again. She was eventually towed to another berth off Haakoy Island where RAF Lancaster bombers sank her in place.

The surviving crews of *X-6* and *X-7* were imprisoned in German POW camps and eventually repatriated after the war. The fate of *X-5* remains a question to this day. Cameron said he saw the Germans sink *X-5* with their heavy guns, but a postwar search of the fjord only found *X-6* and *X-7*. It is more likely that *X-5* never made Kaafjord. To Place it didn't matter. He said later, "It doesn't to me make much of a difference whether he attacked or didn't attack . . . Henty Creer [commander of *X-5*] was a jolly good chap and I know he did the best he possibly could."[31]

X-10, whose target was the *Scharnhorst,* had mechanical difficulties and decided not to attack the pocket battleship for fear of compromising the rest of the operation. The crew of *X-10* eventually rendezvoused with her parent submarine, scuttled *X-10,* and returned to England. The *Seanymph* and *Sceptre* remained in their patrol sectors until 4 October in the event that some of the X-craft crews escaped.* They returned to Lerwick, Scotland, on 7 October, and Operation Source was officially ended. Admiral Barry later remarked,

> I cannot fully express my admiration for the three commanding officers . . . and the crews of *X-5, X-6,* and *X-7* who pressed home their attack and who failed to return. In the full knowledge of the hazards they were to encounter, these gallant crews penetrated into heavily defended fleet anchorages. There, with cool courage and determination and in spite of all the modern devices that ingenuity could devise for their detection and destruction, they pressed home their attack to the full . . . It is clear that courage and enterprise of the very highest order in the close presence of the enemy was shown by these very gallant gentlemen, whose daring attack will surely go down to history as one of the most courageous acts of all time.[32]

ANALYSIS

Critique
The primary objective of Operation Source was to sink the *Tirpitz,* and although the battleship did not settle on the bottom of Kaafjord, it was disabled sufficiently to render it ineffective. One would have to conclude, therefore, that the mission was a success. The failure of *X-5, X-8, X-9,* and *X-10* to reach their targets, and the inability of *X-6* and *X-7* to escape undetected, may have been due, in large part, to the Royal Navy's not having conducted a full-mission profile during the preparation phase. If a ten-day towing exercise had been conducted during the preparation phase, the mechanical failures that manifested themselves during the assault (e.g., periscope leakages, ballast and trim problems, towline

*The British were unaware of the status of *X-5, X-6,* and *X-7* until several months later, and therefore Rear Admiral, Submarines, ordered the *Seanymph* and *Sceptre* to remain on station to pick up possible survivors.

breakages, etc.) could have been identified prior to the mission and possibly corrected. This might have made the difference between escape and capture for the crews of *X-6* and *X-7* and life and death for the crews of *X-5* and *X-9*. What eventually salvaged the operation was the professionalism of the crews, honed by months of repetitive training, and their boldness and perseverance in pressing home their attacks.

Were the objectives worth the risk? While the *Tirpitz* was in Trondheim, she had direct access to the Norwegian Sea and along with the *Scharnhorst* and *Lutzow* was capable of severing or damaging the maritime link between England and Russia. Just weeks before the X-craft raid, the *Tirpitz* and her escorts had attacked and leveled the entire 150-man Norwegian garrison at Spitsbergen, a strategically vital island east of Greenland. The *Tirpitz*'s guns had also destroyed a meteorological station, supply depots, thousands of tons of coal, shiploads of fuel, and a large port facility that supported the British fleet. This action caused concern, not because of the devastation, but because it meant that the British were unable to contain the *Tirpitz* and that it could sortie out into the Norwegian Sea and wreak havoc, apparently at will.

For almost a year the British, Russians, and Americans had been attempting to sink the *Tirpitz*. Even if she had never left her secure harbor for the rest of the war, the battleship would have presented a threat that could not be ignored. Although Operation Source cost the British seven dead and six captured, the *Tirpitz* never posed a significant problem again. The risks were clearly warranted.

Was the plan developed to maximize superiority over the enemy and minimize risk to the assault force? Operation Source began with one goal in mind—sink the *Tirpitz*. The air defense system surrounding Kaafjord was exceptionally dense, and even if a bomber had penetrated the antiaircraft guns, it would have had to drop torpedo bombs to pierce the hull where the ship was least armored. Both feats were highly unlikely. It became evident that there was only one way to deliver enough ordnance to destroy the battleship, and that was by submersible. Consequently, the X-craft was designed specifically for this mission. There were devices to counter the antisubmarine and antitorpedo nets, specially designed attack periscopes, and side charges with enough explosives to buckle the hull. Everything about the plan was aimed at maximizing the relative superiority of the X-craft. However, minimizing the risk in a submersible operation is difficult because to be exposed is to be captured or killed. Nonetheless, the British did everything they could to reduce this risk. They provided extensive intelligence to the planners, properly prepared the crews, and supported the effort throughout the operation.

Was the mission executed according to the plan? If not, what unforeseen circumstances dictated the outcome? The British were unable to fully execute the objectives of Operation Source due to the difficulties encountered while towing the midgets across the Norwegian Sea and owing to the defensive envelope that surrounded the *Tirpitz.*

On the open-ocean crossing, *X-9* was lost at sea when the towrope between the parent submarine and the X-craft parted. *X-8* had to be scuttled when she sustained damage, also related to a parted towrope. This meant that only *X-10* would be available to attack the *Scharnhorst* and *Lutzow*. *X-10* subsequently had mechanical problems and elected not to compromise the main objective (attacking the *Tirpitz*) by attempting to sink the *Scharnhorst.* Consequently, none of the secondary targets were engaged by the midgets of Operation Source.

The plan to sink the *Tirpitz,* however, was adhered to more closely. All three midgets, *X-5, X-6,* and *X-7,* were released approximately on time and began their transit without incident. Although the fate of *X-5* is unknown, the other two X-craft arrived on time at the target. Unfortunately the *Tirpitz* was well protected by a massive antitorpedo net, and although both X-craft cleared the net and placed their charges, their inability to escape was almost preordained. The charges were set to explode less than one hour after placement. This provided no time for the X-craft to extract. The antitorpedo net, which had been relatively easy to enter (in both cases a matter of good fortune), was almost impossible to exit without exposing the midgets. Even if the two X-craft had escaped undetected, it is unlikely they would have gotten very far after the ordnance exploded at 0812. There were several hours of daylight remaining. The Germans could have sealed off the fjords, pursued the X-craft, and captured their quarry fairly quickly in the clear waters of the fjord.

What modifications to the plan could have improved the outcome? The major problem with the plan was having to tow the X-craft across the Norwegian Sea. Although this was unavoidable, it should have been rehearsed more fully and all the towropes should have been nylon or double-wrapped manila. To this day, Admiral Place also questions the viability of dropping the side charges underneath the *Tirpitz* as opposed to having the charges float upward against the ship's hull. He wrote, "Why didn't the *Tirpitz* sink? Several of us questioned the wisdom of releasing the [side cargos] to fall to the sea bed rather than having them float upwards to stick on the bottom of the target. The technical problem of ensuring they stick is easily solved. We were assured the 'tamping effect' would do more damage than simply blowing a hole—*I remain unconvinced.*"[33] The Italians, who used a three-hundred-kilogram contact explosive, did more damage to the British battleships in Alexandria than the X-craft's side charges of eight tons (total) did to the *Tirpitz.** It would appear Place's assumptions were correct. Had the side charge demolitions been positioned as desired, the *Tirpitz* and her crew would have quickly settled to the bottom of Kaafjord, and the X-craft might have escaped.

Relative Superiority

As Figure 6-3 shows, the X-craft (both *X-6* and *X-7*) reached the point of vulnerability at approximately 0400 when they encountered the first of the German defenses, the antisubmarine net. Although the midgets had relative superiority by virtue of their concealment, they were now within the envelope of detection, and the operation hinged on maintaining that clandestine posture. Unfortunately, clearing the antisubmarine net did not dramatically improve their chances of success; the midgets were still three hours from the target and the sun was coming up. Even though the enemy was not

---

*Two of the three Italian crews succeeded in placing their charges on the hulls of their targets. One of the crews, Durand de la Penne and Bianchi, left their charge on the bottom close to the hull. Nevertheless, the bottom of Alexandria Harbor was only a few meters below the HMS *Valiant,* whereas the bottom of Kaafjord was almost one hundred feet below the *Tirpitz.*

Tirpitz Attack

333

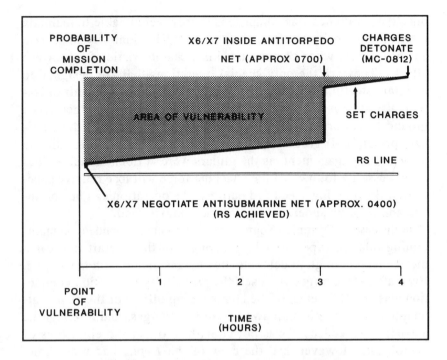

Fig. 6–3. Relative Superiority Graph for the X-Craft Raid on the *Tirpitz*

aware of the X-craft's presence, the area of vulnerability continued to expand because the midgets' probability of detection was increasing, and time was beginning to take its toll on the submersibles' subsystems (i.e., ballast and trim, electrical, periscope, etc.).

At approximately 0700 (three hours after reaching the point of vulnerability), the X-craft penetrated the final obstacle, the antitorpedo net, and their degree of relative superiority improved significantly. Once they were inside the net, there was nothing the crew of the *Tirpitz* could do. There were no weapons in the *Tirpitz* inventory that could stop the X-craft that close to the ship. The massive guns were not able to train down on the midgets, and the *Tirpitz*'s crew was equipped with only small arms and grenades, neither of which could penetrate the steel hull of the X-craft. Once inside the antitorpedo net, all the crew of the X-craft had to do was release their side charges and escape. Unfortunately for the X-craft crews, once their presence was compromised they were unable to maintain relative superiority to effect their escape. This inability to sustain an engagement when compromised is a characteristic of subsurface attacks. They are the only special operations that are designed to maintain stealth throughout the engagement. Ground and air operations use stealth only as a means to gain access to the target. Once ground forces are on target, speed, not stealth, becomes the dominant principle. If ground operations are compromised immediately prior to the engagement, as the gliders were at Eben Emael, it does not necessarily follow that the attacking force will lose relative superiority. By applying speed and purpose, the operation can be continued and relative superiority gained and maintained.

In the case of Operation Source, success was not dependent on maintaining relative superiority long enough for the X-craft to escape, merely long enough to detonate the charges underneath the *Tirpitz*. Even after the charges were set, the probability of mission completion was not 100 percent. The commanding officer of the *Tirpitz* attempted to move his ship away from the charges, and although he partially succeeded, it was not enough to offset the eight tons of demolition. However, had the crew of the *Tirpitz* had more time, they could have completely negated the effects of the demolition by sailing from their anchorage. Relative superiority was maintained at this point by setting the time fuse on the side charges for only forty-five minutes, instead of four hours (to allow ample time for the X-craft to escape). At approximately 0812 the eight tons of demolition exploded, and the *Tirpitz* was rendered inoperable.

What makes the outcome of Operation Source so unusual is that it succeeded in spite of the large area of vulnerability. What should be clear, however, is that given another thirty minutes of vulnerability, *X-6* would not have reached its objective. It was also this large area of vulnerability that probably affected the fate of *X-5*. Had we constructed a relative superiority graph prior to the operation and viewed success as recovery of the X-craft aboard the parent submarines, we would have seen a significant problem with the mission. From the time we reached the point of vulnerability until the time we recovered, the area of vulnerability would have constituted just under 50 percent of the mission. That is not to say that reaching a certain percentage of vulnerability automatically constitutes failure, but it should be a warning to the planners that the greater the area of vulnerability, the greater the frictions of war and the greater the possibility of failure.

Principles of Special Operations

Simplicity. During the planning phase of Operation Source, the Royal Navy constructed six X-craft and assigned each to a single target. This allowed the crews to concentrate on one objective. When *X-8* and *X-9* were put out of action, the Royal Navy remained committed to limiting the objectives. Instead of requiring *X-10* to conduct attacks on both the *Scharnhorst* and *Lutzow,* the navy struck the *Lutzow* from the target list and continued with a focused attack. Although *X-5, X-6,* or *X-7* could have been siphoned off to attack the *Lutzow,* this would have deviated from the final plan, reduced the size of the force attacking the *Tirpitz* (the primary target), and created more confusion.

The intelligence available to the crews of the X-craft was sufficient for the task but could have been better. They had extensive overhead photos, charts, hydrographic and astronomical data, schematics of the targets, and information on the guard routines; and the X-craft crews also knew that the German ship's hydrophones were scheduled to be down for repairs. This detailed intelligence picture of the objective area allowed the Royal Navy to devise a plan that minimized the forces, employed effective tactics to circumvent German defenses, and used technology specifically tailored to the objective.

The one intelligence failure was the inaccurate analysis of the antitorpedo net surrounding the *Tirpitz.* Intelligence estimates concluded that the antitorpedo net extended to a maximum of sixty feet deep. Consequently, Place planned to overcome this obstacle by diving to seventy-five feet and going under the nets. Although divers were trained to cut through the net, this was not a viable option. Place later recalled, "I personally never really visualized we were going to have to cut through the net. There was very little hope of cutting English antitorpedo nets [much less German nets] because it was hardened steel, and it's such a confusion of chain mail there that knowing where to cut is almost impossible."[34]

Place exercised good judgment in planning to go under the net. It was likely that the net would only extend to sixty feet. No "officer who possess a standard of judgement" would have assumed that an antitorpedo net would extend to the bottom of the seabed. Antitorpedo nets were designed to stop either air-dropped or submarine-launched torpedoes, neither of which were capable of diving under a sixty-foot-deep net and then homing on their targets. Therefore, even the best planner would probably not have foreseen this situation. This is a prime example of the frictions of war: poor intelligence sometimes combines with an unforeseen circumstance to create a situation for which one cannot plan or prepare. Even with perfect intelligence and the simplest of plans, one cannot foresee all the possibilities. Fortunately for the crews, they were able to overcome this obstacle and continue on with the mission.

Building on the intelligence picture, the Royal Navy created the X-craft for the purpose of defeating German defenses and sinking the *Tirpitz*. The use of new technology during Operation Source was essential to the mission's success. Previous attempts by British chariots (manned torpedoes) to sink the *Tirpitz* had failed, primarily because the chariots (limited by range and diver exposure) required a support ship to insert them into the immediate vicinity of the target. This failure spurred the requirement for a longer duration, dry, midget submarine. The design of the X-craft considered all the operational parameters of this specific operation. The X-craft was small to negotiate the fjords and penetrate the antisubmarine nets. It was equipped with a wet/dry chamber to lock out the divers to cut the antisubmarine nets, and it had an assault periscope so slender that it barely rippled the calm waters around Kaafjord. Most importantly the X-craft carried two two-ton side charges specifically designed to destroy the fifty-three-thousand-ton *Tirpitz*. By limiting the objective to a single target, focusing the intelligence effort on that objective, and developing new technology to counter the defenses, the planners reduced Operation Source to its simplest form. When asked if he had any reservations about the plan, Godfrey Place responded, "No. I think we were quite confident. It seemed to be quite simple, really." The planning phase, however, was just the beginning, and a simple plan does not equate to a successful operation without a great deal of preparation.

Security. Security was always a concern to the planners of Operation Source; however, it only mildly affected the daily operations of the X-craft crews. When they were training at HMS Varbel in Scotland, the operating area was relatively isolated. Precautions were taken to limit the exposure of the X-craft and their support ships, and the crews were provided a shallow cover story to tell the local townspeople. This notwithstanding, the Germans were fully prepared (antisubmarine and antitorpedo nets as well as daily anti-swimmer drills) to defend the *Tirpitz* against subsurface attacks from both conventional submarines and chariots.* The security for Operation Source, therefore, need only have concealed the time frame of the operation and the unique capabilities of X-craft. This is not to imply that additional security was inappropriate; the less the enemy knew about the forces and means of employment, the better the chance the mission would succeed. In Operation Source, however, security was secondary to proper preparation and the need for repetitive training.

Repetition. As we noted in chapter 1, John Lorimer, a crewman aboard *X-6*, when referring to repetitive training, said, "If you are going to do anything dangerous, the best way to accomplish it is to train, train, train, so that in the excitement of the situation you do the thing automatically."[35]

Operation Source had an advantage not normally associated with special operations: the crews had almost eighteen months to train, from 19 March 1942 until 5 September 1943. Although some of this

---

*Operation Arthur, the attempted attack by British chariots on the *Tirpitz*, failed when the two chariots broke free from their support vessel (*Arthur*) and sank in the fjords. Most of the charioteers and the Norwegian resistance escaped across Norway to Sweden. Unfortunately one of the British frogmen, Bob Evans, was wounded by German police and captured. He was subsequently interrogated and finally shot as a spy. This event occurred in November 1942, almost a year prior to Operation Source. In light of Evans's capture and the success of the Italian manned torpedoes in the Mediterranean, the German defenses at Kaafjord were consistent with the probable threat.

training was basic familiarization, the largest portion was mission-specific. In the early months *X-3* and *X-4* were rotated weekly among the crews to conduct individual training. With the arrival of *X-5* through *X-10* in January through March 1943, each crew conducted daily training in preparation for the mission. Each aspect of the mission was rehearsed multiple times. This included passage training, net cutting, ship attack profiles, emergency procedures, escape and evasion training, and several limited mission profiles against nearby port facilities. As stated earlier the only shortfall in the preparation phase was the lack of a full-mission profile including a full tow. Repetition is essential to the success of any mission; however, repetition based on unrealistic profiles builds a false confidence that erodes quickly during an engagement. Some of the confidence exuded by the X-craft crews fell victim to problems that could have been identified through a more thorough training program: for example, *X-8*'s and *X-9*'s towline breakage and *X-10*'s mechanical problems. Nevertheless, the philosophy of train, train, train insured that four of the six X-craft successfully transited the Norwegian Sea and commenced their insertion into Norway on time. Then it was a matter of reaching the objective and surprising the enemy.

Surprise. The four X-craft that motored into Soroysund on the morning of 20 September 1943 all knew that the element of surprise was absolutely essential to the success of the mission. It was for this reason that Lt. Ken Hudspeth, whose *X-10* was mechanically unsound to operate effectively, decided not to attack the *Scharnhorst*. Hudspeth knew that if his X-craft were compromised prior to the other midgets' arriving on target, it would destroy his companions' chances. One of his crewmen reported later, "Ken Hudspeth asked each of us whether we wanted to go in and do the attack and we all said, 'Yes.' But after consideration he said that we would be bound to be seen and that this would not only do us little good but might also spoil the chances of the others, which was more important."[36]

Hudspeth elected to remain on the bottom (at 195 feet) outside Kaafjord until the window for attacking the *Tirpitz* passed. If he heard no explosions by 0900, he intended to attack the *Scharnhorst* and attempt to complete his mission.

Place and his crew in *X-7* achieved complete surprise, bypassing the antitorpedo net at approximately 0715 and releasing the side charges at 0730. It is conceivable that had *X-6* not alerted the crew of the *Tirpitz*, *X-7* could have escaped. Unfortunately, *X-6* was spotted entering the antitorpedo swing gate at 0707, but confusion aboard the *Tirpitz* provided an additional five minutes before the crew began to react. Although surprise was not complete, the enemy was unprepared to react effectively, which provided Cameron in *X-6* sufficient time to release his charges. Subsurface attacks have several advantages; however, as a rule, sustainability in the face of combat is not one. Once attacks are compromised, speed and purpose become everything and the opportunity for escape vanishes.

Speed. Speed in a subsurface attack must be balanced against the need to maintain surprise. If the attacker can remain undetected, then speed is only a function of the subsurface platform's duration. This phenomenon is more prevalent in a swimmer or manned torpedo attack, where the duration of the diving rig and the temperature of the water directly affect the attacking element's sustainability. In the case of Operation Source, however, speed was important because the mechanical difficulties (damaged periscope, ballast and trim problems, broken gyroscope) that plagued *X-6* and *X-7* became worse with time. Cameron, who had initially planned to cut through the antitorpedo nets, decided it would take too much time, time that would degrade his material condition and reduce the probability of success. Disregarding the risk, Cameron surfaced *X-6* behind a picketboat passing through the antitorpedo net gate. What he lost in surprise he gained in speed. Once through the gate it took the crew of *X-6* only ten minutes, from 0707 until approximately 0717, to reach the *Tirpitz* and release the side charges. The *X-7*, which remained undetected throughout the engagement, took only fifteen minutes to complete its mission once inside the antitorpedo net. Surprise and speed assured relative superiority, but it was the sense of purpose that assured success.

Purpose. In Operation Source, as in all special operations, the men involved in the assault must both understand the primary purpose of the mission and be personally committed to seeing it completed regardless of the costs. The primary purpose of Operation Source was to sink the *Tirpitz*. Everyone from the enlisted divers aboard the X-craft to Rear Admiral, Submarines, understood that, and they always remained focused on what was important. Beginning with the loss of *X-9*, the Royal Navy acted with the primary purpose in mind by not reducing the number of X-craft assigned to attack the *Tirpitz*. The *Tirpitz* was, after all, the primary target. Reducing the number of X-craft might have limited the damage sustained by the *Tirpitz*.

Later in the operation, Hudspeth showed he understood the primary purpose of the mission when he made a command decision not to attack the *Scharnhorst*. He had been ordered, as had the commanders of *X-8* and *X-9*, not to compromise the mission before *X-5*, *X-6*, and *X-7* had an opportunity to make their assaults on the *Tirpitz*. A compromise by Hudspeth would have alerted the nearby crew of the *Tirpitz*, and neither *X-6* nor *X-7* would have penetrated the antitorpedo nets. Place understood the purpose when he bypassed the *Scharnhorst* to remain on schedule to attack the *Tirpitz*. It was exceptionally difficult to pass up a sitting duck in favor of another target some miles away. Place, nevertheless, focused on what was important—the *Tirpitz*.

The men who volunteered for X-craft duty were screened to ensure they understood the hazards of the mission, and throughout training a sense of commitment to king and country was instilled into each man.* This was not by accident but by design. The British, probably more than any other people, fully appreciate the value of patriotism to encourage a man to fight. Encouraging this sense of purpose, or duty, eventually paid dividends when it became a choice of safety or mission accomplishment. When the *X-6*, badly damaged from the long transit, was outside the antitorpedo net, the crew had the option of turning around and attempting to escape or pressing home their attack on the *Tirpitz*. Without hesitation the crew decided to attack. This resulted in all four crewmen being captured and spending the next eighteen months in a POW camp.

---

*Although upon volunteering many of the men did not know that the *Tirpitz* was the objective, they knew that whatever the target was, their chances of survival were slim.

The crew of *X-7* also realized that if they made the attack, escape was unlikely, for when the side charges exploded underneath the *Tirpitz,* the Germans would immediately seal off all escape routes to the open sea. Nevertheless, *X-7* proceeded ahead and dropped her charges. The crews thought about scuttling the X-craft and attempting to cross the snow and ice to Russia, but in reality this was not an option. All the X-craft crews showed from the beginning of training until the completion of the mission that being committed to a cause greater than oneself is necessary for success in battle.

Operation Source was a classic special operation even though the submariners were not classic commandos. There was a specific target whose elimination was a military and political imperative. Men were specially trained, equipped, and supported. A simple plan was developed by limiting the objectives, using good intelligence to identify the obstacles, and then using technology and innovation to overcome those obstacles. The plan was kept concealed, rehearsed numerous times, and executed with surprise, speed (after *X-6* was compromised), and purpose. The frictions of war continuously impeded the progress of the mission, but both the decision makers at the staff level and the submariners in the X-craft showed courage, intellect, boldness, and perseverance. All of this helped achieve and maintain relative superiority long enough to complete the mission.

Notes

1.   Thomas Gallagher, *The X-Craft Raid* (New York: Harcourt Brace Jovanovich, 1971), 11.

2. Richard Compton-Hall, *Submarine Warfare, Monsters and Midgets* (Dorset, England: Blandford, 1985).

3. Adm. Godfrey Place, interview by author, Dorset, England, 18 June 1992.

4. "Attack on 'Tirpitz' by Midget Submarine (Operation Source)," Battle Summary—No. 29.

5. Gallagher, *The X-Craft Raid,* 43.

6. Place, interview.

7. "Attack on 'Tirpitz.'"

8. Adm. Godfrey Place, letter to author, 19 January 1993. These layers of fresh and salt water made it "very tricky" to maneuver the X-craft in shallow water, particularly under eight feet.

9. Donald Cameron, personal diary, September 1942. Graciously provided by Comdr. Richard Compton-Hall.

10. Comdr. Richard Compton-Hall, letter to author, 7 January 1993.

11. Place, interview.

12. Place, letter to author.

13. C. E. T. Warren and James Benson, *The Midget Raiders* (New York: William Sloane, 1954), 272.

14. Place, interview.

15. Ibid.

16. "Attack on 'Tirpitz.' "

17. Warren and Benson, *The Midget Raiders,* 138.

18. "Attack on 'Tirpitz.'"

19. Gallagher, *The X-Craft Raid,* 63.

20. "Attack on 'Tirpitz.'"

21. Gallagher, *The X-Craft Raid,* 82.

22. Ibid., 106.

23. Cameron, diary.

24. Compton-Hall, *Submarine Warfare, Monsters and Midgets,* 130.

25. Lt. Godfrey Place, Report No. Cmd. 38204/993, 107.

26. Place, report.
27. Place, letter to author.
28. Place, interview.
29. Ibid.
30. Ibid.
31. Ibid.
32. "Attack on 'Tirpitz.'"
33. Place, letter to author.
34. Place, interview.
35. Gallagher, *The X-Craft Raid,* 20.
36. Warren and Benson, *The Midget Raiders,* 162.

7

U.S. Ranger Raid on Cabanatuan, 30 January 1945

BACKGROUND

On 9 April 1942, Maj. Gen. Edward P. King Jr., commander of the American and Filipino forces on Bataan, surrendered to the Japanese. This marked the end of four months of fighting by the 90,000 Allied troops holding the Philippine island of Luzon. The Japanese rounded up 72,000 prisoners and began the infamous Bataan Death March, during which more than 20,000 men died from malaria or starvation or were murdered. (Of the 52,000 men who survived the Bataan Death March, approximately 9,200 were American and 42,800 were Filipino.) The survivors were marched sixty-five miles from the peninsula north to the railroad station at San Fernando. Packed one hundred men to a boxcar, the prisoners rode to Capas where they were off-loaded and continued the march to Camp O'Donnell. There they were interned for the next several months. During the stay at Camp O'Donnell another three thousand Americans died. Worse yet, however, were the conditions for the Filipino prisoners who lived in a separate compound across the nearby creek. Dr. Herbert Ott, a survivor of both O'Donnell and Cabanatuan, recalled that "there were 50,000 Filipinos across the creek from us at O'Donnell. In six months, as near as I know, 30,000 of those 50,000 passed away. I got home [from the war] with a diary and . . . I counted 409 dead bodies [Filipinos] carried out [in one day]."[1]* In September 1942, the remaining 6,500 American prisoners were transported by rail from Capas to Cabanatuan City. Five miles east of the small town was Camp Pangatian, their final destination. By December 1943, 2,650 Americans were buried in the camp's cemetery, and by the time the Allies began their fight to retake the Philippines, less than 550 prisoners remained alive in Camp Pangatian.†

On 9 January 1945, the U.S. Sixth Army under the command of Lt. Gen. Walter Krueger landed unopposed at Lingayen Gulf on the island of Luzon. The XIV Corps, which included the 37th and 40th Infantry Divisions, was positioned on the Sixth Army's right flank and advanced along an axis parallel to Tarlac, Clark Field, and San Fernando. On the left flank was I Corps, which drove through the mountains toward the city of Baguio and eventually on toward San Jose in the north. By 26 January advanced units of the Sixth Army held a line from Guimba south to La Paz with Licab in the center. This was to be the jumping-off point for the Rangers' raid on Cabanatuan. (Although the POW camp was officially known as Camp Pangatian it is more commonly referred to as Cabanatuan.)

For months before the Allied invasion, Krueger had been receiving reports on the inhuman treatment of Allied prisoners. He realized that as his forces moved across the island the Japanese would massacre the remaining POWs to hasten their retreat. On 27 January, intelligence provided by American and Filipino guerrillas had located Camp Pangatian just twenty-five miles from the forward edge of the battle area. Between the front lines and the camp, however, were over seven thousand Japanese troops, most positioned in the immediate vicinity of Cabanatuan City.

*During his stay at Cabanatuan, Dr. Ott, a veterinarian, worked in the sick ward and kept health records that indicated the number of prisoners who died of disease and the number who were killed by the Japanese.
†The number in the camp actually grew to ten thousand prisoners at one point. Many of these POWs were later shipped off to other camps in Mindanao and Palawan; nevertheless by January 1945 over three thousand Americans were buried in the camp.

The Sixth Army intelligence officer, Col. Horton White, recommended to Krueger that the newly formed 6th Ranger Battalion be assigned the mission of rescuing the POWs. The plan to reach the POW camp was as follows: "The Rangers would move to Guimba, about seventy-five miles east of base camp, on 28 January and pick up an eighty-man guerrilla force and native guides at a nearby guerrilla camp. They would then march on a route chosen by local civilians and rendezvous with the Alamo Scouts and a second eighty-man guerrilla force at Balincarin, about five miles northeast of the objective, on 29 January. They would complete their plans there and, unless the situation had changed, conduct the operation that night."[2]

The Rangers were commanded by Lt. Col. Henry A. Mucci, a West Point graduate. Mucci chose Capt. Robert W. Prince, commander of Company C, and 1st Lt. John F. Murphy, Company F, 2d Platoon, to lead his operational forces. Additionally, two Sixth Army reconnaissance teams (called Alamo Scouts) headed by 1st Lt. Thomas Rounsaville were assigned to support the mission. The two Filipino guerrilla forces, which were recognized units of the U.S. Army and provided both logistic and combat support, were commanded by Capt. Juan Pajota and Capt. Eduardo Joson respectively.

PANGATIAN POW CAMP—CABANATUAN

The POW site at Camp Pangatian lay five miles east of Cabanatuan City and less than a mile west of the small town of Cabu. Mountains rose in the north and southwest, leaving Cabanatuan nestled in the center of a valley that began at Lingayen Gulf and ended at Manila Bay. Surrounding the camp were rice paddies and elephant grass fed by water from the Platero River on the north and the Cabu River on the east. A main road lay just outside the gate of the camp and connected Cabanatuan City with Baler Bay in the north. This road was the primary transportation route for Japanese troops.

The camp itself had once been a U.S. Department of Agriculture station and later a Filipino army training center. Now it was a death camp where the inhumane treatment of prisoners rivaled the Nazi "work camps," but "the Germans were civilized compared to the

Japanese."[3] In the book *Cabanatuan: The Japanese Death Camp* by Vince Taylor, John McCarty, a survivor of the Bataan Death March and two POW camps—O'Donnell and Cabanatuan—describes the treatment of seven prisoners caught trying to escape. "They beat them awful. Then they tied them to posts . . . They tied them with wire. They left them out there without any cover, clothes torn off. They put two by fours back of their knees and tied up their ankles to their necks and left them in the hot sun without water. Swarms of big black flies and insects crawled all over them . . . They must have kept them there for forty-eight hours, then they moved them to the cemetery and had them dig their own graves . . . and then they shot them all."[4]

This was a frequent occurrence at Cabanatuan. Those who did survive lived a life of pain. Dr. Ott stated:

A daily routine was getting up before [dawn] . . . there were work details that would go to the farm or go to the woods. I was fortunate to be in charge of slaughtering the water buffalos. Occasionally you would get one or two of these for 10,000 people. We were down to as low as 800 calories a day and you had to work on it. It took 1200 calories to maintain you, so a lot of people just worked to death. A scratch would become infected and you would get gangrene. With all the vitamin deficiencies the corners of your mouth would be sore, the backs of your feet and insteps would ache. I've seen men's scrotums the size of your head; so swelled up from beri-beri.[5]

By January 1945, over 3,000 men had died in Cabanatuan. Saving the remaining 512 would require swift action on the part of the Rangers, and obtaining detailed information on the exact layout of the facility was essential. Fortunately for the Americans, one of the guerrilla leaders, Captain Pajota, had once been stationed at the camp while undergoing training as part of the United States Armed Forces in the Far East (USAFFE).

The entire camp was approximately six hundred by eight hundred yards and was enclosed by three barbed wire fences, eight feet high and situated about four feet apart. Four-story wooden guard towers were positioned at even intervals outside the fences. Inside the camp additional barbed wire fences were erected to isolate specific areas, including the entire east section of the camp where the POWs were held.*

The main gate on the north end was an eight-foot-high fence padlocked and guarded by three twelve-foot-high guard towers and one pillbox. The towers were manned by a single guard with another guard at the gate and four heavily armed men in the pillbox. The gate opened onto a dirt road that divided the camp down the middle. To the east were the POWs. They were housed in eight sixty-foot-long thatched-roof barracks. The barracks were originally designed to accommodate 40 troops, but the Japanese had placed 120 prisoners in each building. At the south end of the POW compound were the Japanese guard barracks. These were also protected by a barbed wire fence to prevent POWs from entering the area.

The west side of the camp contained messing and berthing facilities for transient Japanese troops and storage buildings for trucks and tanks. At the time of the raid there were 150 Imperial soldiers from the Kinpeidan Battalion housed in the southwest end of the camp as well as the normal complement of 73 guards. (The guards were a mixture of Japanese, Korean, and Formosan.)

The real threat to the raid force, however, was the Japanese units positioned at both Cabanatuan City and Cabu. At Cabu was the Dokuho 359 Battalion under the command of Tomeo Oyabu. Oyabu's forces numbered over eight hundred men and included six to eight tanks and several artillery pieces. The day prior to the raid, Oyabu had been ordered to rest overnight at Cabu. When the Kinpeidan unit departed Camp Pangatian the following morning, Dokuho 359 Battalion was to move into Cabanatuan City to reinforce the Imperial Army.

Cabanatuan City was the temporary headquarters of the Imperial Army's Command Naotake and harbored over seven thousand troops. Naotake had been ordered to defend Cabanatuan City against the advancing Allied forces and was equipped with a division-level supply of tanks and artillery. All three of the Japanese units, the Dokuho Battalion, the Naotake Command, and the transient Kinpeidan

*The majority of the 512 POWs interned at Cabanatuan were Americans; however there were also 21 British, 3 Dutch, and 2 Norwegians.

Unit, would have to be engaged or delayed in order for the Rangers to have any success rescuing the POWs.

THE 6TH RANGER BATTALION

The 6th Ranger Battalion, which was assigned the mission of rescuing the POWs at Cabanatuan, was originally formed as the 98th Field Artillery Battalion. Activated in January 1941 at Fort Lewis, Washington, the 98th was sent to New Guinea in 1943 but spent most of the time conducting training while the war was going on around them. By April 1944, the 98th had moved to Port Moresby on the southeast end of the island and joined with Lt. Gen. Walter Krueger's Sixth Army.

Krueger was in the process of reorganizing the Sixth Army for the invasion of the Philippines. He had heard about the success of Lt. Col. William O. Darby's newly formed Ranger units in Europe and decided to turn the 98th Field Artillery into the 6th Ranger Battalion. The transition would not be an easy one. Most of the men in the 98th were not infantry trained, and Krueger knew that in order for the Rangers to be a success the men would have to undergo intensive training at the hands of an experienced infantry officer. To this end Krueger chose Lt. Col. Henry Mucci. Mucci was chosen because of both his experience and the fact that he was not from the Sixth Army. Tough decisions would have to be made, probably at the expense of several careers, and Krueger believed an outsider would bring no personal baggage to the decision-making process.

As training began, Mucci made several issues clear. Rangers would not wear insignia in the field, they would not salute other officers, and they would not call officers by their rank. He once said, "I may be Colonel Mucci, but don't dare call me that in the field. The first one who calls me 'Colonel,' I'll call him 'General' and we'll see who the Japs shoot first."[6]

Additionally, Mucci encouraged all married men to look for reassignment elsewhere, and he recommended that those men who did not want to volunteer for the 6th Ranger Battalion be transferred to another unit.[7] By the end of the first week of training, the ranks had thinned considerably, some voluntarily, some not. Eventually the battalion consisted of almost six hundred men divided into six companies, a headquarters staff, and a battalion staff. The companies were subdivided into two platoons with one officer and thirty-one enlisted men as well as a company headquarters element. The platoons were further divided into a headquarters section, two assault teams of eleven men each, and a special weapons section of six men.

The Rangers carried an array of weapons including the Browning automatic rifle (BAR), M1 carbines, Thompson submachine guns, .45-caliber pistols, bazookas, flamethrowers, and 90mm and 60mm mortars. Additionally the Ranger battalion had an integrated medical detachment, communications section, and motor pool.

Basic training for the 6th Ranger Battalion included extensive weapons firing, small-unit tactics, long marches, and amphibious warfare. Sergeant Charles H. Bosard, first sergeant of F Company, kept a diary in which he noted some of the training events. It read in part:

> May 8, 1944—Having a big general inspection today—Have been firing all our weapons, going over Misery Hill, through Torture Flats, landing nets, obstacle course—ran about ten miles. We are all darn good swimmers now—250 yards with a 50 pound pack.
>
> June 4—Working very hard—going through grenade course and bayonet course. Getting ready for amphibious training.
>
> June 19—Getting ready to go out on a night problem . . . night patrol, perimeter defense, etc.[8]

Staff Sergeant Clifton Harris later recalled jokingly, "We always said if we went through the training we never had to worry about getting killed."[9]

On 3 October 1944, the 6th Ranger Battalion got its first assignment. The Rangers would be responsible for securing several Japanese-held islands that guarded the entrance to Leyte Gulf, the site of the planned invasion. On 17 October, three days before the main landing, the Rangers went ashore on the Philippine islands of

Dinagat, Suluan, and Homonhon. Staff Sergeant Harris remembered the tasking clearly. "We were to direct the main invasion fleet into Leyte Gulf. We put up searchlights and brought the convoy through the straits. It was our first mission."[10]

Captain Prince's Company C landed unopposed and saw only limited action, while the remaining companies encountered varying degrees of resistance.[11]* The Rangers were spread out across the three islands and had ringside seats for the ensuing Battle of Leyte Gulf. On 20 October the U.S. Sixth Army landed on the eastern shore of Leyte Gulf and Gen. Douglas MacArthur gave his famous "I have returned" speech. By the end of the month, Leyte was securely in American hands, and by the year's end the Japanese had lost over 50,000 soldiers defending the Leyte Valley. Even with those staggering losses, the Imperial Army still had over 250,000 troops left on Luzon.

On 4 January 1945, the bulk of the Sixth Army departed Leyte and proceeded to the Lingayen Gulf. Five days later, on 9 January, the invasion of Luzon began. The Rangers did not play a significant role in the landing and for the two weeks following the landing remained idle. On 16 January, they received orders to establish a radar station on the Japanese-held island of Santiago. Captain Arthur D. "Bull" Simons, later of Son Tay fame, was tasked with the mission. Simons and a small element arrived on the island that night only to find that the Japanese had departed. Subsequently, the Rangers were ordered to provide two companies to hold the island and erect the radar station. Owing to this requirement, the 6th Rangers were without Bravo and Echo Companies when the mission to rescue the POWs was ordered.

The other unit involved in the operation was the Alamo Scouts. Activated in November 1943, the Alamo Scouts were modeled after the navy's amphibious scouts and formed by Krueger to conduct amphibious and deep reconnaissance, small-unit raids, and demolition. Krueger, a San Antonio native, named the scouts in honor of

---

*Mr. Prince stated that although his company had faced the Japanese prior to the raid on Cabanatuan, none of his C Company had any real combat experience.

the Battle of the Alamo. He said, "They'll be called the Alamo Scouts. I've always been inspired with the story of the Alamo and those brave men who died there. Our Alamo Scouts must have the courage and qualifications of Crockett, Bowie and Travis."[12]

Krueger directed his commanders in the Pacific to identify within their units men who were exceptionally fit, good swimmers, intelligent, and experts with a rifle. The men chosen were sent to New Guinea to begin scout training on Fergusson Island.

Like the participants in the rigorous Ranger course, the trainees spent four weeks conducting long jungle patrols, weapons familiarization (including Japanese weapons), communications training, land and water navigation, self-defense, and rubber-boat training. After the four weeks of this basic indoctrination they underwent two weeks of field-training exercises including joint operations with navy patrol boats, the scouts' primary means of insertion. Part of the final two weeks incorporated a swim test. The prospective scouts were required to swim out through the surf while instructors ashore fired into the water around them. After six weeks of training the prospective scout still had one more hurdle to overcome, peer selection.

"When they wanted to determine who these teams were going to be, they had a secret ballot and the officers voted for the five or six enlisted guys they most wanted on their team, and the enlisted men all voted for the officers they wanted to go on a mission with. They [the instructors] sorted this out so that everyone was compatible," William Nellist, a former Alamo Scout, later recalled.[13]

By February ten teams of seven men had been formed. One of the team members was always a Filipino. "That was a real wise move on somebody's part," said Nellist. "Those people [Filipinos] kept us out of more trouble. They could evaluate the Filipinos [civilians] and their reports and how much stock to put in it. They were completely invaluable to us."[14] Soon after selection, the Alamo Scouts began operations against the Japanese. Inserting by boat, submarine, parachute, or seaplane, the Alamo Scouts would go ashore for three to five days and gather intelligence on enemy activity, conduct beach reconnaissance, spot targets for air strikes, and support guerrilla activities. Within the first year, the scouts conducted sixty missions without a single loss.

Their most successful operation was in October 1944. First Lieutenants Nellist and Rounsaville, and their two teams, all of whom would later play a key role in the rescue of POWs at Cabanatuan, were inserted by patrol boats into Moari, New Guinea. This Japanese-held territory was the site of a POW camp containing thirty-two Dutch and thirty-four Javanese civilians. (According to Nellist most after-action reports indicate that only thirty-three prisoners were rescued instead of the actual number of sixty-six.) The two teams slipped ashore at night and within thirty minutes successfully liberated the civilians and killed the entire Japanese guard force.

Nellist said later, "This mission was just the opposite of the Cabanatuan mission, in that there wasn't anything we didn't know about that prison . . . There was hardly any risk of failure . . . we had such good information."[15]

By late 1944 the Alamo Scouts had racked up an impressive record of combat action, and the men had been awarded nineteen Silver Stars, eighteen Bronze Stars, and four Soldiers' Medals.[16]

LIEUTENANT COLONEL HENRY A. MUCCI— 6TH RANGER BATTALION

Lieutenant Colonel Henry A. Mucci had just turned thirty-three when he reported to New Guinea as the new commander of the 6th Ranger Battalion. A 1936 graduate of the U.S. Military Academy, he had been assigned as a company commander at Fort Warren, Wyoming, attended advanced infantry training at Fort Benning, Georgia, and just prior to his arrival in New Guinea was the provost marshal of Honolulu. In his capacity as provost marshal, Mucci had undergone additional training in jungle warfare and small-unit tactics.

Small in stature and rarely without a pipe in his mouth, Mucci was nevertheless "very well built and muscular" and pushed his Rangers through a rigorous training program in which he fully participated.[17]

Forrest B. Johnson wrote in *Hour of Redemption:* "Whatever Mucci told the men to do, he also did. He seemed to be everywhere . . . on each twenty mile hike, in the middle of bayonet training, jogging along on the five mile runs before breakfast, crawling through the mud to participate in attacks on simulated Japanese pillboxes, firing a variety of weapons and scoring some of the highest grades."[18]

Mucci was known as a born leader. He motivated his men more through inspiration than coercion, but he was also known for his quick temper when soldiers failed to react promptly to an order. With a flare for the dramatic, Mucci once challenged a sergeant to stab him during knife training. When the sergeant attempted to cut the colonel, Mucci sidestepped him and tossed him to the ground, thereby demonstrating to the Rangers the proper technique of avoiding a charging Japanese soldier. This flamboyant style was typical of Mucci. Captain Prince described him as a "great believer in the Ranger concept . . . a terrific officer . . . who had the respect of every man in the outfit."[19] Others said, "He was about as rough as they came . . . as mean as a junkyard dog . . . but everybody liked him. He stood up for us. You had to be right, but he'd go to bat for you."[20]

Mucci was instrumental in both the planning and the execution of the raid on the POW camp. Using basic infantry tactics, Mucci and Prince developed a plan that would incorporate simple, well-known maneuvers. This eliminated the need for the Rangers to undergo extensive rehearsals. Considering the limited time available, this was the only alternative. Mucci also used the Alamo Scouts to reconnoiter the target, and he used the guerrillas to act as a blocking force.

Mucci had the innate ability to deal with people. This proved to be a valuable skill in interacting with both the Filipino guerrillas and the communist insurgents (known as the Hukbalahaps, or Huks for short). In his first meeting with the guerrilla leader Major Pajota, Mucci went out of his way to compliment the Filipino's tactical acumen and obvious "West Point" training. These words of praise helped to win over the guerrilla leader and ensured his support throughout the operation.

While extracting from Cabanatuan, Mucci received news that the Huks were waiting in a nearby barrio and refusing to allow the Filipino guerrillas who were supporting the Rangers to pass. Mucci, gauging the situation, sent back a forceful reply: "Lieutenant, go back and tell those Huks that we all are coming through. If they offer any resistance whatsoever . . . if even a dog snaps at one of my men, I'll call in artillery and level the village."[21]

Unbeknownst to the Huks, Mucci was without radio communication and had no means of calling in either artillery or air support. It was a bluff that worked, and Mucci, his men, the Filipinos, and the POWs passed through the Huk-held village unmolested.

THE RAID ON CABANATUAN

On 27 January, Mucci was summoned from his base camp near Calasio to the Sixth Army Headquarters in Dagupan. There he met the Sixth Army intelligence officer, Col. Horton White; the American guerrilla leader, Maj. Robert Lapham; and the three Alamo Scout officers, Lts. John Dove, William Nellist, and Thomas Rounsaville. White laid out the basic plan for the rescue of the POWs and then informed Mucci of the enemy situation in the area. The operation report said:

> Due to the rapid advance of American forces to the southwest, remnants of the enemy forces were with-drawing [sic] north and east along HIGHWAY #5 running through CABANATUAN-BALOC to SAN JOSE. Due to our air activity enemy troop movement was made during the night. During the day troops rested in concealed areas or transit camps. PANGATIAN was one of these transit rest camps. Heavy concentration of enemy troops were reported at RISAL and CABANATUAN while reports indicated 800 Japs at CABU with tanks. The road nets in this area were used regularly for enemy tank movement of which heavy concentrations were numerous.[22]

The Rangers, White explained, would have to travel by foot the twenty miles from Guimba to the camp, liberate the prisoners, and return to Allied lines. The details of the mission were left entirely up to Mucci, but he was warned that security surrounding the operations must be tight. The assistant G2 cautioned, "One tip to the Japs . . . and . . . you'll find nothing but dead American prisoners when you arrive at the camp."[23]

Mucci spent the remainder of the meeting reviewing the intelligence provided by G2. It was clearly not sufficient to carry out an operation of this magnitude. The Alamo Scouts would have to conduct a detailed reconnaissance of the POW camp and report back to Mucci before the Rangers could make their assault. (The Alamo Scouts worked directly for the G2 section of the Sixth Army. Contrary to other reports, the unit was never attached to MacArthur.) Additionally, Mucci needed Lieutenant Dove to act as a liaison between the Rangers and the Filipino guerrillas. The guerrillas would be coordinating transportation of the POWs and acting as a blocking force, both of which were vital to the success of the mission. Finally, Mucci requested air cover for the return march to Allied lines. White had foreseen this requirement and tasked the Black Widow Night Fighter Squadron to provide one P-61 to act as support. Satisfied that all the headquarters-level coordination was complete, Mucci returned to his base camp.

Upon his return, Mucci summoned his officers together. He had decided upon his force mix. It would include all of Company C, commanded by Captain Prince, and 2d Platoon, Company F, commanded by First Lieutenant Murphy. Additionally, a communications element, medical detachment, and combat camera crew would be included in the list of participants. The total strength of the Ranger rescue unit was 8 officers and 120 enlisted men. Mucci assembled the troops and told them about the mission. "We have been given a tough but rewarding assignment. We're going to hit a Jap POW stockade and free a few hundred of our boys the Nips have held for almost three years . . . They are what's left of our troops who held out on Bataan and Corregidor . . . and if we don't free them now, you can bet they'll be killed by the Japs before our front reaches their area."[24]

After further elaborating on the condition of the POWs and their possible reaction to the Rangers, Mucci continued with the basic plan: "Before daybreak we'll be trucked about seventy-five miles northwest [sic] of here to a town called Guimba. Near there, we'll meet the first guerrilla army who will serve as our escort . . . and, from there we walk through Jap country, all the way . . . no sleep . . . then we attack and walk back!"[25]

At the conclusion of the briefing the troops began to assemble their equipment in preparation for the following morning's departure. Later, at 1900 that evening, the two Alamo Scout teams, guided by Filipino guerrillas, departed their base camp and began the twenty-

four-mile walk to Platero. At Platero, which was the closest barrio
to the POW camp, the local Filipinos would provide a final brief on
the enemy's disposition. From this information the Alamo Scouts
would devise their reconnaissance plan and then move into position
to observe the camp. Mucci had directed the scouts to return to Balincarin, which was just northwest of Platero, by the morning of the
twenty-ninth to give the Rangers a detailed account of the situation.

At 0500 on 28 January 1945, the Rangers left their camp by truck
and proceeded, as planned, to the guerrilla headquarters at Guimba,
arriving at 0715.[26] At Guimba, Mucci met Major Lapham and was
introduced to the Filipino guides who would lead them to Capt.
Edwardo Joson's guerrilla headquarters at Lobong and then onto
Capt. Juan Pajota's base at Balincarin. The next few hours were
spent planning, organizing, and distributing the rations, water, ammunition, and bazookas.* At 1400 the Rangers departed Guimba
and headed east for two miles and then south for a mile until they
intersected the Licab River. After fording the river, they marched
for another mile until they reached Lobong. Upon arriving at
Lobong, Mucci was introduced to Captain Joson. "There his eighty
men [Joson's guerrillas] were attached to our own force and the
entire outfit started east, crossing the national highway into enemy
territory about three miles south of Baloc. We forded the Talavera
River at 2400 and crossed the Rizal Road at 0400, January 29, all
without incident."[27]

At 0600 the Rangers neared the small village of Balincarin. Waiting for Mucci were the two Alamo Scout officers, Lieutenants
Rounsaville and Nellist. The scouts had not had the opportunity to
reconnoiter the POW camp yet, but they had some good information from the local guerrillas concerning the terrain and the enemy
situation. The ground around the camp was flat and open, although
there was a ravine that might allow the Rangers to get close to the
highway without being compromised. Unfortunately, the Japanese

*According to Robert Prince, the short notice tasking combined with the
need to begin marching in the direction of Cabanatuan restricted planning
and rehearsals to approximately six to eight hours. The plans were modified several times as new information became available.

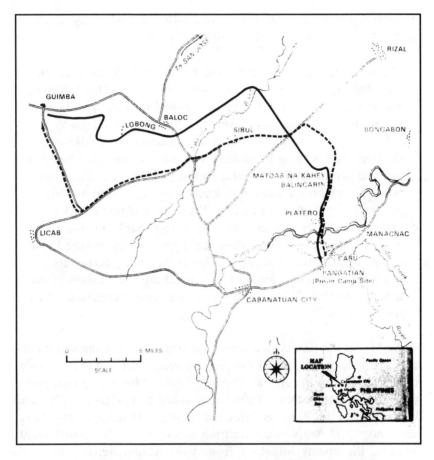

**Fig. 7–1. Rangers' Route to and from the Prisoner of War
Camp at Cabanatuan. From Combat Studies Institute,
Fort Leavenworth, Kansas**

had been traveling the Cabanatuan Highway nonstop for the past
twenty-four hours, apparently reinforcing the Imperial Army at
Cabanatuan, which Pajota's guerrillas estimated at division size.
The Alamo Scouts had also been told there were two to three hundred Japanese (later determined to be almost eight hundred) camped
along the bank of the Cabu River. The lack of cover and concealment around the POW camp had prevented the scouts from gathering the needed information on the physical layout of the facility.

Nellist has tried several times to set the record straight on the scouts' role but to no avail. In his words,

> The scouts didn't get beans done, except interrogate guerrillas until the morning that we were going to attack. This Filipino, Vacular, and I put on Filipino clothes and walked up to [a nipa hut across from] the prison camp . . . I had an aerial photo . . . When I wanted to know something, Vacular was talking out the back of this thing [nipa hut] with other Filipinos. They got out and produced people who had been in there . . . as forced labor. Everything I wanted to know they seemed to be able to produce somebody that could tell us . . . The rest of my team and Rounsaville's team were waiting back in the high grass . . . There is no way they could get up there [to the POW camp] without being seen . . . This thing about the scouts going clear around the camp is a bunch of bullshit. We didn't have time to do that. To make it worse we were exhausted when we got there.[28]

As Mucci continued to discuss the situation with the scout officers, a small contingent of Filipino guerrillas arrived at their location. Leading the group was Captain Pajota. After being introduced to Mucci and the others, Pajota was asked to review the plan and was told that the Rangers intended to attack that night. Pajota responded, "Sir! Are you committing suicide!? . . . You must know, already, the enemy situation from your Alamo Scouts. My own scouts have been reporting to me every hour. Another Jap unit is approaching Cabu Bridge from the north . . . Battalion size . . . There are hundreds of Japs in the camp . . . and tanks. And, maybe five hundred POWs. Only a few POWs can walk. They must be carried if you are going to take them out."[29]

Although irritated by Pajota's comments, Mucci continued to listen, knowing that Pajota was more familiar with the area than any other man. Realizing the difficulty in transporting the POWs, Pajota was organizing a team of carabao (water buffalo) carts to move the POWs from the north side of the Pampanga River back to Allied lines. Pajota's guerrilla force numbered 90 armed and 160 unarmed men. After settling their differences, Mucci and Pajota agreed that the armed guerrillas would hold the Cabu Bridge, preventing any reinforcement from the Dokuho Battalion, while the unarmed men would help carry the POWs, drive the carabao carts, and act as runners and litter bearers.* Captain Prince had requested "that all around security in depth . . . be established and maintained by guerrilla troops; that all civilians in the area north of the CABANATUAN-CABU road remain there and any persons entering this area will be held and not permitted to leave until [the] mission was accomplished; that all chickens be penned and all dogs be tied and muzzled."[30]† Additionally, the civilians along the route would be co-opted to provide food and water for 650 men. At the completion of their initial meeting the Rangers moved into Barrio Balincarin and began final preparations for the raid.

For most of the day Prince, who had been assigned to plan the mission, studied the terrain and general layout of the camp. All the officers and NCOs received a copy of the sketch of the camp so they could begin their respective planning and rehearsals. Details concerning Japanese positions would be filled in by reports from the Alamo Scouts, but not until just before departing Platero. Still under the impression that the operation would commence that night, Prince radioed back to Guimba asking for air cover to begin at 1900.

At 1800 on the twenty-ninth the Rangers departed Balincarin for the short two-and-one-half-mile march to Platero. There Mucci received an updated situation brief on the POW camp and surrounding area from the local guerrillas. The news was all bad. A Japanese unit had moved into the POW camp, and now there were reportedly 500 enemy soldiers within the confines of the barbed wire. (Later the number was determined to be approximately 225.) On the main road leading to Cabanatuan City was a division of troops, tanks, and heavy equipment. In the city itself there were an estimated

---

*Pajota's men were provided bazookas by the Rangers, and unbeknownst to Mucci the guerrillas had acquired four water-cooled .30-caliber machine guns during an earlier raid on the Japanese. Additionally, Pajota had more armed guerrillas in reserve that he "inadvertently" left off his force list.
†In an interview, Mr. Prince stated that the previous day the Rangers' arrival in Balincarin had aroused the dogs and chickens so much that he knew security would be compromised if the animals were left unattended in the area around Cabanatuan.

seven thousand Japanese soldiers. To make matters worse, the scouts had still been unable to thoroughly reconnoiter the POW camp. After getting the report, Mucci made the decision to delay the raid until the following night. A message was subsequently sent back to Krueger's headquarters informing the general of Mucci's decision. The air support was delayed accordingly.

The delay allowed the scouts further time to recon the camp and provided the Rangers extra planning time. Additionally, in anticipation of wounded soldiers and weakened POWs, the Ranger medical officer, Dr. James Fisher, and the local Filipino physician converted the barrio schoolhouse into an emergency hospital.[31] The added time also allowed the Rangers an opportunity to get some rest. They had been up and moving for the past sixty hours. During the Rangers' short stay in Barrio Platero, Pajota's guerrillas provided perimeter security while the towns people fed and cared for the American soldiers.* The following afternoon at 1500, the report from Nellist arrived at Mucci's location. Nellist recalled that he "sent a message back with an aerial photo and [his] other piece of paper with the corresponding numbers . . . On each one [he] wrote everything about it."[32] Nellist's report was extremely detailed and provided Mucci all the information he needed. "The decision was made to attack at dusk. The men were completely briefed on the action to take place and each man was assigned a job and thoroughly instructed as to all duties related to it. The element of surprise was stressed as being of primary importance to the success of the mission; all were cautioned to spare no effort to secure the same."[33]

The plan was as follows. Just prior to dusk, at 1830, a P-61 from the Black Widow Squadron would circle the camp drawing attention away from the Rangers as they attempted to maneuver into position. Second Platoon, Company F, would circle around to the south of the camp and, when in position (approximately 1930), initiate the raid by firing upon the Japanese guard barracks at the rear

---

*Robert Prince stated that the countryside belonged to the Filipinos and at no time did the Rangers feel threatened by the possibility of a Japanese attack. At this point in the war, the Japanese restricted their movements to the highways and did not venture inland to engage the locals.

of the POW compound. (The POW compound was an isolated area within the Japanese camp and held not only the POWs but the guard force as well.) The platoon would isolate the guards, preventing them from reinforcing the section of the POW compound containing the prisoners. Additionally, a six-man squad from 2d Platoon was given the responsibility of destroying a pillbox in the northwest corner of the camp.

As the raid was initiated, 1st Platoon, Company C, which was located to the north, across the highway from the main gate, would assault the camp. The 1st Platoon was divided into two assault sections and a weapons section. The 1st Assault Section would force the front gate and kill the guards at the entrance, in the towers, and at the pillbox. The 2d Assault Section would move across the highway and take up positions outside the fence, providing covering fire for the 1st Section as it moved into the camp. The Weapons Section, equipped with bazookas, would follow the 1st Section through the main gate and pass through their lines, destroying the building containing the tanks. As the Weapons Section entered the compound, the 2d Section would shift fire and then take up security to prevent Japanese from escaping.

Second Platoon, Company C, also located outside the main gate, would follow the 1st Platoon into the camp and proceed to the northeast corner where the POWs were located. After breaking through the entrance to the POW compound, one assault section would proceed toward the rear of the POW compound and engage the guard barracks, preventing any Japanese from reinforcing. A second assault section would position itself on the right flank of the POW compound to prevent a counterattack from the Japanese soldiers on the west side of the camp. The Weapons Section would be held in reserve within the POW compound to escort POWs if needed. The remainder of the platoon's personnel would search the POW barracks and direct or escort the prisoners out to the main gate.

While the Rangers were liberating the POWs, the guerrillas were to provide blocking forces along the highway to prevent reinforcement from either Cabu or Cabanatuan. Captain Joson's guerrilla unit was to set up to the southwest, just eight hundred yards from the main gate. Attached to the guerrillas was a six-man bazooka team from 2d Platoon, Company F. Captain Pajota's guerrillas were to set up a roadblock at the Cabu Creek, three hundred yards northeast of the gate, and cut the telephone lines that connected the camp with other Imperial Japanese units.[34]

When all the POWs were clear of the camp, Captain Prince would initiate the Rangers' withdrawal by firing a red signal flare. The guerrillas were to remain at their roadblocks until the entire column of Rangers and POWs were a mile from the camp. At that time Captain Prince would fire a second red signal flare, and the guerrillas would withdraw, forming a flank and rear guard for the Rangers. What was unknown to Mucci and Prince at the time of the planning was that Captain Pajota had already positioned two hundred armed guerrillas a quarter mile north of the Cabu Bridge. Captain Pajota, who had learned to work closely with the Americans while maintaining a certain autonomy, was planning to use these Filipinos as a reserve element for both himself and Captain Joson. When Captain Prince's second red flare was fired, Pajota would lure the Japanese away from the Rangers' line of march. In order for this maneuver to be successful, Pajota knew he needed more men than Mucci had authorized.[35]

At 1700 on the thirtieth, all units departed Platero. Guided by Pajota's scouts, the column, which numbered almost 375 men, moved southwest through the tall elephant grass and bamboo groves to the Pampanga River. Once at the river, the column divided into its three main tactical groups. Pajota's guerrillas headed upstream and then southwest to their position outside Cabu. Joson moved downstream to his position southeast of the camp, and Mucci and his Rangers crossed midstream to intersect the main gate. For the next three-quarters of a mile the Rangers were able to move without crawling owing to the high grass and falling darkness, which continued to conceal their position.

By 1800 the column was a mile from the river. They had broken through the tall grass and could see the guard towers less than a mile from their position. It was getting dark, but before them lay only rice paddies with no trees or bushes for concealment. Prince ordered 2d Platoon, Company F, to break off and begin heading east. Intelligence from the Alamo Scouts and overhead photography had identified a creek bed that ran underneath the highway and along the east side of the camp. Second Platoon, Company F, would negotiate the creek bed and be in position to initiate the attack at 1930.

After walking a few hundred more yards, Mucci ordered the Rangers to crawl the remaining mile to the highway. "Movement had to be very slow and cautious because the ground was so open."[36] At 1840, a P-61, appropriately named *Hard to Get,* circled the camp, diverting the Japanese's attention away from both Company C approaching from the highway and 2d Platoon, Company F, crawling along the creek east of the camp. Nellist, who had remained in the nipa hut across from the POW camp, saw the P-61 as it made its runs. It "just about ripped the shingles off that damn prison camp. He came by several times and really buzzed it."[37] The diversion was helpful and "by 1925 Company C was all set, in position twenty yards from the front gate, concealed by both darkness and a small ditch."[38]

Second Platoon, Company F, had crossed under the highway at approximately 1830 and had dropped off SSgt. Cleat Norton and a small element midway along the creek bed. This element was tasked with assaulting the guard towers on the east side of the compound. Norton later recalled, "Just as I got underneath that tower a bell went off inside the POW compound. I'm telling the truth, you could feel the hair go right up on the top of your head. Nearly pushed your hat right off . . . It nearly scared the daylights out of us."[39]*

As planned, 2d Platoon, Company F, was in position at the southeast end of the camp at 1930; however, the platoon leader, Lt. John Murphy, spent a few extra minutes to ensure all his troops were ready. At exactly 1945 Murphy opened fire on the guard barracks.

Within seconds all the Japanese in the guard towers and pillboxes around the camp came under fire. An element of 2d Platoon, located in the creek bed to the east of the camp, opened fire on the Japanese positions at the southeast end. Once the guards in the outer positions were killed, the element focused its attention on the guard barracks,

*The bell had been rung by two navy prisoners who were keeping to naval tradition and sounding bells on the half hour. In this case it was 1830.

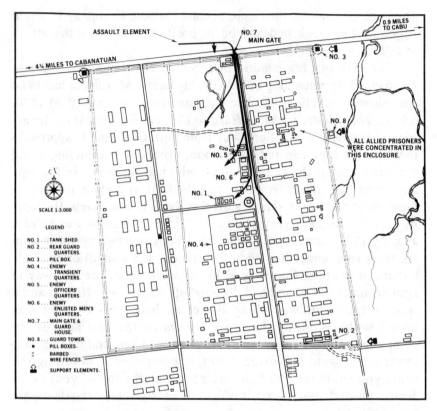

**Fig. 7–2. The Cabanatuan Operation: Actions at the
Objective, January 1945.**

which were also under attack by Lieutenant Murphy's element. "All
guard towers, guard shacks, and pillboxes were neutralized within
thirty seconds after Murphy fired the first shot."[40] When it was
clear that there was no more Japanese resistance at the rear of the
camp, 2d Platoon, Company F, retraced its tracks back up the creek
bed and out to the main road.

At the north end of the camp, elements of Company C had also
killed Japanese guards located in the towers, pillboxes, and concrete
shelters that paralleled the north fence. Staff Sergeant Theodore R.
Richardson, who had been assigned the task of opening the front
gate, quickly crossed the highway and charged the front gate, trying
to smash the lock with the butt of his tommy gun. When this failed

he pulled out his .45-caliber pistol and started to shoot the lock. Two Japanese guards suddenly appeared and fired at Richardson, knocking the pistol from his hand. Private First Class Leland A. Provencher, who was accompanying Richardson, killed one of the guards while Richardson fired his tommy gun and killed the other. Although it was his first real action, Provencher didn't hesitate. "We were so well coached and so well drilled that everything just fell in line instinctively."[41] Richardson recovered his .45-caliber and shot the lock, allowing the gate to open.

Seeing the gate open, the 1st Assault Element from Company C, 1st Platoon, under the command of Lt. William J. O'Connell, jumped from the ditch on the north side of the highway and stormed toward the camp. Immediately behind the 1st Element was the Weapons Section. As the 1st Element and Weapons Section moved, the 2d Assault Element, which was just a few yards down the road, charged the fence line and began firing into the camp. As the two initial elements entered the main gate, the 2d Assault Element ceased firing and took up security positions as assigned.

Inside the camp, the 1st Assault Element moved down the center road and broke to their right (west). The Japanese in the officers' and enlisted men's quarters were now aroused and returning fire. The Rangers quickly subdued the Japanese with grenades and fire from their BARs and tommy guns. The Weapons Section passed through the 1st Assault Element and ran three hundred yards down the center road into position to engage the tank shed. As Sgt. Manton Stewart, the designated bazooka man, dropped into position, he could clearly see two trucks loaded with Japanese troops beginning to emerge from the shed. Stewart aimed his rocket launcher at the shed, received a ready command from his loader, and squeezed the trigger. The 88mm rocket ripped through the thin-skinned building, sending shrapnel flying everywhere and creating secondary explosions that rocked the surrounding area. Stewart received another slap on the shoulder from his loader and squeezed again. The shed exploded, and the Japanese in one of the trucks were quickly engulfed in flames. Those enemy soldiers who managed to escape the fire were cut down by Rangers who flanked Stewart on both sides. Stewart received a third and final ready from his loader and fired once again, this time taking aim on the second truck. The rocket hit the front end of the vehicle, destroying it instantly. The remaining enemy soldiers were killed as they scrambled for cover.

As the assault elements of 1st Platoon, Company C, reached their positions and began to engage the enemy, 2d Platoon, Company C, moved in immediately behind them. The three elements of 2d Platoon, Company C (1st and 2d Assault and the Weapons Section), ran down the center road, and after shooting the lock off the gate, broke into the POW compound. The 1st Assault Element moved toward the POW huts while the 2d Assault Element sprinted toward the south end of the prisoners' section to set up a blocking force. During the planning phase, specific fields of fire had been designated to prevent the various elements from being hit by friendly fire.* The Weapons Section, which was being held in reserve, waited at the entrance to the POW compound, eventually being called upon to assist in evacuating the prisoners.

Inside their nipa huts frightened American prisoners were hiding under beds, in latrines, wherever they could. They were certain that the Japanese had come to kill them. Soon, however, the prisoners heard the Rangers shouting, "We're Americans," and yelling instructions for all POWs to assemble at the main gate. Although many prisoners quickly emerged from the huts, some POWs had to be coaxed out and, in several cases, the prisoners were forcibly escorted to the gate for their own safety. Those who couldn't walk were carried. During the evacuation, one Ranger encountered a POW who said he was dying and told the Ranger to leave him and save the others. The Ranger gently picked the man up and placed him on his back. Unfortunately, before the two men reached the main gate the POW died of apparent heart failure. It was the first casualty of the raid.

---

*Several accounts of the raid show members of 2d Platoon, Company F, positioned at the south end of the camp, presumably firing into the compound to engage the guard barracks. According to recent interviews this was not the case. No member of 2d Platoon ever proceeded around the backside of the camp. This way no cross-fire situation developed between those inside and those outside the compound.

As the POWs began to evacuate, Prince had the task of personally checking each nipa hut to ensure there was no one remaining. "It was kind of spooky. Each nipa hut had a fire burning in a sandbox. I looked in but couldn't see very well. I yelled, 'Is there anyone else left in there?' and then I entered to double-check."[42] At one point Prince encountered the senior POW, Colonel Duckworth, who was trying to assert himself during this state of mass confusion. Duckworth was directing all the POWs to remain where they were until he could figure out exactly what was going on. Prince approached the colonel and asked, "Who are you?" Duckworth fired back, "I'm Colonel Duckworth!" To which Prince responded, "Well, Colonel, get your ass out of here! I'll apologize tomorrow!"[43]

All over the compound similar episodes were taking place. Staff Sergeant Harris still remembers one episode vividly. It was his job to help clear the POWs from inside the nipa huts. "You couldn't see at all. It was dark inside and it stank. Some of the foulest odors you ever smelled in your life. I almost killed one of the prisoners when he jumped on my back."[44]

Prisoners who had witnessed death on a daily basis, who had only dreamed of freedom, were now in the process of being liberated. For many it was an emotionally overwhelming situation, and it required the Rangers to handle each case differently. Mucci described it as follows: "Getting those prisoners out was quite a job. Some were dazed. Some couldn't believe it was true. Some tried to take their belongings, and we had to tell them they had to leave their stuff behind, as there was a tough march ahead. One old United States Marine who had been a prisoner all that time wrapped his arms around the neck of one of the Rangers and kissed him. All he could say was 'Oh boy! Oh, boy! Oh, boy.' "[45]

As the POWs began to flood out of the camp, the Rangers directed or assisted them across the highway and back toward the Pampanga River, where carabao carts were waiting to take them to Allied lines. Mucci, who had remained outside the camp to direct his forces, continued to oversee the evacuation and ensure all the POWs were cared for properly. During the raid, a Japanese soldier had managed to escape the confines of the camp and set up a light mortar on the southern corner of the compound, behind the guard barracks. From this position he began to lob rounds in the direction of the front gate. Three rounds fell in the vicinity of the Rangers, wounding several including the command surgeon Dr. James Fisher.

To the east of the compound, members of 2d Platoon, Company F, were retreating up the creek bed and across the highway as directed. They began to take heavy fire from the compound, and several members dove for a ravine on the north side of the highway. Corporal Roy Sweezy, the BAR man for the platoon, was struck in the back by two rounds and died almost instantly. He was the first and only Ranger killed during the raid.

At approximately 2015, Prince, having inspected all the nipa huts, fired the withdrawal flare. Unknown to Prince or anyone else, however, "one dysentery-weakened British civilian prisoner had hidden in the latrine at the sound of the first shots and never came out. He would be discovered near the camp after midnight by Filipino guerrillas and rescued."[46]

Outside the camp another battle was raging as the guerrilla force under Captain Pajota was holding off the Japanese at the Cabu Bridge. Alamo Scout Bill Nellist later remembered, "This unit that was across the Cabu River was just exhausted. They weren't dug in. They were lying on the ground. The guerrillas just raked the hell out of them."[47]

Pajota caught the Japanese completely by surprise and inflicted heavy casualties within the first few seconds. The Japanese who were not caught in the initial cross fire began to charge across the creek bed in an effort to break the ambush. Pajota had planned for this eventuality and positioned his men accordingly. Additionally, to ensure the Japanese could not bring reinforcements across the Cabu Bridge, Pajota had blown the bridge with a time bomb. Although not completely destroyed by the demolition, the bridge could not support the weight of the Japanese tanks, which were being held in reserve by Commander Oyabu. Even after suffering more than a hundred casualties in the first five minutes, Oyabu continued to order his troops to attack.

At one point several trucks laden with heavy weapons and Japanese troops started for the bridge, hoping to cross on what remained of the structure. As they approached the creek, Pajota's men fired at the trucks with bazookas. Those Japanese who survived the onslaught of the 88mm rockets were killed as they jumped from the vehicles. This fight raged until 2200, and Pajota was forced to disregard Prince's second withdrawal flare until he could ensure that the Japanese would not pursue the retreating column of Rangers and POWs. When Pajota finally broke contact, his guerrillas had killed over three hundred Japanese while suffering only nine casualties, none seriously injured. (Initial reports indicated that twenty-three Filipinos were missing in action, but eventually these men were found and the numbers revised to reflect only nine wounded men.)

The column of POWs and Rangers that departed the Cabanatuan area stretched for over a mile. By the time the small army reached Plateros, there were over twenty-five carabao carts with more being assembled at each barrio. Mucci reported afterward:

The column halted in Plateros [sic] to reorganize, give water and food to the men, and gather more carts. Cots were set up in the schoolhouse by Doctor Layug, local guerrilla doctor, who treated the sick and wounded. The ex-POW's [sic] able to walk were dispatched in groups guarded by Rangers to the next Barrio, Baligcarin [Balincarin], as fast as they could be organized. The first group left Plateros at 2100 hours the 30th. Captain Prince brought the last elements of the column into Plateros protected by the rear guard of 115 men [who] were moved from Plateros to Balincarin in 25 carabao carts.[48]*

Upon reaching Balincarin, the Rangers and POWs halted again. An additional fifteen carabao carts were added to the growing column. The wounded medical officer, Captain Fisher, was left in Balincarin with a small contingent of Rangers. A light plane had been requested to medevac him to a field hospital. Unfortunately, no plane arrived and Fisher died in Balincarin. The column departed Balincarin at 2400 for the next small village, Matoas Na Kahey.

As the Rangers marched along the trails toward the Allied lines, P-61s from the 547th Night Fighter Squadron flew air

---

*Prince did not arrive at Platero with the remaining prisoners until 2140. Mucci, who was trying to keep the column moving toward friendly lines, had already dispatched those who were more mobile.

cover, ensuring that the retreating column would not be intercepted by Japanese. Although few Rangers ever saw the P-61s (other than *Hard to Get*), the Black Widows "destroyed a total of twelve Japanese trucks, one tank and hundreds of foot troops trapped in those vehicles or around camps fires near the roads."[49]

Upon arriving at Matoas Na Kahey, the soldiers and ex-POWs were provided food, water, medical support, and an additional eleven carabao carts. This brought the total of carts to fifty-one and created a column over a mile and one-half long. The length of the column presented a considerable problem for the next phase of the mission, crossing the Rizal Highway. The highway was a main Japanese thoroughfare, and the column would have to travel down the road for almost a mile before crossing.

Mucci ordered 1st Lt. William O'Connell to establish roadblocks on both the north and south end of the highway and to report back when the men were in position. Accompanied by two squads of Rangers, a bazooka team, and some of the Filipino guerrillas, O'Connell set up a blocking force four hundred yards to the north and another three thousand yards to the south. Additionally, Rangers on ponies rode two miles north and two miles south of the crossing to provide added warning time. This would protect both right and left flanks during the crossing. The column began the crossing at 0331 and completed it at 0430. Mucci later recalled, "It was the longest hour I've ever sweated out in all my life."[50]

At 0530 the column arrived at a small barrio, rested for a short while, and then continued the march. By 0800 they had reached the village of Sibul. Mucci received word that the Allied lines had advanced to the Talavera River, which was only a few miles from Sibul. Radio communications were established with Guimba, and Mucci requested that trucks, ambulances, and food be available upon the column's arrival at the front lines. The villagers provided Mucci another twenty carts and at 0900 the march continued.

Within two hours the column was intercepted by an advanced reconnaissance patrol of the Sixth Army. The ambulances and vehicles, which were only a few minutes behind the patrol, evacuated the prisoners and wounded. Soon thereafter the Rangers returned to their base camp near Calasiao, their mission complete. The Ranger logbook of 31 January 1945 reported the following:

Co "C" and 2d Platoon Co "F" returned to Ranger Area. Mission completed. Casualties: Capt. Fisher and Corporal Sweezy killed in action; Pvt Peters, Jack wounded. Enemy casualties estimated at 250 by Rangers and 300 by Guerillas [sic] forces. 510 prisoners released from Japanese prison.[51]*

For their bravery at Cabanatuan, Colonel Mucci and Captain Prince received the Distinguished Service Cross, all other officers and selected enlisted received the Silver Star, and all the remaining enlisted received the Bronze Star. The Filipino guerrillas were all awarded the Bronze Star.

ANALYSIS

Critique
The raid on the Cabanatuan POW camp departs somewhat from my definition of a special operation. Contrary to the stated definition, the 6th Ranger Battalion was neither specially trained nor specially equipped for this specific operation. To make matters more confusing from an analytical viewpoint, at no time during the preparation phase did the Rangers conduct a rehearsal, something that was so essential to the success of previous cases. And yet the mission was clearly special in nature, with the need to rescue the prisoners constituting a political imperative as well as a matter of military honor. This deviation from the model shows how the other principles can sometimes compensate for a missing block in the special operations model. The Cabanatuan mission was extremely simple with a very limited objective and good intelligence. Owing to the no-notice nature of the operation, security had to be tight, but only for a short time frame. Surprise was complete, speed on target was under thirty minutes, and above all each man had a sense of commitment to the mission that overshadowed self-preservation. Lastly, the success of the raid depended as much on the benevolent

*The early reports indicated 510 POWs were rescued from Cabanatuan, but the number was later revised to 512, which included Edwin Rose, the British soldier who was asleep during the raid, and one other prisoner.

frictions of war as on relative superiority and the correct application of the principles of special operations. This, as Clausewitz would say, is the difference between theoretical war and war as it really is—a fact that we should never lose sight of.*

Was the objective worth the risk? In wartime as in peacetime, the taking and holding of hostages or prisoners are direct affronts to the nation's esteem and, if the prisoners are soldiers, to the military's honor. It is, therefore, generally viewed as essential to rescue prisoners regardless of the possible outcome. This maxim not withstanding, the chances of a successful outcome were good provided the Rangers reached the POW camp undetected. The only real threat prior to reaching the camp was crossing the Rizal Highway. Apart from the main roads, the Filipinos owned the countryside, and the Rangers' safety and security were relatively assured. Consequently, rescuing the prisoners was worth the risk.

Was the plan developed to achieve maximum superiority over the enemy and minimize the risk to the assault force? The 375 Rangers and guerrillas were woefully outnumbered. There were over eight thousand Japanese within a five-mile radius of the compound, and the 128 Rangers were outnumbered two to one at the POW camp. This, however, does not reflect the whole story. The division of Japanese troops at Cabanatuan City was not concerned with the escape of 512 prisoners. They were too busy trying to survive the onslaught of the American Sixth Army. The Allied lines were moving forward every day, and the Japanese knew their time was getting short. Even had the Imperial Force at Cabanatuan City received word of the Rangers' attack, it is unlikely they would have siphoned off many troops to give chase. The defense of the city was paramount.

The Dokuho Battalion at Cabu is another story. The close proximity of these troops combined with their superior firepower could

*Clausewitz in his book *On War* talks about the disconnection between war theory and real war. "Why is it," he asks, "that the theoretical concept is not fulfilled in practice? The barrier in question is the vast array of factors, forces and conditions . . . No logical sequence could progress through their innumerable twists and turns as though it were a simple thread that linked the two deductions."

have derailed the entire escape effort. The planners, Prince and Pajota, seemed well aware of this potential and were adequately prepared. Once the column had retreated into the brush, the likelihood of Japanese intervention lessened considerably; nevertheless, had the Japanese pursued, the two P-61s would probably have been sufficient to thwart any serious counterattack.

Was the mission executed according to plan? What unforeseen circumstances affected the outcome? The mission was executed according to plan if one excludes Mucci's twenty-four-hour delay to allow the Japanese troops to move out of the POW camp. Considering the rapidness with which it was planned and executed, this is an impressive achievement. The results of this mission speak for themselves: 512 prisoners were rescued with only two Rangers killed.

What modifications to the plan could have improved the outcome? It is doubtful that any modification to the plan could have improved this outcome.

Relative Superiority

As Figure 7-3 shows, the Rangers' point of vulnerability occurred approximately one hour prior to attacking the POW camp. It was 1800 when Mucci and his men broke out from the tall grass and spotted the guard towers one mile away. After traveling a few hundred yards, Mucci ordered his men to crawl the rest of the way to the highway. It was at this point (1825) that the column of Rangers became vulnerable to detection. The line showing the probability of mission completion does not angle sharply upward; had the Rangers been spotted at any time prior to getting in position, their chance of successfully rescuing the prisoners would have been marginal. After one hour, however, all the Rangers were in position to attack. Although Lieutenant Murphy elected to wait until 1945, the Rangers had gained relative superiority at 1925. At this point, their probability of mission completion jumped dramatically even though no shots had been fired.

Once the attack began, the Rangers quickly dominated the guard force and Kinpeidan Battalion. But as the 511 POWs began to leave the camp and attached themselves to the Ranger column, the degree of relative superiority dropped. The advantage the Rangers had in mobility and self-protection was now diluted by the large number of

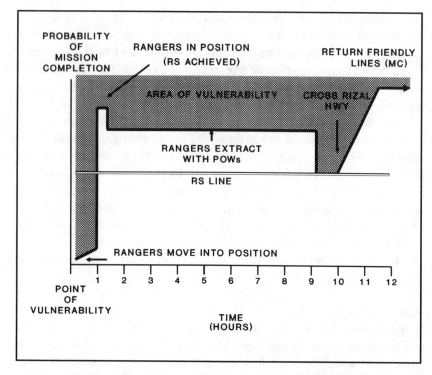

Fig. 7–3. Relative Superiority Graph for the Raid on Cabanatuan

wounded and unprotected POWs. Within thirty minutes the Rangers and POWs were out of the camp and moving inland. The Rangers were able to sustain relative superiority by marching through the countryside and using the guerrillas and P-61s to support their escape.

When the Rangers and POWs reached the Rizal Highway, their area of vulnerability increased dramatically, almost to the point of being unable to sustain relative superiority. Had the Japanese, either inadvertently or by design, intercepted the column of carabao carts and walking wounded, it would have been disastrous. Mucci stated later that the one-hour trek across the exposed Rizal Highway had been the longest in his life. Mucci might have felt less tense during the crossing if he had arranged for additional Ranger companies (of which there were several back at the base camp) to meet the column and provide flank fire support. Another alternative was to ensure the P-61s were in direct support of the column as opposed to looking for targets of opportunity. Once the column crossed the Rizal Highway, mission success was almost assured, and sustaining relative superiority became only a matter of continuing in the right direction.

The Principles of Special Operations

Simplicity. Refering to the need for simplicity, William Nellist, the Alamo Scout in charge of reconnoitering the POW camp, said, "If too many people have something to do with the plan, they can delay the thing and complicate it until it won't work."[52]

The operation order for the raid on Cabanatuan was one page long and directed Mucci to proceed from Guimba to the camp at Cabanatuan, rescue the prisoners, and return to Allied lines. The tactics for conducting this mission were left entirely up to Mucci, who subsequently directed Captain Prince to develop the plan. The plan, if not the implementation, was simple. There were no insertion vehicles to break down, no complicated equipment to rely on, no external forces to coordinate (the guerrillas were attached directly to Mucci, and the P-61s operated independently), and the actions at the objective were literally straightforward—down the road in the middle of the camp.* Each assault element had one objective. There was no attempt, and indeed no time, to develop or brief multiple objectives for the elements. By limiting each element to a single mission it reduced the possibility of confusion, but of course, also increased the possibility of a task not being completed if an element were incapacitated. In reality, though, none of the tasks required special training, with the possible exception of destroying the tank shed which was done by the bazooka element. Therefore had any single element not been able to complete its assigned mission, another element could easily have substituted for it.

The availability of good intelligence was cited as a primary reason for mission success by each individual I interviewed, and this is supported by documentation. The intelligence provided by the guerrillas, as well as the annotated aerial photo produced by the Alamo Scouts, allowed Prince to develop plans that avoided or

*There was a radio relay back to Guimba to call for support. The relay, however, failed to work when needed. The straight road going through the middle of the camp was the path of advance for Company C's platoons and provided the troops an easy landmark to gauge their positions.

eliminated Japanese defenses. For example, the creek bed on the
east side of the camp provided an easy access for 2d Platoon, Company F, to reach the rear of the compound. Had this creek bed not
been identified through good intelligence, 2d Platoon would have
had to enter through the main gate and dash to the guard barracks.
It was eight hundred yards from the main gate to the guard barracks, and it would have taken at least three minutes for the Rangers to run that far. In that time the Japanese could probably have
mounted at least a limited response. Second Platoon's other option
was to crawl the entire distance from the highway to the rear area.
Considering the close proximity of the camp and the time involved
in a dead slow move, this was a dubious prospect at best.

Intelligence also simplified the plan by allowing each Ranger to
know exactly where the enemy was located. The Rangers not only
knew how many Japanese soldiers there were in the camp, but
where they were berthed, how high above the floor they slept,
which way the gate opened, and where the tanks were housed. This
allowed Prince to tailor each man's load. The Rangers carried only
what they needed to eliminate the known threat. Most of the men
marched from Guimba with only their rifle (M1, BAR, or tommy
gun), a pistol, two bandoliers of ammunition, one canteen of water,
and one ration. Only the bazooka men had a heavier load. The
availability of good intelligence simplified the plan and allowed
rapid execution of the mission without any surprises.

Normally innovation is viewed as simplifying a plan by providing the attacking unit a technological force multiplier. In this case
the only advanced technology used was a pair of night binoculars
employed by the P-61 *Hard to Get*. These first-generation night-
vision devices allowed the pilots to identify the Rangers as they
crawled into position as well as to see blacked-out Japanese vehicles traveling the main roads. These binoculars, however, were
hardly instrumental in the success of the mission. The biggest problem facing the Rangers was how to transport over five hundred
prisoners from the camp to Allied lines. Granted the solution was
not high-tech, the use of carabao carts to move the POWs was
nonetheless innovative. Innovation can often be as simple as a UDT
lead line, the klepper canoe, or a Swiss combat bicycle; but as with
the carabao cart, it is often essential to the success of the mission.

Security. The assistant G2 warned Mucci that if one Japanese found out about the raid there would be no Americans left alive when the Rangers reached the camp. In the book *Cabanatuan: Japanese Death Camp,* John McCarty, a former Cabanatuan POW, relates the story of another POW who was interned on Palawan Island. When the American ships began to close on Palawan, the Japanese herded over two hundred prisoners into a cave, ostensibly to protect them from shelling. Once inside the cave, the Japanese doused the prisoners with fuel and then ignited them with hand grenades. Those who survived were machine-gunned. This POW had managed to jump off a cliff and escape, but not before being shot five times.[53] The concern that the Cabanatuan POWs would be annihilated was real. This was the Japanese practice. Security had to be tight.

The advantage of conducting a no-notice operation is that security does not have to be maintained for very long. Mucci received his orders on 27 January and departed the following morning for Balincarin. During the interim period the Rangers never left their base camp, and once they were briefed, they avoided contact even with the other Ranger companies. The Rangers conducted no rehearsals, so there was no opportunity for bystanders to observe and possibly leak information.

The main concern was that communist Huk guerrillas or Japanese sympathizers might inform the guards at the camp. While he was observing the camp, William Nellist spied a young Filipino girl talking to the guards at the main gate. He said, "I just knew that she was telling them that these American soldiers were on the way . . . I thought the whole thing was going down the drain right there . . . It scared the hell out of me."[54] Fortunately for the Rangers, whatever the girl told the guards did not compromise the raid.

There were two factors working in the Rangers' favor. First the Allies were clearly moving rapidly to control Luzon, and those few Filipinos that had supported the Japanese were taking to the hills to hide. Secondly, most of the Filipinos vehemently hated the Japanese and would never have considered compromising the American raid. For these two reasons, the Rangers were able to plan and execute a highly visible behind-the-lines operation without fear of compromise. Their column of over 375 men including the Filipino guerrillas marched twenty-five miles through numerous barrios. By the time they reached the outskirts of the POW camp, the entire Filipino countryside from Guimba to Platero was aware of their presence. Security was important, but Mucci and Prince had to weigh the need for food, water, medical assistance, carabao carts, and guerrilla forces against the requirement to keep the mission top secret. In the end security seemed to have been appropriate and did not unduly impede the preparation or execution.

Repetition. What makes the raid on Cabanatuan so interesting is the overwhelming success of the operation despite the lack of rehearsals. It is easy to understand how a modern-day counterterrorist force, like GSG-9 at Mogadishu, can be successful without a full-dress rehearsal prior to the mission. They train daily on similar targets, and familiarity is born of this repetition. The Rangers, however, had never rehearsed any mission even vaguely similar to the POW rescue. For readers of this case, it is dangerous to generalize about special operations based on the success of this mission. When one peels back the husk of Ranger folklore, success depended as much on luck—that is, on not encountering any Japanese while extracting—as it did on the bravery of the men and proper execution of the plan. And although it is often better to be lucky than well prepared, it is best to be both.

Surprise. Considering the large number of forces within the vicinity of the POW camp, it is amazing that the Rangers were able to achieve surprise. There were four separate elements that had to get into position before the raid could commence: the two guerrilla units, Company C, and 2d Platoon, Company F. Of these four elements only Joson's guerrillas were not in immediate danger of being sighted. The other elements were all sizeable, from platoon to company strength, and maneuvered to within a hundred yards or less of the Japanese guards.

How did the Rangers achieve this advantage? First, the Japanese did not expect the Americans to attempt such a rescue so early in the Luzon offensive. The Allied lines were still several days away, and seven thousand Imperial soldiers were based at Cabanatuan City. The guards, who were a combination of Japanese, Koreans, and Formosans, were in a relaxed state of readiness and content with the knowledge that the Kinpeidan Battalion was in camp and the Dokuho 359 Battalion was a mile down the road.

The terrain and weather also favored the Rangers. The night of the raid there was low cloud cover that concealed a full moon. The darkness allowed the Rangers to move, albeit in most cases crawl, into position without undue fear of detection. The creek bed along the east side of the camp was approximately four feet deep and 2d Platoon, Company F, easily maneuvered to their assigned places. Additionally, there was a ditch on the north side of the Cabanatuan Highway, which allowed Company C to remain unobserved.

All of this notwithstanding, it was the unexpected nature of the raid that allowed the Rangers to gain the element of surprise. Had the Japanese suspected or even halfheartedly prepared for the possibility of an attack, they could easily have prevented the Rangers from gaining surprise. For example, a searchlight making periodic sweeps, a guard placed on the Cabu Bridge, paid sympathizers in the adjoining barrio, or a small Japanese element patrolling the main highway—any of these measures could have seriously jeopardized the raid. As it was, the boldness of the idea and the swiftness with which the plan was executed unquestionably caught the Japanese by surprise, and this element of surprise was the deciding factor in the success of the engagement. The success of the overall mission, however, was equally dependent on other principles.

Speed. Speed during the engagement at the POW camp was important, but owing to good fortune and a well-devised blocking force at the Cabu Bridge, the Rangers had a small cushion of time that could have been extended beyond the amount used.

Captain Prince anticipated that the release of the hostages would take approximately one hour; however, he felt that the Rangers really "needed to be in and out in 30 minutes."[55] If they remained at the camp much longer than thirty minutes, he thought that the chance of being engaged by a superior Japanese force was high. What could not be known ahead of time was the physical condition of the POWs and their ability to move quickly. Fortunately for the Rangers, the POWs had managed to kill a carabao several days before the raid, and although the meat was divided up among the five hundred, most were in the best physical condition they had been in for several years. Nevertheless, there was genuine concern that in the case of any delay beyond thirty minutes, reinforcements from Cabanatuan City could be on the scene. Consequently, Mucci had positioned Captain Joson's guerrilla force along the Cabanatuan Highway to delay the Japanese arrival at the camp. But because the Japanese were more concerned about defending Cabanatuan City, the Imperial soldiers never attempted to reinforce the beleaguered POW camp.

The other concern, of course, was the Japanese at the Cabu Bridge and how long the guerrillas could delay their arrival at the camp. As it turned out, the plan for ambushing the Japanese at Cabu was well thought out and well implemented; and although the battle raged beyond the proposed withdrawal time, the guerrillas appear always to have had the upper hand.

Although accounts vary as to the exact time on target, most Rangers agree that the raid took between twenty and thirty minutes, with the preponderance of Japanese soldiers being subdued or eliminated within the first twelve minutes.[56] Based on the actual events, the actions at the objective probably could have been extended a few minutes more. However, because the Japanese at Cabanatuan City could have been mobilized to counterattack, the thirty minutes on target was the maximum allowable time.

The return to Allied lines, although not measured in minutes, did have a sense of urgency that caused Mucci to push the column all night, allowing them to rest only briefly to reorganize and obtain more carabao carts. Mucci clearly understood his precarious position and wanted to minimize the time spent behind enemy lines.

Purpose. Cleat Norton summed up the need for the principle of purpose in combat when he stated, "The idea of releasing these prisoners motivated the guys to no uncertain terms. They were ready to go for anything! We had a chance to get these prisoners out of there and if there was any way possible we were going to do it."[57]

Purpose is often an overlooked principle because it is a difficult concept to quantify. The soldiers involved in the operation must both understand the purpose or aim of the mission and have a personal commitment to see it succeed. Understanding the purpose keeps the individual focused on the objective and prevents effort being expended unnecessarily. Having a personal commitment, or purpose in the philosophical sense of the word, motivates a man beyond what inspired leadership can accomplish. If a special operation is going to succeed against overwhelming odds, the individual, and to a larger degree the unit, has to have a purpose for fighting that goes beyond mere survival.

In this case the stated purpose was simple: release the prisoners and return them to Allied lines. Each Ranger knew that regardless of whatever else transpired during the engagement at the POW camp, it was their mission to rescue the prisoners. There was no detailed plan delineating which squad would search and clear which nipa hut, there were no assigned escorts for the prisoners, no one mustered the POWs as they departed the camp; the plan was simple and the purpose well understood. It was an all-hands effort that did not need a lot of explanation.

The second aspect of purpose is the sense of personal commitment. In his book *Hour of Redemption,* Forrest Johnson relates the story of how Mucci required each Ranger to go to church and pray. Mucci later wrote an article for the *Saturday Evening Post* entitled "We Swore We'd Die or Do It." He begins the article by saying, "This is the story of how a small group of American soldiers swore an oath that they would die in battle rather than let any harm befall 512 prisoners of war."[58]

This idea of personal commitment is frequently downplayed by today's professional forces who must "answer the call" regardless of the objective. Even a finely honed force, if not committed to the purpose of the mission, will falter at the crucial moment. The raid on Cabanatuan demonstrates how understanding the purpose of the mission and being committed to fulfilling that purpose are essential to success in special operations.

Notes

1. Dr. Herbert Ott, interview by author, tape recording, Monterey, Calif., 14 January 1993.

2. Michael J. King, "Rangers: Selected Combat Operations in World War II," Leavenworth Papers, June 1985, Combat Studies Institute, Fort Leavenworth, Kans., 57.

3. Ott, interview.

4. Vince Taylor, *Cabanatuan: The Japanese Death Camp* (Waco, Texas: Texian Press, 1987), 81.

5. Ott, interview.

6. Forrest B. Johnson, *Hour of Redemption: The Ranger Raid on Cabanatuan* (New York: Manor Books, 1978), 131.

7. Subject letter, "Historical Data," from Capt. Arthur D. Simons, CO, B Company, 6th Ranger Battalion, to the Adjutant General, 7 February 1945, SF-INBN 72-37, roll 6, frames 24–28, Fort Leavenworth, Kans.

8. Johnson, *Hour of Redemption,* 135.

9. Clifton R. Harris, interview by author, tape recording, Monterey, Calif., 14 January 1993.

10. Ibid.

11. Robert W. Prince, interview by author, tape recording, Monterey, Calif., 28 December 1992.

12. Johnson, *Hour of Redemption,* 120.

13. William Nellist, interview by author, tape recording, Monterey, Calif., 15 January 1993.

14. Ibid.

15. Ibid.

16. King, "Rangers," 55.

17. Prince, interview.

18. Johnson, *Hour of Redemption,* 133.

19. Prince, interview.

20. Quotes compiled from author's interviews with Clifton Harris, William Butler, and Cleat Norton, tape recording, January 1993.

21. Johnson, *Hour of Redemption,* 337.

22. Operation Report, 6th Ranger Battalion, Pangatian Prison, 27–31 January 1945, Fort Leavenworth, Kans.

23. Johnson, *Hour of Redemption,* 187–88. Quotes attributed to Col. Horton White and Maj. Frank Rowale respectively.

24. Johnson, *Hour of Redemption,* 198.

25. Ibid. Direction was actually southeast from the camp to Guimba.

26. Operation Report, 6th Ranger Battalion, 1.

27. Lt. Col. Henry A. Mucci, "Rescue at Cabanatuan," *Infantry Journal* (April 1945): 15.

28. Nellist, interview.

29. Johnson, *Hour of Redemption,* 221.

30. Operation Report, 6th Ranger Battalion, 2.

31. King, "Rangers," 61.

32. Nellist, interview.

33. Operation Report, 6th Ranger Battalion, 2.

34. Ibid., 3.

35. Johnson, *Hour of Redemption,* 255.

36. Mucci, "Rescue at Cabanatuan," 18.

37. Nellist, interview.

38. Ibid.

39. Cleat Norton, interview by author, tape recording, Monterey, Calif., 14 January 1993.

40. King, "Rangers," 65.

41. Leland Provencher, interview by author, tape recording, Monterey, Calif., 14 January 1993.

42. Prince, interview.

43. Johnson, *Hour of Redemption,* 300. This story is recounted here but is not attributed to any particular Ranger. During an interview, Mr. Prince told me about encountering the stubborn Colonel Duckworth and the incident that followed.

44. Harris, interview.

45. Henry A. Mucci, "We Swore We'd Die or Do it," *The Saturday Evening Post* (7 April 1945): 110.

46. King, "Rangers," 66.

47. Nellist, interview.

48. Operation Report, 6th Ranger Battalion, 5.

49. Johnson, *Hour of Redemption,* 335.

50. Mucci, "We Swore," 112.

51. Operation Report, 6th Ranger Battalion, Log of 31 January 1945.

52. Nellist, interview.
53. Taylor, *Cabanatuan,* 5.
54. Nellist, interview.
55. Prince, interview.
56. King, "Rangers," 66.
57. Norton, interview.
58. Mucci, "We Swore," 18.

The Albert Canal as seen in 1992. Photo by author

Cupola 24 in 1992. Photo by author

Casemate with three 75mm guns and steel observation cupola on top. Photo by author, 1992

Tunnel leading to cafeteria, infirmary, and bunk room. Photo by author, 1992

Inside turret area of casemate. Photo by author, 1992

Fifty-kilogram shaped charge. Photo by author, 1992

False cupola. Photo by author, 1992

Sergeant Helmut Wenzel (bandaged) and Otto Brautigam. Courtesy Helmut Wenzel

Main entrance #3 in 1992. Note 75mm gun emplacement. Photo by author

Glider men from Witzig's platoon the day after the assault. Courtesy Imperial War Museum

Hitler, Lieutenant Meibner, Lieutenant Witzig, and Captain Koch. Courtesy Imperial War Museum

Alexandria harbor in 1940. Courtesy Imperial War Museum

Italian frogman wearing the Belloni aqualung and dry suit. Courtesy Royal Submarine Museum

Italian submarine *Scire* with manned torpedo transport chambers. Courtesy Royal Submarine Museum

Italian "pig" manned torpedo. Courtesy Royal Submarine Museum

Manned torpedo preparing to cut through antitorpedo net. Courtesy Royal Submarine Museum

Painting of manned torpedo attack. Art by A. Rapkias courtesy Imperial War Museum

Damage sustained by HMS *Valiant*. Courtesy Imperial War Museum

Port Saint-Nazaire, France, 1941. In the foreground is the *avant port,* which leads into Saint-Nazaire and Penhouet Basins. In the background is the Normandie dry dock. Courtesy Imperial War Museum

Normandie dry dock looking from the southern to the northern caisson. Photo by author, 1992

Submarine pens. Photo by author, 1992

Southern caisson of the Normandie dry dock in 1992. Photo by author

Old Mole in 1992. In March 1942 it had fortified German machine gun positions at the front and rear of the pier. Photo by author

HMS *Campbeltown* just hours before the ship exploded. Courtesy Imperial War Museum

The bridge leading from the Old Town area to new Saint-Nazaire in 1992. Photo by author

Otto Skorzeny. Courtesy Imperial War Museum

Mussolini with Hitler. Courtesy Imperial War Museum

Hotel Campo Imperatore in 1992. Photo by author

Looking toward L'Aquila Valley from the top of the funicular railway. Photo by author, 1992

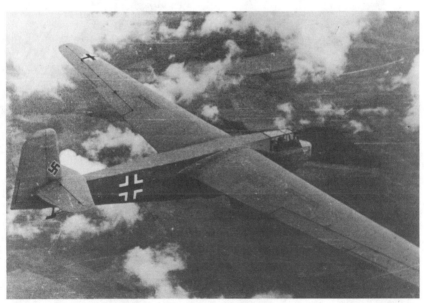

DFS 230 glider. Courtesy Imperial War Museum

Germans and Italians wave as Mussolini and Skorzeny depart Gran Sasso.
Courtesy Imperial War Museum

Hitler greets Mussolini upon the latter's return from Rome. Courtesy Imperial
War Museum

Skorzeny's men pose at Gran Sasso after the departure of Mussolini. Courtesy Imperial War Museum

X-craft preparing to dock. Courtesy Imperial War Museum

Captain of X-craft at periscope. Courtesy Imperial War Museum

X-craft control room. Photo by author, 1992

The *Tirpitz*. Courtesy Imperial War Museum

X-craft side charge. Two tons of amatol. Courtesy Imperial War Museum

Position of *Tirpitz,* in Kaafjord. Courtesy Imperial War Museum

Lieutenants Godfrey Place, *second from right,* and Donald Cameron, *far right with pipe.* Courtesy Imperial War Museum

Ensign Godfrey Place.
Courtesy Imperial War
Museum

Artist's rendering of X-craft
cutting through antisubmarine net. Courtesy Imperial War
Museum

Tirpitz surrounded by antitorpedo net. Courtesy Imperial War Museum

Alamo Scouts. Courtesy U.S. Army

Nipa prisoner hut at Cabanatuan. Courtesy U.S. Army

Carabao cart with liberated prisoners of war 31 January 1945 near Sibul, Luzon. Courtesy U.S. Army

Liberated prisoners of war the morning after the raid on Cabanatuan. Courtesy U.S. Army

Overhead photo of the Son Tay objective area, taken from SR-71. Note location of secondary school, *lower left.* Courtesy U.S. Army

8

Operation Kingpin: The U.S. Army Raid on Son Tay, 21 November 1970

BACKGROUND

In 1968, 356 American prisoners of war (POWs) were being held in camps north of the Demilitarized Zone in the Republic of North Vietnam. One of these facilities was Camp Hope, located near the Son Tay citadel, just twenty-three miles northwest of Hanoi. It had been activated on 24 May 1968, and over the course of the next several months fifty-five American POWs were moved into the small compound. After U.S. intelligence sources located the camp, the Interagency Prisoner of War Intelligence Committee (IPWIC), headed by the Defense Intelligence Agency (DIA), began to focus its reconnaissance efforts to determine whether American POWs were being held at Son Tay.

In May 1970, the U.S. Air Force's 1127th Special Activity Squadron (Headquarters Command) received aerial reconnaissance photos taken of Son Tay that showed a coded message "spelled out" by the prisoners indicating the number of personnel interned and the location of a possible pickup site eight miles to the northeast at Mount Ba Vi. (The 1127th believed that the work parties from Son Tay were being sent to Mount Ba Vi to chop wood either for the kitchen fires or for camp construction projects.) The 1127th provided the information to Brig. Gen. James Allen, the deputy director of plans and policy under the deputy chief of staff for plans and

Operations, Headquarters, U.S. Air Force, who commissioned a preliminary study of rescue possibilities and presented the findings to Brig. Gen. Donald Blackburn, the special assistant for counterinsurgency and special activities (SACSA), Joint Chiefs of Staff (JCS). Blackburn immediately asked the DIA to conduct a photo reconnaissance mission of both Son Tay and another suspected POW camp called Ap Lo. On 2 June, DIA provided Blackburn with SR-71 photos that confirmed the presence of "someone" in both camps. Three days later Blackburn briefed the JCS and recommended an in-depth feasibility study be conducted with options provided to the JCS by 30 June. He later recalled, "The JCS wanted more detail before they would make a determination of whether we should go on with this thing or before they would agree to a joint task force to be set up to plan this operation."[1]

JCS approved the study, and on 10 June SACSA convened a twelve-man study group from all three services and DIA. But Blackburn realized it would be difficult to get a mission approved. "I knew from the start that we would be singing to a reluctant choir. My inhibitions stemmed from my days as Chief SOG in Viet Nam . . . There was an off-and-on policy at the time about bombing in the north, and they did not want to rock the boat by these ground operations."[2]*

The initial concept-of-operations brief to the Joint Chiefs was delayed from 30 June until 10 July, at which time Col. Norman Frisbie, USAF, the senior member of the preliminary study group, told the JCS that a rescue effort was feasible, and he presented an expanded concept of the operation. Initially, Blackburn and his staff considered inserting a controlled American source (CAS) agent (Vietnamese recruited by SOG) into the vicinity of Son Tay. The agent would verify the presence of POWs and call in a helicopter-borne rescue force that would be prepositioned on the Laotian border. This concept was discarded because of fears that prepositioning forces in Laos would alert the North Vietnamese and compromise the mission. Consequently, the planning group recommended that a combined fixed-wing and rotary-wing air element (two C-130Es,

---

*Studies and Observations Group (SOG) was a cover name for the special operations group that conducted clandestine and covert operations throughout the Vietnam War.

five HH-53s, one HH-3, and five A-1Es) be launched from Thailand to insert and support a Special Forces ground-assault force that would rescue the POWs. The navy would provide a massive three-carrier air strike into North Vietnam as a deception to focus enemy air defenses and radars away from the inbound rescue force. The JCS approved the concept and directed commencement of detailed planning and training.

On 8 August, a joint contingency task group (JCGF) was formed under the JCS with SACSA as the office with primary responsibility. Brig. Gen. Leroy J. Manor, USAF, commander of the Special Operations Force at Eglin Air Force Base, Florida, was designated as the commander, and Col. Arthur D. Simons, USA, J4, XVIII Airborne Corps, Fort Bragg, North Carolina, was assigned as the deputy. Admiral Moorer, the chairman of the Joint Chiefs of Staff, told Manor, "You have the authority to put together a task force and train that task force."[3] Manor was pleased with the clear direction and support. He said later, "We had practically a blank check when we left there to go ahead with this. We had the authority we needed to get whatever resources we needed personnel-wise or equipment-wise or whatever. All the resources that were available in the military were ours to put this together. It is the only time in my 36 years of active duty that somebody gave me a job, simply stated, and the resources with which to do it, and let me go do it!"[4]

Immediately upon establishment of the JCT, Colonel Simons returned to Fort Bragg and requested volunteers for a classified mission involving considerable travel and risk. Over five hundred men from the John F. Kennedy Center for Special Warfare showed up for the initial meeting. Some men, not knowing the nature of the operation, elected not to return for a follow-on screening. Each of those men who did return was personally interviewed by Colonel Simons, Lt. Col. Joseph Cataldo, a Special Forces medical officer, and two sergeants major. Eventually 120 men were chosen as the nucleus for the army component of the Son Tay force. "Every one of these people had been to Viet Nam. Some of them had had two or three tours in Viet Nam."[5]*

---

*Although all of those men chosen from the initial screening at Ft. Bragg had combat experience, four of the ground force participants chosen later

At the same time, the air force crews were being selected from personnel assigned to the Aerospace Rescue and Recovery Training Center at Eglin. This squadron possessed the only stateside heavy-lift, air-refuelable H-3 and HH-53 helicopters. Some HH-53 crews from the 40th Air Rescue Squadron and the 703d Special Operations Squadron were even returned to Florida from Southeast Asia to participate in the operation. Additionally, the 1st Special Operations Wing at Hurlburt Field, Florida, and the 56th Special Operations Squadron in Thailand supplied pilots and co-pilots. According to Col. John Allison, "All of the foregoing crew members volunteered, and after being interviewed by General Manor or Lieutenant Colonel Warner Britton, were selected to participate on the mission. Colonel Britton was the Air Force representative who participated in the feasibility study and was pilot of Apple 1 on the mission."[6]

Once chosen, all the men were taken to Duke Field at Eglin to begin training. Eglin was chosen as the training site because it had all the necessary resources and provided the isolation required to maintain security. The training began on 20 August and terminated on 8 November 1970. During the interim, the air and ground planning staffs assumed the joint planning function. Regularly scheduled joint meetings were held to plan the logistic and training activities. In Washington, intelligence agencies continued to gather extensive information on Son Tay. "Both SR-71 and drone (low altitude) resources were programmed to obtain aerial photography of the objective, the surrounding area, and the tentative route."[7]

Operational security was considered essential to the success of the mission. The Security Staff Section was established on 11 August 1970 and given the responsibility of maintaining security and counterintelligence for the project. Work areas were surveyed, visitor control was established, classified material control was instituted within the work space, and all messages leaving the command were screened by the Security Staff. All the personnel involved in the planning, support, or execution of the raid had their phones

---

did not have combat experience. Two were assigned to the rear area communications element and two were assigned as communicators for the assault element.

monitored. Brigadier General Manor received a daily report detailing the highlights of possible violations. Additionally, a cover and deception plan was developed for the training and deployment phase and a counterintelligence plan to provide specialized assistance in gathering information on possible organized threats to the mission.

As training progressed, Brigadier General Manor and Colonel Simons frequently traveled to Washington to assist the SACSA planning cell and brief the necessary senior officials. Manor recalled that on 8 September

> Simons, Don Blackburn, and myself had an appointment to brief the chiefs and I was the briefer, the commander of the task force. I pointed out to the chiefs that we had determined that this [the Son Tay raid] is feasible. It can be done. This is how we plan to do it and I outlined the concept. We will be ready to do this on the 21st of October.[8] Admiral Moorer [Chairman of the JCS] said, "We could approve it here, but of course, it has to go to a higher level for [final] approval. You will have to brief the secretary of defense." Secretary of defense was Mr. Melvin Laird. We weren't able to schedule a briefing before him until the 24th of September. And at the same time, we briefed the Director of CIA [Central Intelligence Agency] [Richard Helms]. Apparently he had been briefed before . . . They were rather noncommittal, although Secretary Laird said that he agreed with the concept and he agreed that it was feasible, and we would have to wait for higher authority. We knew, of course, that it would have to go to the White House. But it wasn't until the 8th of October that we had an opportunity to brief the White House. Then we briefed Dr. Kissinger and General Al Haig. Al Haig, then, was the military assistant to Kissinger. The briefing was well received there. No changes made in concept. They didn't have any problems with how we planned to do this, and they had confidence we could do it.[9]

Kissinger told Manor that the mission might have to be delayed from 21 October to 21 November. Unbeknownst to Manor, President Nixon was working to gain the release of POWs through diplomatic means, and he was concerned that a raid could compromise those initiatives. Kissinger authorized Manor to continue training. On 1 November, Admiral Moorer authorized Manor to conduct in-the-ater coordination. Prior to this time no one beyond CINCPAC (commander in chief, Pacific) (Admiral McCain) was aware of the proposed operation. Blackburn, Manor, and Simons flew to Saigon and briefed General Creighton Abrams (commander, U.S. Military Assistance Command, Vietnam) and General Lucius Clay (commanding general, Seventh Air Force). Both generals wholeheartedly supported the mission and offered "any resources" under their control.

Upon completing the brief in Saigon, Blackburn flew back to Washington, and Manor and Simons flew to the aircraft carrier USS *Oriskany* and briefed VAdm. Fred Bardshar (commander, Task Force [CTF] 77), Capt. Alan Hill (CTF 77 operations officer), and Comdr. P. D. Hoskins (CTF 77 intelligence officer). From these briefings the navy developed a three-carrier diversionary strike into North Vietnam designed to divert attention away from the inbound helicopter raid force. Bardshar was directed not to inform his immediate superior, Admiral Weisner (commander, Seventh Fleet). "I [Manor] later worked for Admiral Weisner, and he would occasionally bring this up to me—in a good natured way—that I had gone around him to get his force to do something."[10]

On 10 November, the raid force with its logistic support departed Eglin, and it arrived at Takhli Royal Thai Air Force Base (RTAFB) on 14 November 1970. Additional C-141s departed on the tenth and twelfth, arriving as scheduled on the sixteenth. On the morning of 18 November, Moorer briefed Nixon on the Son Tay raid. Also present were Kissinger, Laird, Helms, Secretary of State William Rogers, and Haig. Later that afternoon the raid was approved.

CAMP HOPE—SON TAY POW COMPOUND

Camp Hope, located near the Son Tay citadel, was activated on 24 May 1968. Three contingents of American POWs were brought into the camp, the first group on 24 May, the second on 18 July, and the third on 27 November 1968. After confirming the existence of personnel in the camp (June 1970), the U.S. intelligence community began extensive coverage of the compound and surrounding area. Photo intelligence during the planning phase of Son Tay consisted of coordinating the reconnaissance, photo interpretation, and target material production. All photography came from either SR-71 over-flights or Teledyne Ryan's Buffalo Hunter reconnaissance drones and was orchestrated through the DIA. Both Camp Hope and the nearby camp Ap Lo were entered as national intelligence requirements and a priority drone coverage effort from Strategic Air Command (SAC) was requested.

In September 1970, seven drone tracks were drawn up by the Son Tay planners to ensure full coverage of both the camp and surrounding areas. This allowed the planners to identify helicopter landing zones (LZs), infiltration and exfiltration routes, and airborne staging areas, and to develop detailed intelligence on the POW camp itself. From these photos a scale model of the POW camp was produced by the CIA for use by the planners and operators. (The model was codenamed Barbara and now resides in the aviation museum at Wright-Patterson Air Force Base, Ohio.)

Camp Hope, designated Son Tay Prisoner of War Camp N-69, was located at 21 degrees, 08 minutes, and 36 seconds north and 105 degrees, 30 minutes, and 01 second east. It was bordered on the west by the Song Con River which flowed south to north and bent slightly to the east three hundred feet from the camp. The river was about forty feet wide and fordable by foot troops in the dry season. There was a sixty-foot, single-lane, three-span bridge to the north that became a gravel road to the east of the compound. The road was bordered by power lines and air-raid pits. A small canal bordered the compound in the south. The entire area, from the bridge to the canal, including the compound and surrounding buildings, was no larger than three football fields laid side to side.

The compound itself (Fig. 8-1) was approximately 140 feet wide by 185 feet long north to south. Its walls were 6- to 12-inch-thick masonry and between 7-1/2 and 10 feet high. There was concertina wire on the south wall. Entrance into the compound was either by a vehicle access gate on the east wall or a smaller access gate on the south wall. Inside there were five main buildings, three guard

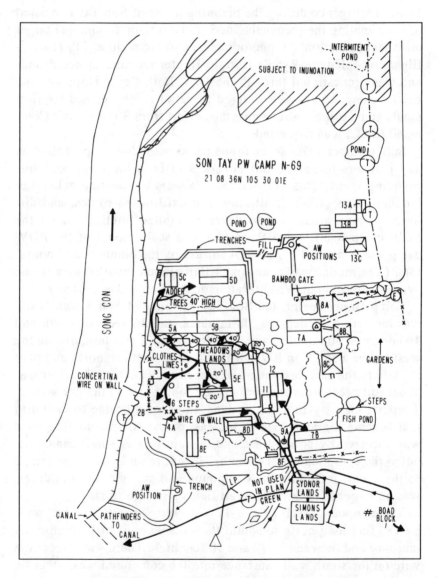

Fig. 8–1. Son Tay Prisoner of War Camp and the Movements of the Assault (Meadows), Command (Sydnor), and Support (Simons) Groups. From JCS

towers, and two latrines. On the north end of the compound were two smaller buildings. The building on the west wall (5C) was surrounded by concertina wire and considered to be a maximum detention cell. The other building, located against the north wall, contained holding cells (5D). The large adjoining buildings in the center of the compound also contained holding cells (5A and 5B), and the large single building housed the guard relief and interrogation cells (5E).[11]

Outside the compound were several structures that supported the guard force including: guard quarters (7B), kitchen and guard mess (11, 12), administration building (7A), family housing (13 A, B, C, and D, E [not shown]), and numerous support buildings (8A–F). The nighttime guard force was estimated to be one guard per watchtower and a minimum of two guards in the compound with possible relief personnel in 5E. The outside force could number up to two platoons, located primarily in the guard quarters in 7B. Although they were probably not manned, automatic-weapon positions were stationed around the camp at the south, east, and north ends.

Located approximately four hundred meters south of the Son Tay POW camp was another facility originally designated as the Son Tay secondary school. This facility was later presumed to be the headquarters for a missile battery and was reclassified as a military installation after the support element mistakenly landed by the compound and was engaged by enemy forces. The installation was similar in size and construction to the Son Tay compound. It had a masonry wall surrounding the outside. A canal resembling the Song Con River ran north of the facility, and a gravel road bordered the compound on the east side. Inside the walls were at least four buildings, three one-story barracks and a two-story headquarters facility. (According to Col. Elliot Sydnor it was never actually determined how these buildings were used.) Very little intelligence was gathered on the installation prior to the mission because it was not part of the objective area. Based on photo interpretation of the Son Tay compound and surrounding area, intelligence experts estimated that a total of fifty-five personnel might be held prisoner at Camp Hope. (Colonel Richard A. Dutton, USAF [Ret.], a former Son Tay POW, stated that on 27 November 1968 there were a total of fifty-two prisoners.) A physical profile of the average Son Tay POW was

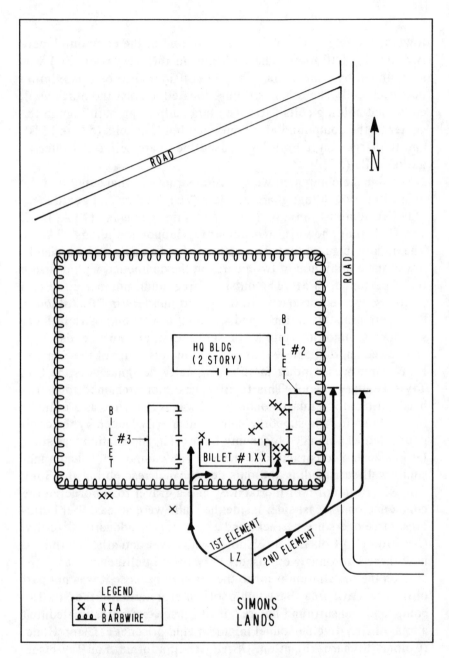

Fig. 8–2. Overhead View of the "Secondary School" Showing the Movements of the Support Group. From JCS

developed by Dr. Cataldo based on World War II and Korean War data. Estimates of body weight, disease, and psychological state were made. It was determined that most of the POWs would have lost 20 percent of their body weight and been inflicted with either malaria, intestinal parasites, goiter, malnutrition, peripheral neuritis, active dysentery, or tuberculosis. A psychological profile based on interrogations of returning POWs was prepared for POW-handling purposes. The profile was as follows:

The POW has heard very little noise, has had very little physical exercise and lives in dimly lit rooms. He has two meals a day, usually consisting of cabbage soup plus bread or rice. Fish and pumpkin occasionally supplement the diet with less than two ounces of meat per week. Sometimes a banana or some other fruit is provided. Flour and sugar cookies are rarely given to the POW. Restriction of total protein intake plus physical inactivity will cause marked muscular atrophy plus a slow reaction to stimuli. A few POWs will maintain a strong hope for liberation, and some will have given up hope, but the majority are probably unsure and live day to day driven only by a natural desire to survive. Therefore, for the most, the sudden realization that "liberation is here" will be shocking.[12]

The North Vietnamese air defense system was one of the most extensive in the world. Each known site was mapped by the planners, and the appropriate anti–air defense measures were used. Of significance were the central and western air defense systems. Fortunately, neither of these systems detected the raid force until five minutes after the time over target (TOT). This was despite the presence of four F-4s and four F-105s in the area ten minutes prior to TOT. Other air defense systems that proved active included the northeastern (Phuc Yen control) sector, which controlled a minimum of seven FanSong (surface-to-air missile or SAM) and two FireCan (antiaircraft artillery or AAA) sites. Intelligence on these sites was excellent. Brigadier General Manor later recalled, "We had the capability to determine what they were seeing on their radar almost as soon as they did—which, of course, was very, very helpful."[13]

THE LEADERS

On 8 August 1970, the joint contingency task group (JCTG) was formed, and Brig. Gen. Leroy J. Manor was selected to command the force. Manor's career began in June 1942 when he enlisted in the army air force and was sent to pilot training as an aviation cadet. Upon graduation he became a fighter pilot in P-48s, flying in the European theater of operation with both the Eighth and Ninth Air Force. He finished the war with seventy-two combat missions.

After the war, Manor returned to New York University and finished his degree in 1947. Later that year he became an instructor at the air tactical school at Tyndal Field, Florida. Following that assignment he went to Maxwell Air Force Base at Montgomery, Alabama, and helped organize the squadron officers' school, staying on to teach the first class. He departed Maxwell for the Tactical Air Command air-ground operations school at Southern Pines, North Carolina.

In 1953 he was assigned to the Sixth Allied Tactical Air Force in Izmir, Turkey. After two years he went to Selfridge Field, Michigan, as the commander of the 2242d Air Reserve Flying Center where he flew F-80s, F-84s, F-86s, and eventually C-119s. In 1958 he attended the Armed Forces Staff College and was subsequently assigned as squadron commander of an F-100 squadron at Cannon Air Force Base, New Mexico. Manor was then reassigned overseas to Germany as the chief of the Tactical Evaluation Division of U.S. Air Forces in Europe (USAFE), where he flew F-100s and F-105s. Upon completion of his tour in Germany, Manor was sent to the Industrial College of the Armed Forces with a four-year follow-on assignment in the Pentagon. For his tour in the Pentagon, he was rewarded with command of the 37th Tactical Fighter Wing (F-100s) in Phu Cat, Republic of South Vietnam.

After one year and 275 combat missions in Vietnam, Manor returned to command the 835th Air Division at McConnell Air Force Base, Wichita, Kansas. While at McConnell, Manor was promoted to brigadier general and in 1970 became commander of the U.S. Air Force Special Operations Forces at Eglin Air Force Base, Florida. While heading the Special Operations Forces, Manor was chosen as the task group commander for the Son Tay raid. Colonel Elliot "Bud"

Sydnor described Manor as "very intelligent . . . the steel hand in a velvet glove."[14]

Another person instrumental in the planning and preparation of the raid was Brig. Gen. Donald D. Blackburn. Blackburn was the JCS SACSA at the time of the Son Tay raid. He was responsible for developing the initial plan, establishing the study group, coordinating all the intelligence and logistic support, and interfacing with the JCS and senior Department of Defense (DOD) and National Security Agency (NSA) personnel. Blackburn was arguably the most knowledgeable senior officer in the army on special operations. He began his career in 1940 as an infantry officer assigned to advise a Filipino infantry battalion in northern Luzon. When the Philippines fell in 1942, Blackburn refused to surrender and helped organize Filipino guerrillas to fight the Japanese. He became a regimental commander of a unit composed largely of Igorot headhunters. On 9 January 1945, the Americans returned in force to Luzon but had to battle the 235,000 well-entrenched Japanese until 5 July 1945. Throughout the interim "Blackburn's headhunters" were instrumental in behind-the-lines operations in support of the ground campaign.

After the war, Blackburn, a highly decorated twenty-nine-year-old full colonel, returned to the United States where he was sent back to service schools to learn about "the real army." After a tour as provost marshal of the Military District, Washington, D.C., he was sent to the Infantry School and then returned to Washington to serve two years in the Pentagon. Following his tour in the Pentagon, Blackburn was sent to parachute training and then in 1950 to be an instructor at the U.S. Military Academy. In 1953 he was assigned to the Allied Northern Forces, Europe. Upon completing his European assignment in 1957, Blackburn was sent to Vietnam as senior adviser to the Vietnamese commanding general, 5th Military Region, Mekong Delta. He was subsequently assigned to Fort Bragg where he assumed command of the 77th Special Forces Group. In 1960 Blackburn was picked to organize a military advisory group to conduct covert operations in Laos. Blackburn chose Lt. Col. Arthur D. Simons to head his "White Star" program. From 1964 to 1965, Blackburn was director of special operations for the deputy chief of staff for operations (DCS Ops) of the army.

He returned to Vietnam in 1965 to be the first commander of the Military Assistance Command, Vietnam, Studies and Observation Group (MACVSOG). This joint military organization included army and air force special operations forces, navy SEALs, marine reconnaissance forces, CIA, and a host of service support personnel. Following his tour in Vietnam, Blackburn returned to Washington as SACSA and retired from the military in June 1971 after that assignment.

Colonel Arthur "Bull" Simons was chosen as the deputy commander of the JCTG for the raid on Son Tay. He graduated from the University of Missouri through the Reserve Officer Training Corps (ROTC) program and received his commission in the army in 1941. His first assignment was with the 98th Field Artillery Battalion in New Guinea. The outfit was disbanded soon thereafter, and Simons, who had become a battery officer and battalion executive officer, joined the 6th Ranger Battalion. He participated in the invasion of the Philippines, commanding B Company, 6th Rangers, during several behind-the-lines operations.

He was out of the service from February 1946 until June 1951. From 1951 until 1954 he served as an instructor at the Eglin Air Force Base Ranger Camp. The Ranger Camp was a department of the Infantry School. Following that tour Simons served three years in Ankara, Turkey, as a military adviser. In 1957 he received orders to Fort Bragg and in 1958 was assigned to the 77th Special Forces Group. He transferred to the 7th Special Forces Group. There Simons met Blackburn, who in 1960 chose him to head his White Star program in Laos.

Simons took 107 Special Forces personnel to Laos and formed a Laotian army by impressing thousands of Meo tribesmen into service. The CIA used White Star teams to train the Meo one-hundred-man *autodéfense de choc* (shock) companies. The Meo were well suited to the task and enjoyed soldiering. The White Star teams sent the Meo into the highlands to ambush the Pathet Lao forces and capture key military territorial objectives.

By July 1962, the White Star program included 433 Special Forces personnel who were responsible for conducting extensive unconventional warfare and training both the Forces Armées du Royaume and the Laotian military schools. Following his six months in Laos, Simons returned to Fort Bragg and then was as-

signed to Panama with the 8th Special Forces Group at Fort Gulick.
In 1965 he reported to Vietnam and joined Blackburn at MAC-
VSOG. While at MACVSOG Simons earned a reputation as a superb unconventional operator, but as Blackburn remembered, "He
didn't believe in 'foolhardy frolics' . . . When Bull Simons under-
took an operation, . . . the research and planning behind it were
'meticulous.' "[15]

In 1966 he returned to the States and was the assistant chief of
staff of the XVIII Airborne Corps at Fort Bragg. Following a one-
year tour in Korea, Simons returned to the XVIII Airborne Corps
and while there was appointed to be the deputy commander of the
Son Tay raid. He retired in July 1971 after thirty-four years of service. In 1979 Ross Perot brought Simons out of retirement to rescue
two executives of the Electronic Data Systems who were trapped in
Tehran. He died of heart failure soon after returning from Iran.

Lieutenant Colonel Bud Sydnor was probably the most influential and yet the most publicly unappreciated officer on the raid. It
is a popular misconception that Simons was the ground force commander, but in fact, it was Sydnor. Sydnor developed the training
curriculum, conducted the rehearsals, and led the force at the
POW compound. For these tasks he was well qualified. At the end
of World War II, Sydnor joined the navy, and after serving in the
Atlantic as an enlisted man aboard the submarine USS *Raton,* he
left the service and attended ROTC at Western Kentucky University, where he graduated in August 1952 as the Distinguished Military Graduate. After several schools Sydnor was assigned to the
11th Airborne Division as a platoon commander and then in 1954
as a company commander with the 2d Infantry Division in Korea.
This was followed by a Stateside tour as the 25th Infantry
Division's battalion operations officer. In 1960–61 he served with
the 22d Special Air Service in England and then returned to Fort
Bragg where he joined the Special Forces in 1962. After three
years in Washington, Sydnor received command of the 1st Battalion, 327th Airborne Infantry Regiment, 101st Airborne Division,
in Vietnam. He held this position until June 1968, at which time
he was sent back to Fort Bragg.

In 1970 Sydnor was selected as the ground force commander for
the raid on Son Tay. For his actions at Son Tay, Sydnor received the

Distinguished Service Cross. In 1973, he assumed command of the
1st Special Forces Group in Okinawa. Following command, Sydnor
was assigned as chief, Infantry Branch, and then chief, Company
Grade Arms Division, at Fort Bragg. In June 1977, he moved to
Fort Benning and became the director of the Ranger Department.
He held that post until May 1980. Sydnor's final assignment was the
director of plans and training at the Infantry Center at Fort Benning.
He retired in August 1981 after thirty-one years of service. In addi-
tion to the Distinguished Service Cross, Sydnor's decorations also
include: the Silver Star, Legion of Merit with two Oak Leaf Clus-
ters, the Distinguished Flying Cross, the Bronze Star for valor, the
Air Medal with nine Oak Leaf Clusters, the Vietnamese Cross of
Gallantry with Silver Star, the Combat Infantryman's Badge, the
Master Parachutist Badge, and the Ranger tab. In June 1992, Col.
Elliot Sydnor was inducted into the Ranger Hall of Fame.

TRAINING

On 13 August 1970, Auxiliary Field 3 at Eglin Air Force Base,
Florida, was selected as the continental United States (CONUS)
training site for the raid. The cantonment included six barracks for
the troops, classroom space, a secure building for the tactical operations center, a mess hall, a BX, a theater, and a motor pool. The
area was isolated from the main base and had an apron space suitable for helicopter training.

A support detachment and five operational detachments were
formed from those Special Forces personnel chosen for the mission.
The training site was activated on 26 August, and the personnel
deployed in two increments from Fort Bragg, with the last group
arriving at Eglin by 8 September. The support detachment was responsible for all administrative and logistical support, providing
backup personnel for the operational units, and maintaining a cover
program by conducting daily training not related to the mission.

The training program was divided into four phases for both the
air and ground forces. Phase I for the ground forces began on 9
September and ended on 16 September. During this time combat
skills were evaluated to help select primary and alternate participants. This training included daily physical exercise (six to eight

repetitions of Army Drill I and a two-mile run), psychological preparation for escape and evasion, land navigation, communications procedures, radio familiarization classes, helicopter orientation (including tactical loading and unloading), demolition charge preparation, patrolling, and extensive range firing with all weapons (M16, M79, M60, and .45-caliber).

The *Son Tay Report* explained that "this relaxed schedule of approximately seven hours per day was designed to allow the individual Ground Force member sufficient time to adapt to the strenuous PT program and to become acclimated."[16]

Throughout Phase I and the remainder of the training, several nonstandard equipment items were obtained for use on the mission. The procurement and employment of this equipment were instrumental in the success of the mission and warrant discussion. This equipment included:

- Two oxyacetylene emergency outfits for cutting through metal hasps or locks.
- Six commercial chain saws for clearing LZs.
- Bolt cutters used by air force fire fighters for cutting locks.
- Miners' electric headlamps for hands-off illumination of the target. In many cases it became impractical to move and shoot with the lamps mounted on the soldiers' heads, so most were secured to their load-bearing gear.
- Armson single-point sights. This sight allowed the Special Forces personnel to identify their target under low-light conditions. (For the actual raid, flares were dropped from a C-130 to provide the needed light.) It was found that during daylight operations the conventional iron sights were marginally better than the single-point; however at night there was no comparison. The single-point sight significantly improved the soldier's ability to engage his target. At a distance of twenty-five meters, the worst marksman could place all rounds in a twelve-inch circle at night. At fifty meters the same individual could place all his rounds in an E-type silhouette.
- A special machete was developed with a heavy blade and a sharp point to be used for prying open doors and barricades.

Some difficulty was encountered in making the blade quickly, and eventually the Eglin machine shop produced the required quantity in a couple of days.

- A fourteen-foot fireman's ladder was acquired for use by the assault platoon in the event they had to scale the compound wall.
- Night-vision devices (NVDs) were obtained for the group and element leaders. During the raid, the NVDs were used by the assault and security groups at the objective site.

Phase II was conducted between 17 September and 27 September and included a review of basic skills and some specialized training, including: night firing on the range with all weapons, close air support, raid and immediate action drills, day and night aerial platform training, house searches, demolition training, medical training, and target recognition (this emphasized engaging targets at unknown distances). To increase realism, some abandoned buildings on Field 1 were used as a training aid.

Phase III was conducted between 28 September and 6 October. This phase concentrated on the joint interoperability aspect of the mission. For the first time, the ground and air forces were joined to develop and exercise detailed insertion and extraction plans necessary for the ground operations. The after-action report stated: "The period culminated with a series of 'profile' flights. The last profile was flown full-time to include a one hour flight simulating the flight from staging base to launch site."[17] This phase also concentrated on day and night live-fire rehearsals, close air control of the A-1s, weapons firing, search and rescue training, and escape and evasion (E&E).

Phase IV was added to the schedule when the execution was delayed. This phase was designed to maintain force readiness and improve any skills that might be deficient. It included a continued emphasis on dress rehearsals, immediate action drills, house-to-house fighting, demolition training, house clearing, E&E, and search and rescue (SAR) (which included a night exercise where all personnel were extracted by HH-53 in a simulated tactical scenario), alternate plan execution, and detailed target studies.

The air forces's training was also divided into four phases and required precision night formation flying at low altitudes. The composition of the force complicated this mission because some of the aircraft were required to perform at the extremes of their capabilities. The *Son Tay Report* states that "this demanded the installation and use of special equipment as well as the development of new tactics and procedures before the Task Group could become mission ready."[18]

The composition of the air force task group included two Combat Talon C-130s to provide precise navigation to the target area. One C-130 was designated to escort the five HH-53s and one HH-3 carrying the assault force. The other C-130 led the five A-1s that were used to provide strike force and air cover. (General Manor later stated, "The primary reason for the second Combat Talon was for redundancy in the event the first [C-130] was lost due to mechanical or other troubles. Redundancy was planned into every phase of the air elements.")

During Phase I (preparation phase) personnel were selected for the mission, deployed to Auxiliary Field 3, and put through complex formation flying to determine their proficiency. In Phase II (specialized training) the HH-3, UH-1, and C-130s conducted day and night formation flying and full-mission profiles. (The UH-1 was designated as an alternative insertion platform in the event the HH-3 was unable to land in the compound owing to the limited size of the landing zone.) During Phase III (joint training phase) actions at the objective were rehearsed, including aerial and ground rescue operations, objective area tactics, emergency procedures, and full-mission profiles. A delay in the execution window from 21 October to 21 November allowed time for additional training (Phase IV) and included continued rehearsal of the basic and alternate plans.

For the training and execution, a forward-looking infrared (FLIR) system was installed aboard each C-130, and an additional navigator was added to the crew to improve precise navigation to the target area. Additionally, ground acquisition responder/interrogator (GAR/I) beacons were used to assist the C-130s in determining their location over the ground.

In the course of training, some important lessons were learned. Formation flying for the air forces was particularly challenging. The

C-130 and either the HH-3 or the UH-1H were both required to exceed their normal limits. The helicopters flew in a draft position, maintaining a speed of 105 knots to keep up with the C-130, which had to fly at 70 percent flaps. At those slow speeds the C-130 had Doppler reliability problems. These problems were overcome by both the FLIR and GAR/I beacon, which added to the reliability of navigation. The narrow operating envelope of the HH-3 meant only essential fuel and equipment could be carried. As tactical requirements increased the size of the assault team, particular attention was paid to weight reduction. After numerous trials it was determined that flying the UH-1H in formation with a C-130 was "not within the capability of the average Army aviator," but after intense training "the tactics of drafting with HH-3 and UH-1H [were] proven and [could] be applied in future plans."[19]*

Another minor problem developed when it was found that the C-130 and A-1 strike force was not capable of maintaining formation with the lead assault force of C-130s and helicopters. A plan was devised to allow the A-1s to make circles or S-turns to remain in contact with the lead helicopter force. This later resulted in the decision to separate the two formations and allow them to arrive on target at a predesignated time.

According to the after-action report, throughout the training, air force "tactics and techniques were in a constant state of revision and modification until the full-dress rehearsal in early October. All missions were jointly briefed and debriefed with every element that participated represented. The building-block concept was constantly stressed and emphasized and practiced. [The air element] would practice each segment separately and single ship, if feasible. Ballast was carried to match planned flight gross weight. Formations were flown at density altitude expected to be encountered . . . Frequently a mission would be flown in the afternoon, and after a debrief and

---

*While attached to the Holloway Commission investigating the failed Iranian hostage rescue mission, Lt. Gen. Manor asked one of the planners why the C-130s and helicopters did not fly in formation to the first staging base at Desert One. He was told that this concept wouldn't work because the air speeds between the C-130 and the HH-53 were not compatible.

discussions of problems with corrective actions, the mission would be repeated after dark. During the proper phase of the moon, some missions were flown as late as 0230 in the morning to achieve as realistic lighting as possible."[20]

By the time training was completed on 13 November 1970, "every facet of the operation [was] exercised [totaling] more than 170 times . . . and over 1000 hours of incident-free flying [were] conducted primarily at night under near combat conditions."[21]

On 10 November 1970 the force deployed to Thailand fully prepared to conduct the mission that lay before them.

THE MISSION

The deployment to Thailand was conducted in two phases. On 10 November the two C-130s left Eglin Air Force Base under cover of darkness, and they arrived at Takhli RTAFB on 14 November. In staggered flights, the remaining personnel and equipment were flown by C-141s on 10, 12, and 16 November. The helicopters and A-1s used during training were left in CONUS, and replacement aircraft were provided by forces in Thailand. Appropriate cover stories were disseminated to prevent "espionage and sabotage from interfering with the movement of the force, to insure surprise, and to deny information regarding the movement."[22] In Thailand, security surveys were conducted at both Takhli and Udorn (the helicopter-staging base) RTAFBs, and secure working areas were established and maintained throughout the final stages.

On 18 November the force was assembled in the base theater at Takhli, where Manor and Simons presented a joint air and ground operations brief. Up to this time only those personnel directly involved in the planning knew what the objective was and where Son Tay was located. Although this brief was fairly extensive it did not include the exact name and location of the POW camp. Following the formal brief, the platoon leaders read the official operation plan and reviewed the schedule of activities for the remaining three days. That evening there were more staff and platoon meetings that included partial mission briefs by key individuals.

At 0330 local time on 19 November, Manor received a red rocket (flash execute) message giving him approval to launch the mission as planned. Unfortunately, the weather situation had deteriorated since the force had arrived in Thailand. Typhoon Patsy was about to make landfall over the Philippines and was expected over Hanoi within twenty-four to forty-eight hours. It was essential for the success of the mission that the air element have a five-thousand- to ten-thousand-foot cloud ceiling en route to Son Tay and suitable moonlight for the ground operations at the objective. Additionally, the coastal ceiling off the Gulf of Tonkin had to be seventeen thousand feet for the navy to conduct their diversionary air raid. Manor received a detailed weather brief the afternoon of the nineteenth, and based on that forecast he made the decision to launch the raid on the twentieth instead of the twenty-first.

The ground force spent the nineteenth conducting equipment checks, range firing, and receiving SAR and E&E briefings. On 20 November a final briefing was conducted in the base theater. "A route briefing and target briefing was given to include the geographical location, the name of the target, its relation to Hanoi's location [cheers went up] and specific instructions concerning the conduct of force in the target area. Included were: decisive action, importance of time to success, care of wounded, SAR operations, and fighting as a complete unit in case of emergency actions."[23]

Following the brief, the ground force moved to the hangar for a final equipment check and to await onload. An advanced party had flown to Udorn earlier in the evening to load the helicopters with special clothing for the POWs and extra batteries and equipment for the ground force. Manor had departed earlier in the day for his command post located at Monkey Mountain just north of Danang. He later reported that "the reason Monkey Mountain was chosen was because it was a communications hub, and it had some special communication put in for [Manor's] use."[24]

In the three days preceding the launch, the air elements were also busy checking aircraft and making final preparations. The two C-130s had arrived on the fourteenth and were test flown for systems checks on both the sixteenth and seventeenth. The 3d Aerospace Rescue and Recovery Group redistributed HH-53s within Southeast Asia so that ten were available at Udorn RTAFB on 15 November. By 17 November all HH-53s were mission ready. Two CONUS-based EC-121T airborne radar platforms were prepositioned at Danang, South Vietnam, for support of the mission and were ready by the seventeenth of November. The A-1 strike aircraft used for the mission were based at Nakhon Phanom RTAFB, Thailand. The A-1 crews from CONUS were moved to Nakhon Phanom and conducted system checks throughout the final three days. The aircraft realignment was conducted using routine daily frag orders or operational patterns. This helped maintain a low profile, and was consistent with the security posture throughout the training and deployment.

At 2125 on 20 November 1970, the ground force departed Takhli by C-130 and after an uneventful flight arrived at Udorn. While at Udorn the ground force transferred to the five HH-53s and one HH-3. At approximately the same time, the A-1s departed Nakhon Phanom RTAFB to effect the rendezvous over Laos with the ground force aircraft. The aircraft were designated as follows:

Aircraft Type	Call Sign	Mission
C-130E	Cherry 1	Raid force lead aircraft and flare drop aircraft
C-130E	Cherry 2	A-1 lead aircraft
HC-130P	Lime 01	Tanker
HC-130P	Lime 02	Tanker
HH-3	Banana 1	Assault element helo (Meadows)
HH-53	Apple 1	Support element helo (Simons)
HH-53	Apple 2	Command element helo (Sydnor)
HH-53	Apple 3	Destroy the guard towers
HH-53	Apple 4	POW helo or spare flare ship
HH-53	Apple 5	POW helo or spare flare ship
A-1s	Peach 1–5	Strike aircraft

In addition to the above aircraft there were also a ten-aircraft MiG combat air patrol (CAP) provided by the 432d Tactical Reconnaissance Wing at Udorn (F-4s), six F-105Gs (SAM and AAA suppression) provided by the 6010th Wild Weasel Squadron at Korat RTAFB, two EC-121T College Eye early warning and command

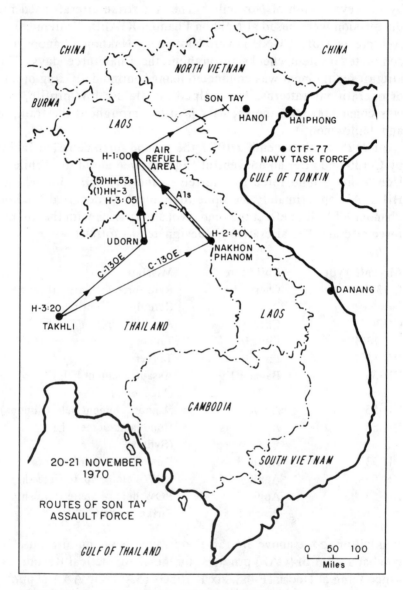

Fig. 8–3. The Route of the Son Tay Raid Force.

and control aircraft, two Combat Apple (airborne mission coordinator aircraft) from Kadena Air Force Base, Okinawa, one KC-135 radio relay aircraft, ten KC-135 reserve tankers from U-Tapao RTAFB, and a three-aircraft carrier diversionary strike force which included seven A-6s, twenty A-7s, twelve F-4 and F-8 aircraft, six ECM/ES-1s, and fourteen support aircraft. In all over 116 aircraft participated in the operation, taking off from seven airfields and three aircraft carriers.

At 2256 on 20 November, the ground forces aboard their designated helicopters departed Udorn to begin the flight to Son Tay. Immediately after takeoff, an unidentified aircraft passed through the formation on a reciprocal heading, causing the helos to disperse. This created only a momentary delay before the helos rejoined in formation. The plan called for the helicopters (led by one C-130) and the A-1s (following the second C-130 out of Nakhon Phanom) to rendezvous over Laos. This provided an in-flight refueling point for the helos and allowed the two elements to join forces prior to the final leg into Son Tay.

The assault formation approached Son Tay from the west. As they arrived at a point 3-1/2 miles from the compound, the lead C-130 relayed a heading of 072 degrees to the helicopters and then pulled up and away, preparing to drop flares and firefight simulators. The first three HH-53s and the HH-3 slowed to approximately eighty knots while the remaining two HH-53s climbed to fifteen hundred feet to stand by as reserve flare ships and to recover POWs. The A-1s had executed their flight plan as scheduled, with the fifth A-1 dropping off over the Black River and the third and fourth A-1s establishing a holding pattern closer to the compound. The primary strike A-1s proceeded to the objective area and established a left-handed orbit at three thousand feet above ground level.

The lead C-130 commenced the flare drop on schedule at 0218. Seeing that the flare drop was satisfactory, Apple 4 and 5 HH-53s proceeded to their holding area on an island in Finger Lake (7 nautical miles west of Son Tay). At the same moment, approaching the coast from the east, the navy diversionary raid was in progress, which "utterly confused the enemy defenses," focusing their attention away from Son Tay.[25]

As the helos approached the objective area, Apple 3 (the gunship

HH-53, which was the lead helo in the formation at this time) began a firing run on what appeared to be the compound. As he approached the target, however, the pilot realized it was not the correct location, and he turned left toward Son Tay. The HH-3 following immediately behind Apple 3 also turned north. Unfortunately, Apple 1 (containing Colonel Simons's support group) landed in a field outside the wrong target. Behind Apple 1 was Apple 2, which contained Sydnor and the command and security group. The pilot of Apple 2 immediately recognized the error and proceeded north behind Apple 3 and the HH-3.

At 0218, Apple 3 commenced his firing run on the Son Tay guard towers. As their aircraft flew between the two wooden structures, the door gunners in Apple 3 opened fire, destroying the watchtowers instantly. After completing the firing run, Apple 3 proceeded to a holding area 1-1/2 nautical miles east of Finger Lake and awaited orders to return and pick up POWs.

Banana 1, the HH-3 with Capt. Richard Meadows and the assault group, made a west-to-east approach crossing the west wall. The door, window, and ramp gunners began firing on their areas of responsibility as the helo executed a controlled crash into the compound. The trees in the LZ had grown significantly since June when they were originally photographed. The blades of the HH-3 severed several small trunks and sheered the tops of the others. The impact of the landing was so violent that the door gunner was thrown clear of the aircraft but landed unhurt. Once on the ground the assault group's mission was "to secure the inside of the POW compound, to include guard towers, gates, and cell blocks and to release and guide POWs to the control point."[26]

The group was divided into five elements: a headquarters element with the mission to secure the south tower and latrines and provide command and control; Action Element 1, which was to clear the cell blocks and north tower; Action Element 2, which was to provide cover for the third element; Action Element 3, which was to clear the front gate; and the air force crew, which would assist in POW handling.

Upon landing, the headquarters element cleared the southwest guard tower, broadcast messages to the POWs, blew a four-foot-by-four-foot hole in the west wall with a twenty-pound satchel charge, and established radio contact with the ground force commander (Sydnor) and all the action elements.

Action Element 1 moved to building 5A where it was believed the prisoners were being held. All the cell blocks were searched by a two-man search team while other members of the element provided security. Members of the element continued to clear their assigned areas including the northwest tower and the areas along the west and north walls. Part of the element proceeded to the holding cells in building 5C and another part to 5D. As the element moved into 5D, three to five NVA (Vietnamese Army troops) rushed from the building and were killed by Action Elements 2 and 3. Outside the building, NVA guards began to initiate a large volume of ineffective automatic-weapons fire. Action Element 2 quickly moved into buildings 5E and 4, clearing the spaces as they went. Inside 5E, two NVA guards were killed. The locks on the cells were cut and all blocks searched as planned. Action Element 3 moved to secure the gate and clear building 5B. Element 3 killed three NVA just inside and north of the gate while two enemy were killed outside near building 7A.

At H hour + 10 minutes the headquarters element received an all-clear from the action elements and was notified that no prisoners had been found. Meadows subsequently ordered all elements to move to the southwest wall and stand by for extraction. He then radioed the command group leader that "zero items" were found in the compound. At H+15 the action elements (minus headquarters) moved to the marshaling position outside the compound. The headquarters element remained behind to destroy the HH-3. At H+18, Meadows initiated the demolition charge and a firefight simulator to replicate the sound of gunfire. Then he proceeded out the southwest wall and linked up with Sydnor.

As the assault group was executing its controlled crash inside the Son Tay compound, Apple 2, with Sydnor and the command element, was landing just outside the south wall. The pilot of Apple 2, realizing that Apple 1 had inadvertently landed at the wrong compound, implemented Plan Green, which provided for the loss of one helicopter. With Plan Green in effect, the door gunners from Apple 2 engaged the prescribed buildings outside the compound while the pilot landed the helicopter a hundred yards from the south wall.

Inside the helo, Sydnor was advised "by the pilot of Apple 2 that
Apple 1 was not present."[27] Sydnor immediately "took hold of Red-
wine's [Captain Daniel Turner—command group leader] equipment
harness [they were seated side by side in the aircraft] and advised
him that Plan Green was in effect."[28] Then he directed his radio operator to notify all elements that the alternate plan was being executed.
All of the command elements (known as security elements) were
redirected except for Security Element 2, which had not established
radio contact and was too far away to be visually alerted.

As soon as the new orders were transmitted, all the elements
responded accordingly. They had practiced the alternate plan so often "all [Turner] had to do was say 'Plan Green in effect' and they
reacted."[29]

"The mission of the Command Group was to secure the south
wall, act as reserve for Assault and Support Groups, and act as control for evacuating prisoners to helicopters."[30] However, with Plan
Green in effect that mission was expanded to include securing the
east wall and all buildings close by as well as destroying the vehicle bridge to the north. The command element came under small-
arms and rifle-grenade fire from building 7B as they exited the helo
and began to direct the security elements. This threat was quickly
subdued but not eliminated. The helo immediately departed the area
for its holding spot. Within minutes Sydnor contacted the circling
A-1s and directed them to attack the footbridge to the southeast.
The A-1s dropped four white phosphorous one-hundred-pound
bombs on the bridge and then expended six Rockeyes on isolated
targets on the road southwest of the camp.

The NVA, now fully alerted, began to return fire and move to secure areas. Three or four NVA were killed running between buildings
11 and 12, and several more were killed as they were caught between
the command element (still situated at the LZ) and Security Element
1 moving toward the south wall. Security Element 1, executing Plan
Green, moved to its objectives at buildings 8E, 8D, and 4A. In the
process small-arms fire from building 7B was suppressed and two
NVA killed. Upon arriving at building 8D, Element 1 came under
heavy fire. Three members of the element assaulted the building and
cleared it with a hand grenade. The number of killed is unknown.
Five NVA were spotted to the east of 8D and were engaged by fire.

At the same time, one NVA engaged Element 1 from the west end of the building, and two NVA fired from the east end of 8D. Element 1 engaged and killed the two NVA at the east end and suppressed the remaining fire. The portion of Element 1 assigned to clear buildings 8E and 4A was engaged by four NVA. The element returned fire, but the results are unknown. They continued clearing the buildings and subsequently linked up with members of the assault group exiting the compound through the hole in the west wall.

Security Element 2 did not receive word about the change in plan and consequently proceeded to execute their basic mission. They disabled the power station with an M72 light antitank weapon (LAW) and then assaulted and cleared it. Immediately following this action, the element began receiving small-arms fire from the southwest and from a position south of the canal. Both enemy threats were subdued with two NVA killed in the process.

Security Element 3 had moved to a position south of the small canal when they received word about the change in plan. Unfortunately, enemy fire and the thick foliage prevented a hasty retreat to their new objective. However, by H+5 the element was in position to engage building 7B. The grenadier and M60 man attacked the building with heavy fire. The element was delayed in assaulting the building owing to a deep drainage ditch and the thick concertina wire that surrounded the target. As they approached the building two NVA were killed. Another ten were killed once they entered the building.

The pathfinder element, which was to set up the primary LZ, cleared the pump station with a concussion grenade and thirty rounds of ammunition and then blew down the nearby power poles to clear the LZ. As this was happening, the support group, which had been delayed at the false compound, arrived at Son Tay. The ground force commander alerted all his security elements that the support group had landed and would take up their original positions. The security elements were ordered to remain in their positions until the support group elements relieved them. At that point they were to return to the ground force commander's location and await extraction.

The support group, which had been aboard Apple 1, was mistakenly inserted at a compound (initially named the secondary school)

four hundred meters southeast of the POW compound. The mistake
was not immediately obvious, and the helo departed, leaving the
support group at the secondary school. The elements were quickly
engaged by the enemy. Reacting to the situation the support group
headquarters element assaulted the secondary school and penetrated
the complex at the south wall. Once inside the school compound,
they assaulted the building located at the south end (building 1)
with grenades and rifle fire. This accounted for ten NVA dead. The
support group commander, Colonel Simons, notified all elements
that a withdrawal was imminent. Element 1 cleared a LZ and provided zone security while Element 2, under heavy fire, moved to
the road east of the compound and established a blocking force.

The support group headquarters element continued to clear the
compound. Significant automatic-weapons fire was coming from
the two-story building (building 4) in the center of the compound.
A grenadier fired 40mm rounds through both the windows and
doors eliminating the threat. By H+3 this building was secure. As
the headquarters element began to clear building 2, four NVA, who
were attempting to reach the two-story building (which was later
reported to have housed the armory), were killed.

Element 2 continued to receive isolated fire from the enemy and
at H+4 was ordered to close the LZ and help establish perimeter
security. By H+6 all elements began moving toward the LZ. Apple
1, who by now realized his mistake, was inbound to extract the
force. As the support group began to load the helo, Element 1 laid
down suppressive machine-gun fire and all personnel reembarked
without any casualties being sustained.

Nine minutes after mistakenly landing at the wrong compound,
the support group arrived at Son Tay. Simons was advised that Plan
Green had been implemented, but with the support group's arrival,
the force would return to the basic plan. Elements from the support
group passed through the lines and linked up with command elements. Support Group Element 1 established a secure position near
building 7A, from which a steady volume of fire had been received.
The grenadier launched several 40mm grenades and the firing
ceased. Element 2 headed toward building 13E, suppressing the
enemy with M60, M79, and M16 fire. The building was subsequently assaulted and two NVA killed.

By the time the support group and command group elements were in position, the word had been passed from Meadows that there were no POWs in the Son Tay compound. Sydnor gave the order for all elements to withdraw to the vicinity of the extraction site. This occurred at approximately H+17. Soon thereafter, the A-1s were ordered to attack the vehicle bridge to the north to prevent any reinforcement from the NVA. Four strafing runs using 20mm were conducted by two different aircraft. At H+23 the helos landed, and by H+27 all elements were extracted with only one minor casualty. The return trip to Udorn, Thailand, was punctuated by several SAM sightings, which required evasive action on the part of all the air force elements. However, after the aircraft refueled over Laos, the remaining trip was relatively uneventful.

As the ground engagement was in progress, the aviation support forces (F-4Ds and F-105s) were busy avoiding and suppressing SAMs. Approximately sixteen SAMs were fired, and the F-105s responded with eight Shrikes. While flying at thirteen thousand feet, one of the F-105s (Firebird 03) was damaged by a SAM that exploded under its left wing and apparently ruptured the fuel tank.* The crew was forced to eject at eight thousand feet over the Plaine des Jarres. They were eventually picked up by the assault formation HH-53s (Apples 4 and 5).

The navy diversionary raid proceeded as planned. It is estimated that twenty SAMs were fired at the force, but no casualties were sustained. It was later reported that "the density of the Navy operations in the Gulf of Tonkin [during the Son Tay raid] was the most extensive Navy night operation of the SEA [Southeast Asia] conflict."[31]

Throughout the entire operation, Manor monitored radio communication between all the participants, and he had a direct link with

---

*Firebird 03 was fired upon by two SAMs. When the missiles were at one mile, the pilot rolled over and descended to five thousand feet. The two missiles followed the F-105, and the pilot was forced to execute a hard pullout. The first SAM passed over the aircraft and detonated behind it. The second SAM detonated under the left wing, damaging the aircraft. Another F-105 also recorded a hit and was forced to crash-land on an airfield in Thailand.

Admiral McCain (CINCPAC) and Admiral Moorer (Chairman, JCS). Additionally he received continuous real-time intelligence on the enemy activity. He said later, "I had information on what they [NVA integrated air defense personnel] were seeing almost as quickly as . . . their decision makers were getting it."[32]

Manor knew that the operation had failed to recover any POWs. He flew to Udorn to meet the returning raid force. "They were a very disappointed group of people. My immediate goal was to have a meeting of some of the key people and get some information from them that I needed right away to put together a top secret message to Admiral Moorer telling him what the status was . . . Later that morning I got a call from Admiral Moorer telling me and Simons to get back to Washington as soon as we could."[33] Within two days the force was returned to CONUS and Operation Kingpin was officially completed.

ANALYSIS

Critique

The failure of the Son Tay raid to recover any POWs created a political fallout of incredible proportions. The media immediately blasted the intelligence community for its inability to verify the existence of POWs prior to the operation, and the administration was vilified for escalating the war. What was overlooked was the exceptional performance of the raiding force and their support elements. The fact that there were no POWs in the compound does not detract from the success of the tactical portion of the raid. The mission was planned, rehearsed, and executed exactly the same as if there had been POWs. The disposition of the enemy force at Son Tay was as expected. The fact that there were no POWs to guard may have relaxed the enemy's posture, but relaxed or not, the raid force executed the mission with such surprise and speed that only substantial opposition could have prevented a successful outcome. Brigadier General Manor stated in his report on the raid on Son Tay that "it should be noted that we were successful not only in what was done, but what could have been done if necessary."[34] The raid on Son Tay is the best modern-day example of a successful special operation and should be considered textbook material for future missions.

Were the objectives worth the risk? The taking of prisoners of war has always generated a call for action. As stated earlier during the case on Cabanatuan, prisoners constitute a direct affront to national and military honor. In Vietnam, this concern may have been more pronounced owing to the perceived failure of the war effort. By 1970 the war claimed an average of five hundred deaths a month, and more than 470 Americans were believed held captive in North Vietnam. All previous efforts to rescue American prisoners had been futile.* All of these issues were compounded by the reluctance of the North Vietnamese government to negotiate with President Nixon concerning de-escalation and the release of POWs. Nixon, who was faced with dwindling political alternatives, clearly saw the rescue as a viable option to restore national dignity and recover American soldiers, many of whom had been held prisoner for years. Any time a nation attempts to rescue prisoners behind enemy lines, they face the risk of having the rescue force captured and thereby adding to the number of POWs. For most nations, however, attempting to rescue prisoners, regardless of the outcome, is generally perceived as a worthwhile endeavor and well worth the risks.

Was the plan developed to maximize superiority over the enemy and minimize the risk to the assault force? Of the eight cases presented in this book, the raid on Son Tay eclipses all others in the level of national support it received. By having the assets of CIA, DIA, NSA, SAC, and military intelligence, the planners and operators were able to identify all the critical nodes in the North Vietnamese air defense system and have enough information to construct a detailed model of the POW camp. As Blackburn described it, this flawless operational intelligence, coupled with four months of mission preparation, allowed the assault force to plan around the North Vietnamese defenses and minimize the risk to the raiders. Additionally, the small raid force was augmented by over one hundred aircraft that provided MiG CAP, air defense suppression, and operational deception, all of which contributed to maximizing superiority over the enemy.

---

*Over ninety-one POW rescue attempts had been mounted between 1966 and 1970. However, none of these were in North Vietnam.

Was the mission executed according to plan, and if not what un-foreseen circumstances dictated the outcome? From the raid force's perspective the mission was conducted by the numbers, with the exception of Simons's misadventure into the secondary school. But this eventuality was planned for, and Simons's failure to arrive at the POW camp on time did not unduly affect the conduct of the operation. Obviously the failure to rescue any POWs was demoral-izing to the raid force, but from a purely operational standpoint, that was beyond the control of the planners and operators. As the secretary of defense, Melvin Laird, said later during a congres-sional hearing, "We have not been able to develop a camera that sees through the roofs of buildings."[35] Had the planners risked plac-ing a CAS in the vicinity of the camp, they might have been able to determine conclusively whether there were POWs. But this option was weighed carefully, and the risks were considered too high. Consequently, the unforeseen circumstances that affected the out-come of the mission were not a result of faulty planning, prepara-tion, or execution and can only be attributed to the frictions of war.

What modifications could have improved the outcome of the mis-sion? Disregarding the failure to rescue any POWs, the mission was almost flawless. Not one soldier or airman was killed or seriously injured on the raid. This includes the navy and air force airmen who supported the deception and cover operations. Considering the dif-ficulty of penetrating a sophisticated air defense system and then conducting combat operations in unfamiliar surroundings, the raid on Son Tay should stand as a tribute to the tremendous preparation and professionalism of the assault force. It is doubtful that any modifications to the plan could have improved the performance of the raiders.

Relative Superiority
Camp Hope, near the Son Tay citadel, was less than thirty miles from Hanoi. The air defense coverage in the immediate vicinity was complete, and even without POWs in the compound, the guard force surrounding the camp numbered over one hundred North Viet-namese regulars. Although there were no prisoners, the raid force was not certain of this fact until fifteen minutes into the assault. Consequently, the force still had to achieve relative superiority in

order to make this determination and then sustain relative superiority long enough to extract from the camp and return to Thailand. Therefore, for purposes of analysis we will view mission completion as the successful return of the raid force and relative superiority as a function of that mission.

When did the raid force achieve a decisive advantage over the North Vietnamese? As Figure 8-4 shows, the point of vulnerability occurred "twelve minutes before [the raid force] reached the objective."[36] It was at this point that the central and western air defense systems could detect the inbound aircraft. Manor remarked later that the raid force was not overly concerned with the FanSong SAMs because they could not engage targets below three thousand feet, and the FireCan AAA sites posed only a limited threat. (Later the North Vietnamese acquired the newer India-version SAMs and were subsequently able to engage and destroy aircraft at much lower altitudes.) As for the North Vietnamese air force, they "had little or no night fighter capability."[37] But, at twelve minutes out, even with the sophisticated electronic warfare used by the U.S. Air Force, the raid force became vulnerable to detection. If it had been detected by the North Vietnamese, the POW camp might have been notified in time to prepare an ambush for the raiders. With each minute that passed, however, the raid force improved their probability of mission completion, although a decisive advantage would not be achieved until the moment the raid force engaged the guards. At H hour, Lieutenant Colonel Donohue, piloting his HH-53, strafed the guard towers, and it became apparent that "the [raid force] had never been detected at all."[38] It was a complete surprise, and the enemy was unprepared to counter the assault. It was at this point that the probability of mission completion outweighed the probability of failure, not marginally but decisively. This is depicted by the significant jump above the relative superiority line. Had the North Vietnamese been alerted five or ten minutes before the raid, the Americans, with their speed and overwhelming firepower, would probably still have achieved relative superiority, but it would have been only slightly above the dotted line, indicating less of an advantage.

Relative superiority or not, the force still had to assault the compound and fight the guards. Therefore they remained vulnerable

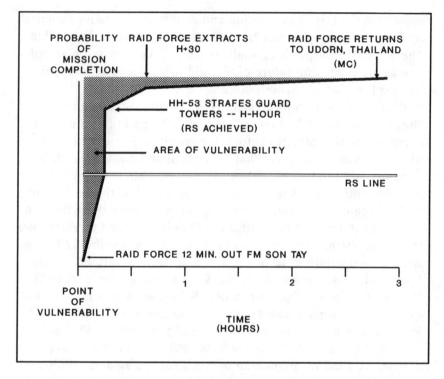

Fig. 8–4. Relative Superiority Graph for the Son Tay Raid

throughout the twenty-six-minute time on target. This vulnerability was minimized somewhat by A-1 strike aircraft that provided close air support and bombing runs to dissuade enemy reinforcements (similar to the Stukas at Eben Emael). Once the assault force was back on the helos, the area of vulnerability decreased to a negligible amount, primarily because Manor had arranged for a host of F-105s and F-4s to provide SAM suppression and MiG CAP. Manor said later that the returning assault force was really only vulnerable until they reached Laos, approximately one hour from Son Tay. But even this vulnerability was minimal. In the end, gaining and sustaining relative superiority became a function of proper planning, preparation, and execution rather than being dependent on benevolent frictions of war or the strong intervention of the moral factors.

The Principles of Special Operations

Simplicity. When referring to the assault plan on Son Tay, Colonel Sydnor said, "I had never seen such a simple plan and so clearly written that even I could understand it."[39]

From the time the special operations plan was formulated until the execution of the mission, the basic scheme of maneuver was virtually unchanged. The only major exception was the change in the assault helo from a UH-1H to an HH-3. The plan was simple enough that it allowed various aspects of the mission to be rehearsed over 170 times, with several full-dress rehearsals. One rehearsal even included exercising the short C-130 flight from Takhli to Udorn and transferring the raid force to the helos. Although the plan was simple enough, there were some difficult objectives to be achieved, including the clandestine penetration of the North Vietnamese integrated air defense and quick seizure of the compound with a minimum of friendly losses. Both of these actions were made simpler by applying good intelligence and innovative technology to the problems.

Although much has been written about the intelligence failure at Son Tay, the intelligence successes generally go unheralded. In assessing the intelligence provided the planning group, General Blackburn later recalled that "operational intelligence was flawless . . . One day we got from Manor, 'Hey, do you realize that to fly from the Plaine des Jarres down into Son Tay, there are two radars? If we fly between those two radars, we are going to make that northeast warning system go hot. What do we do?' I [Blackburn] got a fellow named Milt Zaslov from NSA. I said, 'Zaslov, we have a problem. How do we handle this thing?' . . . In less than a week . . . they were able to solve the problem. There is a five-minute gap in the way these things are rotated and we used that five-minute gap and they flew through it undetected."[40]

Every conceivable asset in the national intelligence network was placed at the disposal of the planners. Other platforms, such as the Buffalo Hunter reconnaissance drones and the SR-71, conducted overflights of the area. These flights (primarily the SR-71) provided complete photo coverage of the raid force's inbound route as well as a detailed look at the POW compound.* These photos were used by the CIA to produce a scale model of the compound for the operators to study. Photo interpreters who studied the drone pictures were able to determine precise details about the POW compound including the height of trees in compound, the composition of the buildings and what they were used for, the approximate number of guards, the NVA fighting positions, and the location of all telephone wires that might affect a helicopter landing. All of this intelligence contributed to simplifying the plan by eliminating unknown factors.

Once inside the POW compound the Special Forces personnel needed to quickly identify and kill the guards. This required rapid target discrimination. Unfortunately, the soldiers' night-firing capability, as shown during the rehearsals at Eglin Air Force Base, proved less than acceptable. Once the army acquired the Armson single-point sight, however, the soldiers' night-firing accuracy improved dramatically. It was this innovative technology that directly contributed to the lack of American casualties. Of the fifty-six men in the raid force, only one man sustained a gunshot wound as opposed to over forty enemy killed. The air element of the raid force also benefited significantly from technological improvements including the forward-looking infrared (FLIR), GAR/I beacons, and the host of airborne command and control and SAM suppression assets.

The Son Tay raid does present a paradox of simplicity. On the one hand the actions by the raid force appear to have been simplified through proper application of intelligence and technology and the limitation of objectives. However, the raid also included one hundred other aircraft launched from seven air bases and three aircraft carriers, none of which had an opportunity to rehearse the mission ahead of time. Can this be called simple? It can if the operation was a matter of routine for those pilots, and it was. All of the flight profiles flown by the support aircraft had been flown doz-

---

*The Buffalo Hunter reconnaissance drones conducted seven overflights, but six of these malfunctioned or were destroyed by the North Vietnamese, and the photos from the last flight were unacceptable.

ens and in some cases hundreds of times by the aircrews. Constant practice had honed the pilots' skills to the point where their mission was not special and therefore didn't require additional training.

Security. At the outset of the mission a conscious decision was made to limit the number of personnel who actually knew the objective and its location. The security staff section was organized on 11 August, well before actual training began. They developed cover and deception plans that provided for every aspect of the operation from training through deployment. While the raid force was training at Eglin Air Force Base, the Security Staff systematically elicited information from military personnel, monitored the news media, and analyzed domestic and foreign intelligence reports to determine if information was leaking. This small army of counterintelligence personnel also monitored all military telephone calls, conducted technical security surveys of all facilities both in CONUS and in Thailand, established document control, and conducted psychological operations to prevent espionage or sabotage from interfering with the mission. All of these precautions were taken without unduly affecting the operation's planning or preparation.

There were, however, two facets of security that did negatively impact on the mission. The first was a minor inconvenience caused by the need to protect classified weather data. The *Son Tay Report* stated: "Protecting the security of the operation imposed some special problems during in-theater coordination. Much of the decision base for the final launch hinged upon timely classified weather data . . . Initial access to the classified weather data was denied by the 1st Weather Group Commander."[41] Eventually Manor had to get the director of operations, U.S. Air Force Headquarters, to send a personal message to the vice commander of the Seventh Air Force, which owned the 1st Weather Group. This created undue interest among personnel at Takhli, and eventually a cover story was generated to avoid further questions.

The second facet of security that negatively impacted the mission was the decision not to deploy a CAS agent into the vicinity of Son Tay to verify the existence of American POWs in the camp. Benjamin Schemmer reported in his book, *The Raid,* that military planners supported inserting a CAS agent who could "'bicycle down the road' outside Son Tay, arrange to have a flat tire or break his drive chain, take a quick glimpse or two inside that front gate, [and] listen for an American voice."[42] Unfortunately, the CIA, which controlled the CAS agents, objected for fear "it could reveal the fact that [we] were zeroing in on that point . . . [and] that the North Vietnamese might find out about the raid and lay an ambush."[43] In hindsight, had a CAS agent been successfully inserted, the planners might have known the status of the American prisoners at Son Tay. With these two exceptions, the security was thorough but not cumbersome. It worked around the basic plan without being the driving factor.

Repetition. In the *Son Tay Report,* Brigadier General Manor commented on the degree to which the mission had been rehearsed. He said, "Every facet of the operation [was] exercised [totaling] more than 170 times. Every conceivable contingency was provided for and exercised. Each man knew precisely what his task was under each contingency . . . The rapid and smooth transition to an alternate plan at the objective testifies to [the] ability of the force to adapt to varying conditions."[44]

Through constant rehearsal, first by individual units, then by the force as a whole, the contingency task force was able to identify and rectify operational shortfalls, develop and exercise alternate plans, and ensure the raid force was confident in its own capabilities. Repetition was instrumental to success in almost every aspect of the mission: achieving formation flying between the helos and the C-130s, executing the HH-53 firing run between the guard towers, controlled crashing of the HH-3, initial ground force actions, and execution of alternate Plan Green. The aviation rehearsals alone included 284 sorties and over 793 total flight hours. When the ground force was required to execute Plan Green, Sydnor remembered, "because of all the rehearsals we had done, it was automatic."[45] Each of these aspects of the mission required special training before the participants could master the evolution: immediate action drills, house searches, target recognition, close air control, search and rescue, and escape and evasion were all new or varied procedures unique to the Son Tay raid. Rehearsals were also required for the use of new equipment, such as Armson single-point sights, night-vision devices, and FLIR and GAR/I beacons for the air crews. Fortunately, the task force had four months to prepare, but even up to the last hour, assault team leaders were briefing and rehearsing their movements on target. Other aspects of the mission, such as SAM suppression and the navy diversionary raid, were not unique to the individual pilots and therefore could safely be executed on short notice.

Surprise. The *Son Tay Report* noted that "the diversionary actions performed by Carrier Task Force 77 were vital to the overall success of the mission. The results of this effort were exactly as foreseen during the planning phase. It caused the enemy defense authorities to split their attention and concern thereby contributing greatly to the confusion and chaos which resulted. In short, it served to deny the enemy the option of concentrating his attention to our true and primary mission."[46]

In order to gain complete surprise on target, the air element carrying the Special Forces personnel had to penetrate North Vietnamese integrated air defenses undetected. They achieved this as a result of the navy's deception operation. Complete surprise, however, was probably not essential to mission success. If during the twelve-minute window of vulnerability the North Vietnamese had detected the force and notified the camp guards, they would have taken several minutes (it was approximatley 0200, and most of the auxiliary guard force was asleep) to muster a substantial resistance. Had the raid force been visually detected on their final approach, it is doubtful the North Vietnamese could have withstood the speed or firepower of the air armada. But, of course, the concern was not that the raid force would be detected, but that the NVA would kill the POWs before the raid force could arrive. It is doubtful, however, that in all the confusion around Hanoi as a result of the navy's air raid, the Vietnamese would have realized that this "massive attack" was all a deception to rescue fifty-five POWs. It is even more doubtful that they would have made this determination and then given the order to kill the POWs, all within twelve minutes.

As it turned out, the raid force was "never picked up at all."[47] This was due in part to the use of the navy deception raid and in part to the good intelligence and superior technology that allowed the air element to navigate terrain and slip through the radar blind spots. The *Son Tay Report* stated: "The initial North Vietnamese Air Defense System reaction against the task force was first noted approximately 20 minutes *after* the first helicopter landed at the landing zone (LZ)."[48] Surprise, when rescuing POWs or hostages, is an essential requirement for success. The Son Tay raiders unquestionably achieved complete surprise. Unfortunately there were no POWs to rescue, but the element of surprise still prevented unnecessary casualties among the raid force and was instrumental in getting in and out alive.

Speed. The decision to land Meadows and his assault force inside the POW compound instead of outside showed that the planners had a thorough understanding of the need to move quickly on target. Sydnor stated later that "originally the plan was to land [the helo with Meadows's assault element] outside the compound, which meant there would be a slight delay. However you were going to negotiate the wall; blow through it, go over it, find an open gate . . . whatever. It was reckoned that those few seconds might lose us some prisoners."[49] But this aspect of the mission was only one of many that minimized the time on the objective. The first attempt to reduce the time on target was a conscious decision by the planners to limit the ground operation to thirty minutes. It was assumed that after thirty minutes the NVA regulars in the surrounding area would begin to reinforce the beleagured POW camp. This would place both the ground force and the helos in jeopardy. Once a limit was established, all the rehearsals were conducted with that time frame in mind. The ground force practiced rapid helo on-load and off-load exercises, POW evacuations, immediate action drills—all designed to reduce their time in the compound. Special equipment such as bolt cutters and acetylene torches was purchased to quickly force the cell doors and extract the POWs. Chain saws were bought to help the pathfinders rapidly clear the helicopter LZs, and demolition charges were used to blow a hole in the compound wall to quickly extract the POWs.

All of this preparation paid off, and the entire ground operation took only twenty-six minutes. Even if the POWs had been present, it is arguable whether the operation would have taken longer than thirty-five minutes. Postwar reports from Son Tay POWs indicated that most of the prisoners were in solitary confinement or doubled up, but none were shackled. Consequently, no time would have been required to cut chains.

Purpose. Every man in the task force understood that the primary objective of the raid was to free the POWs at the Son Tay POW compound. Understanding the purpose of the overall mission is crucial, particularly when elements have supporting roles (i.e., assault, support, command, pathfinder, and marshaling) that are integral to the success of the operation. Too often elements can become distracted by their situation and lose focus on what is important. This did not happen during the Son Tay raid. When the support element, under Simons, landed at the secondary school and came under heavy fire, they could easily have been induced to remain at that location and engage the enemy with both ground and air fire. Instead of becoming preoccupied with killing NVA at the secondary school, the support element disengaged after nine minutes and rejoined the task force at the compound. Although this represents the principle of purpose on a large scale, it applies equally to the individual soldier, who must execute his portion of the mission always cognizant of the primary objective.

Sydnor said later, "The mission statement was clearly written to include the phrase 'To forcibly release and extract the prisoners.' I liked the word 'forcibly' as it provided a lot of flexibility in the use of force against the enemy."

Notes

1. Brig. Gen. Donald Blackburn, comments from the Son Tay panel discussion 29 March 1988, USSOCOM MacDill Air Force Base, Fla.

2. Ibid.

3. Lt. Gen. Leroy J. Manor, interview by author, tape recording, Monterey, Calif., 3 June 1992.

4. Lt. Gen. Leroy J. Manor, interview by Dr. John W. Parton and Richard J. Meadows, tape recording, Tampa, Fla., 23 February 1988.

5. Manor, panel discussion.

6. Col. John V. Allison, panel discussion.

7. Commander, JCS Joint Contingency Task Group, *Report on the Son Tay Prisoner of War Rescue Operation* (Washington, D.C.: Office of the Joint Chiefs of Staff, 1970), parts 1–3.

8. Manor, interview by author.

9. Manor, panel discussion.

10. Manor, interview with Parton and Meadows.

11. *Son Tay Report,* C-8–C-12.

12. *Son Tay Report,* D-2.

13. Manor, interview with Parton and Meadows.

14. Col. Elliot Sydnor, interview by author, tape recording, Monterey, Calif., 29 April 1992.

15. Benjamin F. Schemmer, *The Raid* (New York: Avon Books, 1976), 80.

16. *Son Tay Report,* E-37.

17. Ibid., E-39.

18. Ibid., E-49.

19. Ibid., E-61, E-54.

20. Allison, panel discussion.

21. *Son Tay Report,* ii–iii.

22. Ibid., 31.

23. Ibid., 33.

24. Manor, interview by author.

25. Lt. Col. Donohue featured on West Point instructional video dated February 1977.

26. *Son Tay Report,* 59.
27. Sydnor, interview.
28. Ibid.
29. Ibid.
30. *Son Tay Report,* 54.
31. *Son Tay Report,* 70.
32. Manor, interview by author.
33. Ibid.
34. *Son Tay Report,* iii.
35. Schemmer, *The Raid,* 233.
36. Lt. Gen. Leroy J. Manor, interview by author, telephone tape recording, Monterey, Calif., 23 April 1993.
37. Manor, interview, 1993.
38. Ibid.
39. Sydnor, panel discussion.
40. Blackburn, panel discussion.
41. *Son Tay Report,* 29.
42. Schemmer, *The Raid,* 82.
43. Ibid.
44. *Son Tay Report,* ii–iii.
45. Sydnor, interview.
46. *Son Tay Report,* iv.
47. Manor, interview, 1993.
48. *Son Tay Report,* 6. (Emphasis added.)
49. Sydnor, interview.

9

Operation Jonathan: The Israeli Raid on Entebbe, 4 July 1976

BACKGROUND

On Sunday, 27 June 1976, at approximately 1230, Air France flight number AF 139 was hijacked en route from Lod Airport in Israel to Paris after an intermediate stop in Athens. Aboard the A300 airbus were 254 passengers, a third of whom were Israeli. The four terrorists who hijacked the plane included two Germans, who were members of the Baader-Meinhof Gang, and two Palestinians.

The Israeli government immediately placed the Sayeret Matkal Counterterrorist Unit, referred to as the Unit, on alert. (Sayeret Matkal literally means the reconnaissance unit of the General Headquarters of the Israeli Defense Force. The Unit was under the direct operational and administrative control of the General Headquarters.) It had been the habit of hijackers to return to Israel and make their demands on Israeli soil. In 1972, for example, Arab terrorists hijacked a Sabena airliner and landed at Lod Airport to make their demands to the international media. The Unit was always prepared to conduct a hostage rescue inside the confines of Lod Airport. But by the time the Unit's personnel assembled at Lod, the airbus had landed in Benghazi, Libya. The Unit stood down temporarily and awaited further orders.

After a six-and-one-half-hour delay in Benghazi, the plane refueled and took off heading east. Again the Unit went on alert and prepared to receive the hijackers. After several discussions, the commander of the Unit, Lt. Col. Jonathan Netanyahu, recommended to his superiors that if the plane returned to Lod, the Unit should immediately mount an assault. By midnight, however, it was clear the airbus was heading to Africa. At 0300 the following morning, the plane touched down at Entebbe, Uganda, where three more Palestinians, from the Popular Front for the Liberation of Palestine (PFLP), joined the terrorists.*

The passengers were kept inside the airbus for nine hours after the plane landed at Entebbe. At noon on Monday, 28 June, the terrorists took the passengers from the plane to the main passenger lounge in the old terminal building. Later that day, Idi Amin, president of Uganda, arrived and told the hostages that he was working to negotiate their release and that Ugandan soldiers would remain at the terminal to ensure the passengers' safety. Amin informed the passengers that Israel had already stated that their government would not negotiate with terrorists.

On Tuesday, 29 June, at approximately 1530, the terrorists, now under the command of a Palestinian Arab called the Peruvian, made their specific demands known. They wanted the release of fifty-three prisoners: thirteen Arab and German terrorists held in West Germany, France, Switzerland, and Kenya, and forty terrorists in Israeli prisons. One of those held in Israel was Kozo Okamoto of the Japanese Red Army, who was responsible for the murder of twenty-six people at Lod Airport in 1972.[1] If these prisoners were not released, the terrorists announced that they would begin executing passengers at 1400 (Israeli time) on 1 July.

With the announcement, Prime Minister Yitzhak Rabin convened a group of cabinet members to discuss the alternatives. Prior to the

---

*It is also believed that three additional terrorists joined the group later the next day. This raised the total number to ten terrorists. However, at the time of the assault by Israeli commandos, only seven terrorists were present at the old terminal. The others are believed to have been in the town of Entebbe.

meeting with Rabin, the Israeli Defense Force (IDF) Chief of Staff, Motta Gur, had telephoned his own staff and directed them to review military options. Although not part of Gur's staff, Lt. Col. Joshua Shani, commander of the Air Force's only C-130 squadron, had already conducted some rudimentary flight planning. He later said, "We did some private planning exercises and learned that the C-130 was the only airplane that could get to Entebbe and carry people and equipment. I was sitting with my staff, my two deputies, the chief flight engineer, and the chief navigator. We looked at range, fuel, payload, navigation, weather problems, things that take time to cover. We worked six hours or so . . . Tuesday I was at a wedding in Haifa and the commander of the Air Force called. He asked me some questions and I said yes, yes, yes, yes, and yes."[2] Shani was convinced that his C-130s could make the flight from Israel to Entebbe and carry up to one thousand men if necessary. Refueling would be a problem, but there were several ways to work around it.

During the brief with Rabin, Gur presented his ideas, but for several reasons, military options were not seriously contemplated. First, Idi Amin was considered an impartial actor in the hijacking, and it was hoped that through negotiation the Ugandan dictator could secure the hostages' release. Secondly, the majority of the passengers were non-Israeli, and because the airbus was French, the French government had the lead in the negotiation process. Thirdly, the distance from Israel to Uganda was 2,220 miles. The thought of conducting a raid to rescue hostages was, at first, almost inconceivable.

Later that evening, Maj. Gen. Yekutiel Adam, Deputy Chief of Staff, contacted Col. Ehud Barak, the former head of the Unit. Barak was asked to meet informally with the commando and paratrooper units and review possible military actions. By Wednesday morning, when the meeting with Barak ended, a plan had been proposed to parachute marine commandos and their rubber boats into Lake Victoria, which bordered Entebbe Airport. The marines would transit over water to the airport, rescue the hostages, and then turn themselves over to the Ugandan armed forces. There were several problems with the option, not the least of which was that parachuting rubber boats had never been tried before. Nevertheless, at the time it was believed to be the best alternative.

Throughout Wednesday some intelligence began to filter in slowly, although the bulk of information did not arrive until Thursday and Friday. Forty-seven of the non-Jewish hostages were released to the French ambassador in the afternoon. Immediately upon their arrival in Paris, these passengers were interviewed by French intelligence. Also, Brig. Gen. Baruch Bar-Lev, who had formerly been the Israeli attaché in Uganda, had two telephone conversations with Idi Amin. During these phone calls it became increasingly clear that Amin was not neutral and could actually be collaborating with the PFLP. If this was true, it would change the entire complexion of the operation: it meant that the negotiations were a sham and any chance of resolving the crisis in Israel's favor was slim. Additionally, the plan for the marine commandos to rescue the hostages and then surrender to the Ugandans no longer seemed viable. The status of Amin, however, could not be immediately confirmed, and planning and preparation continued.

Early Thursday morning Shani conducted the first of two rubber boat parachute drops to test the concept. The parachute drop failed; Shani recalled that "the rubber boat exploded." But "immediately [the] problem was found and fixed, and we dropped again the same day. And it worked nicely."[3] That same day information from the released passengers seemed to confirm Amin's support for the PFLP. Consequently, by Thursday evening the idea of using marine commandos was dismissed.

In the meantime, members of the IDF had developed an alternate plan that made use of C-130s to land directly at the airfield. Shani said later, "The plan was relatively simple. It was based on the fact that no one would think we were crazy enough to fly there, so it would be a total surprise."[4]

This operational concept called for the four C-130s to conduct a staggered landing at Entebbe. The airport had been recently upgraded and there was an old terminal complex and a new terminal. It was now known that the hostages were being held in the old terminal. In the first aircraft would be commandos from the Unit who would assault the old terminal. Also in the first aircraft would be a small contingent of paratroopers who would secure the new terminal. The second aircraft would contain armored personnel carriers (APCs) and additional commandos and paratroopers. The third and fourth aircraft would contain a reserve force and space for the hostages.

Brig. Gen. Dan Shomron, the officer who would eventually command the raid, believed the concept of operations presented was sound, but the force structure presented in this plan was too limited. He wanted to rely on numerical superiority to overwhelm the terrorists and Ugandan soldiers. The IDF's Operations Chief, Colonel Shai, directed the command staff officers to return to their bases and continue planning. (Colonel Shai was the deputy commander of the Special Operations Division of the IDF, and although junior in rank to General Shomron, he was the IDF staff focal point for all plans dealing with the raid on Entebbe.) Although several concepts were discussed between Monday and Wednesday evening, "nothing was done during that period of time to treat the subject in depth, to broaden the background planning."[5]

With the deadline only hours away, Rabin once again convened a meeting of his cabinet on Thursday, 1 July, at 0700. Gur informed the prime minister that the military was unable to develop a viable solution to rescue the hostages. Consequently, after lengthy discussions on the political ramifications of submitting to the terrorists' demands, the Israeli government announced that it would release the prisoners in exchange for the hostages. Contrary to previously published information, Rabin was not merely stalling for time. He later stated that the Israeli government was prepared to negotiate the hostages' release. The Israelis were committing themselves to this policy in the belief that the hijacking was not directed solely against Jews. At the time of the announcement, over two hundred passengers of all nationalities were still being held prisoner.

At 1300 Thursday afternoon, the terrorists, in receipt of Israel's exchange proposal, announced that the deadline to execute passengers would be extended until Sunday, 4 July. Additionally, the terrorists had released one hundred passengers earlier that morning. All who remained at Entebbe were Israeli citizens, non-Israeli Jews, and the twelve members of the Air France crew, who refused to accept repatriation. In all, 106 hostages remained with the hijackers. The real purpose behind the hijacking was beginning to emerge. Released passengers told intelligence agents that the Jews

were being segregated and that the Ugandan soldiers were cooper-
ating fully with the PFLP. Now, any military option would have to
consider the Ugandan forces as part of the problem. This fact lent
credence to General Shomron's proposal to insert a large-scale
force to overwhelm the enemy.

Later that day, the Israeli Defense Minister, Shimon Peres, met
with his military advisers. They argued about the viability of a rescue operation. The IDF Chief of Staff, Motta Gur, believed that a
mission of this magnitude would be too difficult to execute with
only two days' planning and preparation; casualties could be high,
and Israel could not afford another military disaster like Ma'alot.*
Additionally, intelligence about the airport, and in particular on the
old terminal, was still very sketchy. These arguments notwithstanding, Peres directed that detailed planning and training commence
immediately and appointed Shomron as the commander of the operation. The feeling among the military advisers was that the mission could always be canceled; therefore any prior preparation
could only work to their advantage.

After the meeting with Peres, Jonathan Netanyahu, who until that
morning had been on a classified operation in the desert, went to
Shomron's paratrooper house in Ramat Gan to receive a briefing on
the proposed raid. At the paratrooper house, Shomron laid out the
roles and missions of each of the three ground combat elements.
The Unit was to secure the old terminal and immediate vicinity,
while the paratroopers and Golani Infantry would seize the new
terminal and control tower and act as reinforcements and escorts for
the hostages. Shomron again stated his position that he wanted a
large force to secure the area. According to Netanyahu's intelligence officer, Netanyahu and others argued for a smaller, more mo-

---

*On 15 May 1974, three terrorists from the Democratic Front, a militant
faction of the PLO, took 105 people hostage in a schoolhouse in the town
of Ma'alot. Most of the hostages were schoolchildren and their teachers.
When Israeli soldiers assaulted the schoolhouse, the terrorists began killing hostages. Twenty-two children died, fifty-six others were wounded,
and an Israeli soldier was killed.

bile force. "They said that Shomron's operation would be too big and unwieldy, and a more limited way had to be found to do it, one that would have a better chance of succeeding."[6]

Shomron elected not to make a final decision on the force composition. He had given his broad guidance and now left the details up to the component commanders. The following morning at 0700, he would present the operations order to all the participants, and rehearsals would begin soon afterward.

Netanyahu returned to his compound with Maj. Muki Betzer, who would be his deputy, and the intelligence officer. They began detailed planning. Fortunately for Netanyahu, Betzer had once served in Uganda and was vaguely familiar with the old terminal.

The Unit's mission was to penetrate the old terminal, kill the terrorists, and rescue the hostages. Additionally, the commandos would have to secure the area around the old terminal to ensure Ugandan troops did not reinforce the terrorists or prevent the hostages from boarding the aircraft. Detailed intelligence was still not available on the exact location of the hostages, the physical layout of the old terminal, or the complete Ugandan order of battle. Therefore, the planning continued based on certain worst-case assumptions.

By Friday morning, Netanyahu and his staff had developed a basic plan of attack. The first C-130, flown by Shani, would conduct a blacked-out landing and taxi to the north end of the runway.* Before the plane came to a complete stop, a small team of paratroopers would jump out and place lights along the runway for the next aircraft. At the north end, Shani would stop the C-130 and lower the ramp. The thirty-five commandos, dressed in Ugandan uniforms, would exit the aircraft in three vehicles: a Mercedes and two Jeep Landrovers. It was decided not to make up the commandos in blackface because target discrimination would be confusing, and at night it was doubtful the Ugandans could tell black from white anyway. The Mercedes would be flying the Ugandan flag and

---

*The Unit did not actually propose the blacked-out landing. This was developed by the planners at the C-130 squadron, but it was coordinated with the Unit.

would appear to be an official vehicle. The rescue force would proceed toward the old terminal with their lights on. It was hoped this
action would reduce suspicion among the guards and gain the Israelis
the time they needed to reach the old terminal. (Originally, the Unit
had explored the possibility of posing as Idi Amin. Amin was
scheduled to return from a meeting of the Organization of African
Unity in Mauritius. This idea was later shelved when Amin returned
early to Uganda.)

Netanyahu realized that speed was vital to success. "The time
spent crossing the large airport had to be cut to a minimum, to reduce the risk of the terrorist and Ugandan sentries at the terminal
being alerted by the control tower—and to make sure that even if
they were warned, they would not have time to understand exactly
what was happening and respond."[7] Any Ugandans who attempted
to stop the vehicles would be immediately killed with silenced pistols. The commandos in the Landrovers would also carry machine
guns and shoulder-fired, rocket-propelled grenades in the event a
heavy force intervened.

Once at the old terminal, three teams would immediately assault
the building's three main entrances, concentrating inside on the areas where the hostages were held. Other elements would follow
behind and move to the second floor, where the Ugandan soldiers
were berthed. Outside the building would be the command and control element, under the direction of Netanyahu, and a support team
that would focus its jeep-mounted weapons on the tactical high
points (control tower and upper deck of the terminal) held by the
Ugandans.* Netanyahu decided not to assault the control tower
because it would require more men and increase the possibility of
casualties.

Two hundred yards east of the old terminal was a Ugandan military base. It was estimated that over one thousand soldiers and airmen

*Originally, Jonathan Netanyahu was not scheduled to be the assault force
leader, in spite of the fact that he was the commanding officer of the Unit.
For political reasons, Col. Ehud Barak, the previous commander of
the Unit, was chosen to supervise the Unit's ground operations. Eventually, this convoluted chain of command was resolved, and Barak did
not participate.

were stationed there, as well as a MiG fighter squadron. It would be necessary to establish a blocking force to prevent the soldiers from spoiling the rescue. Netanyahu planned to add four Buffalo APCs to the equipment list for this purpose. These vehicles would be loaded in the second and third C-130s and operated by commandos from the Unit. The Golani Infantry would also be positioned in the second and third aircraft, but their mission would be to provide protection for the C-130s.

In the final hour of planning, Netanyahu identified the personnel from the Unit who would be participating in the operation. Most of the men selected were chosen on the basis of seniority. There were a few who were picked for their previous combat experience. Netanyahu also chose several men based on his personal experience with these individuals. When this was done, he instructed his secretary to recall the men and have the officers available for an 0100 briefing.

At the first of what were to be many briefings, Netanyahu laid out the proposed plan. Many of the personnel had been involved in missions before that were planned and rehearsed but then never executed. This appeared to be the case with Entebbe. Most of the men were skeptical that the operation would be approved. When the meeting was completed, Netanyahu advised them to get some rest while he returned to his office and began detailed planning. In *Yoni's Last Battle,* Netanyahu's brother Iddo, a former member of the Unit, recalls how Jonathan must have felt while planning the operation. "As he sat alone in his office, it is possible that the full significance of the operation, and the risks it entailed crystallized in Yoni's [Netanyahu's] mind for the first time. The people of Israel had not yet recovered from the devastating blow of the Yom Kippur War in 1973. In many ways, the morale of the country had only deteriorated in the three years since then. If the operation were to fail—if all the hostages were killed, or most of them, and if in addition Israel's elite force were to be captured or annihilated, far from the nation's borders—it would strike at the spirit of the nation with devastating effect."[8] If the mission was approved, Netanyahu knew it would be the most important operation of his life. Failure could affect the honor of his country and the prestige of the Israeli military. Netanyahu, who was known for his obsession with detail, would ensure that Entebbe did not fail for lack of planning and preparation.

In the meantime, Shomron and others had gone to Rabin's office to brief the prime minister on the plan that had been formulated up to that point. Gur intercepted Shomron outside Rabin's office and, after reviewing the proposal, sent Shomron back to continue planning. Although it was Friday morning, six days after the hijacking, Shomron believed that the General Staff was still not taking the possibility of a military rescue seriously. Nevertheless, Shomron and the other commanders were determined to be prepared. When the sun came up, the paratroopers and the commandos would commence full-scale rehearsals, the logistics people would be busy modifying the Landrovers and the Mercedes, the weapons branch would be gathering the Galil assault rifles and the AK-47s, and the intelligence branches would be putting together the final pieces of the Entebbe puzzle.* Unknown to Shomron, however, in a day and a half, his force would take off for Entebbe, ready or not. (Shomron did not actually oversee the Unit's preparation. The Unit was not under the operational control of Shomron until the mission began.)

JONATHAN NETANYAHU

Of all the men studied so far, no one exhibits as much leadership ability as Jonathan Netanyahu. His extensive combat experience, coupled with a flare for motivating his men, stands out above the rest. Born in the United States in 1946, Netanyahu was an extremely bright and industrious young man. When the state of Israel was established, his parents, Benzion and Cela Netanyahu, then on a Zionist mission in the United States, relocated to Israel. Netanyahu became president of his high school student body and leader of his Boy Scout troop. In January 1963, during his junior year in high school, the family moved to Philadelphia where his father was the editor in chief of the *Encyclopedia Judaica*. Young Jonathan, called Yoni by his friends, became extremely homesick for Israel. It

*Most of the commandos preferred the Kalashnikov (AK-47) to the Galil because it fired a 7.62 (39mm) round rather than the 5.56 and the reliability was reportedly better.

was difficult for him to adapt to a new culture, new language, and new friends.

In July 1964, after a year and a half in the United States, Netanyahu returned to Israel and enlisted in the IDF. He joined the paratroopers and was stationed along the ten-mile "waist" that divided the Arabs from the sea. Within two years, Arab terrorists began to launch repeated attacks into Israel. Eventually the Israelis retaliated and attacked the terrorist's base camps. Netanyahu saw his first action in a raid against Es-Samua in Jordan.

In 1966, Netanyahu attended the officers' training school and graduated as the outstanding cadet. He was subsequently assigned back to the paratroopers as a platoon leader. While assigned to the paratroopers, Netanyahu underwent the paratroopers' advanced training course. He wrote in a letter to his parents about the course's final exercise: "We had to parachute in an area that is not a proper drop zone—'somewhere in the Negev'—under cover of smoke and planes, to take over an emergency airfield, capture a number of targets in the area and after that mark the airstrip and land several planes carrying equipment for the continuation of the mission—all of this at night of course."[9] It was this type of training that would later affect Netanyahu's course of action at Entebbe. After the advanced course, he received training in heavy mortars and machine guns. Determined to go to college and get his undergraduate degree, Netanyahu left the regular army in 1966, planning to attend Harvard. After being accepted at Harvard, he decided to delay his entry for a few months to work and raise additional money for school.

In May of 1967, Egypt blockaded the Strait of Tiran, a vital Israeli access route to the Red Sea, and then positioned one hundred thousand Egyptian soldiers in the Sinai Peninsula. On 5 June 1967, believing that an Egyptian invasion was imminent, Israel conducted a surprise attack on Arab strongholds. Within the first day, most of the Egyptian air force was destroyed, and soon afterward, Israeli tanks roared through the Sinai, pushing the Egyptians back past the Suez Canal. Both Jordan and Syria joined in the fighting, creating a three-front war for the Israelis.

Netanyahu, who was called up as part of reserve mobilization, was involved in several battles during the Six-Day War, including a decisive engagement at Um-Katef, which allowed the Israelis access to the Sinai. His paratrooper force was airlifted behind the lines and attacked the Egyptians from the rear. A few days later, the paratroopers were sent to the Golan Heights, where Netanyahu was wounded in the elbow by Syrian gunfire. The wound was severe enough that he was released from the active reserves (although he stayed in the inactive reserves) as a disabled veteran.

In July 1967, Netanyahu was married and by September was enrolled at Harvard. After a year at Harvard, he again got homesick and decided to return to Israel where he entered the Hebrew University in Jerusalem. Soon, however, Netanyahu tired of school, and after receiving a medical waiver for his elbow, he returned to the army. By July 1969, he was back with the army as the second in command of the Sayeret Matkal Counterterrorist Unit. The Unit had the responsibility of antiterrorist operations in the Jordan Valley. While assigned to the Unit, Netanyahu took part in a successful raid into Beirut, and his force killed three members of the PLO high command. Later the Unit kidnapped a group of Syrian generals and exchanged them for Israeli pilots.

In 1972 he was promoted to major and transferred to a tank battalion. On 6 October 1973 Egypt and Syria conducted a surprise attack on Israel, which began the Yom Kippur War. Netanyahu was stationed on the Golan Heights at the beginning of the war. Syrian commandos ambushed his position, killing one officer and wounding others. In what was to become indicative of his leadership style, Netanyahu led a counterattack that routed the Syrians. An Israeli officer who witnessed the action recalled later, "I saw Yoni get up perfectly calm, as though nothing were going on. With hands he motions to us all to get up along with him—and he starts advancing like it's a training exercise. He was upright, giving out orders right and left. I remember my thoughts then as a soldier: Hell, if he can do it, so can I! I got up and started to fight."[10]

At the end of the engagement, forty-five Syrians were dead and only two Israelis. Netanyahu was involved in several other combat operations during the Yom Kippur War, including reconnaissance missions, ambushes, and rescue operations. For his actions he was awarded the Distinguished Conduct Citation. His leadership under fire did not go unnoticed, and in 1975 he was promoted to lieutenant colonel and subsequently assigned to the Sayeret Matkal Counter-terrorist Unit as the commanding officer.

Throughout the book *Yoni's Last Battle,* there are countless recollections of Netanyahu by his fellow officers and enlisted men. They portray a man totally committed to his beliefs, an Israeli who firmly believed in the principles for which his country stood. He was a soldier and a scholar, who preferred reading Machiavelli's *The Prince* to a leisurely night on the town. He was a detail man who realized the value of good planning but also knew that courage and boldness could cut through the fog of war. In his farewell speech to the tank battalion he commanded during the Yom Kippur War, Netanyahu outlined his command principles. These principles, more than any individual man's assessment, show what made Jonathan Netanyahu a great leader. He wrote:

- I believe first of all in common sense, which should guide all of our actions.
- I also believe in the responsibility of commanders. A good commander . . . is one who feels absolutely responsible for anything connected, even indirectly, with his command.
- I believe that the buck should not be passed to anyone else—that it should stop here, with us.
- I believe in getting down to the smallest details. Anyone who fails to do that and tries to spare himself the effort is doing a disservice to our goal, which is preparing the unit for war.
- I believe there can be no compromise with results. Never accept results that are less than the best possible.
- I believe that the greatest danger in the life of a unit is to lapse into self satisfaction.
- I believe that all the battalion's efforts must be subordinated to the main aim—victory in war. Let us never confuse our priorities.
- I believe with all my heart in our ability to carry out any military mission entrusted to us, and I believe in you.
- And I believe in Israel and in the sense of responsibility that must accompany every man who fights for the fate of his homeland.[11]

ENTEBBE AIRPORT

Uganda, located in East Africa, is twenty-two hundred miles from Israel. It is bordered by Sudan on the north, Zaire to the west, Tanzania and Rwanda to the south, and Kenya on the east. At the time of the hijacking, only Kenya had friendly relations with Israel.

From the late 1960s until 1973, Israeli personnel had served in Uganda, training the local air force. In 1971, Idi Amin, the Ugandan army chief of staff, conducted a coup and overthrew Prime Minister Milton Obote. In 1973, after the Yom Kippur War, Amin began to side with the Soviets, who provided him with MiGs and other military hardware.

Entebbe, one of the largest cities in Uganda, is located on the shores of Lake Victoria. The international airport at Entebbe had two runways, the largest a 12,000-foot strip running north on a bearing of 353 degrees. At the north end of this main strip was a taxiway which ran southeast past the old terminal to a small 5,448-foot strip which also ran north-south.

The old terminal, where the hostages were being held, was a two-story building that faced the taxiway and aircraft parking apron. Adjoining the two-story terminal was a single-story west wing. In the past this wing had housed passport control and customs. The west wing led to the old tower. The east wing, another single-story structure, had been a VIP lounge.

The main focus of the attack would be the old terminal. There were six front entrances into the terminal including the east and west wings. The commandos planned to assault through three entrances, thereby ensuring that all areas of the terminal were accessible. The terminal was being guarded by between sixty and one hundred Ugandan soldiers, most equipped with assault rifles. The soldiers had established a perimeter defense and were positioned in key locations including the top of the old tower. The troops presumably rotated the watch and while not on duty were generally stationed on the second floor of the old terminal.

The seven terrorists were inside the old terminal. At the time of the rescue, four of the seven were in the large hall at the center of the terminal, while the other three were in the east wing. They carried AK-47s, and prior to the raid it was thought that the terrorists had rigged the terminal with explosives. Later, it was found that the explosives were only fake. To the north and west of the old terminal were dozens of smaller buildings used to support the daily activities of the Entebbe Airport.

A short distance east of the terminal was the military base, which quartered approximately two battalions of Ugandan troops and the MiG squadron. Additionally, Entebbe was down the road and overlooked the airfield. In the city were the presidential palace and Amin's palace guards.

The new terminal, which was located on the north end of the main runway, was left unguarded except for some Ugandan police. It contained the staging area for passengers departing Uganda and the new tower which now controlled all inbound and outbound traffic. Most importantly, just outside the entrance to the new terminal were underground fuel tanks from which the C-130s might need to refuel. The paratroopers were assigned to secure this facility.

PREPARATIONS

Early Friday morning rehearsals began in ernest. A mock-up of the old terminal had been constructed at the Unit's base, using metal poles covered with burlap sheets to denote the walls and white tape on the ground to identify the rooms. Commandos from the Unit simulated exiting from the vehicles and quickly entering and clearing the building. At the same time, the Unit personnel assigned to drive the Mercedes and the Landrovers met with the air force element at another base and practiced off-loading the vehicles. This exercise was conducted repeatedly until the drivers and loadmasters could unfasten the tie-down straps, lower the ramp, and depart the aircraft in a matter of seconds. Throughout the day, drills covering every aspect of the mission were rehearsed. That evening a full-scale rehearsal was scheduled.

Earlier that morning, all the unit commanders met with Shomron for another briefing. Shomron presented an overview of the plan and a revised force structure. Netanyahu was pleased to see that the general had implemented the force reduction recommended the

previous day. What had been an unwieldy conventional assault was
now a manageable operation. After Shomron finished his brief, he
directed the officers to return to their units and continue planning.

Netanyahu drove back to his base and assembled his men for an
update. Shomron's intelligence officer brought some 8mm films of
the old terminal taken by a sergeant major previously stationed in
Uganda. He showed them to the men in Netanyahu's unit and later
to other key players. Although the films did not show the inside of
the terminal, they did give an exterior view of the area. What concerned Netanyahu was the five-story control tower that tactically
dominated the area. A single soldier with a machine gun could control the entire front of the terminal. The intelligence officer also had
some short clips of the new terminal. This was the first time the
commander of the paratroopers, Col. Matan Vilnai, and the commander of the Golani Infantry, Uri Saguy, had seen pictures of the
new terminal.

Later that evening detailed intelligence arrived from Paris. Israeli
intelligence had interviewed a woman who was released because
she was pregnant. Shani recalled later, "She was a good source of
information. She was very observant. She knew how many terrorists there were, what they were carrying, and where they were located."[12] Other passengers were able to tell the Israelis the general
location of the hostages, although it was still not certain in which of
the rooms they were kept, and the composition of the walls in the
terminal. There was some speculation that the terrorists might have
rigged the building with explosives. "It was good intelligence,"
Shani remembered. "We knew what was going on."[13]

With this information, Netanyahu once again refined the plan and
opened the brief for discussion. The primary concern was the reported heavy concentration of Ugandan soldiers surrounding the building. The passengers indicated that the soldiers were spaced ten to
fifteen yards apart around the entire facility. If this were true, surprise
would be difficult to achieve. The men being briefed were also concerned about the nonstaggered arrival of the APCs. Netanyahu had
initially ordered the first two APCs, arriving on the second C-130,
to wait until the last two APCs, on the next C-130, arrived before proceeding to the old terminal area. This meant that all four APCs
would not be on the target until seven or eight minutes after the

Unit assaulted the old terminal. This scheme was modified to allow the first two APCs to immediately proceed to the old terminal.

The Unit commandos "were also troubled by the numerical inferiority of the force landing in the first plane compared to the terrorists and Ugandan soldiers in the environs of the old terminal . . . This they claimed was contrary to all the rules of combat."[14] Netanyahu told his men that surprise would be on their side and that reinforcements would arrive shortly after the assault. After Netanyahu finished talking, the communications officer and operations officer gave their respective portions of the brief.

Upon completion of the brief, more drills were conducted. The commandos practiced over and over assaulting the mock-up terminal. They timed all the separate evolutions, calculating how long it took to disembark the plane, travel to the terminal, and enter the building. The commandos assigned to ride in the Mercedes during the mission conducted several simulated approaches to the old terminal. The element leaders continued to study the intelligence and discuss the possible options. Even with all this preparation, there was still a feeling among the men that the mission would never be approved.

As the drills continued, Netanyahu drove to Shomron's office to present his modified plan. While waiting to see Shomron, Netanyahu was notified by phone that Ehud Barak, who had initially been tasked with supervising the Unit's assault on the old terminal, had been cut from the force, and that Netanyahu now had complete command of the Unit. This meant that Netanyahu would have to position himself outside the terminal in a command and control position rather than leading one of the elements into the building. After briefing Shomron on his modified plan, which Shomron subsequently approved, Netanyahu returned to base to check on the preparations.

One of the more important requirements was to ensure that the Mercedes sedan, which would be used to deceive the Ugandan soldiers, was mission ready. Unfortunately, the car was in poor mechanical condition: the tires were bare, the frame was dilapidated, the gas tank leaked, and the battery required charging. Additionally, the white exterior had to be painted black to resemble an official Ugandan vehicle, and new Ugandan license plates and flags had to be installed. All of these repairs had to be made between rehearsals, because the portion of the operation requiring the Mercedes was being exercised repeatedly.

After ensuring that the mechanics were making progress on the Mercedes, Netanyahu met with Colonel Shani, the air commander. The two men had been conducting separate planning sessions with their staffs, and now it was time to bring the plan together. Every aspect of the launch, insertion, and extraction was discussed in detail: the exact off-load point, direction of vehicles upon disembarking, which aircraft the hostages would be loaded onto, taxi routes, pickup points, and aircraft protection. Netanyahu wanted to know the alternate plan for landing if the airfield lights were not on. Shani explained that he and his pilots had worked out a method of using the C-130's radar to pick up the runway.* If that failed, Shani was prepared to contact the tower and claim to be a commercial airliner with an in-flight emergency. He later revealed, "My third pilot was an El Al [Airlines] captain, a perfect radio-telephone operator, he spoke perfect English. I told him, if we cannot see the runway, here is the microphone, you are East African Airways flight number 701, you are coming in for an emergency landing . . . 'please turn on the lights.' I don't know an air traffic controller in the world who would not turn on the runway lights."[15]

At the end of the meeting, the two men discussed the evening's full-scale rehearsal. Shani would not actually participate in the exercise; he was scheduled to demonstrate his radar landing procedure to the IDF chief of staff, Motta Gur, and the commander of the air force, Benny Peled, earlier in the evening. As soon as that rehearsal was completed, Shani would return to base, and his second pilot would pick up the Unit's commandos and conduct the full-dress rehearsal.

Once the meeting was completed, Netanyahu continued planning and Shani headed to his base. Shani loaded his C-130 and took off for the prerehearsal exercise. He knew that the entire mission might

---

*The squadron had also been working with night-vision goggles to do blacked-out landings, but Shani felt the pilots were not operationally ready to use this technique.

hinge on convincing Gur and Peled that the C-130 could land on a
dark runway. He was not about to leave that decision to fate. The
demonstration with Gur and Peled was scheduled to be at Sharm-a-
Sheikh, a desert runway in the Sinai. This exercise would be much
harder than the actual mission. Unlike Entebbe, which bordered
Lake Victoria, Sharm-a-Sheikh did not have any distinguishing features that the radar could pick up. Even during the late afternoon,
the prerehearsal landings proved difficult. As expected, the radar
had difficulty identifying the runway.

Shani returned to Lod by early evening and picked up Gur, Peled,
and Brig. Gen. Avihu Ben-Nun. Within the Israeli air force, "Shani
was considered, from an operational standpoint . . . to be top notch."[16]
Nevertheless, he was concerned about making the radar approach
at night. As the C-130 approached Sharm-a-Sheikh, Shani was surprised to find the entire base without lights. The chief of staff had
ordered a complete blackout for the purpose of testing Shani's night
landing skills. Nothing could be distinguished from the air. The radar approach that Shani had so confidently advertised was not
working. All he was able to pick up was a fence that paralleled the
runway.

The first approach fell short of the runway, and Shani pulled out
and came around again. Peled realized that something had gone
wrong but chose to remain quiet. Shani made a second approach.
He remembered later, "It was a beautiful approach, total darkness,
the last thing you could see was the runway, just two feet below. It
was impressive." Gur apparently was impressed, and he congratulated the crew for their fine work. With the demonstration completed, Shani flew the three VIPs to the desert training site to observe the dress rehearsal. It was 2200. In a small office, Netanyahu
and the other component commanders were assembled to brief the
chiefs of staff on the night's rehearsal. Like Shani, Netanyahu had
already conducted two daytime rehearsals in preparation for the
VIP visit. With the chiefs of staff observing, Netanyahu wanted
everything to go right.

After the brief, all the personnel assembled outside and observed
the full-dress rehearsal. The C-130 taxied to the assigned spot and
lowered the ramp. As the ramp touched down, the driver of the
Mercedes tried to start the engine, but the car wouldn't budge. The

driver of the jeep, positioned behind the Mercedes, gave the sedan a nudge and the car came to life. The three vehicles roared down the ramp and toward the mock-up terminal. "Ugandan" guards, alerted by the noise of the C-130, moved to stop the approaching vehicle but were quickly "killed" by silenced pistols. After dispatching the sentries, the commandos hastily moved to the terminal and assaulted the mock-up using blank rounds. Gur, who was watching the entire operation at close range, was impressed. His only criticism was that there were too many men in the jeeps. He ordered each jeep reduced by one man. This was not easily accepted by the Unit. The men knew that a reduction in force meant that someone wasn't going to participate.

Following the rehearsal, Gur met with all the senior officers. He wanted their opinion on the likelihood of success. Shomron stated that the whole mission hinged on the first plane arriving undetected. If that failed, the entire force could be captured and the hostages killed. If Shani was able to land his C-130 and arrive undetected, then the mission stood a good chance of succeeding. When asked his opinion, Netanyahu said confidently, "It can be done."[17]* This seemed to convince the chief of staff of the viability of the military mission. He told the officers that he would recommend to the prime minister that the mission be approved. Later that evening, all the aircraft, vehicles, and equipment were moved to Lod Airport.

Eighteen hours after the first rehearsals began, the training was completed, but there was still a great deal of uncertainty about the preparedness of the force. Several of Netanyahu's officers were vehemently opposed to conducting the mission on such short notice. Normally it took months to prepare for an operation of this magnitude. They were concerned about the shortage of intelligence, the lack of proper training, the unreliability of the vehicles, and the harried nature of the entire preparations. The dissenters wanted to jump the chain of command and let the government know that the force was not ready to conduct this mission. Eventually, Netanyahu

---

*The meeting between Gur and the officers lasted approximately thirty minutes, during which time Netanyahu spoke up several times. However, when Gur asked for Netanyahu's final assessment, this was his response.

was able to "allay this apprehension and ease their uncertainty," but not without much aggravation.[18] Sunrise was only hours away and Netanyahu returned home to get some sleep. Tomorrow, Prime Minister Rabin would approve the operation to rescue Israeli citizens held in Uganda; Netanyahu would lead the initial assault and bear the responsibility of success or failure.

THE MISSION

Early Saturday morning most of the Unit's personnel were at the base well before the assigned time. They were making last-minute alterations and preparing their equipment for the final inspection. In the meantime, the staff continued planning and gathering last-minute intelligence. After the equipment inspection was completed, Netanyahu held a brief for the officers. Once again, he concentrated on the prime objective of the mission, rescuing the hostages. This operation was not to be a "conventional assault on an enemy stronghold."[19] Speed was absolutely essential; the entire rescue operation could not take more than thirty to sixty minutes. All targets that did not immediately affect the rescue of the passengers were to be avoided. When the passengers were secure, then the ancillary targets could be attacked if they presented a problem. The brief turned into a session in tactics and a reiteration of each group's objectives. The what-ifs were discussed, and by the end of the meeting most of the questions were resolved.

By 1130 all the participants were gathered at Lod Airport. The officers and key participants assembled for the final brief. This, however, was only for show. Shani recalled, "It was a general briefing . . . Everybody said a few words. I gave a briefing about how we are going to fly, what is the weather there. It was a bullshit briefing. Nothing serious; big board with all the lines between points . . . a line of generals in front. But, when it was over I was sitting with my crew outside. We discussed again in some detail the mission. We had two more hours and I got with Yoni [Netanyahu] and his deputy, Muki Betzer, and we covered options; what if I missed this turning point, what if I taxi here, what angle should I put the airplane so the Mercedes could go out under the wing. We covered friction points between us [the air crew] and them [the Unit]."[20]

As the force began to depart for its final stop in Sharm-a-Sheikh, there were still considerable details, both of the ground maneuver and of the air plan, that had not been fully coordinated. Many aspects of the flight plan, which were normally prepared as an in-depth mission packet, were handwritten on scraps of paper, the chain of command was still being sorted out, and the decision to launch for Entebbe had still not been made. Nevertheless, at 1320 hours, the five C-130s (one reserve) took off from Lod (in different directions to deceive onlookers) and proceeded to their Sinai air base at Sharm-a-Sheikh. The aircraft flew at low levels to the Sinai to avoid detection by Russian ships and Egyptian radar. The warm desert air caused the flight to be exceptionally turbulent, and by the time the C-130s reached Sharm-a-Sheikh, most of the soldiers were airsick. One commando from the Unit had to be dropped from the mission because he was so weak from vomiting.

At the air base, the C-130s topped off their fuel tanks, and the soldiers got a quick bite to eat. Once again, and for the final time, Netanyahu briefed his element leaders. An intelligence report had been received just prior to departing Lod which stated that the Ugandan soldiers were no longer encircling the old terminal. They had taken up defensive positions around the building and were rotating the guard force. This meant that only half, or maybe one-third, of the guards would be on duty at any one time. The off-duty guards were believed to be positioned on the second floor of the old terminal. Netanyahu emphasized for the last time the importance of focusing on the objective. He told his troops that, the objective of the mission was to save the lives of the hostages. No matter what developments there might be, even when they were under fire and things were not going as anticipated, and even if it turned out that the hostages were not exactly where they were supposed to be, everyone had to remember the purpose of the action, and work towards attaining it. At every stage of the operation, this goal had to be at the front of their minds.[21] Netanyahu also instilled in his men a sense of patriotism. "The entire nation is depending on us," he said.[22] He told his men that he had complete confidence in their ability to succeed. They were the best combat force in the world and now was the time to prove it.

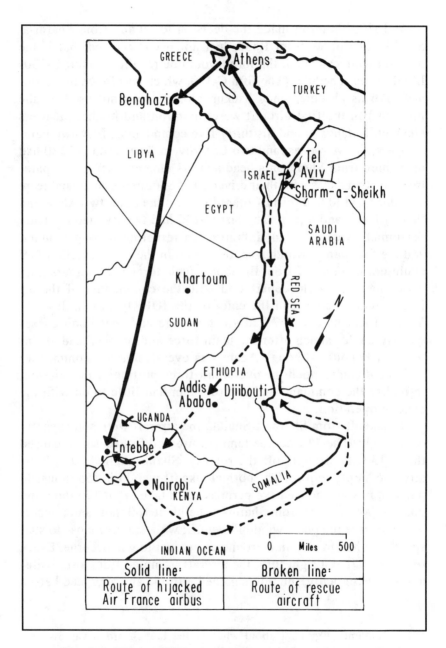

Fig. 9–1. Route of Hijacked Airliner and Israeli C-130s.

At 1530, Shomron made the decision to launch from Sharm-a-Sheikh. The order from Rabin had not been received, but if the mission were canceled, the force would be recalled.* Four C-130s lifted off on schedule. (The fifth C-130, which was flown to Sharm-a-Sheikh as an emergency backup aircraft, was not used on the mission.) In the first aircraft were Shomron and his headquarters element, Netanyahu and his thirty-five commandos, fifty-two paratroopers, the Mercedes, and two Landrovers. The second C-130 had more men from Shomron's headquarters element, seventeen paratroopers, two APCs with their drivers, and Shomron's command jeep. The third C-130 had thirty Golani Infantry, the other two APCs and their drivers, and a jeep. The last C-130 had twenty medical team personnel, twenty Golani Infantry, ten refueling crew personnel, and the fuel pump, which was to be used in the event aviation fuel could not be pumped from Entebbe's fuel storage. Two hours later a Boeing 707 would depart Lod with the commander of the air force, Benny Peled, and the chief of the IDF Operations Branch, Yekutiel Adam. The 707 had greater range and speed and consequently could launch after the main force and be overhead at Entebbe at H hour. Although Adam was overall mission commander and Peled commanded the overall air force portion of the mission, in reality the command and control team had little to do with the combat operation.

On takeoff from Sharm-a-Sheikh, the aircraft were significantly overweight. The 110-degree temperature and full fuel load caused the C-130s to struggle off the runway. Shani recalled later, "The airplane hardly moved. The normal takeoff weight is 155 thousand pounds; in wartime we have permission to take off at 175 thousand pounds. We took off from Sharm-a-Sheikh at 180 thousand pounds. We were sure the plane wouldn't get off; we were very close to stall speed. We had to stay in a ground effect just to get airborne. Every time we started a right turn, the aircraft trembled from a stall situation."[23] Eventually, the pilots gained altitude and air speed before

---

*There is some argument about whether the launch order was ever received or not. Shani never recalls receiving an order to launch from the general staff, while Iddo Netanyahu's research shows that the order was given to launch while the force was at Sharm-a-Sheikh.

once again dropping down to less than fifty feet to avoid enemy surveillance.[24] The flight, which was scheduled for seven and one-half hours, took the C-130s down the length of the Red Sea and across Ethiopia. Once in Ethiopia the planes rose to twenty thousand feet. Ethiopia had no air-search radar, so there was little chance of compromise.

During the flight, Netanyahu, Shani, and Shomron all tried, with varying degrees of success, to get some sleep. Between the planning, briefings, and rehearsals, there had not been much time for rest.

The formation headed south-southwest, eventually passing out of Ethiopia and into the northern corner of Kenya. At 2230, the C-130s reached the far end of Lake Victoria, which was just minutes by air from Entebbe. On their radio the pilots could hear Entebbe control talking with an outbound British Airways passenger liner.

As planned, the last three C-130s broke from the formation. The lead C-130 began its approach. Six minutes after departure of the lead C-130, the other three aircraft would make their descent. The Boeing 707 command plane had arrived on station, and after

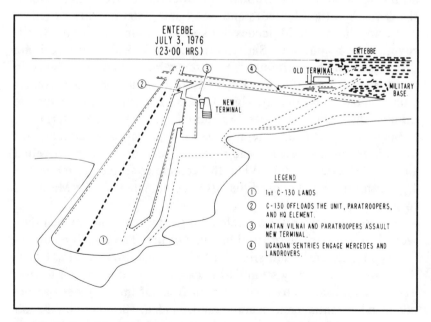

Fig. 9–2. Entebbe International Airport: Mission Overview.

making radio contact with Shani, Peled asked if the runway lights of Entebbe were visible. Not yet, Shani responded. They were still too far out. In the cabin, Netanyahu was trying to talk with each man before they landed. He was giving them final words of encouragement. Although most of the commandos had seen some level of combat, it varied considerably, and Netanyahu was one of the most experienced fighters in the army.

As Shani descended on final approach, he could finally see the runway lights of Entebbe clearly marking his path. Shomron, Vilnai, and Netanyahu had all come into the cockpit to watch the landing and see firsthand what Entebbe looked like. After a quick look, Vilnai and Netanyahu returned to their men and prepared for action. At 2300, 3 July, Israel time, Shani touched down. Inside the C-130, the vehicles started their engines. Aircrew quickly unlashed the tie-down straps and prepared to lower the ramp. As Shani reduced his speed, ten soldiers jumped from the side door of the slow-moving aircraft and began to place their emergency lights. The C-130 spun around as it got to the end of the runway and began to turn onto the access strip leading to the old terminal. On order, the aircrew man lowered the ramp, and the Mercedes and two Landrovers quickly exited.

Netanyahu, in the Mercedes, looked back to make sure the Landrovers were behind him. Satisfied that they were, he began driving directly toward the terminal. The three vehicles had their lights on and kept their speed at a respectable forty miles per hour. Netanyahu wanted to deceive the Ugandans as long as possible. After one minute, the vehicles reached the approach road to the old terminal.

Seemingly out of nowhere, two Ugandan soldiers suddenly appeared, one on each side of the road. The soldier on the right yelled for the Mercedes to stop. When the vehicle continued to move, the Ugandan raised and cocked his rifle and signaled for the Mercedes to pull over.

Netanyahu slowed the vehicle as if to stop, and then, when they were within range, he ordered his men to fire. The Israeli commandos opened up with their silenced Berettas but didn't hit the Ugandan sentry. The sentry stumbled backward and then began to fire. Tracers from the sentry's rifle cut in front of the Mercedes as the commandos continued to shoot at the Ugandan. The sentry on the left began to run toward the terminal, but was killed by the commandos.

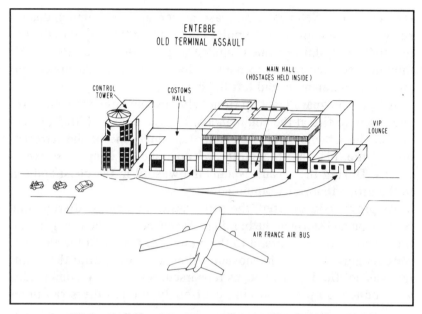

Fig. 9–3. Old Terminal Assault: Exterior View.

Immediately after the shooting began, Netanyahu ordered the driver to head for the terminal at full speed. They were only two hundred yards from the entrance. As they approached, several Ugandan soldiers and a terrorist were seen just outside the main entrance, but the soldiers seemed confused by the action. The driver hurriedly parked the Mercedes by the side of the control tower and all the commandos jumped out. No one had fired yet, and Netanyahu ordered the men to charge the building.

Netanyahu's second in command, Muki Betzer, moved quickly toward the old terminal building, firing at one of the Ugandan soldiers. The terrorist, who was still outside the building, ran back into the terminal shouting, "The Ugandans have gone nuts—They're shooting at us!"[25] The deception appeared to have worked. Soon the assault force had reached the corner of the old terminal and was within a few yards of the entrance. Instead of attacking, however, Betzer stopped the force. Netanyahu yelled several times to move forward, but for some unknown reason Betzer didn't budge. Seeing the hesitation, Netanyahu ran past Betzer, and the commandos resumed their assault with the point man leading the way into the terminal (Netanyahu remained outside to coordinate the attack). Although it seemed longer to them, it had been only fifteen seconds since the commandos had left the car.

A Ugandan guard leapt up from behind some large wooden boxes and began to fire at the commandos. He was quickly killed by several of the Israelis. From inside the terminal, one of the terrorists opened fire, blasting through the window and spraying glass everywhere. During the assault Netanyahu was hit in the chest and fell to the ground mortally wounded.

As previously ordered, the three assault elements disregarded Netanyahu and stormed the building. At this point in the engagement, there wasn't time to attend to the wounded. Although the elements were roughly together, the movement into and throughout the building was not fluid or precise, as rehearsed. Some of the commandos were bunched up and moving cautiously, while others ran inde-

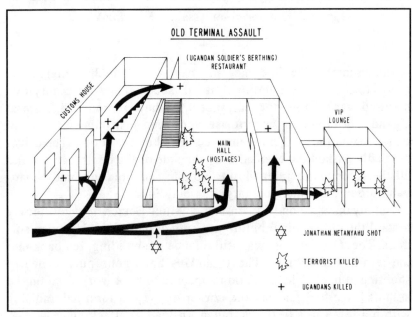

Fig. 9–4. Old Terminal Assault: Inside View.

pendently, darting from room to room in search of terrorists. Nevertheless, the basic scheme of maneuver was being exercised.

One of the Israelis, Amir, was the first man into the terminal. He penetrated through the second door of the main hall. Inside was a large, well-lit room where all the hostages were lying on the floor. A terrorist, who had been lying on the other side of the door, fired a burst from his Kalashnikov but miraculously missed Amir. Amir returned fire. His rounds sliced through the door and killed the terrorist instantly. As trained, Amir turned right and cleared his side of the room. Behind Amir came another commando, who turned left and picked up coverage on the other side of the room. As the second commando entered, he saw two terrorists lying on the floor to his left, their rifles trained on Amir. Immediately he fired and both terrorists were killed.

Betzer and the other part of his element, who should have entered through another door, came into the room directly behind the first two commandos. As the commandos entered, a terrorist jumped out from behind a column but was shot instantly. Within three minutes of landing, four of the seven terrorists were dead, and the hostages were safe. Amir, who had the loudspeaker, began telling the passengers to stay down. The commandos, with weapons at the ready, continued to scan the room. Suddenly, a little girl jumped up from the ground, and the Israeli soldiers turned to fire. Fortunately, they realized in time that the girl was a passenger. Others were not so lucky. In the course of the next several seconds, two passengers were shot as they got up to move. Both later died of their wounds. A third passenger died in the fighting, but apparently from wounds received from one of the terrorists during the initial exchange of fire.*

As Betzer and his men were securing the large room, the other elements were penetrating and clearing the remainder of the terminal. At the next entrance down from the large room, a lone commando

---

*The account of actions in the large room do not indicate that any terrorists, other than the one lying behind the door, fired at the commandos. Nevertheless, an investigation of Ida Borokovitch, the third passenger killed, revealed that the fatal wounds came from terrorist guns and not Israeli. In the confusion, it is conceivable a terrorist fired but was killed so quickly that the incident went unreported.

entered the hallway firing, but no one was inside. By the time he stopped to reload, two other Israeli soldiers entered. They moved down the hall and into a small room that had been used as a kitchen. They entered the room firing, and after the assault they found two dead Ugandan guards. Two commandos from another team, who were disoriented and in the wrong hallway, arrived, only to be yelled at by their companions for being out of position.

Outside the building, the team that was to storm the VIP lounge found their entrance locked. One of the Israelis threw a grenade at the door, only to have the grenade bounce off and explode close by. One commando was slightly wounded from the shrapnel. The team backtracked into an open door and entered the VIP lounge from the building. In the lounge were two men. As the commandos entered, the two men raised their hands slightly and began moving toward the soldiers. The Israelis shouted at them to stop, but the men continued to move. For a moment, the commandos did not know whether the individuals were terrorists or hostages. Then one of the Israelis noticed a grenade belt around one of the men's waist. Without hesitation, the commandos fired. As they did, the terrorist dropped a grenade that had been hidden in his hand. The explosion stunned the commandos, but none were seriously hurt. While clearing the remaining small rooms attached to the VIP lounge, another terrorist was found dead. It is presumed he was killed by an errant round when the commandos fired at the two unidentified terrorists. At this point in the engagement, all known terrorists had been killed; only the Ugandan troops remained.

At the other end of the building, in the old customs hall, the commandos entered and quickly killed a number of Ugandan soldiers. These commandos had the responsibility of clearing the second floor (the Ugandan berthing area) of the terminal. As the commandos climbed the stairs to their objective, two more Ugandans suddenly appeared in the doorway and were killed. A metal door led downstairs into the large hall where the hostages were held, but it was locked. Turning left, the commandos entered a restaurant where the Ugandan soldiers had been living. All that remained were blankets and sleeping bags. The Ugandans had apparently escaped when the fighting began.

Confident that the area was clear, the commandos proceeded to the outside deck above the customs room. From here they could see the Ugandans in the control tower exchanging fire with the commandos in the Landrovers. They found good cover and joined in the firefight. Once the second floor was clear, another smaller team was supposed to provide security, but that team never found the stairs to the second floor.

By this time, the firing in the terminal had abated enough for a doctor to reach Netanyahu, who was still lying outside the main entrance. The doctor found that a round from an AK-47 had pierced Netanyahu's chest just under the collarbone. The internal bleeding was so severe that the doctor knew almost immediately that Netanyahu would not survive. Information on Netanyahu's condition was passed to Betzer, the second in command, who subsequently informed the force that he was taking charge. As soon as the fourth C-130 landed and took its final position on the ground, which was only moments later, Netanyahu was moved by Landrover to that aircraft.

Although there was occasional fire from the control tower, the old terminal was secure, and the Unit began concentrating on their second objective, setting a defensive perimeter around the terminal area. During the fighting at the old terminal, Shomron and his five-man command element had remained at the site where the Mercedes and Landrovers disembarked. Six minutes after the first C-130 landed, the second aircraft touched down. Aboard this aircraft were Shomron's command jeep and the first two APCs. As soon as the plane stopped and the vehicles were off-loaded, Shomron and his element got aboard and proceeded to the old terminal. Shomron arrived at the old terminal to the sounds of sporadic gunfire coming from the control tower. He parked his jeep nearby and directed the APCs to engage the tower with machine guns and rocket-propelled grenades (RPGs). This temporarily quieted the tower.

Within one minute the third C-130 landed, but without the advantage of lights, which had been shut off after the second aircraft touched down. Shani, who watched the approach, recalled later, "The runway just disappeared and the pilot did a 'navy landing.' "[26] In seconds, the last two APCs exited and proceeded to the old terminal. The first two APCs separated, with the first APC remaining in the vicinity of the old terminal and the second APC moving to the Ugandan military base where the MiGs were positioned. The last two APCs drove to the backside of the old terminal and blocked the road coming from the city of Entebbe. Within fifteen minutes of the initial landing, the area inside and outside the old terminal was relatively secure, despite the occasional fire coming from the control tower.

Minutes later, the fourth C-130 landed, taxied south on the access runway, and halted about five hundred yards from the old terminal. This location was further from the old terminal than originally planned, but eventually the pilot corrected his error and moved somewhat closer. A Golani Infantry force of about sixteen officers and men surrounded the aircraft and prepared to assist in the evacuation of the hostages.

Two of the commandos from the Unit met the fourth C-130 after it stopped and began to coordinate the evacuation. At the old terminal, the passengers assembled outside and walked or were shuttled by Landrover or truck to the C-130. Throughout the assembly and evacuation process, the soldiers later reported, the passengers were overly concerned about their personal belongings, some even returning to the terminal to gather lost items. This happened despite pleas from the commandos for the passengers to leave their baggage.

Outside the cabin of the C-130, the medical team set up to assist the wounded. Netanyahu, who was still alive at this point, received a blood transfusion as the doctors worked feverishly to save his life.

As the passengers arrived at the aircraft, they were shuffled to the forward part of the cabin and asked to sit close together. Although efforts were made to get a head count, the darkness and confusion made an accurate count difficult. Several of the passengers at the terminal were hysterical or in shock and had to be physically removed from the building and placed on the C-130. Eventually, however, all the passengers were assembled aboard the aircraft.

While the passengers were being evacuated, the APCs continued to engage the control tower. After all the passengers had been loaded, two vehicles believed to be carrying Ugandan troops appeared on the road from Entebbe. These reinforcements were quickly repelled by the first APC. Meanwhile the second APC requested and eventually received permission to destroy the eight MiGs lined up outside the Ugandan military base. Although this action was ostensibly designed to prevent the MiGs from attacking the retreating C-130s, in reality it was Israel's present to Idi Amin.[27] The APC raked the MiGs with machine-gun fire, and the fighter aircraft exploded in a huge fireball that illuminated the sky. Fortunately for the commandos, who wanted to remain concealed in the darkness, the fire soon died down.

Earlier in the operation, even before the first rounds were fired at the old terminal, paratroopers under the command of Matan Vilnai had left the first C-130 and quickly moved into position outside the new terminal. Intelligence had indicated that the building was only occupied by civilians and a small police unit. As the first shots were heard from the old terminal, the paratroopers advanced on the new terminal. Inside the building were several civilians, but for the most part the facility was deserted. The Ugandan civilians were corralled and kept inside. The only unfortunate incident occurred when one of the Israeli paratroopers was shot by a policeman attempting to escape the building. The Israeli soldier, who, as directed, had his Galil assault rifle on safe, did not react quickly enough to the sudden appearance of the policeman. A round from the policeman's pistol pierced the soldier's neck and paralyzed him for life.

When the new terminal was secure, the C-130s, with the exception of the fourth aircraft, began to assemble on the apron in front of the building. Shani had brought a fuel pump and planned to refuel all the aircraft from the subterranean storage tanks. As the refueling began, the airborne command and control aircraft notified Shani that the Kenyans had granted permission for the C-130s to refuel in Nairobi during their return to Israel. It did not take Shani long to make a decision. He said later, "The chances that something was going to hit you were high. I tried to talk with Shomron, but he was over the hill. We needed forty more minutes on the ground to refuel. It was too risky, so we decided to stop refueling. This decision was supported by everyone."[28] (There was a large mound between the new terminal and the old terminal that made communications between the two positions difficult.) At 2352 Israeli time, the C-130 containing the 106 hostages departed Entebbe. It was fifty-one minutes after the touchdown of Shani's first C-130. The only passenger who remained unaccounted for was seventy-five-year-old Dora Bloch. The previous day Mrs. Bloch had gotten a piece of meat stuck in her throat and was taken by the Ugandans to the Kampala Hospital. The commandos were forced to leave her, hoping that Idi Amin would release the woman later. Unfortunately, Amin had Bloch murdered in retaliation for the raid on Entebbe.

With the passengers safely on their way to Nairobi, the main assault forces began to withdraw. As they extracted to the aircraft, the commandos covered their movements with smoke and left small explosive devices scattered around the parking apron outside the old terminal. These devices were set with a fifteen-minute time fuse and would discourage any Ugandan soldiers from pursuing the force.

Yekutiel Adam, who was aboard the command and control aircraft, had received conflicting reports on the number of hostages rescued. The C-130 aircraft commander reported 93 hostages rescued, but intelligence had previously indicated that there were 106 at the old terminal. Adam directed Shomron to double-check the Air France jet, which was parked at the old terminal, to confirm that no one was still aboard. One of the APCs returned to the terminal and conducted a quick check of the Air France airbus.* Convinced that there was no one left behind, the assault force continued their withdrawal.

By 0012 4 July, Shani had reloaded all his commandos and their vehicles onto the airplane as planned, and they took off for Nairobi. Within thirty minutes the other two C-130s had back-loaded their troops and equipment and lifted off for Nairobi at 0040. Ninety-nine minutes after the first C-130 had landed at Entebbe, all the hostages and Israeli soldiers had been extracted. It was approximately a one-hour flight to Nairobi. As soon as the aircraft landed, they were met by Israeli officials. Some of the passengers were moved to a waiting Boeing 707 mobile hospital that had landed earlier in the evening, while the remainder of the passengers elected to stay with the C-130s. At 0200, after refueling all six aircraft (the airborne command and control, the mobile hospital, and the four C-130s), the task force departed Nairobi bound for Israel. Much to the chagrin of the assault force, the Israeli army radio station broadcast the results of the raid well before the C-130s had returned home. At this point in the flight, it would still have been possible for either Egypt or Saudi Arabia to intercept the unarmed air armada and prevent a successful conclusion to the mission.

---

*The APC commander did not enter the Air France jet for fear that the hatches might be booby-trapped. Instead he looked through the portholes and could see that the aircraft was empty.

About four hundred miles outside of Israel, the C-130s picked up an F-4 fighter escort. At 0943 the C-130s landed at Tel Nof Air Force Base. Here the passengers were debriefed and told not to discuss the tactics employed by assault forces. Following the briefings the passengers were flown to Lod Airport, and Operation Jonathan was completed.

ANALYSIS

Critique

The raid on Entebbe is the best example yet of how the principles of special operations are used to achieve relative superiority. With less than two days to plan and prepare a major assault mission, the Israelis developed the simplest option for success. During the planning phase, they limited their objectives, used intelligence to identify the obstacles, and then applied technology and innovation to overcome those obstacles. During the preparation phase, security surrounding the operation was effective but not overbearing. And in less than eighteen hours the units involved conducted several partial and full-dress rehearsals. During the execution phase, the Israelis gained surprise using boldness and deception to momentarily confuse the Ugandans, and by moving quickly on the target, they were able to secure the hostages within three minutes of landing at Entebbe. Throughout the three phases, the purpose of the operation was emphasized again and again, and it not only meant the rescue of the hostages, but the honor and respect of the state of Israel. Even though the engagement was not executed exactly according to plan, all the commandos and soldiers understood the prime objective and worked toward achieving that goal.

Were the objectives worth the risk? It is difficult to appreciate the risks, both militarily and politically, that were inherent in the raid on Entebbe. The Israeli public had suffered "a great psychological and moral blow" in the Yom Kippur War.[29] Politically, a failure at Entebbe might spell defeat for the Rabin government. Militarily, the Israeli commandos had recently suffered several disasters. In 1974 at Ma'alot, twenty-three children were killed when commandos stormed a schoolhouse, and in 1975 in Tel Aviv, eight hostages and three soldiers died in a rescue attempt at the Savoy Hotel. Had the

IDF failed at Entebbe, it would have had a devastating effect on military pride and morale. Consequently, the choice to use force, from both a political and a military standpoint, was a risky one. When, however, the terrorists turned the hijacking into a purely anti-Zionist action, the Rabin government had little choice but to exercise the military option. Even if the military option had failed, at least it would have failed in defiance of terrorism. To have stood idly by and negotiated with the terrorists would have been a sign of weakness and probably would have perpetuated the terrorist problem. Therefore rescuing the hostages was clearly worth the military and political risks.

Was the plan developed to maximize superiority over the enemy and minimize risk to the assault force? General Shomron initially wanted to use a large force to take Entebbe by storm. Although this probably would have minimized the risk to the assault force, it would not necessarily have maximized superiority over the terrorists. A large force would have been more difficult to control, easier to detect, and slower to launch an assault, all of which could have reduced the effectiveness of the operation. The final plan relied on gaining relative superiority by using surprise and speed to confuse and subdue the terrorists long enough to rescue the hostages. To sustain relative superiority, the Israelis would use conventional force (i.e., APCs, Golani Infantry, and paratroopers). In the first few minutes of the engagement, the risk to the Unit's personnel was high, but once the hostages were secured, the risk abated. The plan, although not without considerable risk, was well conceived. Owing to excellent planning and preparation, it offered the lowest risk possible.

Was the mission executed according to the plan, and if not what unforeseen circumstances dictated the outcome? With the exception of some misdirected commandos entering the wrong hallway, the mission was almost flawless. Although four people died, including Lt. Col. Jonathan Netanyahu, this does not alter the fact that the men and equipment performed as planned and rehearsed. Chance and uncertainty were high; and considering the difficulty of the operation, the loss of four people, although regrettable, nonetheless constitutes a highly successful mission.

What modifications could have improved the outcome? It is doubtful that any change in the plan or the execution of it could have improved the outcome of the raid on Entebbe. Had lightweight body armor been available to the commandos, it might have saved Netanyahu's life. However, in 1976 the only option to the soldiers was a heavy flak jacket. These vests would have restricted movement and, in the heat of the African night, would have been highly undesirable.

In conclusion, the raid on Entebbe stands up well to close scrutiny and even with today's advances in technology and training, it is doubtful that a modern force could have improved on the Israelis' success.

Relative Superiority

In describing the first few minutes of the raid, Iddo Netanyahu captures the essence of relative superiority. "With that, all four of the terrorists who had been in the hall with the hostages, and had posed an immediate danger to them, had been eliminated. At that

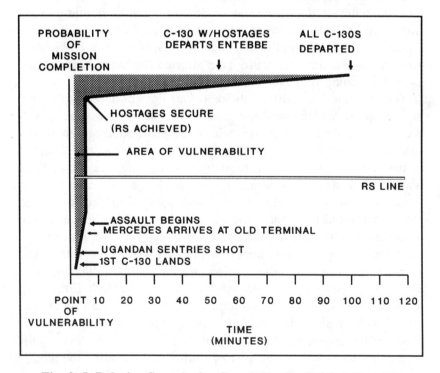

Fig. 9–5. Relative Superiority Graph for the Raid on Entebbe

moment—a blink of an eye after Amir had killed the first terrorist, less than a minute after the force had encountered the Ugandan sentries, and roughly three minutes after it had descended from the Hercules—the operation had essentially achieved success."[30]

The Unit had achieved a decisive advantage over the terrorists and Ugandans within three minutes of arriving at Entebbe. The mission was far from over, but the necessary conditions for success had been achieved. The moment Netanyahu describes did not arrive by coincidence. It was the result of the effective application of the principles of special operations, and it is highly unlikely that a large conventional force, unwieldy by nature, could have achieved the same success.

The relative superiority graph (Figure 9-5) shows that the point of vulnerability occurred immediately upon landing at the airport. Prior to this time, the Ugandans had no capability to detect, much less interdict, the incoming C-130s. Although the aircraft could have been detected by Egyptian or Saudi radars, sufficient precautions were taken to minimize this possibility. Additionally, it is presumed that Israeli intelligence had the capability of monitoring Arab transmissions and could have aborted the mission if the aircraft were compromised.

The terrorists basically established four lines of defense: the new control tower, which could have alerted the terrorists that an assault was taking place; the sentries, who were positioned on the access road; the Ugandan guards outside the old terminal; and the terrorists in the building. After a successful surprise landing, the commandos wasted no time in assaulting the objective. Netanyahu had instructed his men that if the vehicle convoy were interdicted prior to reaching the old terminal, which it was, he and his element in the Mercedes would continue to move toward the objective. Once at the old terminal, the assault element stalled momentarily. Netanyahu, who clearly understood the need to move quickly, took charge and directed the assault force to the door. Once inside the building, the terrorists were killed with a minimum of confusion. The area of vulnerability between gaining relative superiority and mission accomplishment was minimized by the conventional arm of the assault force. Considering that the entire operation, from landing to takeoff, took ninety-nine minutes, the area of vulnerability was just over 3 percent of the total engagement. Fifty-one minutes after the first landing, the fourth C-130 departed with the hostages, and soon thereafter the operation was completed. In this case, the frictions of war were minimal and the moral factors, such as Netanyahu's courage, were strong enough to overcome any attempts to topple the pyramid.

The Principles of Special Operations

Simplicity. All of the forces involved in Operation Jonathan had done missions more complicated than the raid on Entebbe. Shomron, in an effort to convince Gur of the viability of the plan, said, "Believe me, from the moment that we will be on the ground in Entebbe, we can carry it out easily. We have done things a thousand times more complicated."[31] However, in this mission, the forces were working under a severe time constraint, and every attempt to further simplify the plan was worth the effort.

Initially, Shomron wanted to storm Entebbe with a large force, hoping to overwhelm the Ugandan troops. This idea was discarded when Netanyahu and others argued that "such a [force] would be too cumbersome . . . and that a way had to be found to pull [the raid] off in a more limited, more compact way."[32] By limiting the size of the force, Netanyahu understood that the mission "would have a better chance of succeeding."[33] However he also had to limit his objectives to the old terminal in order to maximize the strength of his small force. The adjacent control tower, which clearly presented a threat, was bypassed because penetrating the structure would detract from the primary objective of rescuing the hostages. It was not until the hostages were secure that follow-on forces arrived to cordon off the entire area and provide covering fire for the extraction.

In the early phases of planning there was insufficient intelligence to develop a detailed plan for the hostage rescue operation. By Friday afternoon, however, solid information began to pour in, although it was still somewhat limited for an operation of this magnitude. Israeli intelligence had provided passenger interrogation reports, home movies, and other firsthand accounts of the Entebbe Airport. This information allowed the commandos to construct a clear picture of the threat and develop possible "workarounds."

They now knew how many terrorists there were and basically where they were positioned, and they were able to closely estimate the number of Ugandan soldiers and determine how they might react in combat. This allowed Shomron and Netanyahu to tailor the force structure to simplify the mission. Consequently, with no apparent threat at the new terminal, only a small paratrooper force was used to secure this facility, and with only seven terrorists and a small number of Ugandans inside the old terminal, Netanyahu was able to limit the number of assault elements he employed. Intelligence further simplified the mission by providing additional information about the Ugandan reaction force in the city, the airfield refueling points, and the fact that the old terminal was not wired with explosives, as originally reported. (Although Israeli intelligence was not 100 percent certain that the building was not rigged with explosives, they had verified that Ugandan guards and the terrorists were moving freely throughout the facility without apparent regard for explosives.) By eliminating the unknown factors and identifying obstacles that could reduce surprise and speed on target, intelligence was instrumental in developing a simple plan.

New technology and innovative tactics were also helpful in overcoming obstacles and thereby simplifying the plan. Although it is common practice with today's special operations forces, the raid on Entebbe was the first application of long-range penetration by airborne commandos. The flight from Israel to Entebbe took seven and a half hours. It was virtually unthinkable, at the time, for a force to travel such a distance to conduct a raid. Consequently, the terrorists and Ugandan soldiers were relatively secure in the belief that Entebbe was unapproachable. By using this bold and innovative tactic, the Israelis were able to surprise the enemy, reduce the effectiveness of his defenses, and thereby simplify the mission. Additionally, new or improved technology in the form of Buffalo armored personnel carriers, "sight light" low-light aiming devices, special explosives, and silenced weapons were used as force multipliers against the ill-equipped terrorists and Ugandan soldiers.

The raid on Entebbe, although exceptionally bold and politically risky, turned out to be "a straightforward operation without any complications."[34] The lack of significant problems was a result, in part, of the efforts to simplify the plan through limiting the objectives, obtaining good intelligence, and using innovative tactics and new technology.

Security. The military security that surrounded the planning and preparation for the raid on Entebbe was unusually light by normal standards. This can be attributed, in part, to the sense of national security that prevails throughout Israel. General Shani said it best when he noted that "as a nation, we are always conscious of security . . . We are surrounded by the enemy, so we must be careful."[35] There seemed to be little concern that the raid would be compromised to foreign sources. Some soldiers went home every evening, many of the wives or girlfriends knew that a raid was pending, and personnel from other military units rushed to be considered for the mission. By approaching the raid with a business-as-usual attitude, the Israelis were able to conduct several partial and full-dress rehearsals, borrow home movies from an outside source, and interface with noncleared units (i.e., the air force cadets who set up the mock terminal). Security was tightened, however, once the preparation was in its final stages. On Saturday, when all the personnel arrived for the final briefing, the phones were secured and no one was allowed to leave the base. When the C-130s landed at Sharm-a-Sheikh, the base was sealed off and none of the base personnel were allowed to depart until after the aircraft had returned from the raid. Once in flight, all precautions were taken to avoid enemy air-search radars, and Israeli communications experts listened for possible detection of the mission.

The light security surrounding the raid on Entebbe provides an interesting case study of the cultural appreciation of military operations. The Israelis, by virtue of their national identity and geographic position in the Middle East, are security conscious as a matter of routine. Additionally, Israeli combat operations between 1967 and 1976 were commonplace, so the movement of soldiers and aircraft did not present a unique profile to the average citizen. These two factors—a national appreciation for security and military routinization—provided the assault force sufficient security to maintain their cover without affecting the proper planning and preparation necessary for a successful operation.

Repetition. The principle of repetition, as seen in the raid on Entebbe, takes two forms, routine and rehearsals. Routine was manifested in the thousands of flight hours and hundreds of short-field landings done by the C-130 squadron and in the tens of thousands of rounds fired by the Israeli counterterrorist team. In both cases, because the act of landing or shooting was the same regardless of location, the transition from practice to execution was eased considerably. Shani said later, "As far as the Unit was concerned, they didn't care whether it was Lod or Entebbe. They were trained to do this mission. Their actions were the same either way."[36] This statement was not meant to trivialize the commandos' role but to reinforce the point that by practicing the same action again and again, they were able to somewhat neutralize certain factors, such as location. The same generalization holds true for the pilots. It didn't matter whether they were landing at Ben Gurion or Entebbe; they were trained to do the task.

What the pilots and commandos were not trained to do was to work together on this type of mission. Consequently, when Netanyahu received the order to prepare for Entebbe, he immediately started his men on a series of rehearsals. They began by practicing the hasty off-load from the C-130s. "Everything was rehearsed again and again, each time in order to cut another two or three seconds off the times required to unfasten the vehicles and secure them."[37] At the same time, the men who were assigned to assault the old terminal conducted dozens of drills on a mock-up terminal. By late afternoon on Friday, Netanyahu had his men exercising the entire scenario from off-load to back-load and everything in between. That evening a full-dress rehearsal was conducted that included all the ground and air forces, which had also been conducting drills throughout the day. The scheme of maneuver that was practiced at the rehearsal was constantly reinforced and refined through a series of briefings. By the time the assault force departed Sharm-a-Sheikh, each man knew his responsibility. However, knowing your responsibility and being able to rehearse in a benign environment and quite different from actual combat. During the assault on the old terminal, several commandos entered the wrong hallway, even though they had practiced entering the mock-up a dozen times.* Nevertheless, the Unit's ability to rapidly off-load from the C-130, move to the old terminal, assault the building, and kill the terrorists with a minimum of friendly casualties is a testimony to the importance of rehearsals and constantly practicing basic tactical skills.

Surprise. Rescuing hostages is the most difficult of all special operations. It requires relative superiority to be almost simultaneous with mission completion, because any delay between relative superiority and mission completion provides the enemy an opportunity to kill the hostages—an action which takes only seconds. Consequently, if possible, surprise must be maintained up to the point of entry. In the raid on Entebbe, surprise was not absolute, but, coupled with deception, it was sufficient to confuse the Ugandans and terrorists long enough to allow the commandos to penetrate the old terminal and rescue the hostages.

Interestingly enough, the Israelis were confident they could land at Entebbe uncompromised if not undetected. Entebbe was, after all, an international airport, with "movement in and out of the airport about every half an hour."[38] Shani believed, and was proven correct, that the sound of a C-130 would not arouse undue suspicion. In fact, it was not until the second C-130 landed that the Ugandan Airport personnel became interested enough to investigate the unannounced aircraft. This was approximately six minutes after

---

*In his correspondence with the author, Iddo Netanyahu was quick to point out that entering the mock-up a dozen times could not prevent confusion. The mock-up was just a bare outline of the old terminal, and with all the other preparations necessary for this raid, the commandos could not rehearse as much as they would have liked. This illustrates that the frictions of war are always present in combat. Even if the commandos had rehearsed on a realistic model one hundred times, chance and uncertainty would still have played a major part in success. It is a credit to the Israelis that more tactical problems did not arise.

the first C-130 had landed. (The old terminal was over a kilometer from the new terminal and behind a small ridge, so it is not unbelievable that the noise of the gunfire went unnoticed by the airport personnel.) However, landing at the airport and penetrating Ugandan security at the old terminal were two different problems.

By wearing Ugandan uniforms and using the Mercedes to momentarily confuse the guards, the Israelis were able to maintain surprise right up to the point of entry. The terrorist who ran screaming back into the old terminal apparently did not realize, even at that point, that the Israelis were conducting a rescue. At night, and in the confusion, all the terrorist saw were the mottled camouflage utilities, and he assumed the Ugandans had "gone nuts." Once in the building, the Israelis had a decisive advantage and surprise was no longer an important factor.

Although surprise was manifested in the actions at the airport, those actions were only possible because the idea of rescuing hostages from a sovereign country was so improbable. The boldness of the plan created an environment in which surprise was possible. As Shani said later, the raid was a total surprise, because "nobody [thought] we were crazy enough to fly there." This bold act, coupled with deception, was the key component to gaining surprise at Entebbe.

Speed. In interviews with Iddo Netanyahu members of the Israeli assault force expressed understanding that "the time spent crossing the large airport had to be cut to a minimum, to reduce the risk of the terrorists and the Ugandan sentries at the terminal being alerted by the control tower—and to make sure that even if they were warned, they would not have time to understand exactly what was happening and respond."[39]

In the ideal special operation, speed is so dominant that the enemy has no time to react. This speed allows the attacking force, which has trained for just such a situation, to dictate the tempo of the engagement. The raid on Entebbe demonstrates how speed on the target is necessary for success. From the moment Shani landed the first C-130, it was three minutes until the commandos had relative superiority and the passengers were secure. During most of this time the terrorists guarding the passengers were unaware that a rescue attempt was in progress. Netanyahu fully appreciated the need for speed. Anticipating that the vehicle convoy might be stopped before it got to the old terminal, Netanyahu had ordered the driver of the Mercedes not to stop under any circumstances. Nothing was to delay the initial assault force from reaching the hostages as quickly as possible. When the commandos reached the old terminal and then suddenly hesitated, Netanyahu personally jumped in front of the assault element and ordered them to the door. He knew that "the loss of every second, especially when they were so close to the hostages, could have fatal consequences."[40] Netanyahu had told his men to run as hard as they could, and the commandos heeded his instructions. It was approximately thirty seconds from the time the Mercedes stopped in front of the old tower until the passengers were secure. Considering that the terrorists were not expecting the assault, the thirty seconds was insufficient time for the terrorists to react with any degree of purpose.

Throughout the engagement a sense of urgency always governed the actions of the air and ground elements. For example, Shani had instructed his pilots to take off as soon as they were back-loaded, regardless of the order of departure. This meant that most of the command and control element, Vilnai, Shani, and Betzer, departed before the other aircraft. This was considered acceptable because it reduced the time on target and thereby reduced the number of personnel and aircraft exposed to enemy fire.

Time was also a consideration when planning for the arrival of the APCs. Originally the four APCs, which were to provide security around the old terminal, were scheduled to arrive six minutes apart on the second and third C-130s. Netanyahu had initially ordered the drivers to wait until all four APCs were together before proceeding to the old terminal. Netanyahu's men argued for immediate deployment of the first two APCs, claiming it was better to have two APCs quickly than four APCs later. Logic prevailed and Netanyahu agreed to bring in the first two APCs as soon as they landed.

Any delay that expands the area of vulnerability, or exposure, increases the chance that the mission will fail. Consequently every attempt should be made to reduce the time on target. The raid on Entebbe clearly shows that speed was considered throughout the planning, preparation, and execution and was instrumental to success on the ground.

Purpose. As with most successful operations, the raid on Entebbe shows how identifying the purpose early in the planning instills a sense of commitment and helps the combatants focus on what is important. Time and again throughout the preparation for the raid, Jonathan Netanyahu stressed the purpose of the mission. "The objective of the mission was to save the lives of the hostages . . . everyone [has] to remember the purpose of the action, and work towards attaining it."[41] Since the planners understood the purpose of the mission, they reduced the size of the assault force, ensured the assault on the old terminal was kept to a minimum of time, and bypassed the old tower to reach the hostages quickly. Any action, with the exception of destroying the MiGs, that deviated from rescuing the hostages was discarded from the plan. But a sense of purpose involves more than just understanding the objective; it means being fully committed to the mission. The Unit's intelligence officer recalled that Netanyahu was greatly moved by the moral significance of the operation. "There was another element [that Netanyahu considered] . . . beyond the tactical side of the operation: the Zionist, human element."[42] It was this direct affront to Zionism and the conventions of civilized nations that inspired the Israelis throughout the operation. The success of a mission frequently depends on the actions of one man; consequently indecision and hesitation resulting from misunderstanding and indifference can lead to failure. At Entebbe the purpose was clear and the commitment unwavering.

In conclusion, the raid on Entebbe is the best illustration of the theory of special operations yet presented. Relative superiority, which was achieved within three minutes of the engagement, resulted from the proper application of the principles of special operations: a small force using a simple plan, carefully concealed, repeatedly rehearsed, and executed with surprise, speed, and purpose. The defenses were penetrated before the enemy had time to react, and relative superiority was sustained through the use of superior firepower. Using the principles, the Israelis minimized the frictions of war. Those frictions that did appear were countered by the moral factors of courage and boldness, which were present in abundance throughout the engagement.

Notes

1. Vice President's Task Force on Combatting Terrorism, *Terrorist Group Profiles* (Washington, D.C.: Government Printing Office, 1988), 118.

2. Brig. Gen. Joshua Shani, interview by author, tape recording, Washington, D.C., 19 January 1993.

3. Ibid.

4. Ibid.

5. Iddo Netanyahu, *Yoni's Last Battle,* unpublished manuscript, 19.

6. Ibid., 41. Attributed to Jonathan Netanyahu's intelligence officer.

7. Ibid., 43.

8. Ibid., 55–56.

9. Jonathan Netanyahu, *Self Portrait of a Hero: The Letters of Jonathan Netanyahu (1963–1976)* (New York: Random House, 1980), 97.

10. Netanyahu, *Yoni's Last Battle,* 136. From an Israeli Defense Force radio program of August 1976.

11. Ibid., 266–67.

12. Shani, interview.

13. Ibid.

14. Netanyahu, *Yoni's Last Battle,* 31.

15. Shani, interview.

16. Netanyahu, *Yoni's Last Battle,* 64. Attributed to an officer in the C-130 squadron.

17. Ibid., 78.

18. Iddo Netanyahu, letter to author, 14 May 1993.

19. Netanyahu, *Yoni's Last Battle,* 5.

20. Shani, interview.

21. Netanyahu, *Yoni's Last Battle,* 172. This is an indirect quote based on Dr. Iddo Netanyahu's interviews with Israeli commandos present at the time of Jonathan's brief.

22. Ibid., 27.

23. Shani, interview.

24. Ibid.

25. Netanyahu, *Yoni's Last Battle,* 29.
26. Shani, interview.
27. Ibid.
28. Ibid.
29. Netanyahu, letter.
30. Netanyahu, *Yoni's Last Battle,* 206.
31. William Stevenson, *90 Minutes at Entebbe* (New York: Bantam, 1976), 75.
32. Netanyahu, *Yoni's Last Battle,* 35. Attributed to Netanyahu's intelligence officer.
33. Ibid., 35.
34. Shani, interview.
35. Ibid.
36. Ibid.
37. Netanyahu, *Yoni's Last Battle,* 16.
38. Shani, interview.
39. Netanyahu, *Yoni's Last Battle,* 43.
40. Ibid., 31.
41. Ibid., 172.
42. Ibid., 7.

10

Conclusions

Peter Paret in his book *On Understanding War* outlines Clausewitz's thoughts on what constitutes an effective theory of warfare. First and foremost, a theory must have a powerful capacity to explain. It must be able to show the relationship between the past and the present. It must not be constrained by the temporary trends in military philosophy or technology, and it must be "sufficiently flexible . . . [with] potential for further development."[1] If a theory possesses these characteristics, then the student of war, using his experience and knowledge, will be able to make judgments about the future of warfare.

The theory of special operations meets these criteria by using historical case studies to link the past and the present. These case studies span time and nationality and are not subject to trends in military thought or practice. The theory, particularly as expressed in the relative superiority graph, has ample room for development and provides a framework in which to make judgments about future operations. Most importantly, the theory explains why special operations succeed.

The theory states that special operations forces are able to achieve relative superiority over the enemy if they prepare a simple plan, which is carefully concealed, repeatedly and realistically rehearsed,

and executed with surprise, speed, and purpose. Once relative superiority is achieved, the attacking force is no longer at a disadvantage and has the initiative to exploit the enemy's defenses and secure
victory. Although gaining relative superiority does not guarantee
success, no special operation can succeed without it. Consequently,
by demonstrating how special operations forces achieve relative
superiority, the theory can help explain the success or failure of
a mission.

Analysis of the eight case studies shows that those missions that
adhered to the six principles of special operations achieved relative
superiority. Although all the missions studied had varying degrees
of success, there were aspects of certain missions that failed to adhere to the principles and suffered the consequences.

By using the relative superiority graph to illustrate when relative
superiority was achieved, we can show the relationship between
theory and reality. In most of the cases, the area of vulnerability,
which represents the frictions of war, was minimal, and relative superiority was achieved quickly. In those cases where the area
of vulnerability expanded, we were able to see the tenuous nature of
success. The raid on Cabanatuan had an exceptionally large area
of vulnerability over time, and this correctly portrayed the precari-
ousness of the tactical situation. If we accept the need for relative
superiority and the relationship between relative superiority and the
area of vulnerability, then we can make some judgments about the
viability of future special operations.

The relative superiority graph is not a quantitative mission
analysis. Nevertheless it illustrates the relationship between certain crucial factors in a special operation. Most importantly it
shows the need to quickly gain relative superiority and the importance of reducing the area of vulnerability. How can the area of
vulnerability be reduced to improve the chance of mission success? The best approach, of course, is to enter the engagement
with relative superiority. As shown in Figure 10-1, this automatically reduces the possible area of vulnerability by half. Entering
the engagement with relative superiority can best be accomplished
by using stealth, as shown in the two submersible operations. This
reduces the possible area of vulnerability because half of what

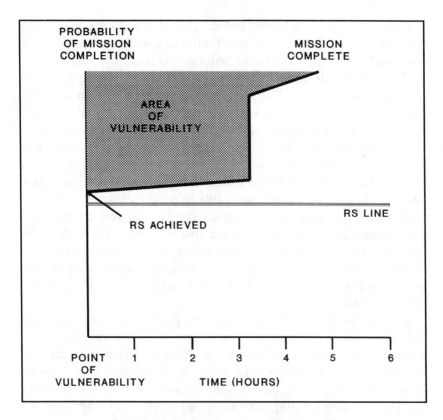

**Fig. 10–1. Relative Superiority Graph:
Entering the Engagement with Relative Superiority**

constitutes area of vulnerability—that is, the will of the enemy—
is not present. In other cases you can achieve relative superiority
before the actual engagement by overwhelming overwhelming
the enemy's defenses at their weakest point. In the latter situation,
overwhelming the enemy does not require numerical superiority,
merely innovative tactics or technology. The best illustration among
the eight case studies is the use of the *Campbeltown* against the dry
dock at Saint-Nazaire. Once the armor-plated *Campbeltown,* which
was loaded with four and a quarter tons of demolition, passed a
certain point in the Loire River, the 20mm guns couldn't prevent the
ship from reaching the dry dock. The *Campbeltown* was, for all

intents and purposes, unstoppable.* The key is to develop a plan
that makes the enemy's defenses ineffective and guarantees an advantage before one reaches the point of vulnerability.

Another way to reduce the area of vulnerability is to move the
point at which the attacking force becomes vulnerable. In a graphic
sense (Figure 10-2) it means pushing the point of vulnerability
closer to mission completion. In a practical sense this means developing enhanced insertion platforms that limit the detectability of
the attacking force until the last possible minute. This technique
was used by both the Germans at Eben Emael and the Americans at
Son Tay. In both cases they were able to push their point of vulnerability closer to mission completion and thereby reduce their area
of vulnerability. Intelligence should also be improved to help determine the extent of the enemy's defenses. By knowing how far the
defenses extend from the target and how sophisticated they are, the
attacking force can determine its point of vulnerability and take
steps to reduce it.

If the point of vulnerability cannot be pushed closer to the target,
then an alternate approach may be to limit what constitutes mission
completion. As noted earlier, area of vulnerability is a function of
the time it takes to complete the mission. Consequently, the longer
it takes to complete the mission, the greater the area of vulnerability. Therefore by limiting what constitutes mission completion, we
can significantly reduce the area of vulnerability. The Italians knew
that if they tried to recover the manned torpedoes after the attack on
the British fleet at Alexandria, the submarine *Scire* would have to
remain off the coast until daylight, and the divers would have to
reduce their time on target to make the rendezvous. By defining
mission completion as a one-way trip, the area of vulnerability was
cut in half and the probability of mission completion significantly
enhanced. Conversely, had the British defined mission completion
as solely the destruction of the Normandie dry dock, they could

---

*If not for the shoal waters of the Loire River, the *Campbeltown* would
have arrived at the point of vulnerability with relative superiority. As it
was, she still achieved relative superiority well before the engagement
with the enemy.

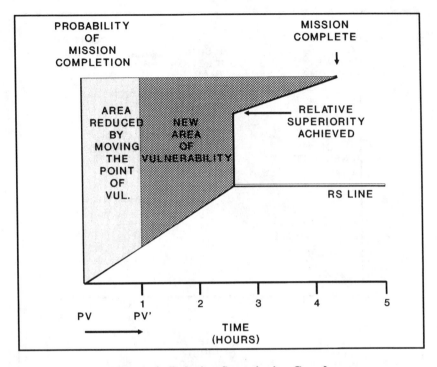

**Fig. 10–2. Relative Superiority Graph:
Moving the Point of Vulnerability**

have achieved their objective within five minutes of being engaged. Instead they planned for two hours ashore to destroy the submarine pens and other targets. This additional time expanded their area of vulnerability to the point of failure. (Although the *Campbeltown* portion of the raid on Saint-Nazaire was successful, the commando assault was not.) Figure 10-3 shows the effect on the area of vulnerability if one moves mission completion closer to the point of vulnerability by limiting the objectives. Although ordering one-way missions is not palatable in today's environment, it certainly has its place during all-out war.

The relative superiority graph also illustrates why certain types of mission, such as holding actions, are not conducive to special operations. If one defines mission completion as holding an objective, special operations forces are required to maintain relative superiority for a lengthy period of time. Figure 10-4 shows the

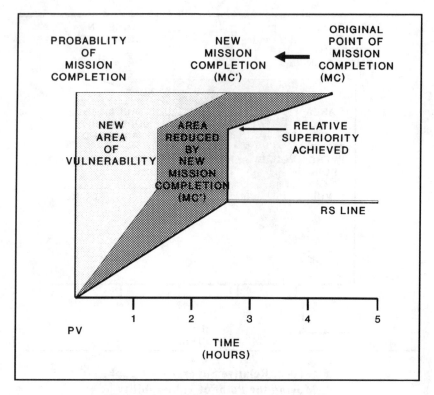

Fig. 10–3. Relative Superiority Graph:
Moving Mission Completion

difference between a raid with a planned withdrawal and a holding action. The holding action obviously has a greater area of vulnerability; and owing to their limited sustainability, special operations forces are placed in a difficult tactical position.

Using the relative superiority graph allows the student of warfare to analyze past special operations and make judgments about future operations. The graph also shows, in somewhat more limited detail, the relationship between the principles of special operations and relative superiority. On the graph, the point of vulnerability is a function of simplicity (innovation and intelligence), security, and surprise; time is a function of speed; and mission completion is related to limiting the objectives and motivating the soldiers. All of

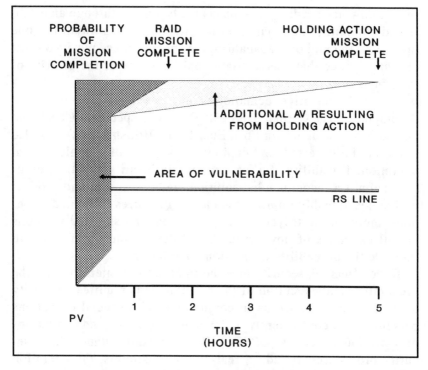

**Fig. 10–4. Relative Superiority Graph:
Raid versus Holding Action**

these principles affect the probability of mission completion and the location of relative superiority along that mission completion curve.

I developed the theory primarily to explain the tactical success of special operations forces, but what does the theory tell us about special operations forces in general? Most importantly, the theory validates the need for a standing special operations force that is trained, equipped, and supported at the best possible levels. This is not parochialism, but an honest reflection of the facts. What allows special operations forces to succeed is their ability to effectively use the principles in concert with each other. A standing force with an institutionalized support mechanism will be better able to employ the principles. For example, simplifying a plan requires good intelligence and innovation. The harder the target, the more detailed the intelligence needed. This means ready access, through an established conduit, to national-level intelligence assets. In all but one operation, the raid on Cabanatuan, the special forces received critical intelligence that was available only because of the priority of their mission.

New and innovative technology requires extensive research and development. The German DFS 230 glider was specifically designed and built for the attack on Eben Emael. The British X-craft was also designed, built, tested, and deployed in support of a single special operation. The ability of a force to rapidly identify a tactical problem, submit a recommended solution, and receive an end product will unquestionably improve the chance of success. Manned torpedoes, modified destroyers, shaped charges, and silenced weapons are all examples of how research and development were used to improve the probability of mission completion.

To be effective, security must be tight but not interfere with the preparation and execution of the mission. This requires a security team that routinely works in conjunction with special operations personnel and consequently understands the needs and limitations of operational security (OPSEC). By establishing standardized security procedures, based on real-world constraints, the operation will have ample room for maneuver while still preventing the enemy from gaining an advantage.

In almost every case where there was direct contact with the enemy (the two submersible operations excluded), the special operations forces personnel were outnumbered approximately ten to one. Yet with the exception of the raid on Saint-Nazaire, the special operations forces inflicted heavy casualties and sustained very few. This ability to effectively shoot, move, and communicate in a chaotic environment is directly related to training. Repetition, as manifested in routine training and realistic rehearsals, requires substantial funding and logistic support. To be proficient, special operations forces personnel need to train daily, preferably in an environment that replicates the conditions of combat. For example, to prepare for their attack on Eben Emael, the glidermen trained for months, traveling throughout Germany and Czechoslovakia and working on targets that closely approximated the fortifications marked for destruction.

Depending on the difficulty of the operation, the logistic support for this training can be extensive and expensive. The logistic support for the preparation phase of the *Tirpitz* attack was phenomenal. It included an entirely new base at HMS Varbel, a dozen support vessels ranging from small trawlers to depot maintenance ships, railroad cars to transport the X-craft, six parent submarines, and a hundred administrative personnel. The task force that was assembled for the raid on Son Tay had similar training and logistic requirements. Although the training of special operations forces personnel is expensive, relative to the return on the investment, the price tag is justified. If Hitler had scrimped on the funding for the glidermen, the Germans might not have taken the fort at Eben Emael, which subsequently helped the entire German army to achieve its objective quickly. Trying to keep the battleship *Tirpitz* trapped in Norway had already cost the British government millions of pounds in manpower and materiel. For the price of a few X-craft and the cost of training, the German battleship threat was virtually eliminated.

Surprise is achieved as a result of all the factors mentioned above, namely intelligence, innovation, security, and training, but it also frequently relies on deception to divert the enemy's attention or delay their actions. Captain Edward McCleskey, USAF, noted in his thesis, "Applying Deception to Special Operations Direct Action Missions," that most missions that used deception succeeded.[2] Depending on the difficulty of the operation, deception can be a major contributor to success. But, in order for operational deception (OPDEC) to be effective, it must be completely synchronized with the assault plan. A failure to achieve this synchronization can result in another Saint-Nazaire.* Once again, this requires an institutionalized integration of the special operations and OPDEC planners.

The rapid execution of the mission (speed) is a function of the training and motivation of the assault force. Training, as previously

*The Royal Air Force was tasked to conduct an air raid as part of the OPDEC for the raid on Saint-Nazaire. The bomber pilots were not told the nature of their mission and consequently executed only a brief portion of the air raid. This resulted in the commandos aboard the motor launches losing the element of surprise, and their mission subsequently failed.

discussed, must be as realistic as possible to replicate the conditions expected on the target. This allows the special operations forces to refine their plan prior to the engagement and, once engaged, move rapidly to achieve their objective. Provided it is properly supported, a standing force has time before the crisis to perfect its combat skills on mock targets such as aircraft, oil rigs, buildings, and ships. All this training will make movement on the target flow smoothly in the face of the frictions of war.

The one constant that prevailed throughout the eight case studies was the motivation of the individual soldier. Every operation was conducted by volunteers, and every volunteer was screened through a rigorous training and selection program. This elite training program did not necessarily make the soldiers either morally, ethically, or even physically stronger than the average soldier. What it did accomplish was to strengthen the bond between the graduates of the selection course. It also developed exceptionally strong unit cohesion and improved the self-esteem and confidence of the graduates. The more physically demanding the course, the tighter the unit became, which was instrumental in the success of the missions. Additionally, the training program established a baseline of performance that could be used by the planners to judge the limitation of the force. It is impossible to determine how an individual will react under fire, but the strength of a special operations force is not its individuals but its unit cohesion. The German glidermen, the British commandos, and the Rangers at Cabanatuan were composed almost entirely of troops with no prior combat experience. The other units had combat veterans but also a large percentage of inexperienced troops. Nonetheless, they all performed with equal bravery and professionalism. Why? They had unit integrity, born not from combat, but from the elite training. Clausewitz says that "a soldier is just as proud of the hardships he has overcome as the dangers he has faced."[3] The hardships encountered at basic Sea, Air, and Land (SEAL), Special Forces, Ranger, and Airborne training are absolutely essential if a special operation is going to succeed in the face of a difficult enemy.

Can a special operation be successfully conducted without a standing force? Absolutely, but the price for establishing and training an ad hoc organization is time. And the more time expended during a political crisis or a military campaign, the less the chances of success.

What else does the theory tell us about special operations? In order to achieve relative superiority, those men leading the operation must understand what actually makes a special operation succeed. It is not just bravado and boldness. Brave men without good planning, preparation, and leadership are cannon fodder in the face of defensive warfare. Lieutenant Rudolf Witzig, Lt. Luigi Durand de la Penne, Capt. Otto Skorzeny, Lt. Godfrey Place, Lt. Col. Henry Mucci, Lt. Col. Bud Sydnor, and Lt. Col. Jonathan Netanyahu were all conventional soldiers before they became special operations soldiers. They understood the importance of detailed planning, constant rehearsals, and precise execution. The view of special operations personnel as unruly and cavalier with a disdain for the brass was not borne out in this study. The officers and enlisted whom I interviewed were professionals who fully appreciated the value of proper planning and preparations, of good order and discipline, and of working with higher authorities. They were also exceptionally modest men who felt that there was nothing heroic in their actions and often sought to downplay their public image.[4] Boldness, courage, perseverance, and intellect unquestionably have their place in combat, but as the theory shows, they must exist in harmony with the principles of special operation in order to achieve success.

In conclusion, what allows special operations forces to achieve relative superiority is their ability to effectively utilize the principles of special operations. The better the principles are integrated, the greater the relative superiority. Although no amount of planning and preparation can guarantee success, by reducing the area of vulnerability an attacking force can achieve relative superiority quickly. Once relative superiority is achieved, success favors those with initiative who, by virtue of their planning, preparation, and rapid execution, can exploit the weaknesses of the defense and defeat the enemy. This is how special operations succeed.

Notes

1. Peter Paret, *Understanding War: Essays on Clausewitz and the History of Military Power* (Princeton, N.J.: Princeton University Press, 1992), 103.

2. Edward R. McCleskey, "Applying Deception to Special Operations Direct Action Missions," Master's thesis, Defense Intelligence College, Washington, D.C., 1991.

3. Carl von Clausewitz, *On War,* ed. and trans. Michael Howard and Peter Paret (Princeton, N.J.: Princeton University Press, 1976), 659.

4. Adm. Godfrey Place, interview by author, tape recording, England, 17 June 1992.

Index

Witzig, Lt. Rudolf, 37–69, 391
Wolf's Lair, 170, 175, 193
Wonck, 36, 54, 67
World War II Magazine, 41
Wynn, Lt. Mickey, 126, 142, 152

X-Craft, 16, 19–22, 110, 202–
241, 388, 389; X-3, 202, 211,
212; X-4, 212; X-5, 212, 214,
215, 218, 219, 228, 230, 231,
234, 235, 238, 240; X-6, 208,
212, 214, 215, 218, 219, 221–
224, 226–232, 234, 235, 237,
238–241; X-7, 204, 209, 212,
214, 215–219, 223, 224, 227–
232, 235, 238–241; X-8, 214–
219, 228–231, 235, 238, 240;
X-9, 214–219, 228–231, 235,
238, 240; X-10, 214, 215, 218,
219, 228–231, 235, 238, 240

Yom Kippur War, 341, 344, 346,
367

Zabbro, 87, 96
Zaslov, Milt, 323
Zehnder, LCol. Herbert, 10